The Irony of Democracy:
An Uncommon Introduction to American Politics

Second Edition

Duxbury Press Series in Politics

General Editor

Bernard C. Hennessy

California State University, Hayward

American Political Interest Groups:
Readings in Theory and Research

Betty H. Zisk
Boston University

The Irony of Democracy: An
Uncommon Introduction to
American Politics

Thomas R. Dye and
L. Harmon Zeigler
The Florida State University,
University of Oregon

The Congressional System: Notes
and Readings

Leroy N. Rieselbach
Indiana University

Techniques of Political Analysis:
An Introduction

Lyman Tower Sargent and
Thomas A. Zant
University of Missouri at St. Louis

Public Opinion, Second Edition

Bernard C. Hennessy
The Pennsylvania State University

An Introduction to the Study
of Public Policy

Charles O. Jones
University of Pittsburgh

A Logic of Public Policy:
Aspects of Political Economy

L. L. Wade and Robert Curry
University of California, Davis,
California State University, Sacramento

Political Life and Social Change:
An Introduction to Political Science

Charles Andrain
California State University, San Diego

Political Life and Social Change:
Readings

Charles Andrain
California State University, San Diego

The People, Maybe: Seeking
Democracy in America

Karl A. Lamb
University of California, Santa Cruz

Analyzing American Politics:
A New Perspective

Walter A. Rosenbaum, John W.
Spanier, and William C. Burris
University of Florida, University
of Florida, Guilford College

The Black Politician:
His Search for Power

Mervyn M. Dymally, Senator,
California State Legislature

The Irony of Democracy:
An Uncommon Introduction to American Politics

Second Edition

Thomas R. Dye
The Florida State University

L. Harmon Zeigler
University of Oregon

Duxbury Press
A Division of Wadsworth Publishing Company, Inc.

Duxbury Press
A Division of Wadsworth Publishing Company, Inc.

ISBN-087872-017-0
L. C. Cat. Card No. -77-189117
Printed in the United States of America

6   7   8   9   10 — 76   75   74

Preface to the Second Edition

We would like to begin the Second Edition of *The Irony of Democracy* with thanks to the instructors who used the first edition of the book and gave us the benefits of their reactions and comments and relayed those of their students. We found such comments unusually instructive; and indeed it is in response to their criticisms that we have added the chief new feature to the Second Edition, the two-part signed Postscript. We are especially grateful to the following people who provided us with extensive pre-revision criticism:

Bernard Hennessy, The Pennsylvania State University;
Murray B. Levin, Boston University;
David H. Tabb, University of California, Berkeley;
Robert G. Striplin and Thomas A. Rhorer, American River College;
Robert Lineberry, University of Texas;
Sherman Lewis, California State College, Hayward; and
Harlan J. Strauss and his students at the University of Oregon.

Aside from the usual updating of material, the major revisions for this Second Edition are: the aforementioned Postscript, described further below; new treatments of mass media and education as instruments for elite instruction of mass attitudes; expanded study of the liberal establishment, including the relationship of elite values and American involvement in war — with special attention to the Pentagon Papers; an expanded discussion of counter-elites (and a more intensive study of George C. Wallace as a focus of the discussion); a substantial revision of our thinking on interest groups; further development of our ideas on voting; and augmented discussion of the weaknesses of pluralist theory.

The first edition of *The Irony of Democracy* produced disquiet and perplexity in many students, for it proposes, and seeks to prove, that in relation to the actual processes and motivating forces of our political and social system many of our most cherished principles of democracy are myths. Many readers have asked, "Where am I left, with my supposed rights and responsibilities as an individual — at the very least, as a voter — in this system?" "What is to be done?" For the Second Edition we have provided what we mean to be guides to the reader who seeks the answers to such questions. In the signed Postscripts, Parts 1 and 2, each author addresses himself to the problem, "What to Do about the Establishment."

In these essays we have stepped out of our roles of political scientist; we speak to the problem from our own respective (and contrary) values — which we hope, of course, have been informed by our work in political science. The first essay takes the "conservative" line and espouses maintenance of an enlightened elite, and proposes means for accomplishing this goal and for keeping the masses tranquil and the system stable. The second essay espouses the more "radical" line that participatory democracy can be made a reality, and proposes means whereby to that end the masses can be enabled to authentically hold and behave by those principles essential to a meaningful and stable democracy.

Again, it should be emphasized that as a work of political science the book ends with Chapter 13. Our essays are not to be construed as the conclusion to the book—nor are they to be treated as our definitive resolutions of that irony of democracy that is delineated in the book. Though they present our own sincere beliefs, they are intended only as guides or aids to the *initiation* of student discussion about the future of American democracy. We hope students will continue the dialogue we have begun in them.

Preface to the First Edition

The prevailing ideology of contemporary political science literature is pluralism. Pluralism portrays the American political process as competition, bargaining, and compromise among a multitude of interest groups that vie for the rewards distributed by the political system. The multiplicity of such groups and the fact that their memberships overlap are believed to ensure the nation against the eventuality that any one group should emerge as a dominant elite. The pluralist ideology characterizes virtually all of the American government textbooks currently in print.

While the underlying value of individual dignity remains at the core of contemporary pluralist thought, the modern pluralist accepts giant concentrations of power as inevitable in a modern, industrial, urban society. The pluralist realizes that the unorganized individual is no match for giant corporate bureaucracy, but he hopes that "countervailing" centers of power will balance each other and thereby protect the individual from abuse. Groups become the means by which individuals gain access to the political system. The government is held responsible not by individuals but by organized groups and coalitions of groups (parties). The essential value becomes participation in, and competition among, organized groups. Pluralism asserts that the dispersed pattern of power among many groups safeguards both individuals and groups against arbitrary and capricious actions of a dominant group. Pluralism contends that the American system is open and accessible to the extent that any interest held by a significant portion of the populace can find expression through one or more groups.

The pluralist ideology went unchallenged for a number of years, not only in American government texts, but also in the general literature of political science. Recently, however, several scholars have challenged the pluralists' claims to empirical validity and, therefore, undermined their claim to normative prescription as well. These scholars, sometimes referred to as "neo-elitists," accept the existence of a multiplicity of groups; however, they look beyond the structural proliferation of interest groups and examine their functional interaction.

Elitism contends that all organizations tend to be governed by a small minority of their membership and that the characteristics of the leaders across all groups tend to be similar. The backgrounds and values of these leaders are so similar, in fact, that they constitute an American socio-political elite. The members of this elite articulate the values of society and exercise control of society's resources. They are bound as much—if not more—by their elite identities as they are by their specific group attachments. Thus, instead of constituting a balance of power systems within American society, organized interest groups are seen as platforms of power from which a relatively homogeneous group—an elite—effectively governs the nation. These leaders are more accommodating toward each other than they are competitive. They share a basic consensus about preserving the system essentially as it is. They are not really held accountable by the members of their group. Members have little or nothing to say about policy decisions. In fact, leaders influence followers far more than followers influence leaders.

A generation or more of Americans have been educated in the pluralist tradition. We do not claim that they have been educated poorly (if for no other reason than that we are among them). Nor do we argue that pluralism is either "wrong" or "dead," for clearly it contains much of value and commands many perceptive adherents. In short, this book was not undertaken to "attack the pluralists". Our primary concern is to make available to students and teachers of political science an introductory analysis of American politics that is *not* based on the pluralist ideology.

The Irony of Democracy is an explanation of American political life based on an elitist theory of democracy. It attempts to organize historical and social science evidence from the American political experience to test propositions derived from elite theory. In view of this specific aim, we have not attempted to discuss or explain the myriad structural aspects and interactive dynamics of the American political system. We have deliberately sacrificed some breadth of coverage to present a coherent exposition of the theory of elitist democracy. Those who seek an encyclopedic presentation of the "facts" of American government are advised to look elsewhere. Nor have we sought to present a "balanced," or theoretically eclectic, view of American politics. The student can find democratic-pluralist interpretations of American politics everywhere.

The Irony of Democracy is not necessarily "anti-establishment." This book challenges the prevailing, pluralistic view of democracy in America, but it neither condemns nor endorses American political life. To say that America is governed by a small, homogeneous elite may be interpreted either as praise or as criticism of this nation, depending on one's personal values. That is, elitism may be thought of as either "good" or "bad," depending on one's preference for elite or mass governance.

Actually, the authors themselves disagree about whether the elitism they perceive in American politics is "good" or "bad." One author values radical reform as a means of establishing a truly democratic political system in America—a system in which individuals partici- pate in all decisions that shape their lives, a system in which individual dignity is preserved and in which equality is realized in the social, economic, and political life of the nation. He believes that, through radical resocialization and a restructuring of educational, economic, and governmental institutions, the anti-democratic sentiments of the masses can be changed. In contrast, the other author values an en- lightened leadership system capable of acting decisively to preserve individual freedom, human dignity, and the values of life, liberty, and property. He believes that a well-ordered society governed by edu- cated and resourceful elites is preferable to the instability of mass society.

In summary, *The Irony of Democracy* challenges the prevailing pluralistic ideology and interprets American politics from the per- spective of elite theory. The reader is free to decide for himself whether the political system described in these pages ought to be preserved, reformed, or restructured.

We are indebted to Harry Scoble (UCLA), John Sproat (Lake Forest College), Richard Young (Stanford), Robert Crew (University of Minnesota), and Bernard Hennessy (Pennsylvania State Univer- sity), for many helpful criticisms and suggestions. We also wish to acknowledge the assistance of Jerry Jenkins, Barbara Smith, Wayne Peak, and Hendrick van Dalen in the preparation of the manuscript. To Bob Gormley of Duxbury Press go special thanks for playing the role of entrepreneur to perfection. Finally, Bea Gormley made a number of helpful stylistic and organizational suggestions.

Contents

Tables

Figures

 The Irony of Democracy

Elites, not masses, govern America. In an industrial, scientific, and nuclear age, life in a democracy, just as in a totalitarian society, is shaped by a handful of men. In spite of differences in their approach to the study of power in America, scholars — political scientists and sociologists alike — agree that "the key political, economic, and social decisions are made by 'tiny minorities.' "[1]

An *elite* is the few who have power; the *masses* are the many who do not. Power is deciding who gets what, when, and how; it is participation in the decisions that allocate values for a society. Elites are the few who participate in the decisions that shape our lives; the masses are the many whose lives are shaped by institutions, events, and leaders over which they have little direct control. Harold Lasswell writes, "the division of society into elite and mass is universal," and even in a democracy "a few exercise a relatively great weight of power, and the many exercise comparatively little."[2]

Elites are not necessarily conspiracies to oppress or exploit the masses. On the contrary, elites may be very "public-regarding" and deeply concerned with the welfare of the masses. Membership in an elite may be relatively open to ambitious and talented individuals from the masses, or it may be closed to all except top corporate, financial, military, civic, and governmental leaders. Elites may be competitive or consensual; they may agree or disagree over the direction of foreign and domestic policy. Elites may form a pyramid, with a top group exercising power in many sectors of the society; or plural elites may divide power, with separate groups making key decisions in different issue areas. Elites may be responsive to the demands of the masses and influenced by the outcome of elections, or they may be unresponsive to mass movements and unaffected by elections. But whether elites are public-minded or self-seeking, open or closed, competitive or consensual, pyramidal or pluralistic, responsive or unresponsive, it is elites and not the masses who govern the modern nation.

[1] Robert A. Dahl, "Power, Pluralism, and Democracy: A Modest Proposal," paper delivered at 1964 annual meeting of the American Political Science Association, p.3. See also Peter Bachrach, *The Theory of Democratic Elitism* (Boston: Little, Brown and Co., 1967).
[2] Harold Lasswell and Abraham Kaplan, *Power and Society* (New Haven, Conn.: Yale University Press, 1950), p. 219.

Democracy is government "by the people," but the responsibility for the survival of democracy rests on the shoulders of elites. This is the irony of democracy: Elites must govern wisely if government "by the people" is to survive. If the survival of the American system depended upon an active, informed, and enlightened citizenry, then democracy in America would have disappeared long ago; for the masses of America are apathetic and ill-informed about politics and public policy, and they have a surprisingly weak commitment to democratic values—individual dignity, equality of opportunity, the right to dissent, freedom of speech and press, religious toleration, due process of law. But fortunately for these values and for American democracy, the American masses do not lead, they follow. They respond to the attitudes, proposals, and behavior of elites. V. O. Key wrote:

> The critical element for the health of the democratic order consists of the beliefs, standards, and competence of those who constitute the influentials, the political activists, in the order. That group, as has been made plain, refuses to define itself with great clarity in the American system; yet analysis after analysis points to its existence. If democracy tends toward indecision, decay, and disaster, the responsibility rests here, not with the mass of people.[3]

Although the symbols of American politics are drawn from democratic political thought, the reality of American politics can often be better understood from the viewpoint of *elite theory*. The questions posed by elite theory are the vital questions of politics: Who governs America? What are the roles of elites and masses in American politics? How do people acquire power? What is the relationship between economic and political power? How open and accessible are American elites? How do American elites change over time? How widely is power shared in America? How much real competition takes place among elites? What is the basis of elite consensus? How do elites and masses differ? How responsive are elites to mass sentiments? How much influence do masses have over policies decided by elites? How do elites accommodate themselves to mass movements?

This book, *The Irony of Democracy*, is an attempt to explain American political life on the basis of elite theory. It attempts systematically to organize the evidence of American history and contemporary social science in order to come to grips with the central questions posed by elite theory. But before we turn to this examination of American political life, it is important that we understand the meaning of *elitism, democracy,* and *pluralism*.

The Meaning of Elitism   The central proposition of elitism is that all societies are divided into two classes—the few who govern and the many who are governed. The Italian political scientist Gaetano Mosca expressed this basic concept as follows:

[3]V. O. Key, Jr., *Public Opinion and American Democracy* (New York: Alfred A. Knopf, 1961), p. 558.

In all societies—from societies that are very undeveloped and have largely attained the dawnings of civilization, down to the most advanced and powerful societies—two classes of people appear—a class that rules and a class that is ruled. The first class, always the less numerous, performs all of the political functions, monopolizes power, and enjoys the advantages that power brings, whereas the second, the more numerous class, is directed and controlled by the first, in a manner that is now more or less legal, now more or less arbitrary and violent.[4]

For Mosca it was inevitable that elites and not masses would govern all societies, because elites possess organization and unity of purpose.

An organized minority, obeying a single impulse, is irresistible against an unorganized majority in which each individual stands alone before the totality of the organized minority. A hundred men acting uniformly in concert, with a common understanding, will triumph over a thousand men who·are not in accord and can be dealt with one by one.[5]

Contemporary writers generally attribute elitism to the impact of urbanization, industrialization, technological development, and the growth of the social, economic, and political organizations in modern societies. Robert Dahl writes, "The key political, economic, and social decisions . . . are made by tiny minorities. . . . It is difficult—nay impossible—to see how it could be otherwise in large political systems."[6] Sociologist Suzanne Keller writes, "The democratic ethos notwithstanding, men must become accustomed to bigger, more extensive and more specialized elites in their midst as long as industrial societies keep growing and becoming more specialized."[7] And according to Harold Lasswell, "The discovery that in all large-scale societies the decisions at any given time are typically in the hands of a small number of people" confirms a basic fact: "Government is always government by the few, whether in the name of the few, the one, or the many."[8]

Elitism also asserts that the few who govern are not typical of the masses who are governed. Elites possess more control over resources—power, wealth, education, prestige, status, skills of leadership, information, knowledge of political processes, ability to communicate, and organization—and elites (in America) are drawn disproportionately from among wealthy, educated, prestigiously employed, socially prominent, white, Anglo-Saxon, and Protestant groups in society. In short, elites are drawn from a society's upper classes, which are made up of those persons in a society who own or control a disproportionate share of the societal institutions—industry, commerce, finance, education, the military, communications, civic affairs, and law.

[4] Gaetano Mosca, *The Ruling Class* (New York: McGraw-Hill Book Co., 1939), p. 50.
[5] Mosca, p. 51.
[6] Dahl, "Power, Pluralism and Democracy," p. 3.
[7] Suzanne Keller, *Beyond the Ruling Class* (New York: Random House, 1963), p. 71.
[8] Harold Lasswell and Daniel Lerner, *The Comparative Study of Elites* (Stanford, Calif.: Stanford University Press, 1952), p. 7.

On the other hand, elite theory admits of some social mobility that enables non-elites to become elites; elitism does not necessarily mean that individuals from the lower classes cannot rise to the top. In fact, a certain amount of "circulation of elites" (upward mobility) is essential for the stability of the elite system. Openness in the elite system siphons off potentially revolutionary leadership from the lower classes, and an elite system is strengthened when talented and ambitious individuals from the masses are permitted to enter governing circles. However, it is important that the movement of individuals from non-elite to elite positions be a slow and continuous assimilation rather than a rapid or revolutionary change. Moreover, only those non-elites who have demonstrated their commitment to the elite system itself and to the system's political and economic values can be admitted to the ruling class.

Elites share in a *consensus* about fundamental norms underlying the social system. They agree on the basic "rules of the game," as well as on the continuation of the social system itself. The stability of the system, and even its survival, depends upon this consensus. According to David Truman, "Being more influential, they (the elites) are privileged; and being privileged, they have, with few exceptions, a special stake in the continuation of the system in which their privileges rest."[9] Elite consensus does not mean that elite members never disagree or never compete with each other for preeminence; it is unlikely that there ever was a society in which there was no competition among elites. But elitism implies that competition takes place within a very narrow range of issues and that elites agree on more matters than they disagree on.

In America, the bases of elite consensus are the sanctity of private property, limited government, and individual liberty. Richard Hofstadter writes about American elite struggles:

The fierceness of political struggles has often been misleading; for the range of vision embodied by the primary contestants in the major parties has always been bounded by the horizons of property and enterprise. However much at odds on specific issues, the major political traditions have shared a belief in the rights of property, the philosophy of economic individualism, the value of competition; they have accepted the economic virtues of capitalist culture as necessary qualities of man.[10]

Hofstadter's analysis of consensus among leaders in American history echoes a central principle of elitism.

Elitism implies that public policy does not reflect demands of "the people" so much as it reflects the interests and values of elites. Changes and innovations in public policy come about as a result of redefinitions by elites of their own values. However, the general conservatism of elites — that is, their interest in preserving the system — means that

---

[9] David Truman, "The American System in Crisis," *Political Science Quarterly* (December 1959), 489.
[10] Richard Hofstadter, *The American Political Tradition* (New York: Alfred A. Knopf, 1948), p. viii.

changes in public policy will be incremental rather than revolutionary. Public policies are frequently modified but seldom replaced.

Basic changes in the nature of the political system occur when events threaten the system. Elites, acting on the basis of enlightened self-interest, institute reforms to preserve the system and their place in it. Their motives are not necessarily self-serving; the values of elites may be very "public-regarding," and the welfare of the masses may be an important element in elite decision making. Elitism does not mean that public policy will ignore or be against the welfare of the masses but only that the responsibility for the mass welfare rests upon the shoulders of elites, not upon the masses.

Finally, elitism assumes that the masses are largely passive, apathetic, and ill-informed. Mass sentiments are manipulated by elites more often than elite values are influenced by the sentiments of the masses. For the most part, communication between elites and masses flows downward. Policy questions of government are seldom decided by the masses through elections or through the presentation of policy alternatives by political parties. For the most part, these "democratic" institutions — elections and parties — are important only for their symbolic value. They help tie the masses to the political system by giving them a role to play on election day and a political party with which they can identify. Elitism contends that the masses have at best only an indirect influence over the decision-making behavior of elites.

Naturally, elitism is frequently misunderstood in America, because the prevailing myths and symbols of the American system are drawn from democratic theory rather than elite theory. Therefore, it is important here to emphasize what elitism is *not,* as well as to briefly restate what it *is.*

Elitism does not mean that those who have power are continually locked in conflict with the masses or that powerholders always achieve their goals at the expense of the public interest. Elitism is not a conspiracy to oppress the masses. Elitism does not imply that powerholders constitute a single impenetrable monolithic body or that powerholders in society always agree on public issues. Elitism does not pretend that power in society does not shift over time or that new elites cannot emerge to compete with old elites. Elites may be more or less monolithic and cohesive or more or less pluralistic and competitive. Power need not rest exclusively on the control of economic resources but may rest instead upon other leadership resources — organization, communication, or information. Elitism does not imply that the masses *never* have any impact on the attitudes of elites but only that elites influence masses more than masses influence elites.

Elitism can be summarized as follows:

1. Society is divided into the few who have power and the many who do not. Only a small number of persons allocate values for society; the masses do not decide public policy.

2. The few who govern are not typical of the masses who are governed. Elites are drawn disproportionately from the upper socioeconomic strata of society.

3. The movement of non-elites to elite positions must be slow and continuous to maintain stability and avoid revolution. Only non-elites who have accepted the basic elite consensus can be admitted to governing circles.

4. Elites share a consensus on the basic values of the social system and the preservation of the system.

5. Public policy does not reflect demands of the masses but rather the prevailing values of the elite. Changes in public policy will be incremental rather than revolutionary.

6. Active elites are subject to relatively little direct influence from apathetic masses. Elites influence masses more than masses influence elites.

The Meaning of Democracy

Ideally, democracy means individual participation in the decisions that affect one's life. John Dewey wrote, "The keynote of democracy as a way of life may be expressed as the necessity for the participation of every mature human being in formation of the values that regulate the living of men together."[11] In other words, democracy means popular participation in the allocation of values in a society.

In traditional democratic theory, popular participation has been valued as an opportunity for individual self-development: Responsibility for the governing of one's own conduct develops one's character, self-reliance, intelligence, and moral judgment—in short, one's dignity. Even if a benevolent despot could govern in the public interest, he would be rejected by the classic democrat. The English political philosopher J. S. Mill asks, "What sort of human beings can be formed under such a regime? What development can either their thinking or active faculties attain under it?" The argument for citizen participation in public affairs is based not upon the policy outcomes it would produce but on the belief that such involvement is essential to the full development of human capacities. Mill argues that man can know truth only by discovering it for himself.[12]

Procedurally, popular participation was to be achieved through majority rule and respect for the rights of minorities. Self-development means self-government, and self-government can be accomplished only by encouraging each individual to contribute to the development of public policy and by resolving conflicts over public policy through majority rule. Minorities who have had the opportunity to influence policy but whose views have not succeeded in winning majority support would accept the decisions of majorities. In return, majorities would permit minorities to openly attempt to win majority support for their views. Freedom of speech and press, freedom to dissent, and

[11]John Dewey, "Democracy and Educational Administration," *School and Society*, (April 3, 1937).
[12]John Stuart Mill, *Representative Government* (New York: E. P. Dutton, Everyman's Library), p. 203.

freedom to form opposition parties and organizations are essential to insure meaningful individual participation. This freedom of expression is also necessary for ascertaining what the majority views really are.

The procedural requirements and the underlying ethics of democracy are linked. Carl Becker writes about democracy:

> Its fundamental assumption is the worth and dignity and creative capacity of the individual, so that the chief aim of government is the maximum of individual self-direction, the chief means to that end, the minimum of compulsion by the state. . . . Means and ends are conjoined in the concept of freedom: freedom of thought so that the truth may prevail; freedom of occupation, so that careers may be open to talent; freedom of self-government, so that none may be compelled against his will.[13]

The underlying value of democracy is, as we have noted, individual dignity. Man, by virtue of his existence, is entitled to life, liberty, and property. A "natural law," or moral tenet, guarantees to every man both liberty and the right to property; and this natural law is morally superior to man-made law. John Locke, the English political philosopher whose writings most influenced America's founding elites, argues that even in a "state of nature"—that is, a world in which there were no governments—an individual possesses inalienable rights to life, liberty, and property. Locke meant that these rights were antecedent to government, that these rights are not given to the individual by governments and that no governments may legitimately take them away.[14]

Locke believed that the very purpose of government was to protect individual liberty. Men form a "social contract" with each other in establishing a government to help protect their rights; they tacitly agree to accept governmental activity in order to better protect life, liberty, and property. Implicit in the social contract and the democratic notion of freedom is the belief that governmental activity and social control over the individual be kept to a minimum. This involves the removal of as many external restrictions, controls, and regulations on the individual as is consistent with the freedom of his fellow citizens.

Moreover, since government is formed by the consent of the governed to protect individual liberty, it logically follows that government cannot violate the rights it was established to protect. Its authority is limited. Locke's ultimate weapon to protect individual dignity against abuse by government was the right of revolution. According to Locke, whenever governments violate the natural rights of the governed, they forfeit the authority placed in them under the social contract.

Another vital aspect of classic democracy is a belief in the equality of all men. The Declaration of Independence expresses the conviction that "all men are created equal." Even the Founding Fathers

---

[13] Carl Becker, *Modern Democracy* (New Haven, Conn.: Yale University Press, 1941), pp. 26–27.
[14] For a discussion of John Locke and the political philosophy underlying democracy, see George Sabine, *A History of Political Theory* (New York: Holt, Rinehart and Winston, 1950), pp. 517–541.

believed in equality for all men *before the law,* notwithstanding the circumstances of the accused. A man was not to be judged by social position, economic class, creed, or race. Many early democrats also believed in *political equality*—equal access of individuals to political influence, that is, equal opportunity to influence public policy. Political equality is expressed in the concept of "one man, one vote."

Over time, the notion of equality has also come to include *equality of opportunity* in all aspects of American life—social, educational, and economic, as well as political. Roland Pennock writes:

> The objective of equality is not merely the recognition of a certain dignity of the human being as such, but it is also to provide him with the opportunity— equal to that guaranteed to others—for protecting and advancing his interests and developing his powers and personality.[15]

Thus, the notion of equality of opportunity has been extended beyond political life to encompass equality of opportunity in education, employment, housing, recreation, and public accommodations. Each man has an equal opportunity to develop his individual capacities to their natural limits.

It is important to remember, however, that the traditional democratic creed has always stressed *equality of opportunity* to education, wealth, and status and not *absolute equality.* Thomas Jefferson recognized a "natural aristocracy" of talent, ambition, and industry, and liberal democrats since Jefferson have always accepted inequalities that are a product of individual merit and hard work. Absolute equality, or "leveling," is not a part of liberal democratic theory.

In summary, democratic thinking involves the following ideas:

1. popular participation in the decisions that shape the lives of individuals in a society;

2. government by majority rule, with recognition of the rights of minorities to try to become majorities. These rights include the freedoms of speech, press, assembly, and petition and the freedom to dissent, to form opposition parties, and to run for public office;

3. a commitment to individual dignity and the preservation of the liberal values of life, liberty, and property;

4. a commitment to equal opportunity for all men to develop their individual capacities.

A Single Elite or Plural Elites? Our discussion of elitism and democracy raises several vital questions: Is power in America concentrated in the hands of a small elite, with the masses permanently barred from exercising power? Or is power in America diffused, with many separate elite groups exercising

---

[15] Roland Pennock, "Democracy and Leadership," in William Chambers and Robert Salisbury (eds.), *Democracy Today* (New York: Dodd, Mead & Co., 1962), pp. 126–127.

power from time to time? Can individuals move in and out of the ranks of decision makers, depending upon their activity and interest in public affairs? Or are the ranks of decision makers closed to all but the top corporate financial, military, and governmental leaders? Is there convergence at the "top" of the power structure in America, with a single group dominating decision making in industry, finance, foreign policy, military affairs, and domestic programs? Or are there separate elites in each area of decision making? Do elite members in America compete with each other over major questions of public policy, or do they share a consensus about the direction of public policy and disagree only on minor details? Can the masses, through elections and party competition, hold elites accountable for their policy decisions, or are elites free from mass influence?

Social scientists have differed over the answers to these questions; at least two separate varieties or models of elitism can be identified in social science literature concerned with the American political system.[16] The *single elite* model views power as concentrated in the hands of relatively few people, usually drawn from the corporate, financial, military, and governmental circles, who make the key decisions in all significant areas of American life and who are subject to very little influence from the masses. In contrast, the *plural elite* model views power as more widely shared among leadership groups representing different segments of society; these separate elites are competitive and are held responsible by the masses through elections, party competition, and interest groups.

Much of the rest of this volume is an examination of the relevance of these models for describing American politics; therefore, special note should be taken of the following outline, of the major ideas expressed in these single elite and plural elite models of power. The single elite model includes the following ideas:

1. Power stems from roles or positions within the socioeconomic system. People acquire power by virtue of occupying important positions in industrial, financial, military, or governmental institutions.

2. Power is "structured"; that is, power relationships tend to persist over time. Issues and elections may come and go, but the same leadership groups continue to exercise power in society.

3. There is a reasonably clear distinction between elites and masses. Members of the masses can join the elite only by acquiring high positions in the institutional structures of society. Members of the masses do not move freely in and out of the ranks of elites.

[16] This literature is so voluminous that it is only possible to cite some of the major summary works: Thomas J. Anton, "Power, Pluralism, and Local Politics," *Administrative Science Quarterly*, 7 (March 1962), 425–457; Lawrence Herson, "In the Footsteps of Community Power," *American Political Science Review*, 55 (December 1961), 817–831; Peter Bachrach and Morton Baratz, "Two Faces of Power," *American Political Science Review*, 56 (December 1962), 947–953; Nelson Polsby, *Community Power and Political Theory* (New Haven, Conn.: Yale University Press, 1963); Robert Presthus, *Men at the Top* (New York: Oxford University Press, 1964); Robert Dahl, *Who Governs?* (New Haven, Conn.: Yale University Press, 1961); Floyd Hunter, *Community Power Structure* (Chapel Hill: University of North Carolina Press, 1953).

4. The distinction between elite and mass is based primarily on control over the economic resources of society. Industrial and financial leaders compose a major part of the elite.

5. There is considerable convergence at the top of the political system, with a small group exercising influence in many sectors of American life — industry, finance, military affairs, foreign policy, domestic affairs, and so on. A diagram of power in America takes the form of a single pyramid.

6. Persons in the elite disagree from time to time, but they share a larger consensus about preserving the system essentially as it is. Their views are conservative, and they act with great cohesion when the system is threatened.

7. The elite is subject to little or no influence from the masses, whether through elections or any other form of political activity.

In contrast, the plural elite model involves the following notions:

1. Power is an attribute of individuals in their relationships with other individuals in the process of decision making. Regardless of social or economic position, an individual has power to the extent that he can induce another individual to do something he would not otherwise do.

2. Power relationships do not necessarily persist over time. A set of power relationships that are formed for a particular decision may be replaced by a different set of power relations when the next decision is made.

3. The distinction between elites and masses may be quite blurred. Individuals move in and out of the ranks of decision makers with relative ease, depending on the nature of the decision.

4. The distinction between elites and masses is based primarily on the level of interest people have in a particular decision. Leadership is fluid and mobile. Access to decision making can be achieved through the skills of leadership — organization, information about issues, knowledge about democratic processes, and skill in public relations. Wealth or economic power is an asset in politics, but it is only one of many kinds of assets.

5. There are multiple elites within society. Persons who exercise power in some kinds of decisions do not necessarily exercise power in other kinds of decisions. No single group dominates decision making in all issue areas.

6. There is considerable competition among elites. While elites generally share a basic commitment to the "rules of the game" in democratic society, they seek many divergent policies. Public policy represents bargains or compromises reached between competing groups.

7. The masses can exercise considerable influence over elites through elections and membership in organizations. Also, competition among elites enables the masses to hold elites accountable for their decisions.

These statements describe ideal or abstract models of power. It may be that power in America really falls somewhere between these single elite and plural elite models of power; that is, somewhere between a monolithic, pyramidal structure of power and a diffused, multi-centered, pluralist structure of power. Yet these ideal models can help us understand the different ways that power *can* be structured in a society. More importantly, they focus attention on vital aspects of politics – how people acquire power, the degree of access to elites, the relationship between political and economic power, the degree of convergence among power holders, the extent of competition among elites, and the role of masses in shaping elite behavior.

So far we have described only models of elite systems. Now we can turn to some research on actual American communities – Atlanta, Georgia, and New Haven, Connecticut – to illustrate elite theory and the single elite and plural elite models.

In an influential book on power in Atlanta, Georgia, sociologist Floyd Hunter describes a pyramidal structure of power and influence, with most of the important community decisions reserved for a top layer of the business and financial leaders.[17] According to Hunter, admission to the circle of influentials in Atlanta is based primarily on one's position in the business and financial community. Hunter explains that the top power structure concerns itself only with major policy decisions and that the leadership of certain substructures – economic, governmental, religious, educational, professional, civic, and cultural – then take their cues and communicate and implement the policies decided at the top level.

[The substructures] are subordinate . . . to the interests of the policy makers who operate in the economic sphere of community life in the regional city. The institutions of the family, church, state, education, and the like draw sustenance from economic institutional sources and are thereby subordinate to this particular institution more than any other. . . . Within the policy-forming groups the economic interests are dominant [p. 94].

The top powerholders seldom operate openly. "Most of the top personnel in the power group are rarely seen in the meetings attended by the associational understructure personnel in Regional City [Atlanta] [p. 90]." Hunter describes the process of community action as follows:

If a project of major proportions were before the community for consideration – let us say a project aimed at building a new municipal auditorium – a policy committee would be formed. . . . Such a policy committee would more than likely grow out of a series of informal meetings, and it might be related to a project that has been on the discussion agenda of many associations for months or even years. But the time has arrived for action. Money must be raised through private subscription or taxation, a site selected, and contracts let. The time for a policy committee is propitious. The selection of the policy committee will fall largely to the men of power in the community. They will

[17] Floyd Hunter, *Community Power Structure* (Chapel Hill: University of North Carolina Press, 1953).

likely be businessmen in one or more of the large business establishments. Mutual choices will be agreed upon for committee membership. In the early stages of policy formulation there will be a few men who make basic decisions. . . . Top ranking organizational and institutional personnel will then be selected by the original members to augment their numbers; i.e., the committee will be expanded. Civic associations and the formalized institutions will next be drawn into certain phases of planning and initiation of the projects on a community-wide basis. The newspapers will finally carry stories, the ministers will preach sermons, the associations will hear speeches regarding plans. This rather simply is the process, familiar to many, that goes on in getting any community project underway [pp. 92–93].

Note that in Hunter's description of community decision making, decisions tend to flow *down* from top policy makers (composed primarily of business and financial leaders) to the civic, professional, and cultural association leaders, the religious and educational leaders, and the government officials who implement the program. The masses of people have little direct or indirect participation in the whole process. Policy does not go *up* from associational groupings or from the people themselves.

The top group of the power hierarchy has been isolated and defined as comprised of policy makers. These men are drawn largely from the businessmen's class in Regional City. They form cliques or crowds, as the term is more often used in the community, which formulate policy. Committees for the formulation of policy are commonplace; and on community-wide issues, policy is channeled by a "fluid committee structure" down to institutional, associational groupings through a lower-level bureaucracy which executes policy [p. 113].

According to Hunter, elected public officials are clearly part of the lower-level institutional substructure that *executes* policy, rather than formulating it. Finally, Hunter found that this whole power structure is held together by "common interests, mutual obligations, money, habit, delegated responsibilities, and in some cases by coercion and force [p. 113]."

Hunter's findings in Atlanta parallel the single elite model, and they are discomforting to those who wish to see America governed in a truly democratic fashion. Hunter's research challenges the notion of popular participation in decision making, or grassroots democracy; it raises doubts as to whether cherished democratic values are being realized in American community life.

In his significant study of power in New Haven, political scientist Robert A. Dahl admits that community decisions are made by "tiny minorities," who are not representative of the community as a whole in terms of social class.[18] However, Dahl challenges the notion that the elite system in American community life is pyramidal and cohesive and unresponsive to popular demands. Dahl studied major decisions

---

[18] Robert Dahl. *Who Governs?* (New Haven. Conn.: Yale University Press. 1961).

in urban redevelopment and public education in New Haven, as well as the nominations for mayor in both political parties. In contrast to Hunter's highly monolithic and centralized power structure in Atlanta, Dahl found a polycentric and dispersed system of elites in New Haven. Influence was exercised from time to time by many elites, each exercising some power over some issues but not over others. When the issue was urban renewal, one set of leaders was influential; in public education, a different group was involved.

Business and financial elites, who in Hunter's study dominate Atlanta, are only one of many influential elites in New Haven. According to Dahl:

> The economic notables, far from being a ruling group, are simply one of many groups out of which individuals sporadically emerge to influence the politics and acts of city officials. Almost anything one might say about the influence of the economic notables could be said with equal justice about a half dozen other groups in the New Haven community [p. 72].

Yet at the same time, Dahl finds that the total number of people who are involved in all community decisions in New Haven are still only a tiny minority of the community. For example, Dahl writes:

> It is not too much to say that urban redevelopment has been the direct product of a small handful of leaders [p. 115].

> The bulk of the voters had virtually no direct influence on the process of nomination [p. 106].

> The number of citizens who participated directly in important decisions bearing on the public schools is small [p. 151].

Moreover, Dahl notes that persons exercising leadership for each issue are of higher social status than the rest of the community, and that these middle- and upper-class elite members possess more of the skills and qualities required of leaders in a democratic system.

Obviously, Dahl's New Haven parallels the plural elite model. It is very important to observe that New Haven is not a democracy in the sense that we defined democracy earlier. Not all of the citizens of New Haven participated in the decisions that affected their lives, and not all of the citizens had an equal opportunity to influence public policy.

Pluralism and Democracy Most scholars today acknowledge that democratic societies are governed by elites. But often they seek to reaffirm democratic values by contending:

1. That there is competition among elites;

2. That voters can influence elite behavior by choosing between competing elites in elections;

3. That elites are not closed and new social groups can gain access to elite positions;

4. That elites dominating various areas of society, such as business, government, education, defense, and the arts, have not formed a common alliance and do not dominate the society as a *single* elite.

In short, scholars generally believe that democratic values can be effectively realized through the plural elite model.[19]

Pluralism, then, is the belief that democratic values can be preserved in a system of multiple, competing elites, in which voters can exercise meaningful choices in elections and in which new elites can gain access to power. But pluralism should not be considered synonymous with democracy; for pluralism does not include *direct* citizen participation in decision making. Pluralists recognize that mass participation in decision making is not possible in a complex, urban, industrial society and that decision making must be accomplished through elite interaction, rather than individual participation. However, the underlying value of individual dignity still motivates pluralism; for it is the hope of pluralists that countervailing centers of elite power — the competition between business elites, labor elites, and governmental elites — can check each other and can keep each interest from abusing its power or oppressing the individual.

Of course, decision making by elite interaction, whether it succeeds in protecting the individual or not, fails to contribute to individual growth and development. In this regard, modern pluralism diverges sharply from classic democracy, which emphasizes as a primary value the personal development that would result from the individual's actively participating in decisions that affect his life.

Another central value of classical democratic politics is *individual* participation in decision making. In modern pluralism, however, individual participation has given way to interaction — bargaining, accommodation, and compromise — between leaders of institutions and organizations in society. Individuals are represented in the political system only insofar as they are members of institutions or organizations whose leaders participate in policy making. Government is held responsible not by individual citizens but by leaders of institutions, organized interest groups, and political parties. The principal actors are leaders of corporations and financial institutions, elected and appointed government officials, the top ranks of military and governmental bureaucracies, and leaders of large organizations in labor, agriculture, and the professions.

Pluralism stresses the fragmentation of power in society and the influence of public opinion and elections on the behavior of elites.

[19] See Robert A. Dahl. *Pluralist Democracy in the United States* (Chicago: Rand McNally. 1967).

But this fragmentation of power is not identical with the democratic ideal of political equality. Who rules, in the pluralist view of America? According to political scientist Aaron Wildavsky, "different small groups of interested and active citizens in different issue areas with some overlap, if any, by public officials, and occasional intervention by a larger number of people at the polls."[20] This is not government by the people. While citizen influence can be felt through leaders who anticipate the reaction of citizens, decision making is still in the hands of the leaders—the elites. According to the pluralists, multiple elites decide public policy in America, each in their own area of interest.

Traditional democratic theory envisions public policy as a rational choice of individuals with equal influence, who evaluate their needs and reach a decision with due regard for the rights of others. This traditional theory does not view public policy as a product of elite interaction or interest group pressures. In fact, interest groups and even political parties were viewed by classical democratic theorists as intruders into an individualistic brand of citizenship and politics.

There are several other problems in accepting pluralism as the legitimate heir to classical democratic theory. First of all, can pluralism assure that membership in organizations and institutions is really an effective form of individual participation in policy making? Robert Presthus argues that the organizations and institutions on which pluralists rely "become oligarchic and restrictive insofar as they monopolize access to government power and limit individual participation."[21]

Henry Kariel writes, "The voluntary organizations or associations which the early theorists of pluralism relied upon to sustain the individual against a unified omnipotent government, have themselves become oligarchically governed hierarchies."[22] The individual may provide the numerical base for organizations, but what influence does he have upon the leadership? Rarely do corporations, unions, armies, churches, government bureaucracies, or professional associations have any *internal* mechanisms of democracy. They are usually run by a small elite of officers and activists. Leaders of corporations, banks, labor unions, churches, universities, medical associations, and bar associations remain in control year after year. Only a small number of people attend meetings, vote in organizational elections, or make their influence felt within their organization. The pluralists offer no evidence that the giant organizations and institutions in American life really represent the views or interests of their individual members.

Also, can pluralism really assume that the dignity of the individual is being protected by elite competition? Since pluralism contends that different groups of leaders make decisions in *different* issue areas, why should we assume that these leaders compete with each other? It seems more likely that each group of leaders would consent to allow

---

[20] Aaron Wildavsky, *Leadership in a Small Town* (Totawa, N.J.: Bedminster Press, 1964), p. 20.
[21] Robert Presthus, *Men at the Top* (New York: Oxford University Press, 1964), p. 20.
[22] Henry Kariel, *The Decline of American Pluralism* (Stanford, Calif.: Stanford University Press, 1961), p. 74.

other groups of leaders to govern their own spheres of influence without interference. Accommodation, rather than competition, may be the prevailing style of elite interaction.

Pluralism answers with the hope that the power of diverse institutions and organizations in society will roughly balance out and that the emergence of power monopoly is unlikely. Pluralism (like its distant cousin, the economics of Adam Smith) assures us that no interests can ever emerge the complete victor in political competition. Yet inequality of power among institutions and organizations is commonplace. Examples of narrow, organized interests achieving their goals at the expense of the broader but unorganized public are quite common. Furthermore, it is usually producer interests, bound together by economic ties, which turn out to dominate less organized consumer groups and groups based upon non-economic interests. The pluralists offer no evidence that political competition can prevent monopoly or oligopoly in political power, any more than economic competition could prevent monopoly or oligopoly in economic power.

Finally, pluralism must contend with the problem of how private non-governmental elites can be held accountable to the people. Even if the people can hold governmental elites accountable through elections, how can corporation elites, union leaders, and other kinds of private leadership be held accountable? Pluralism usually dodges this important question by focusing primary attention on *public* decision making involving governmental elites and by largely ignoring *private* decision making involving non-governmental elites. Pluralists focus on rules and orders which are enforced by *governments*, but certainly men's lives are vitally affected by decisions made by private institutions and organizations—corporations, banks, universities, medical associations, newspapers, and so on. In an ideal democracy, individuals would participate in *all* decisions which significantly affect their lives; but pluralism largely excludes individuals from participation in many vital decisions by claiming that these decisions are "private" in nature and not subject to public accountability.

Peter Bachrach observes:

> In keeping with the democratic principle that those who make decisions should be accountable to the people who are affected by them, it was reasonable for theorists of the eighteenth and nineteenth centuries to think of political as that which involved only government. There was little justification to think otherwise, since government was the only organized institution that possessed sufficient decision-making power to affect large groups of people or the active society. To continue to think in the same way today in the face of immense and powerful non-governmental decision making is difficult to understand.[23]

In summary, the plural elite model diverges from classical democratic theory in the following respects:

---

[23]Peter Bachrach, *The Theory of Democratic Elitism* (Boston: Little, Brown and Co., 1967), p. 74.

1. Decisions are made by elite interaction — bargaining, accommodation, compromise — rather than by direct individual participation.

2. Key political actors are leaders of institutions and organizations rather than individual citizens.

3. Power is fragmented, but inequality of political influence among power-holders is common.

4. Power is distributed among governmental and non-governmental institutions and organizations, but these institutions and organizations are generally governed by oligarchies, rather than by their members in democratic fashion.

5. Institutions and organizations divide power and presumably compete among themselves, but there is no certainty that this competition guarantees political equality or protects individual dignity.

6. *Governmental* elites are presumed to be accountable to the masses through elections, but many important decisions affecting the lives of individuals are made by *private* elites, who are not directly accountable to the masses.

Frequently confusion arises in distinguishing *pluralism* from *elitism*. Pluralists *say* that the system they describe is a reaffirmation of democratic theory in a modern, urban, industrial society. They offer pluralism as "a practical solution" to the problem of achieving democratic ideals in a large complex social system where direct individual participation and decision making is simply not possible. But many critics of pluralism assert that it is a covert form of elitism — that pluralists are closer to the elitist position than to the democratic tradition they revere. Thus Peter Bachrach describes pluralism as "democratic elitism":

> Until quite recently democratic and elite theories were regarded as distinct and conflicting. While in their pure form they are still regarded as contradictory, there is, I believe, a strong if not dominant trend in contemporary political thought incorporating major elitist principles within democratic theory. As a result there is a new theory which I have called democratic elitism.[24]

The Masses in Democratic Society

Democratic theory assumes that liberal values — individual dignity, equality of opportunity, the right of dissent, freedom of speech and press, religious toleration, and due process of law — are best protected by the expansion and growth of mass political participation. Historically, the masses and not elites were considered the guardians of liberty. For example, in the eighteenth and nineteenth centuries, the threat of tyranny arose from corrupt monarchies and decadent churches. But in the twentieth century, it has been the masses who have been most susceptible to the appeals of totalitarianism.

[24] Bachrach, p. xi.

It is the irony of democracy in America that elites, not masses, are most committed to democratic values. Despite a superficial commitment to the symbols of democracy, the American people have a surprisingly weak commitment to individual liberty, toleration of diversity, or freedom of expression for those who would challenge the existing order. Social science research reveals that the common man is not attached to the causes of liberty, fraternity, or equality. On the contrary, support for free speech and press, for freedom of dissent, and for equality of opportunity for all is associated with high educational levels, prestigious occupations, and high social status. Authoritarianism is stronger among the working classes in America than among the middle and upper classes. Democracy would not survive if it depended upon support for democratic values among the masses in America.

Democratic values have survived because elites, not masses, govern. Elites in America—leaders in government, industry, education, and civic affairs; the well-educated, prestigiously employed, and politically active—give greater support to basic democratic values and "rules of the game" than do the masses. And it is because masses in America respond to the ideas and actions of democratically minded elites that liberal values are preserved. In summarizing the findings of social science research regarding mass behavior in American democracy, political scientist Peter Bachrach writes:

> A widespread public commitment to the fundamental norms underlying the democratic process was regarded by classical democratic theorists as essential to the survival of democracy . . . today social scientists tend to reject this position. They do so not only because of their limited confidence in the commitment of non-elites to freedom, but also because of the growing awareness that non-elites are, in large part, politically activated by elites. The empirical finding that mass behavior is generally in response to the attitudes, proposals and modes of action of political elites gives added support to the position that responsibility for maintaining "the rules of the game" rests not on the shoulders of the people but on those of the elites.[25]

In short, it is the common man, not the elite, who is most likely to be swayed by anti-democratic ideology; and it is the elite, not the common man, who is the chief guardian of democratic values.

Elites must be insulated from the anti-democratic tendencies of the masses if they are to fulfill their role as guardians of liberty and property. Too much mass influence over elites threatens democratic values. Mass behavior is highly unstable. Usually, established elites can depend upon mass apathy; but, occasionally, mass activism will replace apathy, and this activism will be extremist, unstable, and unpredictable. Mass activism is usually an expression of resentment against the established order, and it usually occurs in times of crisis, when a counter-elite, or demagogue, emerges from the masses to mobilize them against the established elites.

[25] Bachrach, pp. 47–48.

Mass activism tends to be undemocratic and violent because masses do not have a strong commitment to established institutions and procedures. Populist values—extremism, intolerance, anti-intellectualism, and equalitarianism—generally become the impetus of mass movements, which may be either "left" or "right" in their political ideology. America has experienced a long history of such mass movements, led by a wide variety of counter-elites, from Shays' Rebellion and the Know-Nothings of the eighteenth and nineteenth centuries, to McCarthyism, black ghetto riots, and George C. Wallace's American Independent party in the twentieth century. These seemingly divergent movements have several common characteristics—they were supported by the masses, they expressed resentment toward the established order, and they were opposed by established elites.

Democracies, where elites are dangerously accessible to mass influence, can survive only if the masses are absorbed in the problems of everyday life and are involved in primary and secondary groups which distract their attention from mass politics. In other words, the masses are stable when they are absorbed in their work, family, neighborhood, trade union, hobby, church, recreational group, and so on. It is when they become alienated from their home, work, and community—when existing ties to social organizations and institutions become weakened—that mass behavior becomes unstable and dangerous. It is then that the attention and activity of the masses can be captured and directed by the demagogue, or counter-elite. The demagogue can easily mobilize for revolution those elements of the masses who have few ties to the existing social and political order.

These ties to the existing order tend to be weakest during crisis periods, when major social changes are taking place. According to social psychologist William Kornhauser:

> . . . communism and fascism have gained strength in social systems undergoing sudden and extensive changes in the structure of authority and community. Sharp tears in the social fabric caused by widespread unemployment or by major military defeat are highly favorable to mass politics.[26]

Counter-elites in Mass Politics

Counter-elites are mass-oriented leaders who express hostility toward the established order and appeal to mass sentiments—extremism, intolerance, racial identity, anti-intellectualism, equalitarianism, and violence. Counter-elites can easily be distinguished from elites: *Elites,* whether liberal or conservative, support the fundamental values of the system—individual liberty, majority rule, due process of law, limited government, and private property; *counter-elites,* whether "left" or "right," are anti-democratic, extremist, impatient with due process, contemptuous of law and authority, and violence-prone. The only significant difference between "left" and "right" counter-elites is their attitude toward change: "right" counter-elites express mass

[26]William Kornhauser, *The Politics of Mass Society* (New York: Free Press, 1959), p. 99.

reaction against change—political, social, economic, technological—while "left" counter-elites demand radical and revolutionary change.

All counter-elites claim to speak for "the people." Both "left" and "right" counter-elites assert *the supremacy of "the people"* over laws, institutions, procedures, or individual rights. Right-wing counter-elites, including fascists, justify their policies as "the will of the people," while left-wing radicals cry "all power to the people" and praise the virtues of "people's democracies." In describing this populism, sociologist Edward Shils writes:

the will of the people as such is supreme over every other standard, over the standards of traditional institutions, over the autonomy of insitutions, and over the will of other strata. Populism identifies the will of the people with justice and morality.[27]

What the "will of the people" really is the counter-elites know in a quasi-mystical fashion. The counter-elite "knows" what is in the interest of the people; and there is no need to establish procedures to ascertain popular will. Frequently the counter-elite "knows" what the people want even if the people themselves are not aware of it.

Extremism is another characteristic of counter elites—they view compromise and coalition-building as immoral. Indeed "politics" and "politicians" are viewed with hostility, because they imply the possibility of compromising mass demands.[28] Occasionally counter-elites will make cynical use of politics, but only as a short-term tactical means to other goals. Thus, Stokely Carmichael speaks contemptuously of the "fallacies" of black coalitions with white liberals: "These groups accept the legitimacy of the basic values and institutions of the society and fundamentally are not interested in a major reorientation of society [revolution]."[29] A commentator on radical student activists observes that they are

indistinguishable from the far right. . . . They share a contempt for rational political discussion and constitutional legal solutions. Both want to be pure. They know nothing about the virtue of compromise. They know nothing about the horror of sainthood or the wickedness of saints.[30]

Counter-elites generally charge that a *conspiracy* exists among established elites to deliberately perpetuate evil upon the people. The "left" counter-elite charges that the established order knowingly exploits and oppresses the people for its own benefit and amusement; the "right" counter-elite charges that the established order is falling

[27] Edward A. Shils, *The Torment of Secrecy* (New York: Free Press, 1956); p. 98.
[28] See John H. Bunzel, *Anti-Politics in America* (New York: Knopf, 1967).
[29] Stokely Carmichael and Charles V. Hamilton, *Black Power: The Politics of Liberation in America* (New York: Random House, 1967) p. 60.
[30] Quotation from Nan Robertson, "The Student Scene: Angry Militants" *New York Times,* November 20, 1967, p. 30.

prey to an international communist comspiracy whose goal is to deprive the people of their liberty and property and to enslave them. Richard Hofstadter refers to this phenomena as "the paranoid style of politics."[31] A related weapon in the arsenal of the counter-elite is *scapegoatism* — the designation of particular minority groups in society as responsible for the evils suffered by the people. Throughout American history various scapegoats have been designated — Catholics, immigrants, Jews, Negroes, communists, intellectuals, "Wall Street Bankers," munitions manufacturers, etc.

Counter-elites define politics for the masses in *simplistic* terms. The masses want simple answers to all of society's problems, regardless of how complex these problems may be. Thus, black counter-elites charge that "white racism" is responsible for the complex problems of under-education, poverty, unemployment, crime, delinquency, ill-health, and poor housing of ghetto dwellers. In a similiar fashion the white counter-elites dismiss ghetto disturbances as a product of "communist agitation." These simplistic answers are designed to relieve both black and white masses of any difficult thinking about social issues and to place their problems in simple, emotion-laden terms. Anti-intellectualism and anti-rationalism are an important part of counter-elite politics.

Counter-elites express equalitarian sentiments which appeal to their mass followers. This is true, not only of "left" counter-elites (whom we generally associate with hostility toward the wealthy), but also of "right" counter-elites. Robert Welch, leader of the John Birch society, writes:

The ordinary happy and innocent American will frequently observe about some multimillionaire or some college president whose activities on behalf of the Communists are obvious: "But of course, he couldn't be a Communist himself. He's rich. . . ." To which the proper answer is: "Nuts! Where on earth do you think the leaders of Communism come from. . . . Almost invariably they have been from the wealthy and best-educated classes. . . ."[32]

And George C. Wallace states firmly: "I don't believe all this talk about poor folks turning Communist. It's the damn rich who turn Communist. Do you ever see a poor Communist?"[33]

Counter-elites also reflect mass *propensities toward violence*. Rap Brown inspired black masses in Cambridge, Maryland, in 1967 with:

"Don't be trying to love that honky to death. Shoot him to death. Shoot him to death, brother, cause that's what he's out to do to you. Like I said in the beginning, if this town don't come around, this town should be burned down, it should be burned down, brother."[34]

[31] Richard Hofstadter, *The Paranoid Style of American Politics* (New York: Knopf, 1965).
[32] Quoted in Seymour Martin Lipset and Earl Raab *The Politics of Unreason* (New York: Harper and Row, 1970), p. 257.
[33] *Ibid.* p. 350.
[34] U.S. Congress, Senate, Committee on the Judiciary, Hearings on H.R. 421, "Anti-riot Bill," 90th Congress, 1st Session, 2 August 1967, p. 32.

George C. Wallace's references to violence are only slightly more subtle:

Of course, if I did what I'd like to do I'd pick up something and smash one of these federal judges in the head and then burn the courthouse down. But I'm too genteel. What we need in this country is some Governors that used to work up here at Birmingham in the steel mills with about a tenth-grade education. A Governor like that wouldn't be so genteel. He'd put out his orders and he'd say, "The first man who throws a brick is a dead man. The first man who loots something what doesn't belong to him is a dead man. My orders are to shoot to kill."[35]

The similarity between the appeals of black and white counter-elites is obvious.

In summary, elite theory views the critical division in American politics as the division between elites and masses. "Left" and "right" counter-elites are similar. Both appeal to mass sentiments; assert the supremacy of "the people" over laws, institutions, and individual rights; reject compromise in favor of extremism; charge that established elites are a conspiracy; designate scapegoat groups; define social problems in simple emotional terms and reject rational thinking; express equalitariam sentiments and hostility toward men who have achieved success within the system; and express approval of mass violence.

Elites and Counter-elites

While elites are *relatively* more committed to democratic values than masses, elites may abandon these values in crisis periods. When war or revolution threatens to tear down the existing order, the established elites may move toward the "garrison state." Dissent will no longer be tolerated; the news media will be censored, free speech curtailed, potential counter-elites jailed, and police and security forces strengthened — usually in the name of national security, or "law and order," in the belief that these steps are necessary to preserve liberal democratic values. The irony is, of course, that the elites make society less democratic in order to preserve democracy.

In short, neither elites nor masses in America are totally and irrevocably committed to democratic values. On the whole, however, elites are restrained by their commitments to freedom and individual dignity. This is true for several reasons. In the first place, persons who are successful at the game of democratic politics are more amenable to abiding by the rules of the game than those who are not. Moreover, many elite members have internalized democratic values learned in childhood. Finally, the achievement of high position may bring a sense of responsibility for, and an awareness of, societal values.

[35] Lipset and Raab, *op. cit.*, p. 356.

Selected Additional Readings

Bachrach, Peter. *The Theory of Democratic Elitism*. Boston: Little, Brown, 1966 (paper). This is an excellent essay on the role of elites in a bureaucratic society.

Bell, Roderick, David V. Edwards, and R. Harrison Wagner. *Political Power: A Reader in Theory and Research*. New York: Free Press, 1969. This collection of important articles on power and elites includes works by Dahl, Polsby, Kornhauser, Simon, Banfield, and Bachrach and Baratz.

Kornhauser, William. *The Politics of Mass Society*. New York: Free Press, 1959. Kornhauser examines the threat to democratic values posed by mass activism.

**The Founding Fathers:
The Nation's First Elite**

The Founding Fathers—those 55 men who wrote the Constitution of the United States and founded a new nation—were a truly exceptional elite, not only "rich and well-born" but also educated, talented, and resourceful. When Thomas Jefferson, then serving as the nation's minister in Paris, first saw the list of delegates to the Constitutional Convention of 1787, he wrote to John Adams, who was the minister to London: "It is really an assembly of demigods."[1] The men at the Convention were drawn from the nation's intellectual and economic elites—possessors of landed estates, large merchants and importers, financiers and moneylenders, real estate and land speculators, and owners of public bonds and securities. Jefferson and Adams were among the very few of the nation's "notables" who were *not* at the Convention.

Needless to say, the Founding Fathers were not representative of the four million Americans in the new nation, most of whom were small farmers, debtors, tradesmen, frontiersmen, servants, or slaves. However, to say that these men were not representative of the American people, or that the Constitution was not a very democratic document, does not discredit the Constitution or the Founding Fathers. To the aristocratic society of eighteenth-century Europe, the Founding Fathers were dangerous revolutionaries, who were establishing a government in which men with the talent of acquiring property could rise to political power, regardless of birth or nobility. And the Constitution has survived the test of time, providing the basic framework for an ever-changing society.

Elites and Masses in the New American Nation

Visitors from the old aristocratic countries of Europe frequently remarked about the absence of a nobility in America and about the spirit of republicanism that prevailed. Certainly the yeoman farmer or frontiersman in America gave much less open deference to his "betters" than did the peasant of Europe; yet there were class lines in America. At the top of the social structure there was a tiny elite, most of whom

[1] Lester Cappon (ed.), *The Adams-Jefferson Letters*, Vol. I (Chapel Hill: University of North Carolina Press, 1959), p. 196.

were well-born, although there were some who were self-made. This elite group dominated the social, cultural, economic, and political life of the new nation. The French chargé d'affaires of that time reported that although there were "no nobles" in America, there were "gentlemen" who enjoyed a kind of "preeminence" because of "their wealth, their talents, their education, their families, or the offices they hold."[2] Some of these prominent "gentlemen" were Tories and had been forced to flee America after the Revolution; but there were still the Pinckneys and Rutledges in Charleston; the Adamses, Lowells, and Gerrys in Boston; the Schuylers, Clintons, and Jays of New York; the Morrises, Mifflins, and Ingersolls of Philadelphia; the Jenifers and Carrolls of Maryland; and the Blairs and Randolphs of Virginia.

Below this thin layer of educated and talented merchants, planters, lawyers, and bankers was a substantial body of successful farmers, shopkeepers, and independent artisans—of the "middling" sort, as they were known in Revolutionary America. This early middle class was by no means a majority in the new nation; it stood considerably above the masses of debt-ridden farmers and frontiersmen who made up the majority of the population. This small middle class had some political power, even at the time of the Constitutional Convention. This middle group was entitled to vote, and its views were represented in governing circles, even if they did not prevail at the Constitutional Convention. The middle class was especially well represented in state legislatures and was championed by several men of prominence in the Revolutionary period—Patrick Henry, Luther Martin, and Thomas Jefferson.

The great mass of white Americans in the Revolutionary period were "freeholders," farmers who worked their own land, scratching out a minimum existence for themselves and their families. They had little interest in or knowledge about public affairs. Usually the freeholders who were not barred from voting by property-owning or tax-paying qualifications were too preoccupied with debt and subsistence, or too isolated in the wilderness, to vote anyhow. Nearly eight out of ten Americans made a marginal living in the dirt; one in ten worked in fishing or lumbering; one in ten was engaged in commerce in some way, from the dockhand and sailor to the lawyer and merchant.

At the bottom of the white social structure in the new republic were the indentured servants and tenant farmers; this class comprised perhaps 20 percent of the population at this time. There is no evidence that this group exercised any political power at all. Finally, Negro slaves stood below the bottom of the white class structure. While they also comprised almost 20 percent of the population and were an important component of the American economy, they were considered property, even in a country that proclaimed the natural rights and equality of "all men."

[2] Max Farrand (ed.), *The Records of the Federal Convention of 1787*, Vol. 3 (New Haven, Conn.: Yale University Press, 1937), p. 15.

**Elite
Dissatisfaction
with the
Confederation:
The Stimulus
to Reform**

In July 1775, Benjamin Franklin had proposed to the Continental Congress a plan for a "perpetual union"; and, following the Declaration of Independence in 1776, the Congress appointed a committee to consider the Franklin proposals. The committee, headed by John Dickinson, made its report in the form of Articles of Confederation, which were debated for more than a year before finally being adopted by the Congress on November 15, 1777. It was stipulated that the Articles of Confederation would not go into effect until every state had approved; Delaware withheld its consent until 1779, Maryland until 1781.

The Articles of Confederation, effective from 1781 to 1789, established a "firm league of friendship" among the states "for their common defense, the security of their liberties, and their mutual and general welfare." Each state was reassured of "its sovereignty, freedom, and independence, and every power, jurisdiction, and right, which is not by this confederation expressly delegated to the United States, in Congress assembled." The expressly delegated powers included power to declare war, to send and receive ambassadors, to make treaties, to fix standards of weights and measures, to regulate the value of coins, to manage Indian affairs, to establish post offices, to borrow money, to build and equip an army and navy, and to make requisitions upon the several states for money and manpower. The powers not delegated to Congress remained with the states, and these included two of the most important powers of government—the power to regulate commerce and the power to levy taxes. Congress had to requisition the states for its revenue, but Congress had no authority to compel the states to honor these requisitions. Moreover, since Congress could not regulate commerce, the states were free to protect local trade and commerce even at the expense of destroying the emerging national economy.

Thus, the United States under the Articles of Confederation was comparable to an international organization of thirteen separate and independent governments. The national government was thought of as an alliance of separate *states,* not a government "of the people"; and the powers of the national government were dependent upon state governments.

The Articles of Confederation established Congress as the single branch of the national government. Delegates to Congress were chosen by the legislature of each state, and every state enjoyed one vote in Congress regardless of its population or resources. Executive and judicial functions were performed by committees of Congress, and officials of the United States were appointed and directed by Congress. The Articles guaranteed travel among the states and entitled the citizens of each state to the "privileges and immunities" of citizens of each of the other states, including privileges of trade and commerce. Each state was required to give "full faith and credit" to the records, acts, and judicial proceedings of every other state, and fugitives could be extradited from one state to another. No state could enter into diplomatic relations with foreign governments or engage in war unless it was actually invaded; no state could maintain a navy, but every state was expected to keep a militia force.

Our Founding Fathers were very critical of the first government of the United States under the Articles of Confederation, but the government was not a failure. In the years between 1774 and 1789, the American Confederacy declared its independence from the world's most powerful colonial nation, fought a successful war, established a viable peace, won powerful allies in the international community, created a successful army and navy, established a postal system, created a national bureaucracy, and laid the foundations for national unity.

But despite the successes of the Confederation in war and diplomatic relations, the political arrangements under the Articles were found unsatisfactory, even threatening, by the American elites. Generally, the "weaknesses" of the Articles that were most lamented by the Founding Fathers were the political arrangements that threatened the interests of merchants, investors, planters, real estate developers, and owners of public bonds and securities. Some of these "weaknesses," and the threats that they posed to America's elite, are described below.

The inability of Congress to levy taxes under the Articles of Confederation was a serious threat to those patriots who had given financial backing to the new nation during the Revolutionary War. The war had been financed with money borrowed by the Continental Congress and the states through the issuance of bonds and securities. The United States government owed about $10 million to foreign investors and over $40 million to American investors; in addition, individual states owed over $20 million as a result of their efforts in support of the war.[3]

Congress was unable to tax the people in order to obtain money to pay off these debts; and although Congress continually requisitioned states for money, the states became less and less inclined, as time passed, to meet their obligations to the central government. Only one tenth of the sums requisitioned by Congress under the Articles was ever paid by the states; and during the last years of the Articles, the United States was unable even to pay interest on its foreign and domestic debt. The result was that the bonds and notes of the United States government lost most of their value, sometimes selling on the open market for only one tenth of their original value. Investors who had backed the American war effort were left holding the bag.

Without the power to tax, and with the credit of the United States ruined, the prospects of the central government for future financial support—and for survival—looked dim. Naturally, the rich planters, merchants, and investors who held public securities had a direct financial interest in helping the central government acquire the power to tax and to pay off its debts.

[3] A debt of $70 million is very small by today's standards, but the total taxable land value in all of the thirteen states in 1787 was only about $400 million. Thus, the public debt was about 20 percent of the total value of all of the lands in the thirteen states.

The inability of Congress under the Articles to regulate commerce between the states and with foreign nations and the practice of the states of laying tariffs on the goods of other states as well as on those of foreign nations were creating havoc among commercial and shipping interests. "In every point of view," Madison wrote in 1785, "the trade of this country is in a deplorable condition."[4] The American Revolution had been fought, in part, for the purpose of defending American commercial and business interests from oppressive regulations by the British government. Now the states themselves were interfering with the development of a national economy. Merchants and shippers with a view toward a national market and a high level of commerce were vitally concerned that the central government acquire the power to regulate interstate commerce and that the states be prevented from imposing crippling tariffs and restrictions on interstate trade.

State governments under the Articles posed a serious threat to investors and creditors through the issuance of cheap paper money and the passage of laws impairing the obligations of contract. Paper money issued by the states permitted debtors to pay off their creditors with money that had less value than the money originally loaned. Even the most successful farmers were usually heavily in debt, and many of these farmers were gaining strength in state legislatures. They threatened to pass laws delaying the collection of debts and even abolishing the prevailing practice of imprisonment for unpaid debts. Obviously, creditors had a direct financial interest in the establishment of a strong central government that could prevent the states from issuing public paper or otherwise interfering with debts.

The political success of debtors in Rhode Island particularly alerted men of property to the need for action that would offset the potential power of the agrarian classes. In Rhode Island, the paper-money faction secured a majority in the legislature and issued so much state currency that Rhode Island money was almost valueless. When merchants and creditors refused to accept Rhode Island paper money as "legal tender," the Rhode Island legislature passed a law making such refusal a punishable offense. In one of the first exercises of judicial review in history, the Rhode Island Supreme Court, still safe in the hands of propertied men, declared the law to be a violation of the Rhode Island Constitution. But the lesson to America's elite was clear: Too much democracy could threaten the rights of property, and only a strong central government with limited popular participation could safeguard property from the attacks of the masses.

A strong central government would help to protect creditors against social upheavals by the large debtor class in America. In several states, debtors had already engaged in open rebellion against tax col-

---

[4]Farrand, *Records of the Federal Convention of 1787,* Vol. 3, p. 32.

lectors and sheriffs attempting to repossess farms on behalf of creditors. The most serious rebellion broke out in the summer of 1786 in Massachusetts, when bands of insurgents—composed of farmers, artisans, and laborers—captured the courthouses in several western districts and momentarily held the city of Springfield. Led by Daniel Shays, a veteran of Bunker Hill, the insurgent army posed a direct military threat to the governing elite of Massachusetts. Shays' Rebellion, as it was called, was put down by a small mercenary army, paid for by well-to-do citizens who feared that a wholesale attack on property rights was imminent.

The growing radicalism in the states was intimidating the propertied classes, who began to suggest that a strong central government was needed to "insure domestic tranquility," guarantee "a republican form of government," and protect property "against domestic violence." The American Revolution had a disturbing effect on the tradition among the masses of deferring to those in authority. Extremists, like Thomas Paine, who had reasoned that it was right and proper to revolt against England because of political tyranny, might also call for revolt against creditors because of economic tyranny. If debts owed to British merchants could be legislated out of existence, why not also the debts owed to American merchants? Acts of violence, boycotts, tea parties, and attacks on tax collectors frightened all propertied men in America.

A strong central government with military power sufficient to oust the British in the Northwest and to protect Western settlers against Indian attacks could open the way for the development of the American West. In addition, the protection and settlement of Western land would skyrocket land values and make rich men of land speculators.

Speculation in Western land was a very active pastime for men of property in early America. George Washington, Benjamin Franklin, Robert Morris, and even the popular hero Patrick Henry were involved in land speculation. During the Revolutionary War, the Congress had often paid the Continental soldiers with land certificates. After the war, most of the ex-soldiers sold these certificates to land speculators at very low prices. The Confederation's lack of proper military forces for America's frontiers had kept the value of Western lands at low prices, for ravaging Indians discouraged immigration to the lands west of the Alleghenies, and the British threatened to cut off westward expansion by continuing to occupy (in defiance of the peace treaty) seven important fur-trading forts in the Northwest. The British forts were also becoming centers of anti-American influence among the Indians.

The development of a strong American navy was also important to American commercial interests; for the states seem to have been ineffective in preventing smuggling, and piracy was a very real danger at the time and a vital concern of American shippers.

Manufacturing was still in its infant stages during the Revolutionary era in America, but farsighted investors were anxious to provide pro-

tection for infant American industries against the importation of British goods. While it is true that all thirteen states erected tariff barriers against foreign goods, state tariffs were unlikely to provide the same degree of protection for industry as a strong central government with a uniform tariff policy, because foreign goods could be brought into low-tariff states and then circulated throughout the country.

Finally, a strong sense of nationalism appeared to motivate America's elites. While the masses directed their attention to local affairs, the educated and cosmopolitan-minded leaders in America were concerned with the weakness of America in the international community of nations. Thirteen separate states failed to manifest a sense of national purpose and identity. The United States were held in contempt not only by Britain, as evidenced by the violations of the Treaty of Paris, but even by the lowly Barbary states. Hamilton expressed the indignation of America's leadership over its inability to swing weight in the world community:

> There is something . . . diminutive and contemptible in the prospect of a number of petty states, with the appearance only of union, jarring, jealous, and perverse, without any determined direction, fluctuating and unhappy at home, weak and insignificant by their dissentions in the eyes of other nations.[5]

In short, America's elite wanted to assume a respectable role in the international community and exercise power in world affairs.

The Formation of a National Elite   In the spring of 1785, delegates from Virginia and Maryland met at Alexandria, Virginia, to resolve certain difficulties that had arisen between the two states over the regulation of commerce and navigation on the Potomac River and Chesapeake Bay. It was fortunate, indeed, for the new nation that the most prominent man in America, George Washington, took a personal interest in this meeting. As a rich planter and land speculator who owned over 30,000 acres of Western lands upstream on the Potomac, Washington was keenly aware of commercial problems under the Articles. He lent great prestige to the Alexandria meeting by inviting participants to his home at Mount Vernon. Out of this conference came the idea for a general economic conference for all of the states. The Virginia legislature issued a call for such a convention to meet at Annapolis in September 1786.

In terms of its publicly announced purpose — that of securing interstate agreement on matters of commerce and navigation — the Annapolis Convention was a failure; only twelve delegates appeared to represent five commercial states: New York, New Jersey, Pennsylvania, Delaware, and Virginia. But these twelve men saw the opportunity to use the Annapolis meeting to achieve greater political successes. Alexander Hamilton, with masterful political foresight, persuaded Egbert

[5] See Clinton Rossiter, *1787, The Grand Convention* (New York: Macmillan Co., 1966), p. 45.

Benson, John Dickinson, George Reed, Edmund Randolph, James Madison, and others in attendance to strike out for a full constitutional solution to all of the ills of America. The Annapolis Convention adopted a report, written by Alexander Hamilton, which outlined the defects in the Articles of Confederation and called upon the states to send delegates to a new convention to suggest remedies for these defects. The new convention was to meet in May 1787 in Philadelphia. It was rumored at the time that Hamilton, with the behind-the-scenes support of James Madison in the Virginia legislature, never intended that the Annapolis Convention should be successful in its stated purposes and had planned all along to make Annapolis a stepping stone toward larger political objectives.

Shays' Rebellion could not have occurred at a more opportune time for men like Hamilton and Madison, who sought to galvanize America's elite into action. Occurring in the fall of 1786, after the Annapolis call for a new convention, the rebellion convinced men of property in Congress and state legislatures that there was cause for alarm. Even George Washington, who did not frighten easily, expressed his concern: "I feel . . . infinitely more than I can express . . . for the disorders which have arisen. . . . Good God! Who besides a Tory could have foreseen, or a Briton have predicted them!"

On February 21, 1787, Congress confirmed the call for a convention to meet in Philadelphia "for the sole and express purpose of revising the Articles of Confederation and reporting to Congress and the several legislatures such alterations and provisions therein as shall, when agreed to in Congress and confirmed by the states, render the federal Constitution adequate to the exigencies of government and the preservation of the union." Delegates to the convention were appointed by the state legislatures of every state except Rhode Island, the only state in which the debtor classes had won political control.

Men of Principle and Property.   The 55 men who met in the summer of 1787 to establish a new national government were the most prestigious, wealthy, educated, and skillful group of "notables" ever to be assembled in America for a political meeting. The Founding Fathers were truly the elite of elites—an elite both willing and able to act with creative boldness in establishing a government for an entire nation.

The Founding Fathers quickly chose George Washington, their most prestigious member—indeed, the most prestigious man on the continent—to preside over the assembly. Just as quickly, the Convention decided that its sessions would be held behind closed doors and that all proceedings would be a carefully guarded secret. This decision was closely adhered to, and neither close friends nor relatives were informed of the nature of the discussions underway. Apparently the Founding Fathers were aware that elites are most effective in negotiation, compromise, and decision making when operating in secrecy.

The Convention was also quick to discard its congressional mandate to "revise the Articles of Confederation"; and without much hesitation, it proceeded to write an entirely new constitution. Only men self-confident of their own powers and abilities, men of principle and property, would be capable of proceeding in this bold fashion. Let us examine the characteristics of the nation's first elite more closely.

The Founding Fathers were, first of all, men of *prestige and reputation*. Washington and Franklin were men of world-wide fame; and Johnson, Livingston, Robert Morris, Dickinson, and Rutledge were also well known in Europe. Gorham, Gerry, Sherman, Ellsworth, Hamilton, Mifflin, Wilson, Madison, White, Williamson, Whitney, and Mason were men of continental reputations; and the others were major figures in their respective states.

It is hardly possible to overestimate the prestige of George Washington at this time in his life. As the commander-in-chief of the successful revolutionary army and founder of the new nation, he had overwhelming charismatic appeal among both elites and masses. In addition to his preeminence as soldier, statesman, and founder of the nation, George Washington was one of the richest men in the United States at this time. Despite all the years that he had spent in the Revolutionary cause, he had refused any remuneration for his services. He often paid his soldiers from his own fortune. In addition to his large estate on the Potomac, he possessed many thousands of acres of undeveloped land in western Virginia, Maryland, Pennsylvania, Kentucky, and the Northwest Territory. He owned major shares in the Potomac Company, the James River Company, the Bank of Columbia, and the Bank of Alexandria. Finally, he held large amounts in United States bonds and securities. In short, Washington stood at the apex of America's elite structure.

As men of great reputations, the Founding Fathers knew one another and had *frequent communications and interaction*. The Convention was said to be a happy reunion of old friends and comrades. They had shared many activities in their elite experiences. As Clinton Rossiter points out:

Washington could look around the room and see a half a dozen men who had voted him into command far back into 1775, a dozen who had been with him at Trenton, Monmouth, or Yorktown, and another dozen who had won his friendship by supporting him in Congress or fishing with him in the Potomac. . . . Yates had studied law with Livingston, Livingston had been a patron of Hamilton, Hamilton had brightened the life of Madison, Madison had swapped books with Williamson, Williamson had done experiments with Franklin, Franklin had been amused by Sherman, Sherman had sold books to Baldwin, Baldwin had talked of the ancients with Johnson, Johnson was an old friend of Morris' of Morrisania, and Gouverneur Morris had worked closely with Yates in New York's dark days of 1776–1777. Bedford and Madison were classmates from Princeton; so too were Ellsworth and Luther Martin. Robert Morris knew at least ten men intimately from the early days in Congress; ten others had been his associates in schemes for bolstering the credit of the United States or improving the fortunes of Robert Morris.[6]

The Founding Fathers had extensive *experience in governing,* and a glance at their previous governing responsibilities reveals that these same men had made all the key decisions in American history from the Stamp Act Congress to the Declaration of Independence to the Articles of Confederation. They controlled the Congress of the United States and had conducted the Revolutionary War. Dickinson, Rutledge, and Johnson had been instrumental in the Stamp Act Congress at the very beginning of revolutionary activity. Eight delegates—Sherman, Robert Morris, Franklin, Clymer, Wilson, Gerry, Reed, and White—had signed the Declaration of Independence. Langdon, Livingston, Mifflin, Rutledge, Hamilton, Dayton, McHenry, Mercer, A. Martin, Davie, and Pierce had all served as officers in Washington's army. Forty-two of the 55 Founding Fathers had already served in the Congress of the United States, and Gorham and Mifflin had served as president of the Congress. Even at the moment of the Convention, more than forty delegates held high offices in state governments; Franklin, Livingston, and Randolph were governors. The Founding Fathers were unexcelled in political skill and experience.

In an age when no more than a handful of men on the continent had ever gone to college, the Founding Fathers were conspicuous for their *great educational attainment.* Over half the delegates had been educated at Princeton, Yale, Harvard, Columbia, Pennsylvania, William and Mary, or in England. The tradition of legal training for political decision makers, which has continued in America to the present day, was already evident in Philadelphia. About a dozen delegates were still active members of the bar in 1787, and about three dozen had been trained in law. Aristotle, Plutarch, Cicero, Locke, and Montesquieu were familiar names in debate. The Founding Fathers continually made historical and comparative references to Athenian democracy, the Roman republic, the Belgian and Dutch confederacies, the German empire, the English constitution, and even the Swiss cantons. The Convention was as rich in learning as it was in property and experience.

The 55 men at Philadelphia formed a major part of the nation's economic elite. The *personal wealth* represented at the meeting was enormous. Even Luther Martin, who showed more sympathy for the debtors of the nation than anyone else in attendance, was a Princeton graduate, successful attorney, planter, slaveowner, and bondholder, although his fortune was modest compared to his fellow delegates. It is difficult to determine accurately who were the richest men in America at this time, because the finances of the period were chaotic and because wealth assumed a variety of forms—land, ships, credit, slaves, business inventories, bonds, and paper money of uncertain

[6] Rossiter, pp. 152–153. Rossiter's discussion of the events leading to the Convention of 1787 and of the Convention itself is excellent.

worth (even George Washington had difficulty at times in converting his wealth in land into hard cash). But at least forty of the 55 delegates were known to be holders of public securities; fourteen were known to be land speculators; 24 were moneylenders and investors; eleven were engaged in commerce or manufacturing; and fifteen owned large plantations.[7] (See Table 2–1.)

Robert Morris was perhaps the foremost business and financial leader in the nation in 1787. This Philadelphia merchant owned scores of ships that traded throughout the world; he engaged in iron manufacturing, speculated in land in all parts of the country, and controlled the Bank of North America in Philadelphia, probably the nation's largest financial institution at the time. In business and financial dealings, he associated with many other eminent leaders, including Hamilton, Fitzsimons, G. Morris, Langdon, Clymer, and John Marshall. He earned his title "the patriot financier" by underwriting a large share of the debts of the United States during and after the Revolutionary War. George Washington was later to ask Morris, described as Washington's most intimate friend and closest companion, to become his first Secretary of the Treasury, but Morris declined in order to pursue his personal business interests. Later in his life, his financial empire collapsed, probably because of overspeculation, and he died in debt. But at the time of the Convention, he stood at the apex of the financial structure of America.

Perhaps what set off the men of Philadelphia from the masses more than anything else was their *cosmopolitanism*. They approached political, economic, and military issues from a "continental" point of

TABLE 2–1. Founding Fathers Classified by Known Membership in Elite Groups	Public Security Interests		Real Estate and Land Speculation	Lending and Investments	Mercantile, Manufacturing, and Shipping	Planters and Slaveholders
	Major	Minor				
	Baldwin	Bassett	Blount	Bassett	Broom	Butler
	Blair	Blount	Dayton	Broom	Clymer	Davie
	Clymer	Brearley	Few	Butler	Ellsworth	Jenifer
	Dayton	Broom	Fitzsimons	Carroll	Fitzsimons	A. Martin
	Ellsworth	Butler	Franklin	Clymer	Gerry	L. Martin
	Fitzsimons	Carroll	Gerry	Davie	King	Mason
	Gerry	Few	Gilman	Dickinson	Langdon	Mercer
	Gilman	Hamilton	Gorham	Ellsworth	McHenry	C. C. Pinckney
	Gorham	L. Martin	Hamilton	Few	Mifflin	C. Pinckney
	Jenifer	Mason	Mason	Fitzsimons	G. Morris	Randolph
	Johnson	Mercer	R. Morris	Franklin	R. Morris	Read
	King	Mifflin	Washington	Gilman		Rutledge
	Langdon	Read	Williamson	Ingersoll		Spaight
	Lansing	Spaight	Wilson	Johnson		Washington
	Livingston	Wilson		King		Wythe
	McClurg	Wythe		Langdon		
	R. Morris			Mason		
	C. C. Pinckney			McHenry		
	C. Pinckney			C. C. Pinckney		
	Randolph			C. Pinckney		
	Sherman			Randolph		
	Strong			Read		
	Washington			Washington		
	Williamson			Williamson		

[7]Charles Beard, *An Economic Interpretation of the Constitution of the United States* (New York: Macmillan Co., 1913), pp. 73–151.

view. Unlike the allegiances of the masses, the loyalties of the elites extended beyond their states; they experienced the sentiment of nationalism half a century before this sentiment would begin to seep down to the masses. Professor John P. Roche summarizes the characteristics and strengths of this national elite:

A small group of political leaders with the continental vision and essentially a consciousness of the United States' *international* impotence, provided the matrix of the movement. To their standard other leaders rallied with their own parallel ambitions. Their great assets were (1) the presence in their caucus of one authentic "father figure," George Washington, whose prestige was enormous; (2) the energy and talent of their leadership (in which one must include the towering intellectuals of the time, John Adams and Thomas Jefferson, despite their absence abroad) and their communications "network," which was far superior to anything on the opposition side; (3) the preemptive skill which made "Their Issue" "The Issue" and kept the locally oriented opposition permanently on the defensive; (4) the subjective consideration that these men were spokesmen of a new and compelling credo: *American* nationalism, that illdefined but none the less potent sense of collective purpose that emerged from the American Revolution.[8]

Elite Consensus. By focusing upon the debates *within* the Convention, many historical scholars tend to overemphasize the differences of opinion among the Founding Fathers. While it is true that many conflicting views had to be reconciled in Philadelphia and that innumerable compromises had to be made, the more striking fact is that the delegates were in almost complete accord on the essential questions of politics. They agreed that the fundamental end of government was the *protection of liberty and property.* They accepted without debate many of the precedents set by the English constitution and by the constitutions of the new states.

Reflecting the rationalism of their times, the Founding Fathers were much less devoutly religious than most Americans today. Yet they believed in a law of nature with rules of abstract justice to which the laws of men should conform. They believed that this law of nature endowed man with certain inalienable rights that were essential to a meaningful existence for a man. Man had the right to life, liberty, and property; and these rights should be recognized and protected by law. They believed that all men were equal, in that they were entitled to have their natural rights respected regardless of their station in life. Most of the Founding Fathers were even aware that this belief ran contrary to the practice of slavery and were embarrassed by this inconsistency in American life.

But "equality" did *not* mean to the Founding Fathers that men were equal in birth, wealth, intelligence, talent, or virtue. Inequalities in society were accepted as a natural product of diversity among men. It was definitely not the function of government to reduce these inequal-

[8] John P. Roche. "The Founding Fathers: A Reform Caucus in Action," *American Political Science Review,* 55 (December 1961), 799.

ities; in fact, "dangerous leveling" was a serious violation of man's right to property, his right to use and dispose of the fruits of his industry. On the contrary, it was the very function of government to protect property and to prevent "leveling" influences from reducing the natural inequalities of wealth and power.

The Founding Fathers agreed that *the origin of government is an implied contract among men.* They believed that men pledged allegiance and obedience to government in return for protection of their natural rights, the maintenance of peace, and protection from foreign invasion. The ultimate legitimacy of government — that is, sovereignty — rested with the people themselves, and not with gods or kings; and the basis of government was the consent of the governed.

The Founding Fathers believed in *republican government.* They were opposed to hereditary monarchies, the prevailing form of government in the world at the time. While they believed that men of principle and property should govern, they were opposed to an aristocracy or a governing nobility. By "republican government" they meant a representative, responsible, and non-hereditary government. But by "republican government" they certainly did not mean mass democracy, with direct participation by the people in decision making. They expected the masses to consent to government by men of principle and property out of recognition for their abilities, talents, education, and stake in the preservation of liberty and order. The Founding Fathers believed that the masses should only have a limited part in the selection of government leaders. There was some bickering over how much direct participation should take place in the selection of decision makers, and some bickering over the qualifications of public office. But there was general agreement that the masses should have only a limited and indirect role in the selection of decision makers, and that decision makers themselves should be men of wealth, education, and proven leadership ability.

The Founding Fathers believed in *limited government.* Government should be designed so that it would not become a threat to liberty or property. Since the Founding Fathers believed that power was a corrupting influence and that the concentration of power was dangerous, they believed in dividing governmental power into separate bodies capable of checking each other, in the event that any one branch should pose a threat to liberty or property. Differences of opinion among honest men, particularly differences between elites located in separate states, could best be resolved by balancing representation of these several elites in the national government and by a system of decentralization that permitted local elites to govern their states as they saw fit, with limited interference from the national government.

It should be noted that the laissez-faire principles of Adam Smith were *not* a part of elite consensus in 1787. Quite the contrary, the men who wrote the Constitution believed that government had the obligation not only to protect private property but also to nourish it. They expected government to foster trade and commerce, protect manufacturing, assist in land development, and provide other positive economic assistance. And, to protect the rights of property, they expected government to enforce contracts, maintain a stable money supply, punish thievery, assist in the collection of debts, record the ownership of property in the form of deeds, punish counterfeiting and piracy, protect copyrights and patents, regulate the value of money, establish courts, and regulate banking and commerce.

Finally, and perhaps most importantly, the Founding Fathers believed that only *a strong national government,* with power to exercise its will directly on the people, would be able to "establish justice, insure domestic tranquility, provide for the common defense, promote the general welfare, and secure the blessings of liberty."

The compromises that took place in the Convention were relatively unimportant in comparison to this consensus among the Founding Fathers on fundamentals. It was the existence of a national elite and its agreement on the fundamentals of politics that enabled the American government to be founded. If there had been any substantial cleavage among elites in 1787, any substantial competition or conflict, or any divergent centers of influence, a new government would never have emerged from the Philadelphia convention. Elite consensus in 1787 was profoundly conservative, in that it wished to preserve the status quo in the distribution of power and property in America. Yet, at the same time, this elite consensus was radical in comparison with the beliefs of other elites in the world at this time. Nearly every other government of the time adhered to the principle of hereditary monarchy and privileged nobility, while American elites were committed to republicanism. Other elites asserted the divine right of kings, while American elites talked about government by the consent of the governed. American elites believed in the equality of man with respect to his inalienable rights, while the elites in Europe rationalized and defended a rigid caste system.

An Elite in Operation— Conciliation and Compromise

On May 25, 1787, sessions of the Constitutional Convention opened in Independence Hall, Philadelphia. After the selection of Washington as President of the Convention and the decision that the proceedings of the Convention should be kept secret, Governor Edmund Randolph, speaking for the Virginia delegation, presented a draft of a new constitution.

Under the Virginia Plan, little recognition was given to the states in the composition of the national government. The plan proposed a two-house legislature, the lower house to be chosen by the people of the several states with representation accorded by population. The second house was to be chosen by the first house. This Congress would be empowered to "legislate in all cases in which the separate states are incompetent, or in which the harmony of the United States may be interrupted by the exercise of individual legislation." Moreover, Congress would have the authority to nullify state laws that it felt violated the Constitution, thus insuring national supremacy. The Virginia Plan also proposed a parliamentary form of government, with members of the executive and judiciary branches chosen by the Congress.

It is interesting that the most important line of cleavage at the Convention was between elites of large states and elites of small states over the representation scheme in the Virginia Plan. This was not a great question of economic interest or ideology, since delegates from large and small states did not divide along economic or ideological lines. But the Virginia Plan did not provide certainty that elites from small states would secure membership in the upper house of the legislature.

After several weeks of debate over the Virginia Plan, delegates from the small states presented a counterproposal, in a report by William Patterson of New Jersey. The New Jersey Plan may have been merely a tactic by the small state elites to force the Convention to compromise on representation, for it was debated only a week before it was set aside, and despite this defeat the small state delegates did not leave the Convention nor did they seem particularly upset with their defeat. The New Jersey Plan proposed to retain the representation scheme in Congress under the Articles, where each state was accorded a single vote. But separate executive and judiciary branches were to be established, and the powers of Congress were to be greatly expanded to include the right to levy taxes and regulate commerce.

The New Jersey Plan was *not* an attempt to retain the Confederation. Indeed, the plan included words that were later to appear in the Constitution itself as the famous "national supremacy clause":

> This constitution, and the laws of the United States which shall be made in pursuance thereof, and all treaties made, or which shall be made, under the authority of the United States shall be the Supreme Law of the land; the judges in every state shall be bound thereby, anything in the Constitution or laws of any state to the contrary notwithstanding.

Thus, even the small states did not envision a confederation. Both the Virginia and New Jersey plans were designed to strengthen the national government; they differed only in the degree to which it would be strengthened and in its system of representation.

On June 29, William Samuel Johnson of Connecticut proposed the obvious compromise; namely, *that representation in the lower house of Congress be based upon population whereas representation in the upper house would be equal* — two senators from each state. The Connecticut Compromise also provided that equal representation of states in the Senate could not be abridged, even by constitutional amendment.

The next question to be compromised, that of slavery and the role of slaves in the system of representation, was more closely related to economic differences among America's elite. It was essentially the same question that was to divide America's elite and result in the nation's bloodiest war 75 years later. Planters and slaveholders generally believed that wealth, particularly wealth in slaves, should be counted in apportioning representation. Non-slaveholders felt that "the people" should only include free inhabitants. The decision to apportion direct taxes among the states in proportion to population opened the way to compromise, since the attitude of slaveholders and non-slaveholders was just the reverse as to which person should be counted for the purposes of apportioning taxes. The result was the famous Three-Fifths Compromise, in which *three fifths of the slaves of each state would be counted for the purposes of representation, and three fifths would also be counted in apportioning direct taxes.*

Agreement between Southern planters and Northern merchants was still relatively easy to achieve at this early date in American history. But latent conflict could be observed on issues other than slavery. While all the elite groups agreed that the national government should regulate interstate and foreign commerce, Southern planters had some fear that the unrestricted power of Congress over commerce might lead to the imposition of export taxes. Export taxes would bear most heavily on the Southern states, which were dependent upon foreign markets for the sale of indigo, rice, tobacco, and cotton. However, planters and merchants were able to reach another compromise in resolving this issue: *No tax or duty should be levied on articles exported from any state.*

Finally, a compromise had to be reached on the question of trading in slaves. On this issue, the men of Maryland and Virginia, states that were already well supplied with slaves, were able to indulge in the luxury of conscience and support proposals for banning the further importation of slaves. But the less developed Southern states, particularly South Carolina and Georgia, could not afford to be so moral, since they still needed additional slave labor. Inasmuch as the Southern planters were themselves divided, the ultimate compromise permitted Congress to prohibit *the slave trade—but not before the year 1808.* This twenty-year delay would allow the undeveloped Southern states to acquire all the slaves they needed before the slave trade was cut off.

Another important compromise, one which occupied much of the time of the Convention although it has received little recognition by subsequent writers, concerned qualifications for voting and holding office in the new government. While no property qualifications for voters or officeholders appear in the text of the Constitution, the debates revealed that members of the Convention generally favored property qualifications for voting and almost unanimously favored property qualifications for officeholding. The delegates showed little enthusiasm for mass participation in democracy. Elbridge Gerry of Massachusetts declared that "the evils we experience flow from the excess of democracy." Roger Sherman protested that "the people immediately should have as little to do as may be about the government." Edmund Randolph continually deplored the turbulence and follies of democracy, and George Clymer's notion of republican government was that "a representative of the people is appointed to think for and not with his constituents." John Dickinson considered property qualifications a "necessary defense against the dangerous influence of those multitudes without property and without principle, with which our country like all others, will in time abound." Gouverneur Morris also insisted upon property qualifications: "Give the votes to the people who have no property and they will sell them to the rich who will be able to buy them." Charles Pinckney later wrote to Madison, "are you not . . . abundantly depressed at the theoretical nonsense of an election of Congress by the people; in the first instance, it's clearly and practically wrong, and it will in the end be the means of bringing our councils into contempt." Many more such statements could be cited from the records of the Convention.[9]

There was even stronger agreement that property qualifications should be imposed for senators and for the president. The Senate, according to C. C. Pinckney, "was meant to represent the wealth of the country. It ought to be composed of persons of wealth." He also proposed that no pay be given presidents or senators, because "if no allowance was made, the wealthy alone would undertake the service." Alexander Hamilton ably expressed elitist feeling on the representation of property:

All communities divide themselves into the few and the many. The first are the rich and well-born, the other the masses of people. The voice of the people has been said to be the voice of God; and however generally this maxim has been quoted and believed, it is not true in fact. The people are turbulent and changing; they seldom judge or determine right. Give therefore to the first class a distinct, permanent share in the government. They will check the unsteadiness of the second, and as they cannot receive any advantage by change, they therefore will ever maintain good government. Can a democratic assembly who annually revolves in the mass of the people, be supposed steadily to pursue the public good? Nothing but a permanent body can check the imprudence of democracy.[10]

In the light of these views, how then do we explain the absence of property qualifications in the Constitution? Actually, a motion was carried in the Convention instructing a committee to fix property qualifications for officeholding, but the committee could not agree upon the nature of the qualifications to be imposed. Various propositions to establish property qualifications were defeated on the floor, not because they were believed to be inherently wrong but, interestingly enough, because of differences in the *kind* of property represented by elites at the Convention. Madison pointed this out in the debate in July, when he noted that a requirement of land ownership would exclude from Congress the mercantile and manufacturing classes, who would hardly be willing to turn their money into large quantities of landed property just to make them eligible for a seat in Congress. Madison rightly observed that "landed possessions were no certain evidence of real wealth. Many enjoyed them to a great extent who were more in debt than they were worth." The objections by merchants and investors led to a defeat of the "landed" qualification for Congressmen. Also, a motion to disqualify persons from public office who had "unsettled accounts" with

[9]See especially Beard, *Economic Interpretation of the Constitution.*
[10]Farrand, *Records of the Federal Convention of 1787,* Vol. 1, pp. 299–300.

the United States (an early-day version of conflict-of-interests law) was also struck down by an overwhelming vote of the delegates.

Thus, the Constitution was approved *without any property qualifications on voters, except those which the states themselves might see fit to impose.* Failing to come to a decision on this issue of suffrage, the delegates merely returned the question to state legislatures by providing that "the electors in each state should have the qualifications requisite for electors of the most numerous branch of the state legislatures." At the time, it did not seem that this expedient course of action would result in mass democracy. Only one branch of the new government, the House of Representatives, was to be elected by popular vote anyhow. The other three controlling bodies—the President, the Senate, and the Supreme Court—were removed from direct voter participations. Finally, the delegates were reassured by the fact that nearly all of the state constitutions then in force included property qualifications for voters.[11]

The Constitution as an Elitist Document

The text of the Constitution, together with interpretive materials in *The Federalist* papers written by Hamilton, Madison, and Jay, provide ample evidence that elites in America benefited both politically and economically from the adoption of the Constitution. While both elites and non-elites—indeed, all Americans—may have benefited by the adoption of the Constitution, elites benefited more directly and immediately than non-elites. And it is reasonable to infer that the advantages contained in the document for America's elite provided the direct, impelling motive for their activities on behalf of the new Constitution. Indeed, if elites had not stood to gain substantially from the Constitution, it is doubtful that this document would have been written or that the new government would have been established. We can discover the elitist consensus by examining the underlying philosophy of government contained in the Constitution.

According to Madison in *The Federalist, controlling factions* was "the principal task of modern legislation."[12] A "faction" is a number of citizens united by a common interest that is adverse to the interest of other citizens or of the community as a whole. The causes of factions are found in human diversity: "A zeal for different opinions concerning religion, concerning government, and many other points, as well of speculation as of practice; an attachment to different leaders ambitiously contending for preeminence and power; or to persons of other descriptions whose fortunes have been interesting to human pas-

---

[11] Historians disagree about the number of people who were disenfranchised by property qualifications in 1787. All states had property-owning or tax-paying qualifications for voting and even higher qualifications for officeholding. But we do not really know how many people met these qualifications. For example, Massachusetts conferred the suffrage on all males owning an estate with an annual income of three pounds or a total value of sixty pounds. And a Massachusetts senator was required to be "seized in his own right of a freehold within this Commonwealth of the value of 300 pounds at least, or possessed of a personal estate of the value of 600 pounds at least, or both to the amount of the same sum." It is difficult to estimate what percentage of Massachusetts males owned an estate with an annual income of three pounds. But whether or not many citizens were *legally* disenfranchised, very few voted.

[12] James Madison, Alexander Hamilton, John Jay, *The Federalist* No. 10 (New York: The Modern Library, 1937).

sions." But at the heart of the problem of faction is inequality in the control of economic resources:

> But the most common and durable source of factions has been the various and unequal distribution of property. Those who hold and those who are without property have ever formed distinct interests in society. Those who are creditors and those who are debtors fall under like discrimination. A landed interest, a manufacturing interest, a merchantile interest, a monied interest, with many lesser interests, grow up of necessity in civilized nations, and divide them into different classes, actuated by different sentiments and views. [Federalist No. 10]

In Madison's view, the most important protection against mass movements that might threaten property was the establishment of the national government. By creating a national government encompassing a large number of citizens and a great expanse of territory "you take in a greater variety of parties and interests; you make it less probable that a majority of the whole will have a common motive to invade the rights of other citizens; or if such a common motive exists it will be more difficult for all who feel it to discover their own strength, and to act in unison with each other."

The structure of the new national government was supposed to insure that "factious" issues would be suppressed. And Madison does not hedge on naming the factious issues that must be avoided: "A rage for paper money, for an abolition of debts, for an equal division of property, or any other improper or wicked project . . . ." Note that all of Madison's factious issues are challenges to the dominant economic elites. Madison's defense of the new Constitution was that its republican and federal features would help to keep certain threats to property from ever becoming public issues. In short, the new American government was deliberately designed by the Founding Fathers to make it difficult for any mass political movement to challenge property rights.

Now let us turn to an examination of the text of the Constitution itself and its impact upon American elites. There are seventeen specific grants of power to Congress in Article I, Section 8, followed by a general grant of power to make "all laws which shall be necessary and proper for carrying into execution the foregoing powers." The first and perhaps the most important enumerated power is the "power to lay and collect taxes, duties, imposts, and excises." The *taxing power* is, of course, the basis of all other powers, and it enabled the national government to end its dependence upon states. The taxing power was essential to the holders of public securities, particularly when it was combined with the provision in Article VI that "All the debts contracted and engagements entered into before the adoption of this Constitution shall be valid against the United States under this Constitution as under the Confederation." This meant that the national government would be obliged to pay off all those investors who held bonds of the United States, and the taxing power would give the national government the ability to do this on its own.

The text of the Constitution suggests that the Founding Fathers intended Congress to place most of the tax burden on consumers in the form of custom duties and excise taxes, rather than direct taxes on individual income or property. Article I, Section 2, required that direct taxes could be levied only on the basis of population; it follows that such taxes could not be levied in proportion to wealth. This provision prevented the national government from levying progressive income taxes, and it was not until the Sixteenth Amendment was passed in 1913 that this protection for wealth was removed from the Constitution.

Southern planters, who depended for their livelihood on the export of indigo, rice, tobacco, and cotton, strenuously opposed giving the national government the power to tax exports. Protection for their interests was provided in Article I, Section 9: "no tax or duty shall be laid on goods exported from any state." However, Congress was given the power to tax imports so Northern manufacturers could erect a tariff wall to protect American industries against foreign goods.

Congress was also given the power to "regulate commerce with foreign nations and among the several states." The *interstate commerce clause,* together with the provision in Article I, Section 9, prohibiting the states from taxing either imports or exports, created a free trade area over the thirteen states. In *The Federalist* No. 11, Hamilton describes the advantages of this arrangement for American merchants: "The speculative trader will at once perceive the force of these observations and will acknowledge that the aggregate balance of the commerce of the United States would bid fair to be much more favorable than that of the thirteen states without union or with partial unions."

Following the power to tax and spend, to borrow money, and to regulate commerce in Article I, there is a series of *specific powers designed to enable Congress to protect money and property.* Congress is given the power to make bankruptcy laws, to coin money and regulate its value, to fix standards of weights and measures, to punish counterfeiting, to establish post offices and post roads, to pass copyright and patent laws to protect authors and inventors, and to punish piracies and felonies committed on the high seas. Each of these powers is a specific asset to bankers, investors, merchants, authors, inventors, and shippers. Obviously, the Founding Fathers felt that giving Congress control over currency and credit in America would result in better protection for financial interests than would leaving this essential responsibility to the states. Likewise, control over communication and transportation ("post offices and post roads") was believed to be too essential to trade and commerce to be left to the states.

All of the other powers in Article I deal with *military affairs* — raising and supporting armies, organizing, training, and calling up the state militia, declaring war, suppressing insurrections, and repelling invasions. These powers in Article I, together with the provisions in Article II making the president the commander-in-chief of the army and navy and of the state militia when called into the federal service, and the power of the president to make treaties with the advice and consent of the Senate and to send and receive ambassadors, all combined to centralize diplomatic and military affairs at the national level. This centralization of diplomatic-military power is confirmed in Article I, Section 10, where the states are specifically prohibited from entering into treaties with foreign nations, maintaining ships of war, or engaging in war unless actually invaded.

It is clear that the Founding Fathers had little confidence in the state militia, particularly when it was under state control; General Washington's painful experiences with state militia during the Revolutionary War were still fresh in his memory. The militia had proven adequate when defending their own states against invasion; but when employed outside their own states, they were often a disaster. Moreover, if Western settlers were to be protected from the Indians, and if the British were to be persuaded to give up their forts in Ohio and open the way to American westward expansion, the national government could not rely upon state militia but must instead have an army of its own. Similarly, a strong navy was essential to the protection of American commerce on the seas (the first significant naval action under the new government was against the piracy of the Barbary states). Thus, a national army and navy were not so much protection against invasion (for many years the national government would continue to rely primarily upon state militia for this purpose), but rather for the protection and promotion of its commercial and territorial ambitions. In addition, a national army and navy, as well as an organized and trained militia that could be called into national service, also provided *protection against class wars* and rebellion by debtors. In an obvious reference to Shays' Rebellion, Hamilton warns in *The Federalist* No. 21:

> The tempestuous situation from which Massachusetts has scarcely emerged evinces that dangers of this kind are not merely speculative. Who could determine what might have been the issue of her late convulsions if the malcontents had been headed by a Caesar or a Cromwell? A strong military force in the hands of the national government is a protection against revolutionary action.

Further evidence of the Founding Fathers' intention to protect the governing classes from revolution is found in Article IV, Section 4, where the national government guarantees to every state "a republican form of government" as well as protection against "domestic violence." Thus, in addition to protecting Western land and commerce on the seas, a strong army and navy would enable the national government to back up its pledge to protect governing elites in the states from violence and revolution.

Protection against domestic insurrection also appealed to the Southern slaveholders' deep-seated fear of a slave revolt. Madison drives this point home in *The Federalist* No. 23:

I take no little notice of an unhappy species of population abounding in some of the states who, during the calm of regular government were sunk below the level of men; but who, in the tempestuous seeds of civil violence, may emerge into human character and give a superiority of strength to any party with which they may associate themselves.

As we have already noted, the Constitution permitted Congress to outlaw the *importation of slaves* after the year 1808. But most of the Southern planters were more interested in protecting their existing property and slaves than they were in extending the slave trade, and the Constitution provided an explicit advantage to slaveholders in Article IV, Section 2:

No person held to service or labor in one state, under the laws thereof, escaping into another, shall, in consequence of any law or regulation thereof, be discharged from such service or labor, but shall be delivered upon claim of the party to whom such service or labor may be due.

This was an extremely valuable protection for one of the most important forms of property in America at the time. The slave trade lapsed in America after twenty years, but slavery as a domestic institution was better safeguarded under the new Constitution than under the Articles.

The *restrictions placed upon state legislatures* by the Constitution also provided protection to economic elites in the new nation. States were prevented from coining money, issuing paper money, or passing legal tender laws that would make any money other than gold or silver coin tender in the payment of debts. This restriction would prevent the states from issuing cheap paper money, which could be used by debtors to pay off their creditors with less valuable currency. The authors of *The Federalist* pointed to this prohibition on paper money in their appeal to economic elites to support ratification of the Constitution:

The loss which America has sustained since the peace from the pestilential effects of paper money on the necessary confidence between man and man, on the necessary confidence in the public councils, on the industry and the morals of the people, and on the character of republican government constitutes an enormous debt against the states chargeable to this unadvised measure, which must long remain unsatisfied, or rather an accumulation of guilt, which can be expiated no otherwise than by a voluntary sacrifice on the altar of justice which has been the instrument of it. [*Federalist* No. 44]

In other words, the states had frequently issued paper money to relieve debtors; they were now to be punished for their "unadvised" behavior by removing their power to issue money. Moreover, the states were denied the power to pass legal tender laws obliging creditors to accept paper money in payment of debts.

The Constitution also prevents states from passing any law "impairing the obligation of contracts." The structure of business relations in a free enterprise economy depends upon government enforcement of private contracts, and it is essential to economic elites that the government be prevented from relieving persons from their obligations to contracts. If state legislatures could relieve debtors of their contractual obligations, or relieve indentured servants from their obligations to their masters, or prevent creditors from foreclosing on mortgages, or declare moratoriums on debt, or otherwise interfere with business obligations, the interests of investors, merchants, and creditors would be seriously damaged.

The heart of the Constitution is the *supremacy clause of Article VI:*

> This Constitution, and the laws of the United States which shall be made in pursuance thereof, and all treaties made, or which shall be made under the authority of the United States, shall be the Supreme Law of the Land and the judges in every state shall be bound thereby, anything in the Constitution or laws of any state to the contrary notwithstanding.

This sentence made it abundantly clear that laws of Congress would supersede laws of the states and it made certain that Congress would control interstate commerce, bankruptcy, monetary affairs, weights and measures, currency and credit, communication, and transportation, as well as foreign and military affairs. Thus, the supremacy clause insures that the decisions of the national elite will prevail over the decisions of the local elites in all of those vital areas allocated to the national government.

The structure of the national government—its republicanism and its system of separated powers and checks and balances—was also designed to provide for protection of liberty and property. To the Founding Fathers, a *republican government* meant the delegation of powers by the people to a small number of citizens "whose wisdom may best discern the true interest of their country, and whose patriotism and love of justice will be least likely to sacrifice it to temporary or partial considerations."[13] Madison goes on to explain, in classic elite fashion, "that the public voice, pronounced by representatives of the people, will be more consonant to the public good than if pronounced by the people themselves." It is clear that the Founding Fathers believed that representatives of the people were more likely to be enlightened men of principle and property than the voters who chose them, and thus more trustworthy and dependable.

Moreover, voters had a very limited voice in the selection of decision makers. *Four* major decision-making bodies were established in the Constitution—the House of Representatives, the Senate, the Presidency, and the Supreme Court—but only *one* of these bodies was to be elected by the people themselves. The other bodies were to be at least twice removed from popular control. In the Constitution of 1787, only United States representatives were directly elected by the people, and

[13]Madison, Hamilton, and Jay, *The Federalist* No. 10.

they were elected for short terms of two years. In contrast, United States senators were to be elected by state legislatures, not by the people, for six-year terms. The president was not elected by the people, but by "electors," who themselves were to be selected as state legislatures saw fit. The states could hold elections for presidential "electors," or could appoint the electors through the state legislatures. The Founding Fathers hoped that presidential "electors" would be prominent men of wealth and reputation in their respective states. Finally, federal judges were to be appointed by the president for life, thus removing these decision makers as far from popular control as possible. Of course, it would be unfair to brand the Founding Fathers as "conservative" because of these republican arrangements. In 1787, the idea of republicanism itself was radical, since few governments provided for *any* popular participation in government, even a limited role in the selection of representatives. While the Founding Fathers believed that government ultimately rested upon the will of the people, they hoped that republicanism could reduce the influence of the masses and help insure government by elites.

The system of separated powers in the national government—separate legislative, executive, and judicial branches—was also intended by the Founding Fathers as a bulwark against majoritarianism and an additional safeguard for liberty and property. The doctrine derives from the French writer, Montesquieu, whose *Spirit of Laws* was a political textbook for these eighteenth-century statesmen. *The Federalist* No. 51 expresses the logic of the checks and balances system:

Ambition must be made to counteract ambition . . . It may be a reflection on human nature, that such devices should be necessary to control the abuses of government. But what is government itself, but the greatest of all reflections on human nature? If men were angels, no government would be necessary. If angels were to govern men, neither external nor internal controls on government would be necessary. In framing a government which is to be administered by men over men, the great difficulty lies in this: you must first enable the government to control the governed; and in the next place oblige it to control itself.

The separation of powers concept is expressed in the opening sentences of the first three articles of the Constitution: "All legislative powers herein granted shall be invested in the Congress of the United States. . . . The Executive power shall be vested in a President of the United States. . . . The Judicial power shall be vested in one Supreme Court and such inferior courts as Congress may from time to time ordain and establish." If this system divides responsibility and makes it difficult for the masses to hold government accountable for public policy, then it is achieving one of the purposes intended by the Founding Fathers. Each of the four major decision-making bodies of the national government is chosen by different constituencies—the House by the voters in the several states, the Senate by the state legislatures, the president by electors chosen by the states, and the judiciary by the president and the Senate. A sharp differentiation is made in the terms of these decision-making bodies, so that a complete renewal of government by popular vote at one stroke is impossible. The House is chosen for two years; the Senate is chosen for six, but not in one election, for one third go out every two years. The president is chosen every four years, but judges of the Supreme Court hold office for life. Thus the people are restrained from working immediate havoc through direct elections; they must wait years in order to make their will felt in all of the decision-making bodies of the national government.

Moreover, each of these decision-making bodies has an important check on the decisions of the others. No bill can become law without the approval of both the House and the Senate. The president shares in legislative power through his veto and his responsibility to "give to the Congress information of the state of the union, and recommend to their consideration such measures as he shall judge necessary and expedient." He can also convene sessions of Congress. But the appointing power of the president is shared by the Senate; so is his treaty-making power. Also, Congress can override executive vetoes. The president must execute the laws, but in order to do so he must rely upon executive departments, and these must be created by Congress. Moreover, the executive branch cannot spend money that has not been appropriated by Congress. Thus, the concept of "separation of powers" is really misnamed, for what we are really talking about is a sharing, not a separating, of power; each branch participates in the activities of every other branch.

Even the Supreme Court, which was created by the Constitution, must be appointed by the president with the consent of the Senate, and Congress may prescribe the number of judges. More importantly, Congress must create lower and intermediate courts, establish the number of judges, fix the jurisdiction of lower federal courts, and make "exceptions" to the appellate jurisdiction of the Supreme Court.

All of these checks and counterchecks were defended in *The Federalist* as a means of restraining popular majorities, particularly those which might arise in the House of Representatives. Perhaps the keystone of the system of checks and balances is the idea of *judicial review*, an original contribution by the Founding Fathers to the science of government. In the case of *Marbury* v. *Madison* in 1803,[14] Chief Justice John Marshall argued convincingly that the Founding Fathers intended the Supreme Court to have the power of invalidating not only state laws and constitutions but also any laws of Congress that came in conflict with the Constitution of the United States. Marshall reasoned (1) that the "judicial power" was given to the Supreme Court, (2) that historically the judicial power included the power to interpret the meaning of the law, (3) that the Supremacy Clause made the Constitution the "Supreme Law of the Land," (4) that

[14]*Marbury* v. *Madison*, 1 Cranch 137 (1803).

laws of the United States should be made "in pursuance thereof," (5) that judges are sworn to uphold the Constitution, and (6) that judges must therefore declare void any legislative act that they feel conflicts with the Constitution.

The text of the Constitution nowhere specifically authorizes federal judges to invalidate acts of Congress; at most, the Constitution implies this power. But Hamilton apparently thought that the Constitution contained this power, since he was careful to explain it in *The Federalist* No. 78 prior to the ratification of the Constitution:

> The complete independence of the courts of justice is peculiarly essential in a limited constitution. By a limited constitution, I understand one which contains certain specified exceptions to the legislative authority; such, for instance, as that it shall pass no bills of attainder, no *ex post facto* laws, and the like. Limitations of this kind can be preserved in practice no other way than through the medium of courts of justice, whose duty it must be to declare all acts contrary to the manifest tenor of the constitution void. Without this, all the reservations of particular rights or privileges would amount to nothing. . . . The interpretation of the laws is the proper and peculiar province of the courts. A constitution is, in fact, and must be regarded by the judges as a fundamental law. It therefore belongs to them to ascertain its meaning, as well as the meaning of any particular act proceeding from the legislative body. If there should happen to be an irreconcilable variance between the two, that which has the superior obligation and validity ought, of course, to be preferred; or, in other words, the constitution ought to be preferred to the statute, the intention of the people to the intention of their agents.

Thus, the Supreme Court stands as the final defender of the fundamental principles agreed upon by the Founding Fathers against the encroachments of popularly elected legislatures.

Ratification — an Exercise in Elite Political Skills. When the work of the Constitutional Convention ended on September 17, 1787, the document was sent to New York City, where Congress was then in session. The Convention suggested that the Constitution "should afterwards be submitted to a convention of delegates chosen in each state by the people thereof, under the recommendation of its legislature for their assent and ratification." The Philadelphia Convention further proposed that when *nine* states had ratified the new constitution, it should go into effect. On September 28, Congress sent the Constitution to the states without making any recommendations of its own.

The ratification procedure suggested by the Founding Fathers was a skillful political maneuver. The Convention itself had been held in secret, so there was little advance word that the delegates had not merely amended the Articles of Confederation, as they had been instructed, but instead had created a whole new scheme of government. Their ratification procedure was a complete departure from what was then the law of the land, the Articles of Confederation. The Articles provided that all amendments should be made by Congress only with the approval of *all* of the states. But since Rhode Island was firmly in the hands of small farmers, the unanimity required by the Articles was obviously out of the question; and the Founding Fathers felt obliged to act outside of the existing law. Hence the proclamation that only nine states need ratify the new Constitution.

It is important to note that the Founding Fathers also called for special ratifying conventions in the states, rather than risk submitting the Constitution to the state legislatures. This extraordinary procedure gave clear advantage to supporters of the Constitution. Nathaniel Gorham argued effectively at Philadelphia that submitting the plan to state legislatures would weaken its chances for success:

> Men chosen by the people for the particular purpose will discuss the subject more candidly than the members of the legislature who are about to lose the power which is to be given up to the general movement. Some of the legislatures are composed of several branches. It will consequently be more difficult in these cases to get the plan through the legislatures than through a convention. In the states, many of the ablest men are excluded from the legislatures but may be elected to a convention . . . the legislatures will be interrupted by a variety of little business . . . if the last Article of the Confederation is to be pursued the unanimous concurrence of the states will be necessary.[15]

In other words, it was politically expedient to by-pass the state legislatures and to ignore the requirement of the Articles for unanimity among the states. Thus, the struggle for ratification began under ground rules designed by the national elite to give them the advantage over any potential opponents.

In the most important and controversial study of the Constitution to date, Charles A. Beard compiled a great deal of evidence in support of the hypothesis "that substantially all of the merchants, money lenders, security holders, manufacturers, shippers, capitalists and financiers, and their professional associates are to be found on one side in support of the Constitution, and that substantially all of the major portion of the opposition came from the non-slaveholding farmers and debtors."[16] While historians disagree over the solidarity of class divisions in the struggle for ratification, most concede that only about 160,000 persons voted in elections for delegates to state ratifying conventions and that not more than 100,000 of these voters favored the adoption of the Constitution. This figure represents about one in six of the adult males in the country, and not more than five percent of the population in general. Thus, whether or not Beard is correct about class divisions in the struggle for ratification, one thing is clear: The total

---

[15]Beard, *Economic Interpretation of the Constitution,* pp. 217–238.
[16]Beard, pp. 16–17. Beard's "economic" interpretation differs from an elitist interpretation in that Beard believed the economic elites supported the Constitution and the masses opposed it. Our elitist interpretation asserts only that the masses did not participate in the writing or adoption of the Constitution, and that elites benefited directly from its provisions. Our interpretation does not depend upon showing that the masses opposed the Constitution, but merely upon showing that they did not participate in its establishment. Beard's thesis about class conflict over adoption is a controversial one among historians. Attacks on Beard are found in Forrest McDonald, *We the People: The Economic Origins of the Constitution* (Chicago: University of Chicago, 1963); and Robert E. Brown, *Charles Beard and the Constitution* (Princeton, N.J.: Princeton University Press, 1956). A balanced view is presented in Lee Benson, *Turner and Beard: American Historical Writing Reconsidered* (New York: Free Press, 1960).

number of persons who participated in any fashion in the ratification of the Constitution was an extremely small minority of the population.

Some men of property and education did champion the views of the common people. Men like Patrick Henry and Richard Henry Lee of Virginia vigorously attacked the Constitution as a "counter-revolutionary" document that could undo much of the progress made since 1776 toward freedom, liberty, and equality. According to the opponents of the Constitution, the new government would be "aristocratic," all-powerful, and a threat to the "spirit of republicanism" and the "genius of democracy." They charged that the new Constitution created an aristocratic upper house and an almost monarchial presidency. The powers of the national government could trample the states and deny the people of the states the opportunity to handle their own political and economic affairs. The Antifederalists repeatedly asserted that the Constitution removed powers from the people and concentrated them in the hands of a few national officials who were largely immune from popular control; moreover, they attacked the undemocratic features of the Constitution and argued that state governments were much more representative of the people. The secrecy of the Philadelphia Convention and the actions of the Founding Fathers, which were contrary to both the law and the spirit of the Articles of Confederation, also came under attack.

While the Antifederalists deplored the undemocratic features of the new Constitution, their most effective criticism centered on the absence of any Bill of Rights. The omission of a Bill of Rights is particularly glaring, since the idea of a Bill of Rights was very popular at the time and most of the new state constitutions contained them. It is an interesting comment on the psychology of the Founding Fathers that the idea of a Bill of Rights was never even mentioned in the Philadelphia Convention until the final week of deliberations; even then it was given little consideration. The Founding Fathers certainly believed in the idea of limited government. A few liberties were written into the body of the Constitution — protection against bills of attainder and *ex post facto* laws, a guarantee of the writ of *habeas corpus*, a limited definition of treason, a guarantee of jury trial — but there was no Bill of Rights labelled as such. Perhaps the Founding Fathers were so confident that men of principle and property would control the new government that they believed limitations on this government were unnecessary.

When criticism about the absence of a Bill of Rights began to mount in the states, supporters of the Constitution presented an interesting argument to explain this deficiency: (1) the national government was one of enumerated powers and could not exercise any powers not expressly delegated to it in the Constitution; (2) the power to interfere with free speech or press or otherwise to restrain liberty was not among the enumerated powers in the Constitution; (3) it was therefore unnecessary to specifically deny the new government this power. But this logic was unconvincing; the absence of a Bill of Rights seemed to confirm the suspicion that the Founding Fathers were more concerned with protecting property than with protecting the personal liberties of the people. Many elites and non-elites alike were uncomfortable with the thought that personal liberty depended upon a thin thread of inference from enumerated powers. Supporters of the Constitution were forced to retreat from their demand for unconditional ratification; the New York, Massachusetts, and Virginia conventions agreed to the new Constitution only after receiving the solemn promise of the Federalists that a Bill of Rights would be added as amendments. Thus the fundamental guarantees of liberty in the Bill of Rights were political concessions by the nation's elite. While the Founding Fathers deserved great credit for the document that they produced at Philadelphia, nonetheless, the first Congress to meet under that Constitution was obliged to submit twelve amendments to the states, ten of which were ratified by 1791.

Historians disagree as to whether or not class lines were as clearly drawn in the struggle for ratification as Beard contends. But Beard's summary of the strengths and weaknesses of the Federalist and Antifederalist in the struggle over ratification is a classic statement of the political advantages of an elite over a numerically superior mass:

At all events, the disenfranchisement of the masses through property qualifications and ignorance and apathy contributed largely to the facility with which the . . . [Federalists] carried the day. The latter were alert everywhere, for they knew, not as a matter of theory, but as a practical matter of dollars and cents, the value of the new Constitution. They were well informed. They were conscious of the identity of their interests. They were well organized. They knew for weeks in advance, even before the Constitution was sent to the states for ratification, what the real nature of the contest was. They resided for the most part in the towns or in the more thickly populated areas and they could marshal their forces quickly and effectively. . . . Talent, wealth, and professional abilities were, generally speaking, on the side of the Constitutionalists. The money to be spent in the campaign of education was on their side also; and it was spent in considerable sums for pamphleteering, organizing parades and demonstrations, and engaging the interest of the press. A small percentage of the enormous gain to come through the appreciation of securities, a loan would have financed no mean campaign for those days.[17]

In contrast, Beard describes the plight of the Antifederalists in this struggle:

The opposition, on the other hand, suffered from the difficulties connected with getting a backwoods vote out to the town and country elections. This involved sometimes long journeys and bad weather, for it will be remembered that elections were held in late fall and winter. There were no such immediate personal gains to be made through the defeat of the Constitution, as were to be made by the security holders on the other side. It was true that the debtors knew that they would probably have to settle their accounts in full, and the small farmers were aware that taxes would have to be paid to discharge the national debt if the Constitution was adopted; and the debtors everywhere waged war against the Constitution—of this there is plenty of evidence. But

[17]Beard, pp. 251–252.

they had no money to carry on their campaign; they were poor and uninfluential—the strongest battalions were not on their side. The wonder is that they came so near defeating the Constitution at the polls.[18]

Summary   The Constitution of the United States was not "ordained and established" by "the people." Only a small fraction of "the people" participated in any way in the adoption of the Constitution. The Constitution was prepared in Philadelphia by a small, educated, talented, wealthy elite, representative of powerful economic interests—bondholders, investors, merchants, real estate owners, and planters. The document itself, and the new government it established, included many provisions for the protection of the elites' political and economic interests from threats by the masses. Ratification was achieved because the elite had skills and political influence disproportionate to its members. The masses of people did not participate in the adoption of the Constitution, and there is some reason to believe that these masses would have opposed the Constitution had they the information, know-how, and resources to do so. The Constitution was not a product of a popular mass movement, but instead the work of a talented, educated, wealthy, and politically skilled elite.

Selected Additional Readings   Beard, Charles A. *An Economic Interpretation of the Constitution.* New York: Macmillan Co., 1935. The classic interpretation of the origins of American national government, *An Economic Interpretation* attempts to examine the motives of the Founding Fathers.

Lipset, Seymour M. *The First New Nation.* New York: Basic Books, 1965. *The First New Nation* examines the politics of the independence movement in America.

Madison, James, Alexander Hamilton, and John Jay. *The Federalist.* New York: Modern Library, 1937. *The Federalist* is the most important commentary on American government, written by the men who founded that government.

Rossiter, Clinton L. *1787, The Grand Convention.* New York: Macmillan Co., 1966. This readable and entertaining account of the men and events of 1787 contains many insights into the difficulties the Founding Fathers had writing the Constitution.

[18]Beard, p. 252.

**The Evolution of
American Elites**

A stable elite system depends upon the movement of talented and ambitious individuals from the lower strata into the elite. An open elite system providing for "a slow and continuous modification of the ruling classes" is essential for the continuation of the system and the avoidance of revolution. Of course, only those non-elites who accept the basic consensus of the system can be admitted into the ruling class. Although popular elections, party competition, and other democratic institutions in America have not enabled the masses to govern, these institutions have been helpful in keeping the elite system an open one. They have assisted in the circulation of elites, even if they have never been a means of challenging the dominant elite consensus.

This chapter presents an historical analysis of the evolution of American elites. In this analysis, we shall show that American elite membership has evolved slowly, without any serious break in the ideas or values underlying the American political and economic system. America has never experienced a true revolution, in which governing elites were forcefully replaced with non-elites. Instead, American elite membership has been open to those individuals who have acquired wealth and property and who have accepted the national consensus about private enterprise, limited government, and individualism. Thus, industrialization, technological change, and new sources of wealth in the expanding economy have produced new elite members, and America's elite system has permitted the absorption of the new elites without upsetting the system itself.

It is our contention that America's political leadership over the years has been essentially conservative, in that it has accepted the basic consensus underlying the American political and economic system. Whatever the popular political label has been—"Federalist," "Democrat," "Whig," "Republican," "Progressive," "Conservative," or "Liberal"—American leadership has remained committed to the same values and ideas that motivated the Founding Fathers. No drastic revisions of the American system have ever been contemplated by the American elites.

While it is true that basic changes in public policy and major innovations in the structure of American government have taken place over the decades, we shall argue in this chapter that these changes and innovations have been *incremental* rather than revolutionary. Public policies have been frequently modified but seldom replaced. Structural adaptations have been made in the constitutional system designed by the Founding Fathers, but the original framework of American constitutionalism remains substantially intact.

Finally, we shall contend that policy changes in America have not come about as a result of demands by "the people." Instead, changes and innovations in public policy have occurred when events have threatened the system and when elites, acting in enlightened self-interest, have instituted reforms in order to preserve the system and their place in it. Reforms have been designed to strengthen the existing social and economic fabric of society with a minimum of dislocation for governing elites. Political conflict in America has continually centered on a very narrow range of issues; only once, in the Civil War, have American elites been deeply divided over the nature of American society. The Civil War reflected a deep cleavage between Southern elites—dependent upon a plantation economy, slave labor, and free trade—and Northern industrial and commercial elites, who prospered under free labor and protective tariffs.

Hamilton and the Nation's First Public Policies The most influential figure in George Washington's administration was Alexander Hamilton, Secretary of the Treasury. More than anyone else, Hamilton was aware that the new nation, to survive and prosper, must win the lasting confidence of business and financial elites. Only if the United States were established on a sound financial basis would it be able to attract investors both at home and abroad and to expand its industry and commerce. Great Britain remained the largest source of investment capital for the new nation, and Hamilton was decidedly pro-British. Also, he favored a strong central government as a means of protecting property and stimulating the growth of commerce and industry.

Hamilton's first move was to refund the national debt at face value. Most of the original bonds were no longer in the hands of the original owners but had fallen to speculators who had purchased them for only a fraction of their face value. Since these securities were worth only about 25 cents on the dollar, the Hamilton program for refunding the national debt meant a 300 percent profit for the speculators. But Hamilton's program did not end with refunding the debts owed by the United States; he also undertook to pay the debts incurred by the states themselves during the Revolutionary War. The object was to place the creditor class under a deep obligation to the central government.

Hamilton also acted to establish a Bank of the United States, which would receive government funds, issue a national currency, facilitate the sale of national bonds, and tie the national government even more closely to the banking community. The Constitution did not specifically grant to Congress the power to create a national bank, but Hamilton was willing to interpret the "necessary and proper" clause broadly enough to include the creation of a bank to help carry out the taxing, borrowing, and currency powers enumerated in the Constitution. Obviously, Hamilton's broad construction of the "necessary and proper" clause looked in the direction of a powerful central government that would exercise powers not specifically enumerated in the Constitution. Thomas Jefferson, who was Secretary of State in the same Cabinet with Hamilton, expressed growing concern over Hamilton's tendency toward centralization at the national level. Jefferson argued that Congress could not establish the bank because the bank was not, strictly speaking, "necessary" to carry out delegated functions. But Hamilton won out, with the support of President Washington; and Congress voted to charter a Bank of the United States. For twenty years the bank was very successful, especially in stabilizing the currency of the new nation.

It was not until 1819 that the constitutionality of the Bank of the United States was decided by the Supreme Court. In the famous case of *McCulloch* v. *Maryland,* the Supreme Court upheld the broad definition of national power suggested by Hamilton under the "necessary and proper" clause. At the same time, the Court established the principle that when a state law interferes with a national activity the state law will be declared unconstitutional.[1] "Let the end be legitimate," Chief Justice John Marshall wrote, "let it be within the scope of the Constitution, and all means which are appropriate, which are plainly adopted to that end, which are not prohibited, but consistent with the letter and spirit of the Constitution, are constitutional." The McCulloch case firmly established the principle that Congress has the right to choose any appropriate means for carrying out the delegated powers of the national government. The "necessary and proper" clause is now sometimes referred to as the "implied powers" clause or the "elastic" clause, because it gives to Congress many powers that are not explicitly given in the Constitution. Of course, Congress must still trace all of its activities to some formal grant of power, but this is usually not a difficult task.

By 1793, the centralizing effect of Hamilton's program and its orientation toward merchants, manufacturers, and ship builders had aroused serious opposition in governing circles. Southern planters and large landowners benefitted very little from Hamilton's policies, and they were joined in their opposition by many small farmers and frontiersmen. These agrarian interests, both large and small, resented especially Hamilton's pro-British policy and gave little support to debt refunding, national banking, or other projects designed to strengthen commerce and manufacturing.

The Rise of the Jeffersonians   The opposition to the Hamiltonian or "Federalistic" programs was a coalition of those who had opposed the adoption of the Constitution in the first place—men who feared strong central government as a

[1] *McCulloch* v. *Maryland,* 4 Wheaton 316 (1819).

threat to freedom and the sovereignty of the states; landed interests who sought to export foodstuffs and opposed high tariffs; anti-British elements in the population who denounced the Anglophilia of Federalists; and those small farmers, tradesmen, and frontiersmen who opposed Hamilton's financial program of support for commerce and industry and resented the aristocratic trends in the new government. These groups were first called "Antifederalists," and later "Republicans" and "Democratic Republicans" when these terms became popular after the French Revolution. When Thomas Jefferson resigned from Washington's Cabinet in protest of Hamilton's program, opposition to the Federalists began to gather around Jefferson.

Jefferson is portrayed in history as a great democrat and champion of the common man. And it is true that in writing the Declaration of Independence, the Virginia Statute for Religious Freedom, and the famous *Notes on Virginia,* Jefferson expressed concern for the rights of all men and a willingness to trust in the wisdom of "the people." But when Jefferson spoke warmly of the merits of "the people," he meant those who owned and managed their own farms and estates. He firmly believed that only those who owned their own land could make good citizens. Jefferson disliked aristocracy, but he also held urban masses in contempt. He wanted to see the United States become a nation of free, educated, informed, incorruptible, landowning farmers. Democracy, he believed, could only be founded on a propertied class in a propertied nation.

Jefferson's political views differed very little from those of the Founding Fathers. In 1788 he wrote to James Madison praising *The Federalist* as "the best commentary on the principles of government which was ever written." He shared the concern of the Founding Fathers about unrestrained rule by the masses. While Jefferson expressed more confidence in the judgment of small landowning farmers than most of his contemporaries, he also believed in republican government with its checks and balances and safeguards against popular majorities. Jefferson was willing to base republican government on large and small landowners, but he distrusted merchants, manufacturers, laborers, and urban dwellers. In 1787 he wrote:

I think our governments will remain virtuous for many centuries; as long as they remain chiefly agricultural; and this will be as long as there shall be vacant lands in any part of America. When they get piled upon one another in large cities, as in Europe, they will become corrupt as in Europe.

Later on he exclaimed: "Those who labor in the earth are the chosen people of God, if ever he had a chosen people." His belief that land ownership was essential to virtuous government explains in part his Louisiana Purchase, which he hoped would provide the American people with land "to the hundredth and thousandth generation."[2]

[2] See Richard Hofstadter, *The American Political Tradition* (New York: Alfred A. Knopf, 1948), pp. 18–44.

The dispute between Federalists and Antifederalists in early America was not between aristocrats and democrats, nor was it a dispute between elites and masses. As Richard Hofstadter explains:

> . . . although democratically minded Americans did stand with Jefferson, the line of division was essentially between two kinds of property, not two kinds of philosophy. The Federalists during Hamilton's service as Secretary of the Treasury had given the government a foundation of unashamed devotion to the mercantile and investing classes . . . the landed interests, however, were in a majority, and it was only a matter of time before they could marshal themselves in a strong party of their own. Jefferson's party was formed to defend specific property interests rather than the abstract premises of democracy, and its policies were conceived and executed in the sober, moderate spirit that Jefferson's generation expected of propertied citizens when they entered the political arena.[3]

The Antifederalists, or "Republicans," did not elect their first president, Thomas Jefferson, until 1800. John Adams, a Federalist, was chosen to succeed Washington in the election of 1796. Yet the election of 1796 was an important milestone in the development of the American political system. For the first time, two candidates, Adams and Jefferson, did not campaign as individuals but as members of political parties. For the first time, the candidates for the electoral college announced themselves before the election as either "Adams' men" or "Jefferson's men." More importantly, for the first time, the American political leaders saw the importance of molding mass opinion in organizing the masses for political action. It was the Republican party that first saw the importance of working among the masses to rally popular support. The Federalist leaders made the mistake of assuming that they could maintain the unquestioning support of the less-educated and less-wealthy without bothering to mold their opinions.

Rather than follow the Republicans in attempts to manipulate public opinion, the Federalists tried to outlaw public criticism of government officials by means of the Alien and Sedition Acts of 1798. Among other things, these acts made it a crime to conspire to oppose the legal measures of the government or to interfere with their execution, or to publish any false or malicious writing directed against the president or Congress, or to "stir up hatred" against them. These acts directly challenged the newly adopted First Amendment guarantee of freedom of speech and press. But the Supreme Court had not yet asserted itself in declaring laws of Congress unconstitutional, as it would in *Marbury* v. *Madison*[4] a few years later.

In response to the Alien and Sedition Acts, Jefferson and Madison put forward their famous Kentucky and Virginia Resolutions. These measures proposed that the states should assume the right to decide whether Congress has acted unconstitutionally and, furthermore, that the states might properly "interpose" their authority against "palpable

---

[3] Hofstadter, pp. 32–33.
[4] *Marbury* v. *Madison*, 1 Cranch 137 (1803).

and alarming infractions of the Constitution." The Virginia and Kentucky legislatures passed these resolutions and declared the Alien and Sedition Acts were "void and of no force" in these states.

Republicans in Power—The Stability of Public Policy

In the election of 1800, the Federalists finally went down to defeat; Thomas Jefferson and Aaron Burr were elected over John Adams and C. C. Pinckney. Only New England, New Jersey, and Delaware, where commercial and manufacturing interests were strongest, voted Federalist. The vast majority of American people won their living from the soil, and landed elites were able to mobilize these masses behind their bid for control of the government. The Federalists had failed to recognize the importance of agrarianism in the economic and political life of the nation. Another half century would pass and America's industrial revolution would be in full swing before manufacturing and commercial elites would reestablish their dominance.

But the real importance of the election of 1800 is *not* that landed interests gained power in relation to commercial and industrial interests. The importance of 1800 is that for the first time in America's history control of the government passed peacefully from the hands of one faction to an opposition faction. This may seem commonplace, but there are few nations in the world today where government office changes hands in orderly or peaceful fashion. The fact that an "out" party peacefully replaced an "in" party is further testimony to the strength of the consensus among the elite of the new nation. Despite bitter campaign rhetoric, Federalists and Republicans agreed to abide by the basic "rules of the game," to view an opposition faction as legitimate, and to accept the outcome of an election. The Federalists relinquished control of the government without fear that the fundamental values of the American society would be destroyed by a new governing faction. There was clearly more agreement among American leaders than disagreement.[5]

The "Virginia Dynasty"—Thomas Jefferson, James Madison, and finally James Monroe—was to govern the country for a total of six presidential terms, nearly a quarter of a century. It is interesting to note that, once in office, the Republicans made few changes in Federalist and Hamiltonian policy.[6] No attack was made on commercial or industrial enterprise; in fact, commerce and industry prospered under

[5]The original text of the Constitution did not envision an opposition faction. Presidental electors were permitted to cast two votes for president, with the understanding that the candidate with the second highest vote total would be vice-president. A total of 73 Republican electors pledged to Jefferson were sent to the electoral college, and 65 Federalists pledged to Adams. Somewhat thoughtlessly, all of the Republicans cast one vote for Jefferson and one vote for Aaron Burr, his running mate, with the result that, when the votes were tallied, each man was equally eligible for the Presidency. Because of the tie vote, the decision went to the Federalist-controlled House of Representatives, where a movement was begun to elect Burr, rather than Jefferson, in order to embarrass the Republicans. But Alexander Hamilton used his influence in Congress to swing the election to his old political foe Jefferson, suggesting again that their differences were not so deep that either would deliberately undermine the presidency to strike at the other. Once in power, the Republicans passed the Twelfth Amendment to the Constitution, providing that each presidential elector should thereafter vote separately for president and vice-president. This reform was promptly agreed to by both Federalists and Republicans in the states and was ratified in time for the election of 1804.
[6]The only major pieces of legislation to be repealed by the Republicans were the Alien and Sedition Acts. And it seems clear that in these acts the Federalists had violated elite consensus. Even John Marshall, who was elected as a Federalist congressman in 1798, pledged to support repeal of these acts.

Republican rule as never before. No attempt was made to recover money paid out by Hamilton in the refunding of national or state debts. Speculations in public lands continued. Instead of crushing the banks, Republicans were soon flirting with the financial interests they were sworn to oppose. Jefferson's Secretary of the Treasury, Albert Gallatin, wrote:

I am decidedly in favor of making all of the banks Republican by sharing deposits among them in proportion to the disposition they show. . . . It is material to the safety of Republicanism to detach the mercantile interest from its enemies and incorporate them into the body of its friends. A merchant is naturally a Republican and can be otherwise only from a vitiated state of things.[7]

When the Bank of the United States expired in 1811, problems of cheap currency and unreliable state banks began to plague Republican men of property; and by 1816, the Republicans themselves chartered a Second Bank of the United States. Soon Republican newspapers were reprinting Alexander Hamilton's arguments in favor of the constitutionality of the First Bank of the United States! Jefferson was an ardent expansionist; to add to America's wealth in land, he purchased the vast Louisiana Territory. Later a stronger army and a system of internal roads were required to assist in the development of Western land. Jefferson's successor, James Madison, built a strong navy and engaged in another war with England, the War of 1812, to protect American commerce on the high seas. The Napoleonic Wars and the War of 1812, by depressing trade with Britain, stimulated American manufacturing. In 1816 Republicans passed a high tariff in order to protect domestic industry and manufacturing from foreign goods. As for Republican tax policies, Jefferson wrote in 1816:

To take from one, because it is thought his own industry and that of his fathers has acquired too much, in order to spare to others, who, or whose fathers have not, exercised equal industry and skill, is to violate arbitrarily the first principle of association, 'the guarantee to everyone of free exercise of his industry and the fruits acquired by it.'[8]

In short, the Republicans had no intention of redistributing wealth in America. Indeed, before the end of Madison's second term, the Republicans had taken over the whole complex of Hamiltonian policies — a national bank, high tariffs, protection for manufacturers, internal improvements, Western land development, a strong army and navy, and a broad interpretation of national power. So complete was the elite consensus that by 1820 the Republicans had completely driven the Federalist party out of existence, largely by taking over their programs.

[7] Hofstadter, *American Political Tradition*, pp. 36–37.
[8] Hofstadter, p. 38.

The Rise of the Western Elites

According to Frederick Jackson Turner, "The rise of the New West was the most significant fact in American history."[9] Certainly the American West had a profound impact on the political system of the new nation. People went West because of the vast wealth of fertile lands that awaited them there; nowhere in the world could one acquire wealth so quickly as in the new American West. Because aristocratic families of the Eastern seaboard seldom had reason to migrate westward, the Western settlers were mainly middle- or lower-class immigrants. With hard work and good fortune, a penniless migrant could become a wealthy plantation owner or cattle rancher in a single generation. Thus, the West meant rapid upward social mobility.

New elites arose in the West and had to be assimilated into America's governing circles. This assimilation had a profound effect on the character of America's elites. No one exemplifies the new entrants into America's elite better than Andrew Jackson. Jackson's victory in the presidential election of 1828 was not a victory of the common man against the propertied classes but rather a victory of the new Western elites against established Republican leadership in the East. Jackson's victory forced America's established elites to recognize the growing importance of the West and to open their ranks to the new rich who were settled west of the Alleghenies.

Since Jackson was a favorite of the people, it was easy for him to believe in the wisdom of the common man. But "Jacksonian Democracy" was by no means a philosophy of leveling equalitarianism. The ideal of the frontier society was the self-made man, and wealth and power won by competitive skill was very much admired. It was only wealth and power obtained through special privilege that offended the frontiersmen. They believed in a *natural aristocracy*, rather than an aristocracy by birth, education, or special privilege. Jackson himself best expressed this philosophy in his famous message vetoing the bill to recharter the national bank:

> Distinctions in society will always exist under every just government. Equality of talents, of education, or wealth cannot be produced by human institutions. In the full enjoyment of the gifts of heaven and the fruits of superior industry, economy, and virtue, every man is equally entitled to protection by law; but when the laws undertake to add to these natural and just advantages artificial distinctions, to grant titles, gratuities, and exclusive privileges, to make the rich richer and the potent more powerful, the humble members of society — the farmers, mechanics, and laborers, — who have neither the time nor the means for securing like favors to themselves, have a right to complain of the injustice of their government.[10]

Thus it was not absolute equality that Jacksonians demanded but rather a more open elite system — a greater opportunity for the rising middle class to acquire wealth and influence through competition.

[9] Frederick Jackson Turner, "The West and American Ideals," in *The Frontier in American History* (New York: Holt, 1921).
[10] See Hofstadter, *American Political Tradition*, pp. 45–67.

In an attempt to win a place for themselves in America's governing circles, the new Western leaders attempted to convince the public that politics and administration should be taken from the hands of social elites and opened to men like themselves, who could boast of natural ability and talent. Jackson himself expressed this philosophy in his first annual message to Congress in December 1829: "The duties of all public offices are, or at least admit of being made, so plain and simple that men of intelligence may readily qualify themselves for their performance, and I cannot but believe that more is lost by the long continuance of men in office than is generally to be gained by experience." Rotation in office became a leading principle of Jacksonian Democracy.

In their struggle to open America's elite system, the Jacksonians appealed to mass sentiment. Jackson's humble beginnings, his image as a self-made man, his military adventures, his frontier experience, and his rough, brawling style served to endear him to the masses. As beneficiaries of popular support, the new elites of the West developed a strong faith in the wisdom and justice of popular decisions. All of the new Western states that entered the Union granted universal white male suffrage, and gradually the older states fell into step. Rising elites, themselves often less than a generation away from the masses, saw in a widened electorate a chance for personal advancement that they could never have achieved under the old regime. Therefore, the Jacksonians became noisy and effective advocates of the principle that all men should have the right to vote and that no restrictions should be placed upon officeholding. They also launched a successful attack upon the Congressional caucus system of nominating presidential candidates. Having been defeated in Congress in 1824, Jackson wished to sever Congress from the nominating process. In 1832, when the Democrats held their first national convention, Andrew Jackson was renominated by acclamation.

Jacksonian Democracy also brought changes in the method of selecting presidential electors. The Constitution left to the various state legislatures the right to decide how presidential electors should be chosen, and in most cases the legislatures themselves chose the electors. But after 1832 all states selected their presidential electors by popular vote. In most of these states the people voted for electors who were listed under the name of their party and their candidate.

The Jacksonian drive to open America's elite system did not stop with electoral reforms. The Western elites also tried to curtail the privileges of the established Eastern elites. As a Westerner, Jackson despised the Bank of the United States, which was controlled by conservative Eastern bankers, and supported the free lending policies of the state banks. State bank men were prominent in Jackson's first administration; Roger Taney, for instance, was a lawyer for and stockholder of the Union Bank of Maryland before Jackson appointed him Chief Justice of the United States Supreme Court. Thus when, prior to the election of 1832, Easterners Daniel Webster and Nicholas Biddle pushed through Congress a new charter for the Bank of the

United States to replace the charter that was to expire in 1836, Jackson vetoed the new charter with a ringing message that cemented his popularity with the masses. He denounced the banks as a "granted monopoly and exclusive privilege." Again, Jackson emerged as the apparent champion of the common man.

Following his re-election in 1832, Jackson decided to make war upon the Bank and its president, Nicholas Biddle. Jackson withdrew all deposits of the United States government from the bank and placed them in selected state banks — "pet banks," as they were called — which were prepared to extend credit to the new empire builders and land speculators of the Western states. The result was that money began to move from east to west in America and the way was paved for the rise of new Western capitalism. Jacksonian Democracy broke the exclusive monopoly of the Eastern elites over money and political power in America.

Yet the evidence is clear that the changes in the character of elites, from the administration of John Adams through Thomas Jefferson to Andrew Jackson, were very minor. Historical research by sociologist Sidney H. Aronson reveals that, contrary to the general assumption, Jackson's administration was clearly upper class in origin, college educated, prestigiously employed, professionally trained, and probably wealthy. (See Table 3–1.) In fact, Jackson's administration is not much different in class character from that of Thomas Jefferson's or even that of the Federalist, John Adams! Over half of Jackson's top appointees were born into America's distinguished upper-class families, and three-quarters enjoyed high class standing, prior to their appointment, either through birth or achievement.

Elite Cleavage — The Civil War

America's elites were in substantial agreement about the character and direction of the new nation during its first 60 years. Conflicts over the Bank, the tariff, internal improvements (roads, harbors, etc.), and even the controversial war with Mexico in 1846 did not threaten the basic underlying consensus in support of the American political system. In the 1850s, however, the role of the Negro in American society — the most divisive issue in the history of American politics — became an urgent question that drove a wedge among America's elites and ultimately led to the nation's bloodiest war. The American political system was unequal to the task of negotiating a peaceful settlement to the problem of slavery because America's elites were themselves deeply divided over the question.

In 1787, the Southern elites — cotton planters, land owners, exporters, and slave traders — had been prepared to envision an end to slavery; but after 1820, the demand for cotton became insatiable, and cotton could not be profitably produced without slave labor. Over half the value of all American goods shipped abroad before the Civil War was in cotton; and a broad belt of Southern land, ranging in width from about 500 miles in the Carolinas and Georgia to 600 or 700 miles in the Mississippi Valley, was devoted primarily to cotton culture.

Table 3–1.
Social Class
Characteristics of
Presidential
Appointments of
Adams, Jefferson,
and Jackson

Characteristic	Adams (N = 96)	Jefferson (N = 100)	Jackson (N = 127)
Father held political office	52%	43%	44%
Father attended college	17	13	12
Class I¹ family social position	62	58	51
High-ranking occupation	92	93	90
Political office prior to appointment	91	83	88
Class I¹ social position	86	74	74
Family in America in seventeenth century	55	48	48
Attended college	63	52	52
Professional training	69	74	81
Relative an appointive elite	40	34	34

¹"Class I" is the highest of four classes described as follows:

Class I: "national and international aristocracy";
Class II: "prosperous and respectable";
Class III: "respectable";
Class IV: "subsistence or impoverished."

Breakdowns by each class are as follows:
Adams: I: 62%, II: 19%, III: 5%, IV: 1%, unknown: 13%.
Jefferson: I: 58%, II: 15%, III: 6%, IV: 1%, unknown: 20%.
Jackson: I: 51%, II: 25%, III: 11%, IV: 2%, unknown: 11%.

Source: Sidney H. Aronson, *Status and Kinship in the Higher Civil Service* (Cambridge: Harvard University Press, 1964), p. 195.

While Virginia did not depend upon cotton, it sold great numbers of slaves to the cotton states, and "slave raising" itself became immensely profitable. The price of a good slave for the fields increased from $300 in 1820 to over $1,000 in 1860, in spite of the fact that the slave population grew from about a million and a half to nearly four million during this period.

It was the white *elites* and not the white *masses* of the South who had an interest in the slave and cotton culture. On the eve of the Civil War, probably not more than 400,000 Southern families—approximately one in four—held slaves. And many of these families held only one or two slaves each. The number of great planters—men who owned fifty or more slaves and large holdings of land—was probably not more than 7,000. Yet the views of these men dominated Southern politics.

The Northern elites were merchants and manufacturers who depended upon free labor. However, Northern elites had no direct interest in the abolition of slavery in the South. Some Northern manufacturers were making good profits from Southern trade; and with higher tariffs, they stood a chance to make even better profits. Abolitionist activities imperiled trade relations between North and South and were often looked upon with irritation even in Northern social circles. But both Northern and Southern elites realized that control of the West was the key to future dominance of the nation. Northern elites wanted a West composed of small farmers who produced food and raw materials for the industrial and commercial East and provided a market for Eastern goods. Southern planters feared the voting power of a West composed of small farmers and wanted Western lands for the expansion of the cotton and slave culture. Cotton ate up the land and, because it required continuous cultivation and monotonous rounds of simple tasks, was suited to slave labor. Thus, to protect the cotton economy, it was essential to protect slavery in Western lands. This conflict over Western land eventually precipitated the Civil War.

Yet despite these differences, the underlying consensus of American elites was so great that compromise after compromise was devised to maintain unity. In the Missouri Compromise of 1820, the land in the Louisiana Purchase exclusive of Missouri was divided between free territory and slave territory at 36° 30'; and Maine and Missouri were admitted as free and slave states, respectively. After the war with Mexico, the elaborate Compromise of 1850 caused one of the greatest debates in American legislative history, with Senators Henry Clay, Daniel Webster, John C. Calhoun, Salmon P. Chase, Steven A. Douglas, Jefferson Davis, Alexander H. Stevens, Robert Tombs, William H. Seward, and Thaddeus Stevens all participating. Elite cleavage was apparent, but it was not yet so divisive as to split the nation. A compromise was achieved, providing for the admission of California as a free state; for the creation of two new territories, New Mexico and Utah, out of the Mexican cession; for a drastic fugitive slave law to satisfy Southern planters; and for the prohibition of slave trade in the District of Columbia. Even the Kansas-Nebraska Act of 1854 was intended to be a compromise; each new territory was supposed to decide for itself whether it should be slave or free, with the expectation that Nebraska would vote free and Kansas slave. But gradually the spirit of compromise gave way to cleavage and conflict.

Beginning in 1856, pro- and anti-slavery forces fought it out in "bleeding Kansas." Senator Charles Sumner of Massachusetts delivered a condemnation of slavery in the Senate and was beaten almost to death on the Senate floor by Preston Brooks, a relative of Senator Andrew P. Butler of South Carolina. Intemperate language in the Senate became commonplace, with frequent threats of secession, violence, and civil war.

In 1857, the Supreme Court decided, in *Dred Scot* v. *Sanford*,[11] that the Missouri Compromise was unconstitutional because Congress had no authority to forbid slavery in any territory. Slave property, said Chief Justice Roger B. Taney, was as much protected by the Constitution as was any other kind of property.

In 1859, John Brown and his followers raided the United States arsenal at Harper's Ferry, as a first step to freeing the slaves of Virginia by force. Brown was captured by Virginia militia under the command of Colonel Robert E. Lee, tried for treason, found guilty, and executed. Southerners believed that Northerners had tried to incite the

[11]*Dred Scott* v. *Sanford*, 19 Howard 393 (1857).

horror of slave insurrection, while Northerners believed that Brown died a martyr.

The conflict between North and South led to the complete collapse of the Whig party and the emergence of a new Republican party composed exclusively of Northerners and Westerners. For the first time in the history of American parties, one of the two major parties did not spread across both sides of the Mason-Dixon line. Robert Dahl describes the decline of unity among American elites:

Congress, hitherto the forum of compromise, became in the 1850s a battleground where almost every issue split the membership in the same two camps. In 1858–1859, Congress had lengthy deadlocks on almost every issue: The admission of Kansas, transcontinental railroads, rivers and harbors appropriations, a homestead bill, the tariff. Deadlock and conflict so much dominated the session that the Congress was not even able to agree on the annual appropriation for the post office; at the end of the session the post office department was left without funds.[12]

1860 was the only year in American history that four, rather than two, major parties sought the Presidency. The nation was so divided that no party came close to winning the majority of popular votes. Lincoln, the Republican candidate, and Douglas, the Democratic candidate, won most of their votes from the North and West, while Breckenridge, the Southern Democratic candidate, and Bell, the Constitutional Union candidate, received most of their votes from the South (see Table 3–2).

Table 3–2.
The Election of 1860

	Percent of Total Vote	Percent of Vote from North and West	Percent of Vote from South
Republicans: Lincoln	40	98.6	1.4
Democrats: Douglas	30	88.0	12.0
Southern Democrats: Breckenridge	18	33.0	67.0
Constitutional Union: Bell	12	13.0	87.0

Source: Robert A. Dahl, *Pluralist Democracy in the United States* (Chicago: Rand McNally, 1966), pp. 312–313; data from W. Dean Burnham, *Presidential Ballots, 1836–1892* (Baltimore: Johns Hopkins Press, 1955).

More important, the cleavage had become so deep that many prominent Southern leaders announced that they would not accept the outcome of the presidential election if Lincoln won. Threats of secession were not new, but this time it was no bluff. For the first and only time in American history, prominent elite members were prepared to destroy the American political system rather than compromise their interests and principles. Shortly after the election, on December 20, 1860, the state of South Carolina seceded from the Union. Within six months, ten other Southern states had followed.

[12]Robert A. Dahl, *Pluralist Democracy in the United States* (Chicago: Rand McNally, 1966).

Yet even in the midst of this disastrous conflict, one finds extensive evidence of continued devotion to the principles of constitutional government and private property among both Northern and Southern elites. There were many genuine efforts at compromise and conciliation. Abraham Lincoln never attacked slavery in the South; his exclusive concern was to halt the spread of slavery in the Western territories. He wrote in 1845: "I hold it a paramount duty of us in the free states, due to the union of the states, and perhaps to liberty itself (paradox though it may seem), to let the slavery of the other states alone."[13] Throughout his political career he consistently held this position. On the other hand, with regard to the Western territories he said: "The whole nation is interested that the best use shall be made of these territories. We want them for homes and free white people. This they cannot be, to any considerable extent, if slavery shall be planted within them."[14] In short, Lincoln wanted the Western territories to be tied economically and culturally to the Northern system. As for Lincoln's racial views, as late as 1858 he said:

I will say, then, that I am not, nor ever have been, in favor of bringing about in any way the social and political equality of the white and black races; that I am not, nor ever have been, in favor of making voters or jurors of Negroes, nor qualifying them to hold office, nor to intermarry with white people . . . and in as much as they cannot so live while they do remain together, there must be a position of superior and inferior; and I as much as any other man am in favor of having the superior position assigned to the white race.[15]

Lincoln's political posture was essentially conservative: He wished to preserve the long-established order and consensus that had protected American principles and property rights so successfully in the past. He was not an abolitionist, and he did not set as his goal the destruction of the Southern elites or the rearrangement of the South's social fabric. His goal was to bring the South back into the Union, to restore orderly government, and to establish the principle that the states cannot resist national authority with force. At the beginning of the war, Lincoln knew that a great part of conservative Northern opinion was willing to fight for the Union but might refuse to support a war to free Negroes. Lincoln's great political skill was his ability to submerge all of the issues of the Civil War into one single overriding theme—the preservation of the Union. On the other hand, he was bitterly attacked throughout the war by radical Republicans who thought that he had "no anti-slavery instincts."

As the war continued and casualties mounted, opinion in the North became increasingly bitter toward Southern slave owners. Many Republicans joined the abolitionists in calling for emancipation of the slaves simply to punish the "rebels." They knew that the power of the South was based on the labor of slaves. Lincoln also knew that if he

[13] Hofstadter, *American Political Tradition*, p. 109.
[14] Hofstadter, p. 113.
[15] Hofstadter, p. 116.

proclaimed to the world that the war was being fought to free the slaves, there would be less danger of foreign intervention. Yet even in late summer of 1862, Lincoln wrote:

My paramount object in this struggle is to save the Union. If I could save the Union without freeing any slaves, I would do it; if I could save it by freeing some and leaving others alone, I would also do that. I shall do less whenever I shall believe what I am doing hurts the cause, and I shall do more whenever I believe doing more will help the cause. I shall adopt new views as fast as they shall appear to be true views.[16]

Finally, on September 22, 1862, Lincoln issued his preliminary Emancipation Proclamation. Claiming his right as commander-in-chief of the army and navy, he promised that "on the first day of January 1863, all persons held as slaves within any state or designated part of a state, the people whereof shall then be in rebellion against the United States shall be then, thence forward, and forever free." Thus one of the great steps forward in human freedom in this nation, the Emancipation Proclamation, did not come about as a result of demands by the people, and certainly not a result of demands by the slaves themselves. It was a political and military action by the President for the sake of helping to preserve the Union. It was not a revolutionary action but a conservative one.

The Rise of the New Industrial Elite The importance of the Civil War for America's elite structure was the commanding position that the new industrial capitalists won during the course of the struggle. Even before 1860, Northern industry had been altering the course of American life; the economic transformation of the United States from an agricultural to an industrial nation reached the crescendo of a revolution in the second half of the nineteenth century. Canals and steam railroads had been opening up new markets for the growing industrial cities of the East. The rise of corporations and of stock markets for the accumulation of capital upset old-fashioned ideas about property. The introduction of machinery in factories revolutionized the conditions of American labor and made the masses dependent upon industrial capitalists for their livelihood. Civil War profits compounded the capital of the industrialists and placed them in a position to dominate the economic life of the nation. Moreover, when the Southern planters were removed from the national scene, the government in Washington became the exclusive domain of the new industrial leaders.

The protective tariff, long opposed by the Southern planters, became the cornerstone of the new business structure of America. The industrial capitalists realized that the Northwest Territory was the natural market for their manufactured goods, and the protective tariff restricted the vast and growing American market to American industry alone. When the passage of the Homestead Act threw the national

[16] Hofstadter, pp. 132–133.

domain wide open to settlers, Eastern capital hastened to build a system of transcontinental railroads to link expanding Western markets to Eastern industry. Northeast America was rich in the natural resources of coal, iron, and water power; and the large immigrant population streaming in from Europe furnished a dependable source of cheap labor. The Northeast also had superior means of transportation — both water and rail — to facilitate the assembling of raw materials and the marketing of finished products. With the rise of the new industrial capitalism, power in America flowed from the South and West to the Northeast and Jefferson's dream of a nation of free farmers faded.

The new industrial elite found a new philosophy to justify its political and economic dominance. Drawing an analogy from the new Darwinian biology, Herbert Spencer undertook to demonstrate that just as an elite was selected in nature through evolution, so also society would near perfection as it allowed natural social elites to be selected by free competition. In defense of the new capitalists, Herbert Spencer argued: "There cannot be more good done than that of letting social progress go on unhindered; an immensity of mischief may be done in . . . the artificial preservation of those least able to care for themselves."[17] Spencer hailed the accumulation of new industrial wealth as a sign of "the survival of the fittest." The "social Darwinists" found in the law of survival of the fittest an admirable defense for the emergence of a ruthless ruling elite, an elite which defined its own self-interest more narrowly, perhaps, than any other in American history. It was a philosophy that permitted the conditions of the masses to decline to the lowest depths in American history.

Spencer's social Darwinism forbade restrictive "meddling" legislation. If trusts and monopolies proved to be the natural results of competition, worshippers of competition could not logically prohibit them. Yet, ironically, the industrial elites saw no objection to legislation if it furthered their success in business. Unrestricted competition might prove who was the "fittest"; but as an added precaution to insure that industrial capitalists themselves emerged as the "fittest," these new elites also insisted upon government subsidies, patents, tariffs, loans, and massive giveaways of land and other natural resources.

Railroads were at the heart of the early industrial expansion in America. The excitement over the completion of the first transcontinental railroad in 1869 was accentuated by the fact that railroad progress was general throughout the United States. The expansion of the railroads created new elites: Leland Stanford of the Union Pacific, Commodore Vanderbilt of New York Central, Jay Gould of the Erie, Henry Villard of the Northern Pacific, and James J. Hill of the Great Northern. So ruthless were these men in exploiting their customers, the Western farmers, that an organization called the Patrons of Husbandry, or the Grange, emerged to battle with the railroads. The Grangers actually succeeded in winning control of some Western state legis-

[17] Herbert Spencer, *Social Statics* (1851).

latures, including Illinois, and in passing some state legislation regulating railroad practices. But these Granger Laws, the railroad attorneys claimed, were unconstitutional "impairments of contracts" and took private property without "due process of law."

In 1877, the Supreme Court, which still reflected pre-Civil War landed interests, ruled against the railroads in *Munn* v. *Illinois*. The Court asserted the "right of a state to regulate a business that is public in nature though privately owned and managed."[18] However, *Munn* v. *Illinois* was soon relegated to an obscure position in court policy when the makeup of the court finally caught up with the industrial revolution. In the 1880s, Justice Stephen A. Field gave a new interpretation to the Fourteenth Amendment. Business corporations were "persons" under the Fourteenth Amendment, and no "corporate person" could be deprived of property by a state without "due process of law."[19] Since legislative regulation of railroad rates or other business decisions might reduce a corporation's profits, such regulations were unconstitutional under the Fourteenth Amendment, Field held. The Court soon became a bulwark against the occasional attempts by states to challenge industrial dominance. In a dissenting opinion in 1905, Justice Oliver Wendell Holmes said that "the Fourteenth Amendment does not enact Mr. Herbert Spencer's *Social Statics*."[20] But Holmes' observation was a *dissenting* opinion; the majority of the Court helped to sustain the capitalist impulse by using the "due process clause" of the Fourteenth Amendment to halt all challenges of industrial dominance.

After the Civil War, businessmen became more numerous in Congress than at any other time in American history. They had little trouble in voting high tariffs and hard money, both of which heightened profits. Very little effective regulatory legislation was permitted to reach the floor of Congress. After 1881 the Senate came under the spell of Nelson Aldrich, son-in-law of John D. Rockefeller, who controlled Standard Oil. Aldrich served 30 years in the Senate. He believed that geographical representation in the Senate was old-fashioned and openly advocated a Senate manned officially by representatives from the great business "constituencies" — steel, coal, copper, railroads, banks, textiles, and so on.

As business became increasingly national in scope, only the strongest or most unscrupulous of the competitors survived. Great producers tended to become the cheapest producers, and little companies tended to disappear. Industrial production rose rapidly, while the number of industrial concerns steadily diminished. Total capital investment and total output of industry vastly increased, while ownership became concentrated. One result was the emergence of monopolies and near monopolies in each of the major industries of America. Another result was the accumulation of great family fortunes.[21] (See Table 3–3, which was compiled from 1924 tax returns and admittedly fails to record

[18] *Munn* v. *Illinois* 94 U.S. 113 (1877).
[19] *San Mateo County* v. *Southern Pacific Railroad Co.* 116 U.S. 138 (1885).
[20] *Lochner* v. *New York*, 198 U.S. 45 (1905).
[21] See Gustavus Myers, *A History of the Great American Fortunes*, 3 vols. (Chicago: 1910).

other great personal fortunes, such as Armour and Swift in meat packing, Candler in Coca-Cola, Cannon in textiles, Fleischman in yeast, Pulitzer in publishing, Golet in real estate, Harriman in railroads, Heinz in foods, Manville in asbestos, Cudahy in meat packing, Dorrance in Campbell's Soup, Hartford in A & P, Eastman in film, Firestone in rubber, Sinclair in oil, Chrysler in automobiles, Pabst in beer, and others.)

Typical of the great entrepreneurs of industrial capitalism was John D. Rockefeller. By the end of the Civil War, Rockefeller had accumulated a modest fortune of $50,000 in wholesale grain and meat. In 1865, with extraordinary good judgment, he invested his money in the wholly new petroleum business. He backed one of the first oil refineries in the nation and continually reinvested his profits into his business. In 1867, backed by two new partners—H. M. Flagler and F. W. Harkness—Rockefeller founded the Standard Oil Company of Ohio, which in that year refined 4 percent of the nation's output. By 1872, with monopoly as his goal, he had acquired 20 of the 25 refineries in Cleveland and was laying plans that within a decade would bring him into control of over 90 percent of the oil refineries of the country. Rockefeller bought up pipelines, warehouses, and factories and was able to force railroads to grant him rebates. In 1882, he formed a giant trust, the Standard Oil Company, with a multitude of affiliates. Thereafter, the Standard Oil Company became a prototype of American monopolies. As Rockefeller himself put it: "The day of combination is here to stay. Individualism has gone, never to return."

Perhaps the greatest American success story is that of Andrew Carnegie, a Scottish immigrant boy who came penniless to America. He worked first as a bobbin boy for $1.25 a week in a western Pennsylvania cotton factory, then as a messenger at $2.50 a week in a Pittsburgh telegraph office. Quite soon, he became the private secretary of Thomas A. Scott of the Pennsylvania Railroad and began to amass railway and oil stocks. Then, on a trip to England, he saw steel being made by the new Bessemer process, and he returned to the United States determined to begin manufacturing steel. In Pittsburgh, in 1873, he opened the J. Edgar Thompson Steel Mill, carefully named after the president of the Pennsylvania Railroad. Carnegie soon monopolized the steel industry in Pittsburgh and much of the nation, and steel replaced railroads as the backbone of the new industrialism. In 1901, Carnegie Steel plus three other steel giants—the Tennessee Coal and Iron Company, the Illinois Steel Company, and the Colorado Fuel and Iron Company—arranged one of the nation's most colossal business mergers, creating the United States Steel Corporation. Unlike his fellow capitalists Carnegie believed that "The amassing of wealth is one of the worst species of idolatry" and he gave away over $350,000,000. Most of his philanthropy went to public libraries in cities throughout the nation.

At the apex of America's new corporate and industrial elite stood J. Pierpont Morgan, master of industrial finance. Morgan knit together the U.S. Steel Corporation, America's first billion dollar corporation, and later established International Harvester Corporation. During World War I, J. P. Morgan and Company was the purchasing agent in America for the Allies at a commission of 1 percent. J. P. Morgan himself was not the wealthiest of America's wealthy men, but the Morgan firm derived its unprecedented power from the combined resources of many families and corporations in which it had an interest. The extent of Morgan power in American industry and finance defies statistical measurement. Direct Morgan *control* of banking and non-banking corporations often shades into Morgan *dominance,* and Morgan dominance often shades into Morgan *influence.* Morgan partners or executives were found in dominant positions on the boards of American Telephone and Telegraph Company, U.S. Steel Corporation, General Electric Company, Consolidated Edison Company, United Gas Improvement Company, American & Foreign Power Company, Electric Bond and Share Company, Niagara Hudson Power Corporation, Montgomery Ward and Company, International Telephone and Telegraph Corporation, American Can Company, Kennecott Copper Corporation, Chesapeake and Ohio Railroad, New York Central Railroad, General Motors Corporation, E. I. du Pont de Nemours and Company, and many others. The Morgan firm exercised dominance over the Guarantee Trust Company of New York, the Banker's Trust Company, the First National Bank of New York, and the New York Trust Company. The combined Morgan commercial banks outweighed all other banking interests in total assets, deposits, and resources. As late as 1932, it was estimated that the Morgan interests, with their varying degrees of control, dominance, and influence, totaled more than one quarter of all American corporate wealth. The boards of directors of most of these banks and corporations reveal the same names again and again and point up the close interlocking community of interest among America's industrial elite.

The American Telephone and Telegraph Company is an excellent example of the interlocking nature of America's industrial, corporate, and banking elites. This company has a virtual monopoly on telephone and telegraph communications in America. This monopoly was in part a product of government patent laws, which protected Alexander Graham Bell's invention of the telephone in 1876. On the other hand, while the A. T. & T. advertises that no individual owns as much as 1 percent of its stock, actual working control of the corporation resides in a small and elite board of directors. In the mid-1930s, this board was composed as follows:

The Morgan men on the A. T. & T. board are George F. Baker, president of the First National Bank of New York; Samuel A. Walldon, vice-president of the First National Bank of New York; John W. Davis (Democratic presidential candidate in 1924), chief council for J. P. Morgan and Co.; and Myron C. Taylor, chairman of the finance committee of the U.S. Steel Corp. The Rockefellers are represented by Winthrop Aldrich (brother of Senator Nelson

Table 3–3.
The Industrial Fortunes, 1924

Family and Number of Tax Returns	Primary Source of Wealth	Aggregate 1924 Tax	Approximate Net Aggregate Income Taxed	Net Aggregate Fortune Taxed	Gross Adjusted Fortune after Multiplying by 3	Maximum Estimated Fortune
1. 21 Rockefellers	Standard Oil	$7,309,989	$17,955,000	$359,100,000	$1,077,300,000	$2,500,000,000
2. 34 Morgan Inner Group	J. P. Morgan & Co.	4,796,263	12,620,000	276,000,000‡	728,000,000‡	
(Including Morgan partners and families and eight leading Morgan corporation executives)						
3. 2 Fords	Ford Motor Co.	4,766,863	11,000,000	220,000,000	660,000,000	1,000,000,000
4. 5 Harknesses	Standard Oil	2,776,735	7,550,000	150,200,000	450,600,000	800,000,000
5. 3 Mellons	Aluminum Company	3,237,876	7,500,000	150,000,000	450,000,000	1,000,000,000
6. 22 Vanderbilts	N.Y. Central R. R.	2,148,892	6,005,000	120,100,000	360,300,000	800,000,000
7. 4 Whitneys	Standard Oil	2,143,992	5,375,000	107,500,000	322,000,000	750,000,000
8. 28 Standard Oil Group	Standard Oil	1,737,857	5,435,000	118,700,000	356,000,000	
(Including Archbolds, Rogerses, Bedfords, Cutlers, Flaglers, Pratts, and Benjamins, but excepting others)						
9. 20 Du Ponts	E. I. du Pont de Nemours	1,294,651	3,925,000	79,500,000	238,500,000	1,000,000,000
10. 8 McCormicks	Int. Harvester and Chi. Tribune	1,332,517	3,520,000	70,400,000	211,200,000	
11. 2 Bakers	1st National Bank	1,575,482	3,500,000	70,000,000	210,000,000	500,000,000
12. 5 Fishers	General Motors	1,424,583	3,225,000	64,500,000	193,500,000	500,000,000
13. 6 Guggenheims	Amer. Smelting & Rfg. Co.	817,836	2,185,000	63,700,000	190,100,000	
14. 6 Fields	Marshall Field & Co.	1,197,605	3,000,000	60,000,000	180,000,000	
15. 5 Curtis-Boks	Curtis Pub. Co.	1,303,228	2,900,000	58,000,000	174,000,000	
16. 3 Dukes	Am. Tobacco Co.	1,045,544	2,600,000	52,000,000	156,000,000	
17. 3 Berwinds	Berwind-White Coal Co.	906,495	2,500,000	50,000,000	150,000,000	
18. 17 Lehmans	Lehman Brothers	672,897	2,150,000	43,000,000	129,000,000‡	
19. 3 Wideners	Am. Tob. & Pub. Utilities	772,720	1,975,000	39,500,000	118,500,000	
20. 7 Reynolds	R. J. Reynolds Tobacco Co.	652,824	1,950,000	39,000,000	117,000,000	
21. 3 Astors	Real Estate	783,002	1,900,000	38,000,000	114,000,000	300,000,000
22. 6 Winthrops	Miscellaneous	651,188	1,735,000	34,700,000	104,100,000	
23. 3 Stillmans	National City Bank	623,614	1,700,000	34,000,000	102,000,000	500,000,000
24. 3 Timkens	Timken Roller Bearing Co.	781,435	1,850,000	37,000,000	111,000,000	
25. 4 Pitcairns	Pittsburgh Plate Glass Co.	752,545	1,660,000	33,200,000	99,600,000	
26. 8 Warburgs	Kuhn, Loeb & Co.	598,246	1,620,000	32,400,000	97,200,000‡	
27. 4 Metcalfs	Rhode Island textile mills	623,817	1,510,000	30,200,000	90,600,000	
28. 3 Clarks	Singer Sewing Mach. Co.	583,087	1,475,000	29,500,000	90,000,000	
29. 16 Phipps	Carnegie Steel Co.	431,969	1,485,000	29,700,000	89,100,000	600,000,000
30. 4 Kahns	Kuhn, Loeb & Co.	565,608	1,440,000	28,800,000	86,400,000‡	
31. 2 Greens	Stocks and real estate	443,021	1,200,000	24,000,000	72,000,000	
32. 2 Pattersons	Chicago Tribune, Inc.	365,211	1,015,000	20,300,000	60,900,000	
33. 2 Tafts	Real Estate	329,689	900,000	18,000,000	54,000,000	
34. 3 Deerings	International Harvester	315,701	825,000	16,500,000	49,500,000	
35. 6 De Forests	Corp. law practice	202,013	685,000	13,700,000	41,100,000‡	400,000,000
36. 5 Goulds	Railroads	154,563	565,000	11,300,000	33,900,000	400,000,000
37. 3 Hills	Railroads	226,827	360,000	7,200,000	21,600,000	150,000,000
38. 2 Drexels	J. P. Morgan & Co.	131,616	350,000	7,000,000	21,000,000	100,000,000

39.	Thomas Fortune Ryan*†	Stock market	791,851	1,800,000	36,000,000	108,000,000
40.	H. Foster (Cleveland)	Auto Parts	569,894	1,700,000	34,000,000	106,000,000
41.	Eldridge Johnson	Victor Phonograph	542,627	1,250,000	25,000,000	75,000,000
42.	Arthur Curtiss James	Copper and railroads	521,388	1,200,000	24,000,000	72,000,000
43.	C. W. Nash	Automobiles	459,776	1,100,000	22,000,000	66,000,000
44.	Mortimer Schiff	Kuhn, Loeb & Co.	459,410	1,100,000	22,000,000	66,000,000
45.	James A. Patten	Wheat market	425,348	1,000,000	20,000,000	60,000,000‡
46.	Charles Hayden*	Stock market	427,979	1,000,000	20,000,000	60,000,000
47.	Orlando F. Weber	Allied Chemical & Dye Corp.	406,582	900,000	18,000,000	54,000,000
48.	George Blumenthal	Lazard Frères	415,621	900,000	18,000,000	54,000,000‡
49.	Ogden L. Mills	Mining	372,827	800,000	16,000,000	48,000,000
50.	Michael Friedsam*†	Merchandising	292,396	700,000	14,000,000	42,000,000
51.	Edward B. McLean	Mining	281,125	700,000	14,000,000	42,000,000
52.	Eugene Higgins	New York real estate	279,265	700,000	14,000,000	42,000,000
53.	Alexander S. Cochran*†	Textiles	271,542	700,000	14,000,000	42,000,000
54.	Mrs. L. N. Kirkwood		268,556	625,000	12,500,000	37,500,000
55.	Helen Tyson		258,086	600,000	12,000,000	36,000,000
56.	Archer D. Huntington*†	Railroads	226,353	575,000	11,500,000	34,500,000
57.	James J. Storrow*†	Lee Higginson & Co.	222,571	575,000	11,500,000	34,500,000‡
58.	Julius Rosenwald*†	Sears, Roebuck & Co.	208,812	500,000	10,000,000	30,000,000
59.	Bernard M. Baruch	Stock market	268,142	625,000	12,500,000	37,500,000
60.	S. S. Kresge	Merchandising	188,608	500,000	10,000,000	30,000,000

*Deceased.
†Fortune left to family.
‡Partly theoretical as income consisted in varying measure of fees.

Source: Ferdinand Lundberg. *America's Sixty Families* (New York: Citadel Press, 1937).

Aldrich), chairman of the Chase National Bank. A Boston group, closely identified with J. P. Morgan and Co., is represented by Charles Francis Adams (of the famous Adams family), director of the Union Trust Co. of Boston and numerous corporations and former Secretary of the Navy and father-in-law of Henry Sturgis Morgan, J. P. Morgan's son; W. Cameron Forbes, of J. M. Forbes and Co., a Boston enterprise, and former governor-general of the Philippines; George P. Gardner, director of the Morgan controlled General Electric Co.; Thomas Nelson Perkins, lawyer; Philip Stockton, director of the First National Bank of Boston. Presidents of three railroads dependent upon J. P. Morgan Co. for financing, two insurance company heads, and James F. Bell of General Mills, Inc., fill out the board, along with three A. T. & T. executives, who have little to say outside the technical field.[22]

In the 1930s, the assets of A. T. & T. exceeded the total wealth of 21 states in the United States and were greater than the assets of 8,000 average-sized corporations.

The Political Dominance of the Industrial Elite

The condition of the masses during the age of great industrial expansion was perhaps the lowest in American history. At the turn of the century, American workers earned, on the average, between $400 and $500 a year (or only $1,500 a year by today's standards). Unemployment was frequent, and there were no unemployment benefits. A working day of ten hours, six days a week, was taken for granted. Accidents among industrial employees were numerous and lightly regarded by employers. The presence of women and children in industry tended to hold down wages but was an absolute necessity for many families. Child labor was ruthlessly exploited in the cotton mills of the South, in the sweat shops of the East, and in the packing plants of the West.

By 1900, almost 40 percent of the population lived in urban areas, in which the living conditions for the masses varied from bad to unspeakable. Very few owned their own homes; from 80 percent to 90 percent rented the space in which they lived.

Both the Republican and Democratic parties reflected the dominance of the industrial elites. Richard Hofstadter comments on the influence that the industrial capitalists exercised over the party system in America:

The Republicans were distinguished from the Democrats chiefly by being successful. From the war and Reconstruction onwards, when it sought actively to strengthen its social base by espousing policies of American industrialists, the Republican party existed in an unholy and often mutually hostile conjunction with the capitalistic interests. Capitalists, seeking land grants, tariffs, bounties, favorable currency policies, freedom from regulatory legislation, and economic reform, supplied campaign funds, fees, and bribes, and plied politicians with investment opportunities. Seward had said that "a party is in one sense a joint stock company in which those who contribute the most direct the action and management of the concern."[23]

[22] Ferdinand Lundberg, *America's Sixty Families* (New York: Citadel Press, 1937), pp. 43–44.
[23] Hofstadter, *American Political Tradition*, p. 170.

V. O. Key also describes the Republican Party machine of the 1870s and 1880s:

> The inner strength of Republicanism did not rest on sentiment alone. Sentiment clothed the bonds of substance. To the old soldiers — old Union soldiers — went pensions. To manufacturers of the Northeast went tariffs. To the farmers of the Northwest went free land under the Homestead Act. To railroad promoters went land grants for the construction of railroads that tied together the West and the North — and assured that the flow of commerce would bypass the South. The synthesis of self-interest and glory formed a cohesive combination. The G.O.P. represented a wonderfully effective contrivance, not only for preserving the Union but for holding together East and West, for the magnate and factory worker, homesteader and banker, and the great enterprise of continental unification, development, and exploitation.[24]

The Democratic Party under Grover Cleveland was little different from the Republican Party. Perhaps the single exception was that Cleveland called upon businessmen to improve their morals and become trustees of the public interest. Nevertheless, Cleveland used federal troops to break the Pullman strike in 1894 and to help keep down the urban working class. He supported the gold standard and alienated the debt-ridden farmers of the West. He hedged on the tariff question, refusing to adopt the traditional position of landed interests on behalf of low tariffs. He even negotiated a much-publicized gold purchase loan from J. P. Morgan. Hofstadter remarks: "Out of heartfelt conviction he gave to the interests what many a lesser politician might have sold them for a price."[25]

The only serious challenge to the political dominance of Eastern capital came over the issue of "free silver." Leadership of the "free silver" movement came from mine owners in the silver states of the Far West. Their campaigns convinced thousands of Western farmers that free silver was the answer to their economic distress. The Western mine owners did not care about the welfare of small farmers, but the prospect of inflation, debt relief, and expansion of the supply of money and purchasing power won increasing support among the masses in the West and South.

When William Jennings Bryan delivered his famous "Cross of Gold" speech at the Democratic Convention in 1896, he swept the Cleveland "Gold Democrats" out of control of the Democratic Party. Bryan was a Westerner, a talented orator, an anti-intellectual, and a deeply religious man; he was antagonistic to the Eastern industrial interests and totally committed to the cause of free silver. Bryan tried to rally the nation's have-nots to his banner; he tried to convince them they were being exploited by Wall Street finance. Yet it is important to note that he did not severely criticize the capitalist system, nor did he call for increases in the regulatory powers of the federal government. In

---

[24] V. O. Key, Jr., *Politics, Parties, and Pressure Groups* (New York: Thomas Y. Crowell Co., 1942), pp. 185–186.
[25] Hofstadter, *American Political Tradition*, p. 185.

his acceptance speech he declared, "our campaign has not for its object the reconstruction of society. . . . Property is and will remain the stimulus to endeavor and the compensation for toil."[26] He was uninterested in labor legislation; his only issue was free silver.

The Republican campaign, directed by Marcus Alonzo Hanna of Standard Oil, was aimed at persuading the voters that what was good for business was good for the country. Hanna raised an unprecedented $16,000,000 campaign fund from his wealthy fellow industrialists (an amount that would not be matched in Presidential campaigns until the 1960s) and advertised his candidate, William McKinley, as the man who would bring a "full dinner pail" to all. The heavy expenditures of the Republicans suggests that Bryan was considered capable of rallying the masses. Republican machines were mobilized across the nation. As the end of the campaign drew near, threats were cast about freely. Working men were told that the election of McKinley would mean high wages and prosperity, whereas the election of Bryan would bring the loss of their jobs. Some employers bluntly told their employees that if Bryan were elected they could not come back to work. Farmers were told that a Democratic victory might mean their mortgages would not be renewed.

Bryan's attempt to rally the masses was a dismal failure; McKinley won by a landslide. Bryan would run twice again under the Democratic banner, in 1900 and 1908, but he would lose by even greater margins. Although Bryan carried the South and some Western states, he failed to rally the masses of the populous Eastern states or the people of America's growing cities. Republicans carried working-class, middle-class, and upper-class neighborhoods in the urban industrial states. As V. O. Key explains:

> While the election of 1896 is often pictured as a lasting fight between the haves and have-nots, that understanding of the contest was evidently restricted to the plains of leadership and oratory. It did not extend to the voting actions of the electorate. . . . In 1896 the industrial cities, in their aggregate vote at least, moved toward the Republicans in about the same degree as did the rural farming communities . . . the Republicans gained in the working class wards, just as they did in the silk stocking wards, over their 1892 vote. . . . Instead of a sharpening of class cleavages within New England, the voting apparently reflected a more sectional antagonism and anxiety, shared by all classes, expressed in opposition to the dangers supposed to be threatening the West.[27]

The Liberal Establishment: Reform as Elite Self-interest

In 1882, William H. Vanderbilt of the New York Central Railroad expressed the ethos of the industrial elite in his famous declaration, "The public be damned." There was little sense of public responsibility among America's first generation of great capitalists. They had built their empires in the competitive pursuit of profit. They believed that their success could be attributed to the immutable laws of natural

[26] Hofstadter, p. 190.
[27] Key, *Politics, Parties, and Pressure Groups*, pp. 189–191.

selection, the survival of the fittest; and they believed that society was best served by allowing these laws to operate freely. In 1910, Woodrow Wilson, forerunner of a new elite ethos, criticized America's elite for its lack of public responsibility. At a widely publicized lecture to a meeting of bankers, with J. P. Morgan sitting at his side, Wilson declared:

The trouble today is that you bankers are too narrow-minded. You don't know the country or what is going on in it and the country doesn't trust you. . . . You take no interest in the small borrower and the small enterprise which affect the future of the country, but you give every attention to the big borrower and the rich enterprise which has already arrived. . . . You bankers see nothing beyond your own interests. . . . You should be broader-minded and see what is best for the country in the long run.[28]

Wilson urged America's elite to reject a narrowly self-interested view of things and to take the welfare of others, especially that of "the community," into account as an aspect of their own long-run welfare. Wilson did not wish to upset the established order; he merely wished to develop a sense of public responsibility within the establishment. He believed that the national government should see that industrial elites operated in the public interest, and his New Freedom program reflected these high-minded aspirations. In the Federal Reserve Act, the nation's banking and credit system was placed under public control. The Clayton Antitrust Act attempted to define specific business abuses, such as charging different prices to different buyers, granting rebates, or making false statements about competitors in order to take business away from them. A Federal Trade Commission was established and authorized to function in the "public interest" to prevent "unfair methods of competition and unfair and deceptive acts in commerce." An eight-hour day was established for railroad workers in interstate commerce; and the Child Labor Act attempted to eliminate the worst abuses of children in industry (this act was declared unconstitutional, however, by a much less public-regarding Supreme Court). Wilson's program aimed to preserve competition, individualism, enterprise, opportunity — all things that were considered vital in the American heritage. But he also believed fervently that elites must function in the public interest and that some government regulation might be required to see that they do so.

Wilson's New Freedom was forgotten during America's participation in World War I, and its gains were largely wiped out by the postwar reaction to reform. During the 1920s, America's elite rejected Wilsonian idealism. The established order clung to the philosophy of rugged individualism and rejected Wilson's appeal to a higher public interest.

Herbert Hoover was the last great advocate of the rugged individualism of the old order. The economic collapse of the Great Depression

---

[28]Hofstadter, *American Political Tradition*, p. 251.

undermined the faith of both elites and non-elites in the ideals of the old order. Following the stock market crash of October 1929, and in spite of elite assurances that prosperity lay "just around the corner," the American economy virtually stopped. Prices dropped sharply, factories closed, real estate values declined, new construction practically ceased, banks went under, wages were cut drastically, and unemployment figures mounted. By 1932, one of every four persons was unemployed, and one of every five persons was listed on welfare roles. Persons who had never known unemployment before lost their jobs, used up their savings or lost them when banks folded, cashed in their life insurance, gave up their homes and farms because they could not continue the mortgage payments. Economic catastrophe struck far up into the ranks of the middle classes. Once a man lost a job, he could not find another. Tramps abounded, panhandlers plied the streets, transients slept on the steps of public buildings, on park benches, on lawns, or on highways. Mines were no longer worked; steel mills, iron foundries, and every variety of industrial plant put out only a fraction of the goods that they could produce; trains ran with only a handful of passengers; stores lacked customers, and many closed their doors; ships stayed in port; hospitals were empty, not because they were unneeded but because people could not afford them.

The election of Franklin Delano Roosevelt to the Presidency in 1932 ushered in a new era in American elite philosophy. The Great Depression did not bring about a revolution; it did not result in the emergence of new elites; but it did have important impact on the thinking of America's governing elites. The economic disaster that had befallen the nation caused American elites to consider the need for economic reform. The Great Depression also gave force to Wilson's advice that elites acquire a greater public responsibility. The victories of fascism in Germany and communism in the Soviet Union and the growing restlessness of the masses in America combined to convince America's elite that reform and regard for the public welfare were essential to the continued maintenance of the American political system and their dominant place in it. In December 1933, John M. Keynes wrote an open letter to Roosevelt, emphasizing the importance of saving the capitalist system:

> You have made yourself the trustee for those in every country who seek to mend the evils of our conditions by reasoned experiment *within the framework of the existing social system.* If you fail, rational change will be gravely prejudiced throughout the world, leaving orthodoxy and revolution to fight it out.[29]

And Roosevelt himself was aware of the necessity of saving capitalism from itself:

[29]Hofstadter, p. 332 (emphasis added).

As I see it, the task of government in its relation to business is to assist the development of an economic declaration of rights, an economic constitutional order. . . . Happily, the times indicate that to create such an order not only is the proper policy of government, but it is the only line of safety for our economic structures as well.[30]

Roosevelt sought to elaborate a New Deal philosophy that would permit government to devote much more attention to the public welfare than did the philosophy of Hoover's somewhat discredited "rugged individualism." The New Deal was not a new or revolutionary system but rather a necessary reform of the existing capitalist system. There was no consistent unifying plan to the New Deal; it was a series of improvisations, many of them adopted very suddenly and some of them even contradictory. Roosevelt believed that more careful economic planning by government was required in order to adapt "existing economic organizations to the service of the people." And he believed that the government must act humanely and compassionately toward those who were suffering hardship. Relief, recovery, and reform, not revolution, were the objectives of the New Deal. Roosevelt called for "full, persistent experimentation. If it fails, admit it frankly and try something else. But above all try something. The millions who are in want will not stand by silently forever while the things to satisfy their needs are within easy reach."[31]

For anyone of Roosevelt's background, it would have been surprising indeed if he had tried to do other than preserve the existing social and economic order. Roosevelt was a descendant of two of America's oldest elite families, the Roosevelts and the Delanos, patrician families whose wealth predated the Civil War and the industrial revolution. The Roosevelts were not schooled in social Darwinism or the survival of the fittest or the scrambling competition of the new industrialists. From the beginning Roosevelt expressed a public-regarding philosophy. In Hofstadter's words:

At the beginning of his career he took to the patrician reform thought of the progressive era and accepted a social outlook that can best be summed up in the phrase "noblesse oblige." He had a penchant for public service, personal philanthropy, and harmless manifestos against dishonesty in government; he displayed a broad easy-going tolerance, a genuine liking for all sorts of people; he loved to exercise his charm in political and social situations.[32]

Roosevelt's personal philosophy was soon to become the prevailing ethos of the new liberal establishment.

In his first Administration, Roosevelt concentrated on relief (a Federal Emergency Relief program, a Public Works Administration program, and a Works Project Administration) and on national economic planning through the National Recovery Administration (NRA).

[30] Hofstadter, p. 330.
[31] Hofstadter, p. 316.
[32] Hofstadter, pp. 323–324.

MY FATHER SAYS THAT "THANK GOD, IT'S A BLESSING WE DON'T LIVE IN THE SOUTH WITH ALL THIS GOING ON."

ABSOLUTELY. MY FATHER AGREES.

MY FATHER SAYS THAT, "THANK GOD THERE'S NONE OF THIS NONSENSE HERE IN NEW YORK."

MY FATHER GOES RIGHT ALONG WITH YOUR FATHER. THEY CAN THROW THE REST OF THE COUNTRY AWAY AS FAR AS MY FATHER IS CONCERNED

MY FATHER SAYS "HA! AND THEY CALL THIS A **DEMOCRACY**! DON'T THEY KNOW HOW THIS LOOKS TO THE UNCOMMITTED COUNTRIES?"

EXACTLY WHAT MY FATHER SAYS. MY FATHER IS VERY INTERESTED IN UNCOMMITTED COUNTRIES.

WHERE DO THEY SEND YOU?

THORSTEIN VEBLEN ACADEMY IN SCARSDALE. HOW ABOUT YOU?

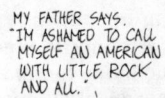

MY FATHER SAYS. "I'M ASHAMED TO CALL MYSELF AN AMERICAN WITH LITTLE ROCK AND ALL."

MY FATHER QUITE DEFINITELY AGREES. HE'S ALWAYS BEING ASHAMED OF CALLING HIMSELF AN AMERICAN.

THE PANDIT NEHRU SCHOOL. IT'S IN RYE.

© 1957 JULES FEIFFER

The NRA sought unsuccessfully to organize businessmen for the purposes of self-regulation in the public interest. The NRA failed, as did the Agricultural Adjustment Administration, which had tried to compensate farmers in various ways for reducing output. The National Labor Relations Act of 1935 was not a product of demands by the workers for government protection but rather a scheme for alleviating the depression by protecting unions, in the hopes that unions could raise wage rates and hence income levels in the nation. Established leaders of the American Federation of Labor actually opposed the measure at its time of passage. The Social Security Act of 1935 was designed to reduce the burdens of government welfare programs by compelling people to purchase insurance against the possibility of their own poverty. Later, the Housing Act of 1937 and the Fair Labor Standards Act continued the President's efforts to restore the health of capitalism.

In the New Deal, American elites accepted the principle that the entire community, through the agency of the national government, had a responsibility for mass welfare. In Roosevelt's second inaugural address he called attention to "one third of a nation, ill housed, ill clad, ill nourished." Roosevelt succeeded in saving the existing system of private capitalism and avoiding the threats to the established order of fascism, socialism, communism, and other radical movements.

Of course, some capitalists were unwilling to be "saved" by the New Deal. Roosevelt was genuinely hurt by criticisms from American industrialists, whom he felt he had protected with his reforms; he cried out in anger against the "economic royalists" who challenged his policies. He believed that the economic machinery of the nation had broken down and that the political fabric of America was beginning to disintegrate. He believed he had stabilized the economy and turned politics safely back to its normal democratic course. While he had engaged in some novel experiments (including the dangerous concept of public ownership, in TVA), he believed that for the most part he had avoided disturbing vital property interests. He rejected cries to nationalize America's banks during the bank crisis of 1933 and instead merely urged the American people to have greater confidence in their bankers. His basic policies in industry and agriculture had been designed by the large industrial and agricultural interests themselves. He believed that his relief and reform measures were mainly of the kind that any wise and humane conservative would admit to be necessary. He believed he had headed off the demagogues—Huey Long, Father Coughlin, and others—who had attempted to stir up the masses.

Eventually, Roosevelt's philosophy of noblesse oblige—elite responsibility for the welfare of the masses—won widespread acceptance within America's established leadership. The success of Roosevelt's liberal philosophy was in part a product of the economic disaster of the Great Depression and in part a tribute to the effectiveness of Roosevelt himself as a mobilizer of opinion among both elites and masses. But the acceptance of liberal establishment ideas may also be attributed in part to the changes that were occurring in the economic system.

One of these was a decline in the rate of new elite formation. Most of America's great entrepreneurial families had built their empires before World War I. The first-generation industrialists and entrepreneurs were unfriendly toward philosophies of public responsibility and appeals to "the public interest." But among the children and grandchildren of the great empire builders these ideals won increasing acceptance. Those who are born to wealth seem to accept the idea of noblesse oblige to a greater degree than those who had to acquire wealth for themselves, and available evidence indicates that there were more self-made men in 1900 than in 1950. Table 3–4 shows that only 39 percent of the richest men in America in 1900 came from the upper classes, while 68 percent of the nation's richest men in 1950 were born to wealth. Thirty-nine percent of the richest men in 1900 had struggled

Table 3–4.
Social Origins
of America's
Richest Men,
1900–1950

Social Origin	1900	1925	1950
Upper class	39%	56%	68%
Middle class	20	30	20
Lower class	39	12	9
Not classified	2	2	3

Source: Adapted from C. Wright Wills, *The Power Elite* (New York: Oxford University Press, 1956), pp. 104–105. The percentages are derived from biographies of the 275 people who were and are known to historians, biographers, and journalists as the richest people living in the United States—the 90 richest of 1900, the 95 of 1925, and the 90 of 1950. At the top of the 1900 group is John D. Rockefeller; at the top in 1925 is Henry Ford I; at the top in 1950 is H. L. Hunt.

up from the bottom, whereas only 9 percent of the richest men of 1950 had done so. This suggests that America's elite in the mid-twentieth century was more receptive to the ideas of responsibility for the common good and concern for the welfare of the masses. In other words, while Wilson's appeals for elite responsibility fell on the deaf ears of John D. Rockefeller in 1910, a sense of public responsibility would motivate the careers of John D. Rockefeller's grandsons—Nelson Rockefeller, Governor of New York; Winthrop Rockefeller, Governor of Arkansas; David Rockefeller, President of Chase Manhattan Bank of New York; and John D. Rockefeller III, Chairman of the Board of the Lincoln Center for Performing Arts in New York City.

Summary

Elite theory states that to maintain stability and avoid revolution, the movement of non-elites into elite positions must be slow and continuous. The competition among elites is less important than their shared concern for the preservation of the system.

The political history of the United States is consistent with elite theory; the ruling American elite has absorbed widely varying groups, from the Federalists to the Jeffersonians to the Westerners to the Industrialists to the Liberals, without any real break in the continuity of values in the American political and economic system. At only one time in American history, during the Civil War, did the elite consensus break down. Even then, both Northern and Southern elites continued to strive for compromise and for the preservation of the system that protected their liberty and property.

Elite theory also states that public policy changes are a result of the redefinition by elites of their own self-interest, rather than the result of direct influence by the masses. Lincoln issued the Emancipation Proclamation not because the slaves wanted to be free, or because the white masses wanted the slaves to be free, but because it was politically and militarily expedient to free the slaves. Likewise, the condition of the masses improved with the coming of the New Deal, not because the masses gained political power, but because elites acquired a sense of noblesse oblige. Furthermore, both of these seemingly radical measures, the Emancipation and the New Deal, were taken to preserve the system rather than to revolutionize it.

Finally, elite theory maintains that changes in public policy are incremental rather than revolutionary. When, for instance, the leadership of Hamilton and Adams was replaced by that of Jefferson, Monroe, and Madison, the policies of the United States government changed very little. One reason for the gradualness of the change in government is that potential elites must demonstrate their commitment to the basic elite consensus before being admitted to elite positions. When the new Western elites were assimilated into the governing elite, public policies were modified but not radically changed.

In short, political conflict in America has involved a very narrow range of issues. Consensus rather than conflict characterizes America's elite history.

Selected Additional Readings

Hofstadter, Richard. *The American Political Tradition.* New York: Alfred A. Knopf, 1948. This excellent analysis of the political philosophy of American leaders throughout the nation's history reveals the fundamental conservatism of American politics.

Lundberg, Ferdinand. *America's Sixty Families.* New York: The Citadel Press, 1937. Lundberg's book is a revealing description of America's entrepreneurial elite in the early twentieth century.

Men at the Top:

Positions of Power

in America

Power in America is organized into large institutions — corporate, governmental, educational, military, religious, professional, occupational. Positions at the top of the major institutions in American society are sources of great power. Not all power, it is true, is anchored in and exercised through institutions. And the potential for power lodged in giant institutions is not always exercised by the leadership. But institutional positions provide a continuous and important base of power. Sociologist C. Wright Mills describes the relationship between institutional authority and power as follows:

> If we took the one hundred most powerful men in America, the one hundred wealthiest, and the one hundred most celebrated away from the institutional positions they now occupy, away from their resources of men and women and money, away from the media of mass communication that are now focused upon them — then they would be powerless and poor and uncelebrated. For power is not of a man. Wealth does not center in the person of the wealthy. Celebrity is not inherent in any personality. To be celebrated, to be wealthy, to have power, requires access to major institutions, for the institutional positions men occupy determine in large part their chances to have and to hold these valued experiences.[1]

In this chapter we shall describe men who occupy high positions in the major private and governmental institutions of American society. We include high positions in the major *private* institutions — in industry, mass media, finance, and other "non-governmental institutions" — because we believe that these institutions allocate values for our society and shape the lives of all Americans. Our definition of an elite member is anyone who participates in decisions that allocate values for society, not just those who participate in decision making as part of the government. The decisions of steel companies to raise prices, of defense industries to develop new weapons, of banks to raise or lower interest rates, of electrical companies to market new products, of the mass media to determine what is "news," and of educational institutions to decide what shall be taught — all affect the lives of

---

[1]C. Wright Mills, *The Power Elite* (New York: Oxford University Press, 1956), pp. 10–11.

Americans as much as do governmental decisions. Moreover, these private institutions have the power and resources to enforce their decisions. As Harold Lasswell says, "Those who are called [governmental] officials do not always make severely sanctioned choices, and the severely sanctioned choices are not necessarily made by persons called officials."[2]

Very often the men at the top of institutional structures need not overtly exercise their power. Decisions may reflect the values of the persons in high institutional positions, even if these persons do not directly participate in the decisions, because the subordinates who carry on the day-to-day business of industry, finance, government, and so on, know the values of the top elite and understand the great potential for power that the top elite possesses. These subordinates were selected for their jobs in part because they reflected dominant values in their thinking and actions. Whether consciously or unconsciously, their decisions reflect the values of the men at the top.

It should be noted also that high positions in industry, finance, government, education, and the military, as well as great wealth, do not necessarily *guarantee* great power. Persons who occupy high formal positions in the institutions of society may have great potential for power and yet be restrained in the actual *exercise* of power.

The institutional structure of society exercises power when it limits the scope of public decision making to issues that are relatively harmless to the elite. Institutions facilitate the achievement of some values while they obstruct the achievement of other values. For example, we already know that the American governmental system was deliberately constructed to suppress certain values and issues. James Madison, in *The Federalist* No. 10, defended the structure of the new American government, particularly its republican and federal features, on the grounds that it would suppress "factious issues." And Madison named outright the factious issues which must be avoided: "a rage for paper money, for an abolition of debts, for an equal division of property, or any other improper or wicked project . . ."[3] It is interesting that all of the issues that Madison wished to avoid involved challenges to the dominant economic interests. To select a non-governmental example: By placing owners of large blocks of company stock on governing boards of directors and by increasingly allocating large blocks of stock to top management personnel, the American business corporation tends to encourage the values of profit and investment security in corporate decision making. The structure of the American corporation deters it from pursuing a policy of public welfare at the expense of profit.

The fact that institutional structures maximize certain values (private enterprise, limited government, the profit system) while obstructing other values (absolute equality or "leveling," government

---

[2] Harold Lasswell, Daniel Lerner *et al.*, *The Comparative Study of Elites* (Stanford; Calif.: Standford University Press, 1952), p. 16.
[3] James Madison, Alexander Hamilton, and John Jay, *The Federalist* No. 10 (New York: Modern Library, 1937).

ownership of industry) is an important aspect of American politics, one which was recognized even by our Founding Fathers. It is another reason for examining the major institutions of society and the men who occupy high positions in them.

Social Class and Governmental Leadership

Governmental leaders are seldom recruited from the masses. This is true in the case of top cabinet officials and presidential advisors; of congressmen, governors, and state legislators; even of mayors and city councilmen. Government officials are recruited primarily from the well educated, prestigiously employed, successful, and affluent upper and upper middle classes (see Table 4–1).

TABLE 4–1.
Social Background of Congressmen (in percentages)

	Population (1900)	Senate (1947–1957)	House (1949–1951)
Father's Occupation			
Professional	6	24	31
Proprietor, managerial	7	35	31
Farmer	22	32	29
Other	66	9	9
Occupation	Population (1960)		
Lawyer	0.2	50	56
Other professional	11	14	13
Managerial	8	29	22
Farmer	4	7	4
Clerical, sales	22	–	1
Skilled labor	14	–	–
Unskilled labor, service	34	–	2
Other	7	–	2
Education			
College	16	84	91
High school	44	14	9
Grade school	40	1	–
Religion	Population (1950)	Congress (1961–1963)	
Protestant	59	87	83
Catholic	34	12	16
Jewish	6	1	1

Sources: Donald Matthews, *Social Background of Political Decision Makers* (New York: Doubleday & Co., 1954); U.S. Bureau of the Census, *Census of Population 1960*, PC1-1C (Washington, D.C.: Government Printing Office, 1961); U.S. Bureau of the Census, *Historical Statistics of the United States* (Washington, D.C.: Government Printing Office, 1962).

The occupations of the fathers of congressmen are a reasonably accurate indicator of the class origins of congressmen; and with few exceptions, congressmen are the sons of professional men, business owners and managers, or successful farmers and land owners.[4] Only a small minority are the sons of wage earners or salaried workers. When this fact is compared with the occupational characteristics of the labor force in 1900, which is about the period when the congressmen in the table were born, the overrepresentation of upper-class families is clear.

[4]See Donald Matthews, *Social Background of Political Decision Makers* (New York: Doubleday & Co., 1954).

The occupational characteristics of congressmen themselves also show that they are generally of higher social standing than their constituents; professional and business occupations dominate the halls of Congress. One reason for this is, of course, that candidates for Congress are more likely to be successful if their occupations are socially "respectable" and provide opportunities for extensive public contacts. The lawyer, insurance man, farm implement dealer, and real estate man establish in their business the wide circle of friends necessary for political success. Another more subtle reason is that candidates and elected congressmen must come from occupational groups with flexible work responsibilities. The lawyer, landowner, or business owner can adjust his work to the campaign and then the legislative schedule, but the office manager cannot.

The overrepresentation of lawyers as an occupational group in Congress and other public offices is particularly marked, since lawyers constitute no more than two tenths of 1 percent of the labor force.[5] Lawyers have always played a prominent role in the American political system. Twenty-five of the 52 signers of the Declaration of Independence and 31 of the 55 members of the Continental Congress were lawyers. The legal profession has also provided 70 percent of the presidents, vice-presidents, and Cabinet officers of the United States; 50 percent of the United States senators from 1947 to 1957; and 56 percent of the members of the House of Representatives from 1949 to 1951. Lawyers are in a reasonably high-prestige occupation, but so are physicians, businessmen, and scientists. Why then do lawyers, rather than members of these other high-prestige groups, dominate the halls of Congress?

It is sometimes argued that the lawyer brings a special kind of skill to Congress. The lawyer's occupation is the representation of clients; therefore, he makes no great change in occupation when he moves from representing clients in private practice to representing constituents in Congress. Also, the lawyer is trained to deal with public policy as it is reflected in the statute books, so he may be reasonably familiar with public policy before entering Congress. But professional skills alone cannot explain the dominance of lawyers in public office. One answer is evident in the fact that of all the high-prestige occupations, only lawyers can really afford to neglect their careers for political activities. The physician, the corporate businessman, and the scientist find the neglect of their vocation for political activity very costly. But political activity can be a positive advantage to the occupational advancement of a lawyer—free public advertising and opportunities to make contacts with potential clients are two important benefits. Another answer is the fact that lawyers naturally have a monopoly on public offices in the law and the court system, and the offices of judge or prosecuting attorney often provide lawyers with steppingstones to higher public office, including Congress.

[5] Heinz Eulau and John D. Sprague, *Lawyers in Politics* (Indianapolis, Ind.: Bobbs-Merrill Co., 1964).

To sum up, information on the occupational background of congressmen indicates that more than high social status is necessary for election to Congress. It is also helpful to have experience in interpersonal relations and public contacts, easy access to politics, and a great deal of free time to devote to political activity.[6]

Congressmen are among the most educated occupational groups in the United States. They are much better educated than the populations they represent. Of course, their education reflects their occupational background and their middle- and upper-class origins.

White Anglo-Saxon Protestants (WASPs) are substantially overrepresented in Congress. The main minority groups—Negroes, Catholics, Jews, and foreign-born—have fewer seats in Congress than their proportion of the population would warrant. Religious denominations of high social status, such as Episcopalians and Presbyterians, are regularly overrepresented in Congress. About one third of the United States senators and representatives are affiliated with the Congregational, Presbyterian, Episcopalian, or Unitarian churches. Although the representation of Catholics and Jews has been increasing in recent years, evidence indicates that these minorities can only win representation in Congress in districts in which they constitute a majority or near majority. Nearly all Catholic and Jewish congressmen are elected from Northern and industrial states, notably from major cities; Mississippi, Georgia, and South Carolina send Congressional delegations composed largely of Baptists and Methodists; whereas New York City sends delegations almost solidly Catholic and Jewish. Apparently congressmen must be of the religious and ethnic backgrounds dominant in their districts.

If Negroes were to have representation in Congress equal to their proportion of the population, there would be 43 Negroes in the House of Representatives and ten in the Senate. However, until 1966, when Republican Edward Brooke of Massachusetts was elected, no Negro was ever popularly elected to the Senate; and in the Ninety-second Congress (1970–1972), there were 12 Negroes in the House of Representatives. Their districts were chiefly the Negro ghetto areas of these large cities—Chicago, New York, Philadelphia, Los Angeles, Cleveland, and Baltimore. All were Democrats.

Roughly the same conclusions apply for top civil servants and the more exalted positions of the executive. And these characteristics are even more applicable to members of the federal judiciary. Schmidhauser has discovered that about 95 percent of the Supreme Court justices during the period 1789–1957 had ethnic origins in Western Europe, most often in England.[7] Nagel has observed that the ethnic origins of lower federal and state court judges follow similar patterns; 51 percent of these judges are of British ancestry, and 87 percent are Protestant.[8]

[6] See Joseph A. Schlesinger, *Ambition and Politics* (Chicago: Rand McNally, 1966).
[7] John Schmidhauser, "The Justices of the Supreme Court: A Collective Portrait," *Midwest Journal of Political Science*, 3 (1959), 1–10.
[8] Stuart Nagel, "Ethnic Affiliation and Judicial Propensities," *Journal of Politics*, 24 (1962), 92–110.

Outside the national government, the tendency toward domination by middle and upper classes is diminished somewhat. State legislators, for example, are more likely than national legislators to have come from families in which the father was a skilled or unskilled laborer. While 59 percent of the United States senators came from families in which the father was engaged in a business or professional occupation, only 47 percent of the state legislators in California, New Jersey, Ohio, and Tennessee have similar status, and only about one third of the state legislators in Wisconsin and Pennsylvania come from upper-status families.[9] Nevertheless, compared to the general population, the family status background of state legislators is very high.

The current occupational status of American state legislators is also lower than the occupational status of national legislators. More than 90 percent of the members of the United States Senate and House of Representatives are professionals, proprietors, managers, or officials. The proportion of state legislators in the same category varies from 33 percent in Minnesota to 83 percent in California and New Jersey; the average is about 70 percent. Educationally, the same patterns persist; state legislators are more educated than the general population but less educated than national legislators. About 85 percent of the members of the Senate and House of Representatives are college graduates, while the proportion of college graduates among state legislators varies from 40 percent in Georgia to 63 percent in New Jersey.

The "fit" between the characteristics of the elite and those of the masses is closer if we examine religious and ethnic origin. We have noted the general dominance of Protestant Anglo-Saxons among national legislators, but at the state level the proportion of Protestant Anglo-Saxons varies substantially with the ethnic composition of the state. For example, Southern legislatures, such as that of Tennessee, are almost entirely Protestant, while more than 40 percent of the New Jersey legislators are Catholic or Jewish. One certainly cannot argue that non-WASPs are *over*represented in the state legislative arenas, but there is more of a balance between elite and mass social characteristics at the state level.

At the local level, the position of ethnic and religious minorities is much improved.[10] During the era of the urban political machines, three fourths of the "city bosses" were either foreign-born or second-generation Americans. In many cases, of course, the "city boss" was an informal leader rather than an elected official, but elected officials at the local level also seemed to be drawn more equitably from the minority groups. In larger cities, minority groups have a fairly good chance of achieving representation on city councils. However, the possibility of representation varies according to whether the council is elected at large or by wards. If the council is elected at large, ethnic and racial minorities will probably be excluded; when the council is fairly large and elected by wards, ethnic groups (which are generally

[9]John Wahlke et al., The Legislative System (New York: John Wiley, 1962).
[10]See Thomas R. Dye, Politics in States and Communities (Englewood Cliffs, N. J.: Prentice-Hall, 1969).

segregated into given areas of the city) will find it easier to achieve some degree of representation. When city councils are elected by non-partisan elections, or when the political process is dominated by the business community, ethnic minorities have a more difficult time.

The typical city council member is a local businessman, well respected in the community and active in community affairs. The smaller the town, the greater the likelihood that the town's elected officials will almost all be local businessmen, primarily owners and operators of retail stores. Generally in the typically tightly knit and homogeneous small town, additional informal qualifications are also imposed for elected officials. Normally, a member of the municipal government is a long-time resident who is committed to the traditional low-tax, low-expenditure policies of the town. The fact that small cities are dominated by businessmen should not be taken as evidence of a conspiracy against underrepresented groups. In fact, the business dominance in small cities is probably as representative of the values of these cities as is the ethnic representation in larger cities.

In conclusion, lower-status segments of the population are systematically, although not overtly, excluded from positions of formal and informal influence in government.

The Governing Elites

Top governmental executives — Cabinet members, presidential advisors, department officers, special ambassadors — are generally men who have occupied key posts in private industry and finance or who have sat in influential positions in education, in the arts and sciences, or in social, civic, and charitable associations. These men move easily in and out of government posts from their positions in the corporate, financial, and educational world. They often assume government jobs at a financial sacrifice, and many do so out of a sense of public service.

Obviously, there is some overlapping of top leadership in America, but it is difficult to measure precisely *how much*. The plural elite model of power (described in Chapter 1) suggests that there is very little overlap, that *different* groups of individuals exercise power in different sectors of American life. In contrast, the single elite model of power envisions extensive overlap, with a single group of men exercising power in many different sectors of American life. In order to understand position overlap among American elites, let us examine the career backgrounds of several key governmental executives in recent Presidential administrations.[11]

Neil H. McElroy: Secretary of Defense, 1957–1959; former president and member of the board of directors of Procter and Gamble Co.; member of the board of directors of General Electric Company, of Chrysler Corporation, and of Equitable Life Insurance Company; member of the board of trustees of Harvard University, of the National Safety Council, and of the National Industrial Conference.

[11] Biographical data in this chapter compiled from various volumes of *Who's Who in America* (Chicago: Marquis Who's Who).

Charles E. Wilson: Secretary of Defense, 1953–1957; president and member of the board of directors of General Motors Corporation.

Robert S. McNamara: Secretary of Defense, 1961–1967; president and member of the board of directors of the Ford Motor Company; member of the board of directors of Scott Paper Company; president of the World Bank, 1967 to date.

John Foster Dulles: Secretary of State, 1953–1960; partner of Sullivan and Cromwell (one of twenty largest law firms on Wall Street); member of the board of directors of the Bank of New York, of the Fifth Avenue Bank, of the American Bank Note Company, of the International Nickel Company of Canada, of Babcock and Wilson Corporation, of Gold Dust Corporation, of the Overseas Security Corporation, of Shenandoah Corporation, of United Cigar Stores, of American Cotton Oil Company, of United Railroad of St. Louis, and of European Textile Corporation. He was a trustee of the New York Public Library, of the Union Theological Seminary, of the Rockefeller Foundation, and of the Carnegie Endowment for International Peace; a delegate to the World Council of Churches.

Dean Rusk: Secretary of State, 1961–1968; former president of Rockefeller Foundation.

George M. Humphrey: Secretary of the Treasury, 1953–1957; former chairman of the board of directors of the M. A. Hanna Company; member of the board of directors of the National Steel Corporation, of Consolidated Coal Company, of Canada and Dominion Sugar Company; a trustee of the Massachusetts Institute of Technology.

Robert B. Anderson: Secretary of the Treasury, 1957–1961; Secretary of the Navy, 1953–1954; Deputy Secretary of Defense, 1954–1955; member of the board of directors of the Goodyear Tire and Rubber Company; member of the executive board of the Boy Scouts of America.

Douglas Dillon: Secretary of the Treasury, 1960–1963; chairman of the board of Dillon, Reed, and Company, Inc. (Wall Street investment firm); member of the New York Stock Exchange; director of U.S. and Foreign Securities Corporation and of U.S. International Securities Corporation; member of the board of governors of the New York Hospital and of the Metropolitan Museum.

Clark Clifford: Secretary of Defense, 1967–1969; senior partner of Clifford and Miller (Washington law firm); member of the board of directors of the National Bank of Washington, and of the Sheridan Hotel Corporation; Special Counsel to the President, 1949–1950; member of the board of trustees of Washington University in St. Louis.

David Kennedy: Secretary of the Treasury, 1969–1971; President and chairman of the board of Continental Illinois Bank and Trust Company; a director of International Harvester Company, of Commonwealth Edison, of Pullman Company, of Abbott Laboratories, of Swift and Company, of U.S. Gypsum, and of Communications Satellite Corporation; and a trustee of the University of Chicago, of the Brookings Institution, of the Committee for Economic Development, and of George Washington University.

George Romney: Secretary of Housing and Urban Development, 1969–   ; former President, American Motors Corporation; Governor of Michigan.

All of the individuals mentioned above held cabinet posts. But of almost equal importance are the men who serve as special assistants to the president or as special ambassadors in periods of international crisis.

W. Averell Harriman: U.S. Ambassador-at-Large and Under Secretary of State for Political Affairs, 1961–1969; chief United States negotiator at Paris Peace Conference on Vietnam; former Governor of the State of New York, 1955–1958; former chairman of the board of directors of the Union Pacific Railroad and of the Merchant Ship Building Corporation; partner in Brown Brothers, Harriman, and Company (Wall Street investment firm).

John J. McCloy: Special Advisor to the President on Disarmament, 1961–1963: chairman of the Coordinating Committee on the Cuban Crisis, 1962; member of the President's commission on the assassination of President Kennedy; U.S. High Commissioner for Germany, 1949–1952; President of the World Bank, 1947–1949; partner in Milbank, Tweed, Hadley, and McCloy (Wall Street law firm); member of the board of directors of Allied Chemical Corporation, of American Telephone and Telegraph Company, of Chase Manhattan Bank, of Metropolitan Life Insurance Company, of Westinghouse Electric Corporation, of E. R. Squibb and Sons; member of the board of trustees of the Ford Foundation, of the Council of Foreign Relations, and of Amherst College.

Arthur H. Dean: chairman of the U.S. Delegation on Nuclear Test Ban Treaty; chief U.S. negotiator of the Korean Armistice Agreement; partner, Sullivan and Cromwell (Wall Street law firm); member of the board of directors of American Metal Climax, of American Bank Note Company, of National Union Electric Corporation, of El Paso Natural Gas Company, of Crown Zellerbach Corporation, of Campbell Soup Company, of Northwest Production Corporation, of Lazard Fund, Inc., and of the Bank of New York; a member of the board of trustees of New York Hospital, of Cornell Medical Center, of Cornell Medical College, of Cornell University, of the Carnegie Foundation, and of the Council of Foreign Relations.

Ellsworth Bunker: former Ambassador to India, Ambassador to Vietnam; former president and chairman of the board of National Sugar Refining Company; member of the board of directors of the Centennial Insurance Company, of the Curtis Publishing Company, of Lambert International Corporation, and of Atlantic Mutual Insurance Company; former president of the American Red Cross; a trustee of the Hampton Institute, of the Asia Foundation, of the Council on World Affairs, and of the Foreign Policy Association.

There was some tendency for the Kennedy administration to rely more on educational elites in staffing key governmental executive posts, whereas the Eisenhower administration relied more upon business and financial elites. The Kennedy administration brought into government McGeorge Bundy as Special Assistant to the President for National Security Affairs, 1961–1966; Bundy was formerly Dean of the Faculty of Arts and Sciences at Harvard University. Kennedy appointed Gardner Ackley as chairman of the Council of Economic Advisors; Ackley had been an economics professor at the University of Michigan, a director of the Social Science Research Council, and a Fulbright Scholar. Walt Whitman Rostow, who was made Special Assistant to the President for National Security Affairs in 1961 and chairman of the Policy Planning Council of the Department of State, had been a professor of economic history at Massachusetts Institute of Technology and a member of the staff of the Center for International Studies. Walter Heller was made chairman of the Council of Economic Advisors in 1961; he had been a professor of economics at the University of Minnesota.

In contrast, Eisenhower tended to rely upon people like Marion B. Folsom, Under Secretary of the Treasury, 1953–1955, and Secretary of Health, Education, and Welfare, 1955–1958. Folsom had been director of the Eastman Kodak Company, of the Eastman Savings and Loan Association, and of Rochester Savings Bank. He had also served as a trustee of the Committee for Economic Development, of the National Bureau of Economic Research, of the University of Rochester, of the Brookings Institution, and of Harvard College. Eisenhower's Secretary of Commerce was Sinclair Weeks, chairman of the board of the United Car Fastener Corporation, and a director of John Hancock Mutual Life Insurance Company, of West Point Manufacturing Company, of the First National Bank of Boston, of Reed and Barton Corporation, of New Hampshire Insurance Company, and of Lancaster National Bank. Eisenhower's first Secretary of Health, Education, and Welfare was Oveta Culp Hobby, president of the Houston Post Publishing Company, and a member of the board of directors of the Bank of Texas and of the Mutual Insurance Company of New York.

The Wall Street Law Firms

1. Shearman, Sterling, and Wright
2. Cravath, Swaine, and Moore
3. White and Case
4. Dewey, Ballantine, Bushby, Palmer, and Wood
5. Simpson, Thacher, and Bartlett
6. Davis, Polk, Wardwell, Sunderland, and Kiendl
7. Milbank, Tweed, Hope, and Hadley
8. Cahill, Gordon, Reindel, and Ohl
9. Sullivan and Cromwell
10. Chadbourne, Parke, Whiteside, and Wolff
11. Breed, Abbott, and Morgan
12. Winthrop, Stimson, Putnam, and Roberts
13. Cadwalader, Wickersham, and Taft
14. Willkie, Owen, Farr, Gallagher, and Walton
15. Donovan, Leisure, Newton, and Irvine
16. Lord, Day, and Lord
17. Dwight, Royall, Harris, Koegel, and Caskey
18. Mudge, Stern, Baldwin, and Todd
19. Kelley, Drye, Newhall, and Maginnes
20. Cleary, Gottlieb, Friendly, and Hamilton

The top personnel in the Nixon administration resemble the Eisenhower team in many respects. In fact, several of Nixon's lieutenants served in the Eisenhower administration—Secretary of State William P. Rogers, a partner in the Wall Street law firm of Dwight, Royall, Harris, Koegal, and Caskey, had served as Attorney General, 1957–61; Treasury Secretary David Kennedy and Commerce Secretary Maurice Stans had both served under President Eisenhower. Nixon's selection of Wisconsin Congressman Melvin Laird as Secretary of Defense was somewhat surprising, inasmuch as previous appointees to this influential position had been top corporate elites. But in an apparent attempt to overcome this deficiency, Nixon appointed as Deputy Secretary of Defense David Packard, whose elite credentials are impeccable: the president of Hewlett-Packard Company, a director of the Palo Alto Mutual Savings and Loan Association, of Pacific Gas and Electric Company, of Systems Development Corporation, and of National Airlines; a trustee of Stanford University, of the Stanford Research Institute, of the Hoover Institute on War and

Revolution, and of the World Affairs Council. Packard was required to put over 300 million dollars in trust in order to accept the $30,000-a-year government job.

Other top Nixon appointments included Secretary of Housing and Urban Development George Romney, who was former president of American Motors Corporation and governor of Michigan; Agricultural Secretary Clifford Hardin, who was former chancellor at the University of Nebraska, a director of Fairmont Foods and of Bankers Life Insurance Company of Nebraska, a trustee of the Rockefeller Foundation, former president of the Association of State Universities and Land Grant Colleges and director of the American Council of Education; and Attorney General John M. Mitchell, who was Nixon's partner in the Wall Street law firm of Nixon, Rose, Guthrie, Alexander, and Mitchell. Just like his predecessors, Nixon sought the advice of Harvard University intellectuals—Henry Kissinger, special Presidential Assistant for foreign affairs, was Professor of Government at Harvard; and Daniel P. Moynihan, Nixon's chief advisor on domestic affairs, was Professor of Education and Urban Politics.

The Corporate Elites

Formal control over the economic life of the nation is concentrated in the hands of a very few men: the presidents, vice-presidents, and boards of directors of the nation's corporate institutions. A major reason for this concentration of control is the increasing consolidation of economic enterprise into a small number of giant corporations. The following statistics can only suggest the scale and concentration of modern corporate enterprise in America: In 1964, the 500 largest corporations in America held over two thirds of all industrial assets in the nation. The fifty largest corporations held over one third of all industrial assets; the five largest industrial corporations in the United States possessed over 12 percent of all of the assets of the nation. The combined revenues of three industrial corporations—General Motors, Standard Oil of New Jersey, and Ford Motor Company—exceed the total revenues of all of the American states combined. The revenues of General Motors alone were fifty times those of Nevada, eight times those of New York, and slightly less than one fifth those of the federal government.[12] The rate of corporate mergers in recent years suggests that this concentration continues to increase.

A. A. Berle, Jr., a corporation lawyer and corporate director who has written extensively on the modern corporation, explains that corporate power is lodged in the hands of the directors of these corporations plus the holders of large "control blocks" of corporate stock:

> The control system in today's corporations, when it does not lie solely in the directors as in the American Telephone and Telegraph Company, lies in a combination of the directors of a so-called control block (of stock) plus the directors themselves. For practical purposes, therefore, the control or power element in most large corporations rests in its group of directors, and it is

[12]"The 500 Largest Industrial Corporations," *The Fortune Directory*, August 1964.

1. American Telephone & Telegraph
2. Standard Oil (New Jersey)
3. General Motors
4. Ford Motor
5. U.S. Steel
6. Texaco
7. Socony Mobil Oil
8. Gulf Oil
9. Sears, Roebuck
10. Standard Oil of California
11. General Telephone & Electronics
12. International Business Machines
13. Standard Oil (Indiana)
14. Consolidated Edison (N.Y.)
15. General Electric
16. Pacific Gas & Electric
17. Pennsylvania RR
18. Southern Pacific
19. E. I. du Pont de Nemours
20. Chrysler
21. Bethlehem Steel
22. Tennessee Gas Transmission
23. New York Central RR
24. Shell Oil
25. Western Electric
26. Union Carbide
27. Santa Fe RR
28. Commonwealth Edison (Chicago)
29. Phillips Petroleum
30. Southern Calif. Edison
31. Southern Co.
32. Union Pacific RR
33. American Electric Power
34. Public Service Electric & Gas
35. International Telephone & Telegraph
36. International Harvester
37. Sinclair Oil
38. Aluminum Co. of America
39. Norfolk & Western Ry
40. Westinghouse Electric
41. Cities Service
42. Continental Oil
43. Monsanto
44. Columbia Gas & Electric
45. El Paso Natural Gas
46. Goodyear Tire & Rubber
47. Procter & Gamble
48. Eastman Kodak
49. Anaconda
50. Republic Steel
51. Dow Chemical
52. Consumers Power
53. Philadelphia Electric
54. Niagara Mohawk Power
55. General Public Utilities
56. Firestone Tire & Rubber
57. Allied Chemical
58. Radio Corp. of America
59. International Paper
60. Texas Eastern Transmission
61. Celanese
62. Detroit Edison
63. Armco Steel
64. Texas Utilities
65. Reynolds Metals
66. National Steel
67. Northern Pacific Ry
68. R. J. Reynolds Tobacco
69. Tidewater Oil
70. Great Northern Ry
71. American Natural Gas
72. American Can
73. Olin Mathieson Chemical
74. Atlantic Refining
75. Sun Oil
76. Inland Steel
77. Southern Ry
78. Middle South Utilities
79. Consolidated Natural Gas
80. Jones & Laughlin Steel
81. Kaiser Aluminum
82. Virginia Electric & Power
83. Union Oil of California
84. Kennecott Copper
85. W. R. Grace
86. Louisville & Nashville RR
87. Sperry Rand
88. Deere
89. Montgomery Ward
90. F. W. Woolworth
91. Chicago, Burl & Quincy RR
92. Continental Can
93. Caterpillar Tractor
94. Youngstown Sheet & Tube
95. Singer
96. Pacific Lighting
97. National Dairy Products
98. American Tobacco
99. U.S. Rubber
100. Great Atlantic & Pacific Tea

autonomous — or autonomous if taken together with a control block. . . . This is a self-perpetuating oligarchy.[13]

Corporate power does not rest in the hands of the masses of corporate employees or even in the hands of the millions of middle- and upper-middle-class Americans who own corporate stock.

Corporate power is further concentrated by a system of interlocking directorates and by a corporate ownership system in which control blocks of stock are owned by financial institutions rather than by private individuals. Interlocking directorates, in which a director of one corporation also sits on the board of other corporations, enable key corporate elites to wield influence over a large number of corporations. It is not uncommon for top elites to hold six, eight, or ten directorships. Let us illustrate the concept of interlocking directorates by examining the positions held by a few top corporate elite members. We shall also

[13] A A. Berle, Jr., *Economic Power and the Free Society* (New York: Fund for the Republic, 1958), p. 10.

note the key positions that these top corporate elites hold outside the corporate system—in government, in the arts and sciences, and in charities, education, and civic affairs.

Richard King Mellon: chairman of the board of Mellon National Bank and Trust Company; president, Mellon and Sons; member of the board of directors of Aluminum Company of America, of General Motors Corporation, of Gulf Oil Corporation, of the Koppers Company, of the Pennsylvania Company, and of the Pennsylvania Railroad. *Fortune* magazine lists Mellon's personal wealth in excess of one-half billion dollars. He is a lieutenant general in the Reserves, a member of the board of trustees of the Carnegie Institute of Technology, of the Mellon Institute, and of the University of Pittsburgh.

David Rockefeller: chairman of the board of directors of the Chase Manhattan Bank; member of the board of directors of the B. F. Goodrich Company, of the Rockefeller Brothers, Inc., and of the Equitable Life Insurance Society; a trustee of the Rockefeller Institute for Medical Research, of the Council on Foreign Relations, of the Museum of Modern Art, of Rockefeller Center, and of the Board of Overseers of Harvard College.

Paul C. Cabot: partner, State Street Research and Management Company (investment firm); member of the board of directors of J. P. Morgan and Company, of the Continental Can Company, of the Ford Motor Company, of the National Dairy Products Corporation, of the B.F. Goodrich Company, and of the M.A. Hanna Company; former treasurer of Harvard University, and a trustee of the Eastern Gas and Fuel Association.

Crawford H. Greenewalt: chairman of the board of directors of E. I. du Pont de Nemours; member of the board of the Equitable Trust Company, of the Christiana Securities Company, and of the Morgan Guaranty Trust Company; a trustee of Massachusetts Institute of Technology, of Wilmington General Hospital, of the Philadelphia Academy of Natural Sciences, of the Philadelphia Orchestra Association, of the American Museum of Natural History, of the Carnegie Institute of Technology, and of the Smithsonian Institute.

Arthur A. Houghton: president and chairman of the board of directors of Corning Glass Works; member of the board of directors of the Steuben Glass Company, of the Erie-Lackawanna Railroad Company, of the New York Life Insurance Company, and of the United States Steel Corporation; trustee of the Corning Museum of Glass, of the J. Pierpont Morgan Library, of the Philharmonic Symphony Society of New York, of the Fund for the Advancement of Education, of the Lincoln Center of Performing Arts, of the Cooper Union, of the Metropolitan Museum of Art, of the New York Public Library, of the Rockefeller Foundation, and of the Institute for Contemporary Art of Boston.

James R. Killian, Jr.: member of the board of directors of the American Telephone and Telegraph Company, of the Cabot Corporation, of the Polaroid Corporation, and of General Motors Corporation; former Special Assistant to the President for Science and Technology; member of the Board of Visitors of the U. S. Naval Academy; a trustee of Mt. Holyoke College, of Mellon Institute, of the Alfred.P. Sloan Foundation, and of the National Merit Scholarship Corporation; chairman and member of the board of the Institute for Defense Analysis.

Federick R. Kappel: chief executive officer of American Telephone and Telegraph Company; a member of the board of directors for Western Electric Company, for Chase Manhattan Bank, for Metropolitan Life Insurance Company, and for General Foods Corporation; trustee of the Boys Clubs of America, of the National Safety Council, of the Grand Central Art Galleries, of the Salvation Army, of Columbia University, of the Tax Foundation, and of the Committee for Economic Development.

James Stillman Rockefeller: chairman and director of First National City Bank of New York; member of the board of directors of the International Banking Corporation, of the National City Foundation, of the First New York Corporation, of the First National City Trust Company, of the Mercantile Bank of Canada, of the National City Realty Corporation, of Kimberly-Clark Corporation, of the Northern Pacific Railway Company, of the National Cash Register Company, of Pan American World Air Lines, and of Monsanto Company.

Some of these top corporate elite members, such as Rockefeller, Mellon, Cabot, and Houghton, inherited their position and power. Others, such as Greenewalt, Killian, and Kappel, came to power through the ranks of corporate management. But almost all members of the American business elite, according to recent studies, share similar social backgrounds. Suzanne Keller, in a study of more than 1,000 business leaders, reports that 57 percent of the business leaders had fathers who were businessmen (owners or managers).[14] Only one fourth of the businessmen studied originated in lower-class homes — laborers, farmers, clerks, or salesmen. Over 60 percent of the business leaders were college graduates, and almost one half had postgraduate training in either law (15 percent), engineering (15 percent), or other professions (15 percent).

Concentration of power among corporate elites occurs not only through interlocking directorates but also through the system of ownership in which one corporation or financial institution owns controlling blocs of the common stock of other corporations or financial institutions. It is very difficult to trace the ownership of a corporation. For example, because the Federal Power Commission requires that the ten largest stock holders of electric utilities companies be reported, one might assume that it would be easy to identify the owners of these companies. However, this is not the case, because these utilities are owned by other corporations rather than by individuals. The list of the ten top stockholders of Pacific Gas and Electric, the fifth largest utility in the country, was reported as follows:[15]

1.	Merrill Lynch	6.	King and Company
2.	Equitable Life	7.	Raymond and Company
3.	New York Life	8.	Sigler and Company
4.	Savings Fund and Plan	9.	Mack and Company
5.	Prudential Life	10.	Cudd and Company

Some of these companies are identifiable; but others are "street names," or aliases, of leading banks and investment firms, which hold the stock in trust for unnamed individuals. Mack and Company, for example, translates into Mellon National Bank, which represents the Mellon family interest, headed by Richard King Mellon.

[14] Suzanne Keller, *Beyond the Ruling Class* (New York: Random House, 1963).
[15] See William Domhoff, *Who Rules America?* (Englewood Cliffs, N.J.: Prentice-Hall, 1967), p. 55.

We have defined management and controlling stockholders as the corporate elites. A. A. Berle, Jr., has suggested that managers, rather than major stockholders, have come to exercise dominant influence in American corporations. Berle describes power in corporations as follows:

Management control is a phrase meaning merely that no large concentrated stock holding exists which maintains a close working relationship with the management or is capable of challenging it, so that the board of directors may regularly expect a majority, composed of small and scattered holdings, to follow their lead. Thus, they need not consult with anyone when making up their slate of directors, and may simply request their stock holders to sign and send in a ceremonial proxy. They select their own successors. . . . Nominal power still resides in the stockholders; actual power in the board of directors.[16]

In contrast to Berle's thesis, other scholars continue to assert the importance of large stockholders operating through holding companies, "street names," and family trusts.[17] It is generally conceded that a five percent ownership stake in a large corporation is sufficient in most cases to give corporate control. The Rockefellers, Fords, Du Ponts, Mellons, and others are still said to exercise prevailing influence over the large corporations. One example is the Mellon interest group which controls, among others, Mellon National Bank, Gulf Oil, Westinghouse Electric, Aluminum Company of America, and Koppers. *Forbes* magazine reports:

When Gulf executives speak reverently of "The Board," they are normally referring to a single man, diffident Richard King Mellon, senior member of one of the world's richest families. The only Mellon on Gulf's board, Dick Mellon looks after his family's two billion, 32 percent interest in Gulf—though he rarely is concerned with the day-to-day operations.[18]

But it does not matter a great deal whether the managers or the owners of the controlling blocks of stock really control America's largest corporations; the end result appears to be the same. Management is just as interested in profits as stockholders. Moreover, managers themselves generally own sizeable blocks of stock in their own corporations. For example, Charles E. Wilson of General Motors had accumulated $2.5 million in stock in that company before he became Secretary of Defense; and Robert McNamara had accumulated $1.5 million worth of stock in the Ford Motor Company before he became Secretary of Defense. It is doubtful that the values of management and of large stockholders differ a great deal.

Economist Gabriel Kolko summarizes what we know about corporate power in America:

[16] A. A. Berle, Jr., *Power Without Property* (New York: Harcourt, Brace & World, 1959), p. 73.
[17] See Ferdinand Lundberg, *The Rich and the Super Rich* (New York: Lyle Stuart, 1968).
[18] *Forbes*, May 1, 1964, p. 22; also cited by Domhoff, *Who Rules America?*, p. 49.

The concentration of economic power in a very small elite is an indisputable fact. . . . A social theory assuming a democratized economic system—or even a trend in this direction—is quite obviously not in accord with social reality. Whether the men who control industry are socially responsive or trustees of the social welfare is quite another matter: it is one thing to speculate about their motivations, another to generalize about economic facts. And even if we assume that these men act benevolently toward their workers and the larger community, their actions still would not be the result of social control through a formal democratic structure and group participation, which are the essentials for democracy; they would be an arbitrary noblesse oblige by the economic elite. When discussing the existing corporate system, it would be more realistic to drop all references to democracy.[19]

Corporate ownership in America is highly concentrated. Despite the publicity given the idea of "people's capitalism"—the official concept of the New York Stock Exchange, which urges American families to buy stock—fewer than 10 percent of the American people own any stock at all. And, as might be expected, stock ownership is very inequitably distributed among income classes. In 1959, only 6 percent of the persons with an income of $5,000 or less owned stock, while 55 percent of the persons with an income of $15,000 or more owned stock.

Moreover, many individual owners of stock own very small numbers of shares. A Brookings Institution study of stock ownership in nearly 3,000 major corporations discovered that the top 2 percent of the shareholders owned nearly 58 percent of the common stock of these corporations.[20] The next 31 percent of the shareholders owned 32 percent of the shares. But fully two thirds of all common stock shareholders owned only one tenth of the shares. (See Figure 4–1.)

FIGURE 4–1.
The Distribution of Common Stock In Publicly Owned Corporations

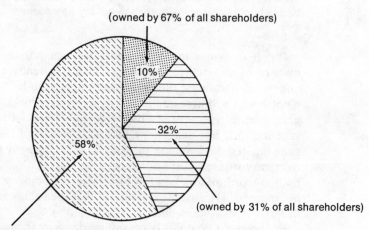

(owned by 67% of all shareholders)

10%

32%

58%

(owned by 2% of all shareholders)

(owned by 31% of all shareholders)

Source: Lewis H. Kimmel, *Share Ownership in the United States* (Washington, D.C.:Brookings Institution, 1952), pp. 43, 46.

[19]Gabriel Kolko, *Wealth and Power in America* (New York: Praeger, 1962), pp. 68–69.
[20]Lewis H. Kimmel, *Share Ownership in the United States* (Washington D.C.; Brookings Institution, 1952).

Contrary to optimistic predictions about "democratization" of the American economy, there is little evidence that inequality is lessening much over time. The class structure of American society is heavily influenced by, and in turn influences, the distribution of income; and income inequality is and has always been a significant component of American social structure.[21] The top tenth of income recipients in America receives nearly thirty percent of all income in the nation, while the bottom tenth receives only about one percent (see Table 4–2). The income share of the top tenth has declined slightly since the pre-World War II years, but the bottom half of the population still receives about the same share of the national income that it has always received. The only significant rise in income distributions has occurred among the upper middle classes, in the second- and third-richest income tenths. It is widely believed that the progressive income tax substantially levels incomes in America, but this is not really the case. Large portions of the national income of the nation are not subject to income taxation. The best available evidence suggests that taxation has not altered the unequal distribution of income.

Millionaires in America are no longer considered among the *really* rich of the nation. In 1968 it was estimated that there were at least

TABLE 4–2. Percentage of National Personal Income, Before Taxes, Received by Each Income-Tenth*

	Highest tenth	2nd	3rd	4th	5th	6th	7th	8th	9th	Lowest tenth
1910	33.9	12.3	10.2	8.8	8.0	7.0	6.0	5.5	4.9	3.4
1918	34.5	12.9	9.6	8.7	7.7	7.2	6.9	5.7	4.4	2.4
1921	38.2	12.8	10.5	8.9	7.4	6.5	5.9	4.6	3.2	2.0
1929	39.0	12.3	9.8	9.0	7.9	6.5	5.5	4.6	3.6	1.8
1934	33.6	13.1	11.0	9.4	8.2	7.3	6.2	5.3	3.8	2.1
1937	34.4	14.1	11.7	10.1	8.5	7.2	6.0	4.4	2.6	1.0
1941	34.0	16.0	12.0	10.0	9.0	7.0	5.0	4.0	2.0	1.0
1945	29.0	16.0	13.0	11.0	9.0	7.0	6.0	5.0	3.0	1.0
1946	32.0	15.0	12.0	10.0	9.0	7.0	6.0	5.0	3.0	1.0
1947	33.5	14.8	11.7	9.9	8.5	7.1	5.8	4.4	3.1	1.2
1948	30.9	14.7	11.9	10.1	8.8	7.5	6.3	5.0	3.3	1.4
1949	29.8	15.5	12.5	10.6	9.1	7.7	6.2	4.7	3.1	0.8
1950	28.7	15.4	12 7	10.8	9.3	7.8	6.3	4.9	3.2	0.9
1951	30.9	15.0	12.3	10.6	8.9	7.6	6.3	4.7	2.9	0.8
1952	29.5	15.3	12.4	10.6	9.1	7.7	6.4	4.9	3.1	1.0
1953	31.4	14.8	11.9	10.3	8.9	7.6	6.2	4.7	3.0	1.2
1954	29.3	15.3	12.4	10.7	9.1	7.7	6.4	4.8	3.1	1.2
1955	29.7	15.7	12.7	10.8	9.1	7.7	6.1	4.5	2.7	1.0
1956	30.6	15.3	12.3	10.5	9.0	7.6	6.1	4.5	2.8	1.3
1957	29.4	15.5	12.7	10.8	9.2	7.7	6.1	4.5	2.9	1.3
1958	27.1	16.3	13.2	11.0	9.4	7.8	6.2	4.6	3.1	1.3
1959	28.9	15.8	12.7	10.7	9.2	7.8	6.3	4.6	2.9	1.1

*In terms of "recipients" for 1910–1937 and "spending units" for 1941–1959.

Source: Gabriel Kolko, *Wealth and Power in America* (New York: Praeger, 1962), p. 14. Data for 1910–1937 are from National Industrial Conference Board, *Studies in Enterprise and Social Progress* (New York: National Industrial Conference Board, 1939), p. 125. Data for 1941–1959 were calculated by the Survey Research Center. Figures for 1941–1946 are available in rounded form only. Previously unpublished data for 1947–1958 are reproduced by permission of the Board of Governors of the Federal Reserve System, and data for 1959 by permission of the Survey Research Center.

153 Americans who were "centi-millionaires" — worth more than $100,000,000 each, and the numbers of these great fortunes are multi-

[21] See Kolko, *Wealth and Power in America;* see also Clair Wilcox, *Toward Social Welfare* (Homewood, Ill.: Richard D. Irwin, 1969), pp. 7–24.

plying rapidly in America. The editors of *Fortune* report that in 1957, 45 persons in the United States had fortunes over $100,000,000. In the following ten years, the "centi-millionnaire" population tripled; those with $150,000,000 or more grew to 66. *Fortune* also states that half of the people with $150,000,000 or more inherited most of it and that the Du Ponts, the Fords, the Mellons, and the Rockefellers *are* among America's wealthiest citizens.[22]

Economist Gabriel Kolko observes:

Insofar as economic power in the United States derives from savings and income, it is dominated by a small class, comprising not more than one tenth of the population, whose interests and style of life mark them off from the rest of American society. And within this class, a very small elite controls the corporate structure, the major sector of our economy, and through it makes basic price and investment decisions that directly affect the entire nation.[23]

Most of the capital in America is owned not by individuals but by corporations, banks, insurance companies, mutual funds, investment companies, and pension trusts. Adolf A. Berle writes:

Of the capital flowing into non-agricultural industry, 60 percent is internally generated through profits and depreciation funds (within corporations). Another 10 or 15 percent is handled through the investment staffs of insurance companies and pension trusts. Another 20 percent is borrowed from banks. Perhaps 5 percent represents individuals who have saved and chosen the application of their savings. This is the system. . . . The capital system is not in many aspects an open market system. It is an administered system.[24]

The Managerial Elite

Today the requirements of technology and planning have greatly increased the need in industry for specialized talent and skill in organization. Capital is something that a corporation can now supply to itself. Thus there is a shift in power in the American economy from capital to organized intelligence, and we can reasonably expect that this shift will be reflected in the deployment of power in society at large.

Individual capitalists are no longer essential to the accumulation of capital for investment. Approximately three fifths of industrial capital now comes from retained earnings of corporations, rather than from the investments of individual capitalists. Another one fifth of industrial capital is borrowed, chiefly from banks. Even though the remaining one fifth of the capital funds of industry come from "outside" investments, the bulk of these funds are from large insurance companies, mutual funds, and pension trusts, rather than from individual investors. Thus, the individual capitalist investor is no longer in a position of dominance in American capital formation.

American capital is primarily administered and expended by managers of large corporations and financial institutions. Stockholders are

[22]*Fortune*, May 1968.
[23]Kolko, *Wealth and Power in America*, p. 127.
[24]Berle, *Power Without Property*, p. 45.

1. J. Paul Getty (oil)
2. Howard Hughes (Hughes Tool Co., real estate)
3. H. L. Hunt (oil)
4. Edwin H. Land (Polaroid)
5. Daniel K. Ludwig (shipping)
6. Alisa Mellon Bruce (Mellon)
7. Paul Mellon (Mellon)
8. Richard King Mellon (Mellon)
9. N. Bunker Hunt (oil, son of H. L. Hunt)
10. John D. MacArthur (Bankers Life and Casualty)
11. William L. McKnight (Minnesota Mining and Manufacturing)
12. Charles S. Mott (General Motors)
13. R. E. (Bob) Smith (oil)
14. Howard F. Ahmanson (Home Savings & Loan Association)
15. Charles Allen, Jr. (investment banking)
16. Mrs. W. Van Alan Clark, Sr. (Avon Products)
17. John T. Dorrance, Jr. (Campbell Soup)
18. Mrs. Alfred I. Du Pont (Du Pont)
19. Charles W. Engelhard, Jr. (mining and metal fabricating)
20. Sherman M. Fairchild (Fairchild Camera, I.B.M.)
21. Leon Hess (Hess Oil & Chemical)
22. William R. Hewlett (Hewlett-Packard)
23. David Packard (Hewlett-Packard)
24. Amory Houghton (Corning Glass Works)
25. Joseph P. Kennedy (banking, real estate, investments; father of John F. Kennedy)
26. Eli Lilly (Eli Lilly & Co.)
27. Forrest E. Mars (Mars candy)
28. Samuel I. Newhouse (newspapers)
29. Marjorie Merriweather Post (General Foods)
30. Mrs. Jean Mauze (Abby Rockefeller)
31. David Rockefeller
32. John D. Rockefeller III
33. Laurance Rockefeller
34. Nelson Rockefeller
35. Winthrop Rockefeller
36. Cordelia Scaife May (Mellon)
37. Richard Mellon Scaife (Mellon)
38. DeWitt Wallace (*Reader's Digest*)
39. Mrs. Charles Payson (Joan Whitney)
40. John Hay Whitney
41. James S. Abercrombie (oil, iron)
42. William Benton (*Encyclopaedia Britannica*)
43. Jacob Blaustein (Standard Oil of Indiana)
44. Chester Carlson (inventor of xerography)
45. Edward J. Daly (World Airways)
46. Clarence Dillon (investment banking)
47. Doris Duke (tobacco)
48. Lammot Du Pont Copeland (Du Pont)
49. Henry B. Du Pont (Du Pont)
50. Benson Ford (Ford Motor)
51. Mrs. W. Buhl Ford II (Ford Motor)
52. William C. Ford (Ford Motor)
53. Helen Clay Frick (steel)
54. William T. Grant (variety stores)
55. Bob Hope (entertainment)
56. Arthur A. Houghton, Jr. (Corning Glass)
57. J. Seward Johnson (Johnson & Johnson)
58. Peter Kiewit (construction)
59. Allan P. Kirby (Woolworth heir, Alleghany Corp.)
60. J. S. McDonnell, Jr. (McDonnell Douglas, aircraft)
61. Mrs. Lester J. Norris
62. E. Claiborne Robins (A. H. Robins, drugs)
63. W. Clement Stone (insurance)
64. Mrs. Arthur Hays Sulzberger (New York *Times*)
65. S. Mark Taper (First Charter Financial Corp.)
66. Robert W. Woodruff (Coca-Cola)

*In descending order of approximate wealth, from $1.5 billion to $150 million. These assessments include holdings of spouses and minors, of trusts, and of foundations established by the individuals or their spouses.

Source: *Fortune*, May 1968.

supposed to have ultimate power over management, but individual stockholders seldom have any control over the activities of the corporations they own. Usually "management slates" for the board of directors are selected by management and automatically approved by stockholders. Occasionally banks and financial institutions and pension trust or mutual fund managers will get together to replace a management-selected board of directors. But more often than not, banks and trust funds will sell their stock in corporations whose management they distrust, rather than use the voting power of their stock to replace management. Generally, banks and trust funds vote their stock for the management slate. The policy of non-action by institutional investors means that the directors and managements of corporations whose stock they hold become increasingly self-appointed and unchallengeable; and this policy freezes absolute power in the corporate managements.

Of course, the profit motive is still important to the corporate managers, since profits are the basis of capital formation within the corporation. Increased capital at the disposal of corporate managers means increased power; losses mean a decrease in the capital available

Banks with the Largest Total Assets

1. Bank of America National Trust & Savings Assn. (California)
2. The Chase Manhattan Bank, N. A. (New York)
3. First National City Bank
4. Manufacturers Hanover Trust Co. (New York)
5. Morgan Guaranty Trust
6. Chemical Bank N.Y. Trust
7. Bankers Trust Co. (New York)
8. Continental Illinois National Bank & Trust Co. of Chicago
9. First National Bank of Chicago
10. Security First National Bank (Los Angeles)
11. Wells Fargo Bank (San Francisco)
12. Crocker-Citizens National Bank (San Francisco)
13. United California Bank
14. Irving Trust Co. (New York)
15. Mellon National Bank & Trust Co. (Pittsburgh, Pa.)
16. National Bank of Detroit
17. The First National Bank of Boston
18. Franklin National Bank (Mineola, N.Y.)
19. Cleveland Trust Co.
20. First Pennsylvania Banking and Trust Co. (Philadelphia)
21. Marine Midland Grace Trust Co. of New York
22. The Detroit Bank & Trust Co.
23. Philadelphia National Bank
24. Manufacturers National Bank of Detroit
25. Seattle First National Bank

Insurance Companies with the Largest Total Assets

1. The Prudential Insurance Co. of America
2. Metropolitan Life Insurance Co. (New York)
3. Equitable Life Assurance Society of the United States (New York)
4. New York Life Insurance Co.
5. John Hancock Mutual Life Insurance Co. (Boston)
6. Aetna Life & Casualty Co.
7. Northwestern Mutual Life Insurance Co. (Milwaukee)
8. Travelers Insurance Co. (Hartford, Conn.)
9. Connecticut General Life Insurance Co. (Hartford)
10. Massachusetts Mutual Life Insurance Co. (Springfield)
11. Mutual Life Insurance Co. of New York
12. New England Mutual Life Insurance Co. (Boston)
13. Connecticut Mutual Life Insurance Co. (Hartford)
14. Mutual Benefit Life Insurance Co. (Newark, N.J.)
15. Penn Mutual Life Insurance Co. (Philadelphia)
16. Lincoln National Life Insurance Co. (Fort Wayne, Ind.)
17. Bankers Life Co. (Des Moines)
18. Teachers Insurance & Annuity Assn. of America (New York)
19. Western & Southern Life Insurance Co. (Cincinnati)
20. National Life & Accident Insurance Co. (Nashville, Tenn.)
21. Continental Assurance Co. (Chicago)
22. Occidental Life Insurance Co. of California (Los Angeles)
23. American National Insurance Co. (Galveston, Tex.)
24. National Life Insurance Co. (Montpellier, Vt.)
25. Phoenix Mutual Life Insurance Co. (Hartford, Conn.)

to the managers, a decrease in their power, and perhaps eventual extinction for the organization.

There is some evidence that management today has more concern for the interests of the public than did the individual industrial capitalists of a few decades ago. The management class is more sympathetic to the philosophy of the liberal establishment, to which they belong; they are concerned with the public interest and express a devotion to the "corporate conscience." As Adolph Berle explains:

> This is the existence of a set of ideas, widely held by the community and often by the organization itself and the men who direct it, that certain uses of power are "wrong," that is, contrary to the established interest and value system of the community. Indulgence of these ideas as a limitation on economic power, and regard for them by the managers of great corporations, is sometimes called — and ridiculed as — the "corporate conscience." The ridicule is pragmatically unjustified. The first sanction enforcing limitations imposed by the public consensus is a lively appreciation of that consensus by corporate managements. This is the reality of the "corporate conscience."[25]

Management fears loss of prestige and popular esteem. While the public has no direct economic control over management, and government control is more symbolic than real, the deprivation of prestige is one of the oldest methods by which any society enforces its values upon individuals and groups. Moreover, most of the values of the prevailing liberal consensus have been internalized by corporate managers themselves; that is, they have come to believe in a public-regarding philosophy.

It is also important to the corporate management elite that it maintain a continuing and intimate relationship with public officials. In the past, industrialists tended to affiliate themselves strongly with the Republican party and to denounce the Democratic party as an enemy of business. But the modern corporate manager avoids close identification with one party or the other, keeping the doors open to easy access for political figures from both parties. He does not speak out on partisan issues. According to John K. Galbraith:

> In this role the corporation can participate in the decisions that count. It can help shape the highly technical choices which, in turn, govern the demand for its own military and other products. It will have access to the decisions on military strategy which establish the need for such products. And it will help to shape the current beliefs or assumptions on foreign policy. These obviously are a far more important power than arguing partisan issues].[26]

Galbraith summarizes the changes in America's economic elite:

> Seventy years ago the corporation was the instrument of its owners and a projection of their personalities. The names of these principals — Carnegie,

[25] Berle, *Power Without Property*, pp. 90–91.
[26] John K. Galbraith, *The New Industrial State* (Boston: Houghton Mifflin, 1967), p. 323.

Rockefeller, Harriman, Mellon, Guggenheim, Ford — were well known across the land. They are still known, but for the art galleries and philanthropic foundations they established and their descendents who are in politics. The men who now head the great corporations are unknown. Not for a generation did people outside Detroit in the automobile industry know the name of the current head of General Motors. In the manner of all men, he must produce identification when paying by check. So with Ford, Standard Oil, and General Dynamics. The men who now run the large corporations own no appreciable share of the enterprise. They are selected not by the stockholders but, in the common case, by a board of directors which narcissistically they selected themselves.[27]

Corporations and Government

The economic system is inextricably associated with the political system. Often there is no clear line of division between government and business enterprise, or between government elites and business elites. The modern corporation is highly dependent upon government. As Galbraith explains:

> The mature corporation . . . depends on the state for trained manpower, for the regulation of aggregate demand, for stability in wages and prices. All are essential to the planning with which it replaced the market. The state, through military and other technical procurement, underwrites the corporations' largest commitments in its area of most advanced technology. . . . The state is strongly concerned with the stability of the economy. And with its expansion and growth. And with education. And with technical and scientific advance. And most notably with the national defense. These are *the* national goals; they are sufficiently trite so that one has a reassuring sense of the obvious in articulating them. All have their counterparts in the needs and goals of [management]. It requires stability in demand for its planning. Growth brings promotion and prestige. It requires trained manpower. It needs government underwriting of research and development. Military and other technical procurement support its most developed form of planning. At each point the government has goals with which [management] can identify itself.[28]

C. Wright Mills comments in a critical fashion about the interrelationships of business and government:

> The decisions of a handful of corporations bear upon military and political as well as upon economic developments around the world. The decisions of the military establishment rest upon and grievously affect political life as well as the very level of economic activity. The decisions made within the political domain determine economic activities and military programs. There is no longer, on the one hand, an economy, on the other hand a political order containing a military establishment unimportant to politics and to money making. There is a political economy linked, in a thousand ways, with military institutions and decisions. On each side of the world split running through Central Europe and the Asiatic rimlands, there is an ever increasing interlocking of economic, military, and political structures . . . At the pinnacle of each of the three and large centralized domains, there have arisen those higher circles which make up the economic, the political, and the military elites. At the top of the economy, among the corporate rich, there are the chief executives; at

[27] Galbraith, p. 14.
[28] Galbraith, p. 316.

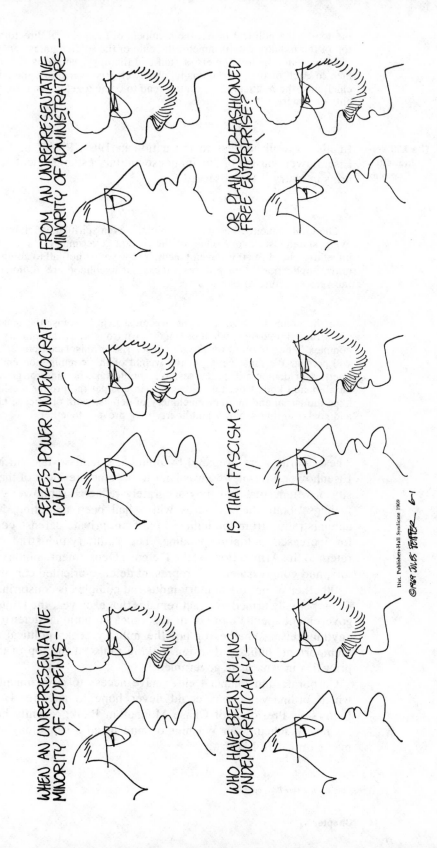

WHEN AN UNREPRESENTATIVE MINORITY OF STUDENTS—

SEIZES POWER UNDEMOCRATICALLY—

FROM AN UNREPRESENTATIVE MINORITY OF ADMINISTRATORS—

WHO HAVE BEEN RULING UNDEMOCRATICALLY—

IS THAT FASCISM?

OR PLAIN OLD-FASHIONED FREE ENTERPRISE?

the top of the political order, the members of the political directorate; at the top of the military establishment, the elite of the soldier statesmen. Clustered in and around the joint chiefs of staff and the upper echelons . . . the leading men in each of the three domains of power—the war lords, the corporation chieftains, the political directorate—tend to come together, to form the power elite of America.[29]

The Military-Industrial Complex

In his farewell address to the nation in 1961, President Dwight D. Eisenhower warned of "an immense military establishment and a large arms industry." He observed:

The total influence—economic, political, even spiritual, is felt in every city, every statehouse, every office of the federal government. We recognize the imperative need for this development. Yet we must not fail to comprehend its grave implications. Our toil, resources, and livelihood are all involved; so is the very structure of our society.

In the councils of government, we must guard against the acquisition of unwarranted influence, whether sought or unsought, by the military industrial complex. The potential for the disastrous rise of misplaced power exists and will persist. We must never let the weight of this combination endanger our liberties or democratic processes. We should take nothing for granted. Only an alert and knowledgeable citizenry can compel the proper meshing of the huge industrial and military machinery of defense with our peaceful methods and goals, so that security and liberty may prosper together.

These words were prepared by political scientist Malcolm Moos, an Eisenhower advisor who was later to become president of the University of Minnesota. But they accurately reflect Eisenhower's personal feelings about the pressures which had been mounting during his administration from the military and from private defense contractors for increased military spending. The "military-industrial complex" refers to the Armed Forces, the Defense Department, military contractors, and congressmen who represent defense-oriented constituencies.

Whether or not the military-industrial complex is conspiring to keep us perpetually armed, the fact remains that each year the United States government spends more of its resources on national defense than on anything else. Whether or not the military seeks political power is unimportant: military decision making ranks at the top of the list of priorities in American government.

Corporate and financial elites have access to government officials which ordinary citizens could never hope to acquire. Herbert P. Patterson, President of Chase Manhattan Bank, recently bemoaned his heavy schedule in Washington and listed a single day's appointments on Capitol Hill:

[29] Mills, *The Power Elite*, pp. 7–8.

8:30 A.M.	Arrive National Airport
9:15 A.M.	Sen. Ernest Hollings of South Carolina
9:45 A.M.	Rep. William Widnall of New Jersey
10:30 A.M.	Sen. Warren Magnuson of Washington
11:00 A.M.	Sen. Alan Cranston of California
11:45 A.M.	Rep. Gerald Ford of Michigan, House Minority Leader. (I'm asked to note that if he's delayed at a White House conference the appointment will be rescheduled for 3:45 p.m.)
Noon	Luncheon in House dining room with Rep. Leslie Arends of Illinois, the House Minority Whip, and Rep. Harold Collier of Illinois
1:30 P.M.	Sen. Henry Jackson of Washington
2:00 P.M.	Sen. Wallace Bennett of Utah
2:30 P.M.	Sen. Robert Packwood of Oregon
3:15 P.M.	Rep. Hale Boggs of Louisiana, the House Majority Leader
3:45 P.M.	Rep. Gerald Ford (who *was* delayed at the White House)

Also on the schedule, if time permitted and they could break free, were Rep. Benjamin Blackburn of Georgia and Sen. William Brock of Tennessee.[30]

Needless to say, it is unlikely that very many Americans would ever be able to schedule meetings with so many Congressmen in a lifetime, let alone in a single day. Mr. Patterson goes on to note with approval that:

My banking colleague, A. W. Clausen of the Bank of America, is no stranger to Capitol Hill. Men like Edward Cole of General Motors, John Connor of Allied Chemical and Charles Myers of Burlington Industries, among others, have made a real effort to provide legislators with information, to discuss with them problems of mutual interest, and to give them their best judgment as to how particular issues can be handled in the national interest.[31]

A frequent criticism of the military-industrial complex is that defense-oriented industries have become dependent on military hardware orders. Any reduction in military spending would result in a severe economic setback for these industries, so they apply great pressure to keep defense spending high. This is particularly true of the industries that are almost totally dependent upon defense contracts. The military, always pleased to receive new weapons, joins with defense industries in recommending to the government that they purchase new weapons. The military identifies and publicizes "gaps" in United States weapon strength relative to that of the Soviet Union—the missile gap, the bomber gap, the atomic submarine gap, the surface ship gap—frequently overestimating Soviet military capabilities to obtain new weapons. Finally, Congressmen from constituencies with large defense industries and giant military bases can usually be counted on to join with the armed forces and defense industries in support of increased defense spending for new weapons. Of course, heavy military spending by the United States prompts the Soviet Union to try to keep pace, thus accelerating the arms race.

[30] Herbert P. Patterson in *Nation's Business*, February 1971, p. 61.
[31] Patterson.

An interesting example of industrial pressures on the Defense Department could be observed in the decision to build an anti-ballistic missile system (ABM) to protect the United States against a possible missile attack. As Secretary of Defense, Robert McNamara had long opposed an ABM system as too expensive, unreliable, and unproven in ability to actually halt incoming missiles. McNamara had been the only Secretary of Defense ever to exercise control over the Pentagon and the military establishment. During his administration, in a radical departure from past Pentagon practices, McNamara, rather than the military itself, made the key decisions about which weapons the services could buy and how much could be spent for them. In so doing, he incurred the wrath of both the military and their industrial contractors.

McNamara argued that the best deterrent to a sneak attack was a strong United States offensive missile force. But an ABM system, ineffective or not, meant $10 to 20 billion or more in defense contracts. It was estimated that 28 major contractors for the ABM project employed about one million persons in 172 congressional districts in 42 states; among these were such major defense contractors as General Electric Company, Sperry-Rand Corporation, Raytheon Company, Texas Instruments, the McDonnell Douglas Corporation, and the Thiokol Chemical Corporation. The prime contract was held by Western Electric Corporation, an affiliate of American Telephone and Telegraph. McNamara held out stubbornly against industry demands (as a member of the top corporate elites himself, he was not over-awed by industrial salesmen or bemedaled generals), but when intelligence reports disclosed that the Soviet Union was deploying some ABMs, the pressure became irresistible. The White House feared that in the 1968 election campaign its political opponents would claim that the incumbent administration had failed to provide adequately for the nation's security (John F. Kennedy used this tactic well in 1960). The result of this pressure was a decision from the White House in September of 1967 that the United States would now deploy a "thin" antiballistic missile system against a possible missile attack by Communist China. Not long afterward, Secretary McNamara resigned. His resignation was generally considered a victory for the military-industrial complex.

The Nixon administration's "Safeguard" ABM system is a revised version of the Johnson plan. Instead of placing ABM sites near American cities, the Safeguard system places ABMs around offensive missile sites to reduce the likelihood that an enemy first-strike could knock out United States retaliatory power. After a prolonged and bitter debate in the Senate, in which the reliability as well as the expense of this weapons system was seriously challenged, the Nixon administration secured its approval by a close margin.

The military has come to exercise great influence in America, not only because of the importance of defense spending in the economy but also because of the increased prestige of military people during World War II and the Cold War years. During the years immediately following World War II, there was an influx of military officers into

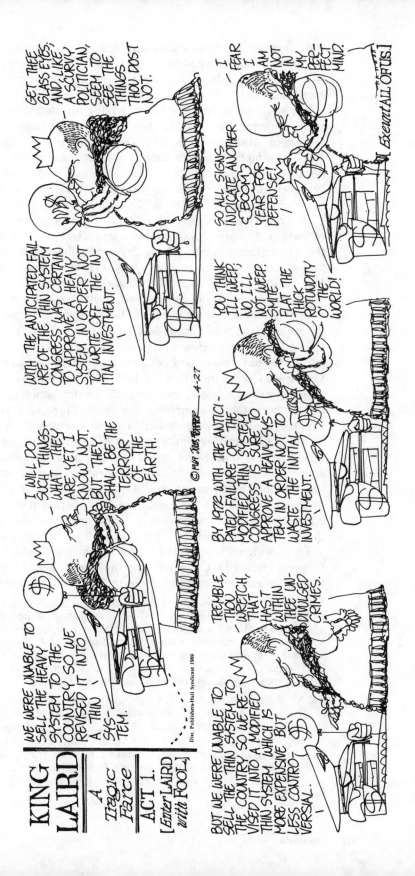

top corporate positions and a development of close ties between military leaders and corporations. The Cold War ideology of governing elites elevated military decisions to prime importance, and military men joined the ranks of the nation's elites.

Military men were often recruited directly into top corporate positions. General Douglas McArthur became chairman of the board of Remington-Rand (now Sperry-Rand Corporation). General Lucius D. Clay, who commanded American troops in Germany after the war, became board chairman of Continental Can Company; General James H. Doolittle, head of the Air Force in World War II, became vice-president of Shell Oil. General Omar M. Bradley, Commander of the 12th Army Group in Europe in World War II, became board chairman of Bulova Research Laboratories. General Leslie R. Groves, head of the Manhattan Project, which developed the atomic bomb, became vice-president of Remington-Rand. General Walter Bedell Smith, Eisenhower's Chief of Staff, became vice-president of the board of directors of American Machine and Foundry Company. General Matthew B. Ridgway, Army Chief of Staff during the Korean War, became chairman of the board of the Mellon Institute of Industrial Research.[32]

The two largest defense contractors in the United States since the late 1950s have been the Lockheed Aircraft Corporation and General Dynamics Corporation (see Table 4–3). Lockheed has over 200 high-ranking retired officers, including 22 former generals and admirals, in top corporate management positions. General Dynamics is the nation's leading missile maker. The president and chairman of the board of General Dynamics since 1962 has been Roger Lewis, who served as Assistant Secretary of the Air Force during the Eisenhower administration. These private corporations are so much a part of the national government that President Nixon and Congress felt obligated to bail out the Lockheed Corporation with a multi-million dollar loan in 1971, when cost overruns and other management errors threatened bankruptcy.

The positional backgrounds of former military leaders — for example, General Lucius D. Clay and Admiral Arleigh Burke — suggest the extent of military and corporate interlocks among top elites.

Lucius D. Clay, Commander in Chief of United States forces in Europe and military governor of Germany 1947–1949; chairman of the board of directors of Continental Can Company; senior partner in Lehman Brothers (Wall Street investment firm); member of the board of directors of Aerospace Corporation, of Allied Chemical Corporation, of Chase Manhattan Bank, of General Motors Corporation, of Lehman Corporation, of United States Lines, of Metropolitan Life Insurance Company, of American Express Company.

Arleigh Burke, Chief of Naval Operations 1955–1961; member of the board of Directors of Texaco Inc., of Chrysler Corporation, of Newport News Shipbuilding and Dry Dock Company, of Thiokol Chemical Corporation, of First National Bank of Washington, of Capital Radio Engineering Institute, of DuKane Corporation, of Federal Services Finance Corporation; a member of the board of trustees of the Freedom Foundation, of the Center for Strategic Studies of Georgetown University, of the Fletcher School of Law and Diplomacy.

[32] See Mills, *The Power Elite*, pp. 136–137.

	1961	1962	1963	1964	1965	1966	1967	7-Year Total	Percent of Total Sales
1. Lockheed Aircraft	$1,175	$1,419	$1,517	$1,455	$1,715	$1,531	$1,807	$10,619	88%
2. General Dynamics	1,460	1,197	1,033	987	1,179	1,136	1,832	8,824	67
3. McDonnell Douglas	527	779	863	1,360	1,026	1,001	1,125	7,681	75
4. Boeing Co.	920	1,133	1,356	1,365	583	914	912	7,183	54
5. General Electric	875	976	1,021	893	824	1,187	1,290	7,066	19
6. North American-Rockwell	1,197	1,032	1,062	1,019	746	520	689	6,265	57
7. United Aircraft	625	663	530	625	632	1,139	1,097	5,311	57
8. American Tel. & Tel.	551	468	579	636	588	672	673	4,167	9
9. Martin-Marietta	692	803	767	476	316	338	290	3,682	62
10. Sperry-Rand	408	466	446	374	318	427	484	2,923	35
11. General Motors	282	449	444	256	254	508	625	2,818	2
12. Grumman Aircraft	238	304	390	396	353	323	488	2,492	67
13. General Tire	290	366	425	364	302	327	273	2,347	37
14. Raytheon	305	407	295	253	293	368	403	2,324	55
15. AVCO	251	323	253	279	234	506	449	2,295	75
16. Hughes	331	234	312	289	278	337	419	2,200	u
17. Westinghouse Electric	308	246	323	237	261	349	453	2,177	13
18. Ford (Philco)	200	269	228	211	312	440	404	2,064	3
19. RCA	392	340	329	234	214	242	268	2,019	16
20. Bendix	269	286	290	257	235	282	296	1,915	42
21. Textron	66	117	151	216	196	555	497	1,798	36
22. Ling-Temco-Vought	47	133	206	247	265	311	535	1,744	70
23. Internat. Tel & Tel.	202	244	266	256	207	220	255	1,650	19
24. I. B. M.	330	155	203	332	186	182	195	1,583	7
25. Raymond International*	46	61	84	196	71	548	462	1,568	u
26. Newport News Shipbuilding	290	185	221	400	185	51	188	1,520	90+
27. Northrop	156	152	223	165	256	276	306	1,434	61
28. Thiokol	210	178	239	254	136	111	173	1,301	96
29. Standard Oil of N. J.	168	180	155	161	164	214	235	1,277	2
30. Kaiser Industries	u	87	49	152	219	441	306	1,255	45
31. Honeywell	86	127	170	107	82	251	306	1,129	24
32. General Tel.	61	116	162	229	232	196	138	1,124	25
33. Collins Radio	94	150	144	129	141	245	202	1,105	65
34. Chrysler	158	181	186	170	81	150	165	1,091	4
35. Litton	u	88	198	210	190	219	180	1,085	25
36. Pan. Am. World Air.	127	147	155	164	158	170	115	1,046	44
37. F. M. C.	88	160	199	141	124	163	170	1,045	21
38. Hercules	117	182	183	137	101	120	195	1,035	31

u-unavailable.

*Includes Morrison-Knudsen, Brown & Root, and J. A. Jones Construction Co.

Source: Dr. Ralph E. Lapp, *The Weapons Culture* (1968), pp. 186-187.

Military and corporate elites, while they have come to share a common interest, are of somewhat dissimilar social backgrounds. Sociologist Morris Janowitz calls attention to the unusually high nativism of the American military.[33] The military is even more heavily dominated by white Anglo-Saxon Protestants than is the political elite. The nativism of the American military elite is buttressed by an over-representation of rural areas. The rural tradition of the American military elite may stem from the stronger nationalism prevailing in rural areas, or from the more limited civilian career opportunities in these areas, or both. As Janowitz observes: "In contrast with the almost 70 percent of contemporary military leaders with social backgrounds with rural settings, only 26 percent of business leaders have rural backgrounds."[34] Another contrast between military and corporate elites is their regions of birth. The South has one-third more representation in the Army than it would have on a purely random basis, but only a small portion of the business leadership comes from the South.

[33] Morris Janowitz, *The Professional Soldier* (New York: Free Press, 1960).
[34] Janowitz, p. 87.

While the military elite as a whole draws disproportionately from middle- and upper-class groups, in recent years the social backgrounds of military elites suggest that the military elite is becoming more open. A general infusion of persons from lower- and middle-class backgrounds has occurred in all branches of the Armed Services, with the Air Force leading the way. However, a majority of top military elite come from professional, managerial, and business families.

Since World War II, American military elites have acquired sufficient power, independence, and scope to influence the shaping of high-level policies. What has been the effect of this increase in military influence among American elites? Political scientists Burton M. Sapin and Richard C. Snyder have described what they call the "military mind" in policy making:

(A) Rigidity in thought and problem analysis—the rejection of new ideas and reliance on tradition rather than lessons learned from recent experience;

(B) Inadequate weighing of non-military factors in military problems, and inability to understand complex·political-military relationships;

(C) An authoritarian approach to most social issues and situations, accompanied by disrespect and disregard of civilian authority;

(D) Insulation from non-military knowledge and anything beyond what is narrowly defined as militarily relevant;

(E) Judgment of policy goals and techniques primarily in terms of force and total victory from total war.[35]

If this description of the "military mind" is accurate, then the increased role of the military among American elites may help to explain the tendency of United States policy to rely on military solutions to complex political problems.

The Liberal Establishment The prevailing philosophy of America's elite is liberal and public-regarding. By this we mean a willingness to take the welfare of others into account as an aspect of one's own sense of well-being, and a willingness to use governmental power to correct perceived wrongs done to others.[36] It is a philosophy of noblesse oblige—elite responsibility for the welfare of the poor and downtrodden, particularly blacks. Today's liberal elite believes that it can change men's lives through the exercise of governmental power: end discrimination, abolish poverty, eliminate slums, insure employment, uplift the poor, eliminate sicknesses, educate the masses, and instill dominant culture values in everyone. The prevailing impulse is to *do good,* to perform public

---

[35] Burton M. Sapin and Richard C. Snyder, "The Role of Military Institutions and Agencies in American Foreign Policy," in Richard C. Snyder and Edgar S. Furniss, Jr. (eds.), *American Foreign Policy* (New York: Holt, Rhinehart and Winston, 1954), p. 369.

[36] See Edward C. Banfield and James Q. Wilson, "Public-regardingness as a Value Premise in Voting Behavior," *American Political Science Review,* 58 (December 1964), 876–887.

services, and to assist the poorest in society, particularly blacks. This philosophy is *not* widely shared among America's masses.

Leadership for liberal reform has always come from America's upper social classes. This leadership is more likely to come from established "old family" segments of the elite, rather than "new rich," self-made men. Before the Civil War, abolitionist leaders were "descended from old and socially dominant Northeastern families"[37] and were clearly distinguished from the new industrial leaders of that era. Later, when the children and grandchildren of the rugged individualists of the industrial revolution inherited positions of power, they turned away from the Darwinist philosophy of their parents and toward the more public-regarding ideas of the New Deal. Liberalism was championed not by the working class but by men like Franklin D. Roosevelt (Groton and Harvard), Adlai Stevenson (Choate School and Princeton), Averell Harriman (Groton and Yale), and John F. Kennedy (Choate School and Harvard).

The liberal, public-regarding character of America's elite defies simplistic Marxian interpretations of American politics; wealth, education, sophistication, and upper-class cultural values do not foster attitudes of exploitation, but rather of public service and do-goodism. Liberal elites are frequently paternalistic toward segments of the masses they define as "underprivileged," "culturally deprived," "disadvantaged," etc., but they are seldom hostile toward them. Indeed, hostility toward blacks is more characteristic of white masses than of white elites. Political divisions in America do not take the form of upper classes versus lower classes, but rather upper class, allied with certain minority segments of the lower classes, notably blacks, in opposition to the white middle-class and working-class masses.

The Liberal Establishment and War

Our contention is that the liberal philosophy of noblesse oblige — elite responsibility for the welfare of the masses — leads inevitably to a sense of national responsibility for the welfare of the world, which in turn involves the United States in war. The missionary spirit of liberalism strives to bring freedom — self-determination, civil liberty, limited government, and private enterprise — to all the peoples of the world. America's major wars of the twentieth century occurred during the administrations of liberal Democratic presidents — Wilson (World War I), Roosevelt (World War II), Truman (Korea), and Johnson (Vietnam). Is it accidental that wars occurred during these administrations? Or is it this element of the liberal philosophy which propels the nation toward international involvement and war?

Both World Wars were fought to "make the world safe for democracy." Following World War II, the United States embarked upon a policy of worldwide involvement in the internal and external affairs of nations in an effort to halt the expansion of communism. The "con-

---

[37] David Donald, *Lincoln Reconsidered* (New York: Knopf, 1956), p. 33.

tainment policy," as it came to be known, was a commitment by America's liberal elite to halt revolutionary Communist movements and to support non-Communist governments attempting to resist revolutionary influences either within or outside their borders. Cold war ideology accepted the notion of an international Communist conspiracy directed from Moscow and committed to world conquest through external aggression and internal subversion. Communism had to be halted everywhere in the world for fear that a victory anywhere would topple all non-Communist governments like a row of dominoes. The first official statement of the containment policy came in an address to Congress in 1947 by President Harry S. Truman, requesting that the United States provide military and economic aid for the Greek and Turkish governments, which were then engaged in civil wars with Communist-led insurgents. The Truman Doctrine called upon America to help all "free peoples who are resisting attempted subjection by armed intervention or by outside pressure."

In Europe, the containment policy was implemented by the North Atlantic Treaty Organization (NATO), a military alliance of western European nations led by the United States and directed against the Soviet Union, and by the Marshall Plan, an economic aid program designed to end the post-war paralysis of western Europe and, by improving living conditions in these nations, to reduce the appeal of communism to their masses. The test of containment came in Korea, where the United States had established a pro-Western government south of the thirty-eighth parallel; this government was attacked in June 1950 by forces of the Communist-led Democratic People's Republic of Korea. By December 1950, U.S. troops had defeated the North Korean Army and occupied most of North Korea to the Chinese border. When Chinese troops intervened, U.S. forces were threatened with total defeat, but eventually the Chinese were driven back to the thirty-eighth parallel. After three years of bloody fighting and bitter criticism of Truman's conduct of the war, the Eisenhower administration negotiated a settlement that left the battle lines not much different from the original border between North and South Korea.

The Korean War stimulated a massive rearmament program and directed elite interest to Asian affairs. Secretary of State John Foster Dulles sought to create a military alliance similar to NATO, in Southeast Asia, but the major non-Communist powers—India, Indonesia, and Burma—did not care to be "protected" by a military alliance with the United States. The best that could be achieved was a union of Pakistan, Thailand, the Philippines, and Western nations—Britain, France, Australia, and New Zealand. The United States also signed bilateral agreements with the Republic of China (Formosa) and Japan.

The United States did not support France and Britain when they attempted to recapture the Suez Canal from the Egyptians in 1956, but in 1958 we joined Britain in sending troops to Lebanon and Jordan to bolster tottering pro-Western regimes. In 1957, the Eisenhower Doctrine proclaimed a United States commitment to use armed force to prevent Communist regimes from seizing power in the Middle East.

In 1961, the Central Intelligence Agency led an army of Cuban refugees in an invasion of Cuba at the Bay of Pigs, but the result was a humiliating failure for the United States. When aerial photography revealed the presence of Soviet missiles in Cuba in October 1962, President Kennedy ordered a naval blockade of the island to halt Soviet military shipments and threatened an invasion of Cuba if the Soviets did not remove their missiles. Since fortunately they agreed to do so, the United States took no further military action against Cuba. In 1965, President Johnson rushed troops to the Dominican Republic to prevent what he believed was a "Communist takeover" of that nation.

As a result of this containment policy and cold war ideology, the United States has acquired a staggering number of international obligations (see Figure 4–2). In addition to specific treaty commitments, the containment policy commits the United States to resist the expansion of communism in every non-communist nation in the world. We are committed to resist not only overt military aggression, but also internal takeovers, economic penetration, and even successful campaigning in free elections.

Many nations of Asia, Africa, and Latin America are more concerned with shaking off the bonds of colonialism and seeking rapid economic development than they are with struggles between the great powers or between "democracy" and "communism." Both elites and masses of these nations are often revolutionaries in their politics. They desire rapid industrialization, freedom from colonial influence, land reform, social justice, the elimination of poverty and disease, and even social revolution. Yet the containment policy commits the United States to oppose all revolutionary movements, if "Communists" appear to be involved in them.

Many peoples of the world are ignorant and ungrateful; they do not wish to "improve" their lives and their society by accepting American social, political, and economic ideals. The "good" that the liberals seek to do throughout the world is neither appreciated nor understood by the elites and masses of many nations. The result has been a great deal of bloodshed and violence committed by well-meaning liberal administrations for the finest of motives. An American field commander in Vietnam summed up the liberal dilemma: "It was necessary to destroy the village in order to save it."

Finally, there is the tragic record of United States involvement in Vietnam. After the French withdrawal from Indochina in accord with the Geneva Agreements of 1954, the United States supported the pro-Western regime in South Vietnam. It encouraged the Saigon government to cancel elections promised in 1956, and began a large-scale military buildup in South Vietnam and Thailand. But despite the efforts of the United States, the governments of Ngo Dinh Diem and later military dictators steadily lost ground to the National Liberation Front, or Vietcong, which was receiving assistance from the Democratic Republic of Vietnam in Hanoi. In 1965, following an alleged attack on a United States destroyer in the Gulf of Tonkin, the

NORTH ATLANTIC TREATY (15 NATIONS)

A treaty signed April 4, 1949, by which "the parties agree that an armed attack against one or more of them in Europe or North America shall be considered an attack against them all; and . . . each of them . . . attacked by taking . . . will assist the . . . attacked by taking forthwith, individually and in concert with the other Parties, such action as it deems necessary including the use of armed force . . ."

1 UNITED STATES
2 CANADA
3 ICELAND
4 NORWAY
5 UNITED KINGDOM
6 NETHERLANDS
7 DENMARK
8 BELGIUM
9 LUXEMBOURG
10 PORTUGAL
11 FRANCE
12 ITALY
13 GREECE
14 TURKEY
15 FEDERAL REPUBLIC OF GERMANY

PHILIPPINE TREATY (BILATERAL)

A treaty signed August 30, 1951, by which the parties recognize "that an armed attack in the Pacific Area on either of the Parties would be dangerous to its own peace and safety" and each party agrees that it will act "to meet the common dangers in accordance with its constitutional processes."

1 UNITED STATES
38 PHILIPPINES

JAPANESE TREATY (BILATERAL)

A treaty signed January 19, 1960, whereby each party "recognizes that an armed attack against either Party in the territories under the administration of Japan would be dangerous to its own peace and safety and declares that it would act to meet the common danger in accordance with its constitutional provisions and processes." The treaty replaced the security treaty signed September 8, 1951.

1 UNITED STATES
39 JAPAN

ANZUS (Australia-New Zealand-United States) TREATY (3 NATIONS)

A treaty signed September 1, 1951, whereby each of the parties "recognizes that an armed attack in the Pacific Area on any of the Parties would be dangerous to its own peace and safety and declares that it would act to meet the common danger in accordance with its constitutional processes."

1 UNITED STATES
36 NEW ZEALAND
37 AUSTRALIA

RIO TREATY (22 NATIONS)

A treaty signed September 2, 1947, which provides that an armed attack against any American State "shall be considered as an attack against all the American States and . . . each one . . . undertakes to assist in meeting the attack . . ."

1 UNITED STATES
16 MEXICO
17 CUBA
18 HAITI
19 DOMINICAN REPUBLIC
20 HONDURAS
21 GUATEMALA
22 EL SALVADOR
23 NICARAGUA
24 COSTA RICA
25 PANAMA
26 COLOMBIA
27 VENEZUELA
28 ECUADOR
29 PERU
30 BRAZIL
31 BOLIVIA
32 PARAGUAY
33 CHILE
34 ARGENTINA
35 URUGUAY
44 TRINIDAD AND TOBAGO

SOUTHEAST ASIA TREATY (8 NATIONS)

A treaty signed September 8, 1954, whereby each Party "recognizes that aggression by means of armed attack in the treaty area against any of the Parties . . . would endanger its own peace and safety" and each will "in that event act to meet the common danger in accordance with its constitutional processes."

1 UNITED STATES
5 UNITED KINGDOM
11 FRANCE
36 NEW ZEALAND
37 AUSTRALIA
38 PHILIPPINES
41 THAILAND
42 PAKISTAN

REPUBLIC OF CHINA (Formosa) TREATY (BILATERAL)

A treaty signed December 2, 1954, whereby each of the parties "recognizes that an armed attack in the West Pacific Area directed against the territories of either of the Parties would be dangerous to its own peace and safety," and that each "would act to meet the common danger in accordance with its constitutional processes." The territory of the Republic of China is defined as "Taiwan (Formosa) and the Pescadores."

1 UNITED STATES
43 REPUBLIC OF CHINA (FORMOSA)

REPUBLIC OF KOREA (South Korea) TREATY (BILATERAL)

A treaty signed October 1, 1953, whereby each party "recognizes that an armed attack in the Pacific area on either of the Parties . . . would be dangerous to its own peace and safety" and that each Party "would act to meet the common danger in accordance with its constitutional processes."

1 UNITED STATES
40 REPUBLIC OF KOREA

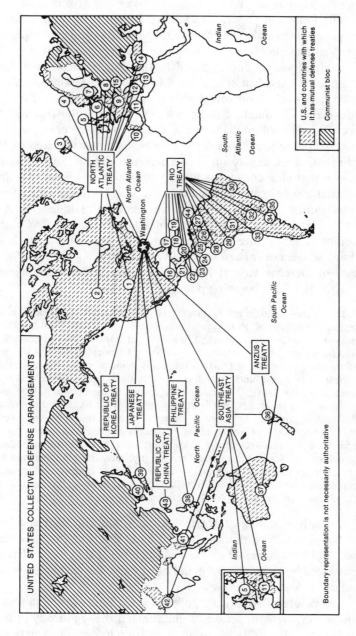

FIGURE 4–2. Summary of U.S. Treaty Obligations

Source: Department of State Bulletin, Vol. 57 (October 9, 1967).

United States initiated bombing attacks on North Vietnam and eventually committed more than half a million men to the battle in the South. The United States dropped more bombs on Vietnam than on all of the Axis powers in World War II, and took more casualties than in the bloody Korean War. Yet victory was nowhere in sight.

The Pentagon Papers — a Defense Department-commissioned study of government policy in relation to the genesis and evolution of the war in Vietnam, documented with reports by government participants in policy making, and released to the American press in July 1971, despite its classified status, by a former RAND Corporation scholar who had worked on the study — confirm the fact that five American presidents — Truman, Eisenhower, Kennedy, Johnson, and Nixon — were committed to halting the development of communist governments in Southeast Asia. Elite consensus never wavered on the value of resisting the expansion of communism. In fact, the Pentagon Papers reveal that elite consensus was so strong on this point that the advice of intelligence agencies (including the C.I.A.) to the effect that armed intervention would likely fail was ignored. Ultimately, America's liberal leadership changed its mind about the *feasibility* of halting communism by direct military intervention, but the *desirability* of doing so has never been seriously questioned. As early as 1966, Secretary of Defense Robert McNamara began to have doubts about the feasibility of our bombing policy:

> The increased damage to targets is not producing noticeable results. No serious shortage of POL [petroleums, oils, lubricants] in North Vietnam is evident, and stocks on hand, with recent imports, have been adequate to sustain necessary operations. No serious transport problem in the movement of supplies to or within North Vietnam is evident; most transportation routes appear to be open, and there has recently been a major logistical build-up in the area of the DMZ. The raids have disrupted the civil populace and caused isolated food shortages, but have not significantly weakened popular morale. Air strikes continue to depress economic growth and have been responsible for abandonment of some plans for economic development, but essential economic activities continue. The increasing amounts of physical damage sustained by North Vietnamese are in large measure compensated by aid received from other Communist countries. Thus, in spite of an interdiction campaign costing at least $250 million per month at current levels, no significant impact on the war in South Vietnam is evident.[38]

Eventually bombing of North Vietnam was curtailed and American forces gradually withdrawn from South Vietnam, but it is clear from both public statements and secret documents that these changes were prompted by tactical failure and not by any basic change in American policy in Asia.

The failure of America's political and military leadership to achieve victory in Vietnam seriously undermined the legitimacy of the established elite. By 1970, the original decision to commit American troops to a land war in Vietnam was viewed as a serious mistake — militarily and politically — by both elites and masses. The obvious errors in

---

[38] The New York Times, *The Pentagon Papers* (New York: Bantam Books, 1971), pp. 554–555.

S.D.S. STEALS SECRET PAPERS FROM HARVARD.

HARVARD IS EMBAR- RASSED BY SENSA- TIONAL DISCLOSURES.

REVOLUTIONARIES STEAL SECRET PAPERS FROM F.B.I. IN MEDIA, PA.

F.B.I. IS EMBAR- RASSED BY SENSATIONAL DISCLOSURES.

NEW YORK TIMES OB- TAINS SECRET PAPERS FROM GOVERNMENT.

GOVERNMENT IS EMBARRASSED BY SENSATIONAL DISCLOSURES.

IN A COLD WAR SOCIETY IF YOU WANT LIES—

YOU GO TO A PRESS CON- FERENCE.

IF YOU WANT THE TRUTH—

YOU STEAL IT.

political and military judgment, the heavy loss of life over a prolonged period of time, the humiliation of the military establishment in a war with a third-rate power, the revelations of incompentency and brutality, and the moral and philosophical questions posed by American involvement in a distant war, all combined to spawn a rash of counter-elite movements. Not since the Depression of the 1930s had America seen as many counter-elites of both the "left" and the "right" or as much mass unrest.

Summary Power in America resides in the large institutions, private as well as public—corporations, banks and financial institutions, universities, law firms, churches, professional associations, and military and governmental bureaucracies. Naturally, the men in high positions in these institutions have the potential for great power. These governmental, corporate, financial, and military elites are recruited disproportionately from the upper socioeconomic classes. There is considerable overlap in high positions among elites in America. Top governmental elites are generally men who have occupied key posts in private industry and finance or who have sat in influential positions in education, in the arts and sciences, and in social or civic charitable associations; and high-ranking military officers often occupy top corporate positions. Economic power in America is increasingly concentrated in the hands of a very few men who occupy key posts in a small number of giant corporations; and the economic system is inextricably intertwined with the political system, particularly with the military.

Selected Additional Readings Domhoff, William G. *Who Rules America?* Englewood Cliffs, N.J.: Prentice-Hall (Spectrum Books edition), 1967. *Who Rules America?* is a descriptive account of the overlapping structures of elites in American life. Although the author is a psychologist, he has attempted to answer the political question of who controls the political machinery of America. His findings substantiate the hypothesis that a small elite is in control.

Galbraith, John K. *The New Industrial State*. New York: Houghton Mifflin Co., 1967. Galbraith's thesis is that industrial and technical development has produced a decision-making elite of government officials and corporate specialists. He also discusses the goals on which elite decisions are based.

Kolko, Gabriel. *Wealth and Power in America*. New York: Frederick A. Praeger, 1962. Kolko uses economic analysis to define his elite system, but unlike Galbraith, refuses to distinguish between managers and owners.

Lundberg, Ferdinand. *The Rich and the Super-Rich*. New York: Lyle Stuart, 1968. *The Rich and the Super-Rich* posits an elite, based on ownership and wealth, that also has political power.

Mills, C. Wright. *The Power Elite*. New York: Oxford University Press, 1956. Mills contends that three elites—political, corporate, and military—together control the United States.

5

Elites and Masses:
The Shaky Foundations
of Democracy

One might suppose that the survival of democracy depended upon a substantial and widespread consensus among the American people on the principles of democratic government. Actually, only a small portion of the population is committed to the principles of democracy. While most people voice agreement with abstract expressions of democratic values, they are not willing to translate abstract principles into democratic patterns of behavior. The question is not whether most Americans are in accord with the principles of democracy. The question is how democracy and individual freedom can survive in a country where most people do *not* support these principles in practice.

Mass Attitudes toward Democracy
The readiness of the American public to restrict the civil rights of deviant groups has been known for quite some time. As early as 1937, it was found that the majority of voters were in favor of banning Communist literature and denying Communists the right to hold public office, or even to hold public meetings.[1] During World War II, when the United States and the Soviet Union were allies, tolerance of the rights of Communists rose somewhat; but even after the Battle of Stalingrad, two out of five Americans would have prohibited any Communist party member from speaking on the radio. This proportion rose during the Cold War years; it was 77 percent by 1952 and 81 percent by 1954.[2] Willingness and, occasionally, eagerness to abridge the civil liberties of groups other than Communists is also very much in evidence.

The first systematic examination of the intolerant frame of mind was made by sociologist Samuel Stouffer in 1954.[3] Stouffer realized that he was conducting his surveys of attitudes toward communism and other minority ideologies during one of the periodic reactions to communism that characterize our nation. He argued, however, that he was concerned not with transient opinions but with

[1] *Fortune* (June 1940).
[2] Herbert H. Hyman and Paul B. Sheatsley, "Trends in Public Opinion on Civil Liberties," *Journal of Social Issues*, 9 (1953), 6–16.
[3] Samuel A. Stouffer, *Communism, Conformity and Civil Liberties* (New York: John Wiley, 1966). Originally published in 1955.

deeper attitudes. For example, he measured popular support for freedom of speech, a fundamental democratic value. Stouffer asked a national sample of Americans whether various minorities should be allowed to "speak in your community." Twenty-one percent would not permit a man to speak if his loyalty had been *questioned* before a congressional committee, even if *he swore he was not a Communist.* Nearly a third of Stouffer's sample would not permit a socialist to speak; 60 percent would not permit an atheist to speak; and fully two thirds would not permit a communist to speak (Table 5-1).

TABLE 5-1.
Mass Support
for Free Speech

	Yes	No	Don't Know
Consider a man whose loyalty has been questioned before a congressional committee, but who swears under oath he has never been a Communist. Should he be allowed to make a speech in your community, or not?	70%	21%	9%
If a person wanted to make a speech in your community favoring government ownership of all the railroads and big industries, should he be allowed to speak, or not?	58	31	11
If a person wanted to make a speech in your community against churches and religion, should he be allowed to speak, or not?	37	60	3
Suppose an admitted Communist wants to make a speech in your community. Should he be allowed to speak, or not?	27	68	5

Source: Samuel A. Stouffer, *Communism, Conformity, and Civil Liberties* (Garden City, N.Y.:Doubleday & Co., 1955), pp. 29–42. Based on a national sample of 4,933 respondents.

This important study indicates that the extension of democratic rights to Communists, socialists, and other minorities cannot be accepted by the average American. Granted, these minorities are very unpopular groups in the United States, but the important point is that the questions are phrased in terms of *legitimate activities.* The respondents were not asked to approve sabotage or other conspiratorial behavior; they were only asked whether these minorities should be given the right to speak.

Another test of the commitment of elites and masses to democratic values was undertaken by political scientist Herbert McClosky, in a national sample of "political influentials" (over 3,000 leaders, drawn from delegates and alternates to the Democratic and Republican National Conventions) and nearly 1,500 adults in the general population.[4] McClosky found that both elites and masses responded favorably to abstract statements about freedom; his results, shown in Table 5-2, tempt one to conclude that a far-reaching consensus regarding freedom

[4]Herbert McClosky, "Consensus and Ideology in American Politics," *American Political Science Review,* 58:2 (June 1964), 361–382.

has been achieved. But when these abstract principles of freedom were given specific meaning, elites differed significantly from masses in their commitment to free speech. (See Table 5-3.) As Robert Dahl once remarked, it is a "common tendency of mankind . . . to qualify universals in application while leaving them intact in rhetoric."[5] This observation holds true of elites as well as masses, but to a noticeably lesser degree. Not only do elites exhibit greater support for democratic values than do masses, but they are also more consistent in applying the general principle to the specific instance.

TABLE 5-2.
Elites and Masses:
Responses to Items
Expressing Support
for General
Statements of Free
Speech and Opinion

Items	Percentage Who Agree	
	Political Influentials (N = 3,020)	General Electorate (N = 1,484)
People who hate our way of life should still have a chance to talk and be heard.	86.9	81.8
No matter what a person's political beliefs are, he is entitled to the same legal rights and protection as anyone else.	96.4	94.3
I believe in free speech for all no matter what their views might be.	89.4	88.9
Nobody has a right to tell another person what he should and should not read.	81.4	80.7
You can't really be sure whether an opinion is true or not unless people are free to argue against it.	94.9	90.8
Unless there is freedom for many points of view to be presented, there is little chance that the truth can ever be known.	90.6	85.2
I would not trust any person or group to decide what opinions can be freely expressed and what must be silenced.	79.1	64.6
Freedom of conscience should mean freedom to be an atheist as well as freedom to worship in the church of one's choice.	87.8	77.0

Source: McClosky, "Consensus and Ideology in American Politics," *American Political Science Review*, 58:2 (June 1964), 361-382.

Social Class
and Democratic
Attitudes

The studies cited above suggest the correctness of Senator Fulbright's comment that Americans believe in the right of freedom of speech until someone tries to exercise that right.[6] The evidence seems quite clear that "a large proportion of the electorate has failed to grasp certain of the underlying ideas and principles on which the American political system rests."[7] We are left with the question, why does the system survive?

One possible answer to this question can be found in the distribution of anti-democratic attitudes, for commitment to the norms and procedures of a democratic system is directly related to social class. Seymour Lipset has observed that "extremist and intolerant move-

[5] Robert A. Dahl, *Who Governs?* (New Haven, Conn.: Yale University Press, 1961), p. 319.
[6] William Fulbright, *The Arrogance of Power* (New York: Vintage 1966), p. 27.
[7] McClosky, "Consensus and Ideology in American Politics," 365.

TABLE 5–3.
Elites and Masses:
Responses to Items
Expressing Support
for Specific
Applications of Free
Speech and
Procedural Rights

Items	Percentage Who Agree	
	Political Influentials (N = 3,020)	General Electorate (N = 1,484)
Freedom does not give anyone the right to teach foreign ideas in our schools.	45.5	56.6
A man oughtn't be allowed to speak if he doesn't know what he's talking about.	17.3	36.7
A book that contains wrong political views cannot be a good book and does not deserve to be published.	17.9	50.3
When the country is in great danger we may have to force people to testify against themselves even if it violates their rights.	28.5	36.3
No matter what crime a person is accused of, he should never be convicted unless he has been given the right to face and question his accusers.	90.1	88.1
If a person is convicted of a crime by illegal evidence, he should be set free and the evidence thrown out of court.	79.6	66.1
If someone is suspected of treason or other serious crimes, he shouldn't be entitled to be let out on bail.	33.3	68.9
Any person who hides behind the laws when he is questioned about his activities doesn't deserve much consideration.	55.9	75.7
In dealing with dangerous enemies like the Communists, we can't afford to depend on the courts, the laws and their slow and unreliable methods.	7.4	25.5

Source: McClosky, "Consensus and Ideology in American Politics," *American Political Science Review*, 58:2 (June 1964), 361–382.

ments in modern society are more likely to be based on the lower classes than on the middle and upper classes."[8] Analyzing the ideologies of the lower classes, Lipset notes:

The poorer strata everywhere are more liberal or leftist on economic issues; they favor more welfare state measures, higher wages, graduated income taxes, support of trade unions, and so forth. But when liberalism is defined in non-economic terms — as support of civil liberties, internationalism, and so forth — the correlation is reversed. The more well-to-do are more liberal; the poorer are more intolerant.[9]

Lipset has expanded these ideas into his concept of "working class authoritarianism." He observes, from Stouffer's data, that only 30 percent of those in manual occupations are "tolerant," compared with 66 percent of the professionals. The question that Lipset sought to answer is, what aspects of lower-class life make an authoritarian or anti-democratic personality? He argued that a number of elements, such as low education, low participation in political organizations, little

[8]Seymour Martin Lipset, *Political Man* (Garden City, N.Y.: Doubleday & Co., 1963), p. 87.
[9]Lipset, p. 92.

reading, economic insecurity, and rigid family patterns, contribute to the making of the anti-democratic personality.

Taken collectively, many features of the subculture of the working and lower classes support the idea of a class-linked, anti-democratic pattern. There is no doubt, for example, that the childrearing patterns of the lower classes are substantially more authoritarian than those of the middle and upper classes. Also, the work life of the lower classes is depressing. Unskilled workers are substantially less satisfied with their jobs than are skilled workers and, as a partial consequence of their job dissatisfaction, have a more fatalistic attitude toward life. Workers who are conscious of having little control over their own lives show a tendency to view the social and political worlds as unchangeable. Unskilled workers are also more likely to view both big business and big government as cynically manipulative. Most important, the skill level in manual jobs is clearly related to mental health. Anxiety, hostility, negative self-feelings, and social alienation are associated quite consistently with unskilled labor; and people in skilled occupations have higher mental health scores than those whose jobs require a repetitive unskilled operation.[10] In addition to the relationship between mental health and work-life, there is a very strong link between the socioeconomic status of one's parents and the probability of poor mental health. The higher the social class of one's parents, the better one's mental health.

Given this impressive evidence, Claude Bowman has concluded that "the world of the semi-skilled and especially of unskilled workers is an unhealthful environment for them and their families."[11] Political scientist Robert Lane's more optimistic research indicates that the support for the democratic system found among the "common men" is related to their work situation. Most of his sample have some independence at work, find their jobs quite rewarding, and feel competent to perform their jobs well. Lane argues that high self-esteem derived from the work situation leads to support for the ambiguities of a democratic political system.[12] However, Lane's happy worker is not, judging from the evidence of other studies, typical of the American working class. Lipset provides the following depressing summary of the lower-class individual:

He is likely to have been exposed to punishment, lack of love, and a general atmosphere of tension and aggression since early childhood — all experiences which tend to produce deep-rooted hostilities expressed by ethnic prejudices, political authoritarianism, and chiliastic transvaluational religion. His educational attainment is less than that of men with higher socioeconomic status, and his association as a child with others of similar background not only fails to stimulate his own intellectual interests but also creates an atmosphere which prevents his educational experience from increasing his general social sophisti-

[10] Lewis Lipsitz, "Work Life and Political Attitudes: A Study of Manual Workers," *American Political Science Review*, 58:4 (December 1964), 959.
[11] Claude E. Bowman, "Mental Health in the Worker's World," in Arthur B. Shostk and William Gomberg (eds.), *Blue Collar World: Studies of the American Worker* (Englewood Cliffs, N. J.: Prentice-Hall, 1964), p. 374.
[12] Robert E. Lane, *Political Ideology* (New York: Free Press, 1962), p. 95.

cation and his understanding of different groups and ideas. Leaving school rather early, he is surrounded on the job by others with a similarly restricted cultural, educational, and family background.[13]

Education and Commitment to Democracy. The main thrust of the preceding argument is that the circumstances of lower-class life make commitment to the democratic system virtually impossible. However, the relative contribution of each of these circumstances to the making of the anti-democratic personality is not clear. Is it family life, or work life, or education that produces the authoritarian or anti-democratic personality?

Lipset suggested that lack of education might be more important than any of the other characteristics of lower-class life. By examining the tolerance responses of people of various educational and occupational strata, he found that within each occupational level, higher educational status makes for greater tolerance. He also found that increases in tolerance associated with educational level are greater than those related to occupation. And no matter what the occupation, tolerance and education were strongly related.

Stouffer found that commitment to free speech was also closely related to educational levels; college graduates were far more tolerant of the speech of unpopular minorities than were persons with only a grade school or high school education (see Table 5-4). Kornhauser found that within a given occupation (auto workers) those with poor education were more authoritarian than were those with more education.[14]

Lewis Lipsitz, by examining a variety of surveys administered in the 1950s, finds that the upper and middle classes are less authoritarian primarily because of the greater frequency in these classes of post-high school education. Very few of the relationships between class and authoritarianism remain strong when education is held constant. Thus, the greater authoritarianism of the working classes is largely a product of low education.[15]

Comparable findings are reported by Trow in his analysis of political tolerance and support for Senator Joseph McCarthy. He finds that, among those with less than four years of high school education, the manual workers are less tolerant than small businessmen; but, among those who have some college training, occupational differences are virtually destroyed. He concludes:

Occupation and economic class, and all the variant discontents that flow from membership in different class and occupational groups, seem to have little bearing on political tolerance, certainly as compared with the bearing of formal education and cultural sophistication. . . . Tolerance of dissidence appears to be almost wholly a function of the degree to which men have

[13] Lipset, *Political Man,* p. 114.
[14] Lipset, p. 110.
[15] Lewis Lipsitz, "Working-class Authoritarianism: A Re-evaluation," *American Sociological Review,* 30 (1965) 103–109.

TABLE 5–4.
Education and
Support for
Free Speech

		Percentage Willing to Allow Various Classes of Individuals to Speak "in Your Community"				
	General Public	College Graduates	Some College	High School Graduates	Some High School	Grade School
An accused Communist who denies the charge	70	82	83	75	71	61
An advocate of government ownership of industry	58	82	74	68	55	45
An opponent of churches and religion	37	66	57	48	36	20
An admitted Communist	27	50	41	30	24	18

Source: National survey reported in Samuel A. Stouffer, *Communism, Conformity, and Civil Liberties* (Garden City, N.Y.: Doubleday & Co., 1955), pp. 29–42. The breakdowns reported above are based on a reanalysis of the original IBM cards, which are on file at the Roper Public Opinion Research Center, Williamstown, Massachusetts.

learned and internalized the rules of the democratic political game: in the United States this, in turn, is closely related to general political awareness and sophistication, acquired in part through formal education and through exposure to the serious political media which support those norms, rather than through economic or occupational experience.[16]

Education and the Anti-democratic Personality. Another opportunity to examine the relationship between education and commitment to democratic norms is provided by Herbert McClosky, whose research provides the most thorough inventory available of the psychological underpinnings of a democratic society.[17] McClosky administered a variety of attitude and personality scales to a national cross-section of 1,484 respondents. Most of the scales were also administered by a mail survey to 3,000 Democratic and Republican leaders, ranging from federal officials to local officials and precinct workers.[18] By dividing the national sample into educational categories, we can compare the responses of both well educated and poorly educated people with the responses of the sample of national leaders.

McClosky examines the following attributes of elites, of the educated public, and of the uneducated public: (1) psychological flexibility, (2) feelings of marginality or lack of identification with one's class, (3) intellectuality, (4) dichotomous, or black-and-white, thinking, (5) liberalism and conservatism, (6) attitudes toward democracy and politics, (7) political alienation, and (8) extreme beliefs. The analysis measures both personality and attitude (Table 5–5). A good introduction to the characteristics of elites and masses can be gained from

[16]Martin Trow, "Small Businessmen, Political Tolerance, and Support for McCarthy," *American Journal of Sociology,* 64:270 (November 1958), 280.
[17]Herbert McClosky, "Personality and Attitude Correlates of Foreign Policy Orientation," Publication A-48, Survey Research Center, University of California at Berkeley, in J. Rosenau (ed), *Domestic Sources of Foreign Policy* (New York: Free Press, 1967), pp. 51–110.
[18]One might quarrel with McClosky's definition of leaders; certainly it is not intended to be inclusive. However, political party leaders are at least a part of the elite as we have defined it.

determining what proportion of each of the three groups scores high on the rigidity scale. A person who scores high on this scale is likely to view the world in black-and-white terms and is especially given to stereotypic categorizations and overgeneralizations. The world consists of "them" and "us." "They" are unquestionably bad, while "we" are unquestionably good. A division of the world into two opposing camps simplifies problems that would otherwise require thought and makes the world manageable. Notice that rigidity is higher among low-education groups than among either the leaders or the high-education group.

A more explicit measure of dichotomous thinking can be observed in the we-they scales, the chauvinism scale, the ethnocentrism scale, the anti-Semitism scale, and the segregation-integration scale. All of these scales indicate quite clearly that leaders are distinguished from followers by their rejection of dichotomous thinking. Such simplistic views of the world are compatible with those who have a feeling of marginality. The alienation scale (which refers to feelings of personal isolation), the anomie scale (which measures the degree to which individuals feel society is lacking in direction and meaning), and the cruel-world scale (which measures the tendency to regard the world as cold and indifferent) point up some of the problems of the poorly educated individual. Clearly, these individuals feel estranged, bewildered, and overwhelmed by a complex world and seek simple explanations of this world.

A hostile, dangerous, or indifferent world can be explained most easily as the consequence of a conspiracy; and lower-class movements are typically concentrated upon a scapegoat. Scapegoating is linked with intellectuality, since prejudice declines with information about the "out-group." The under-educated strata do not read and are poorly informed about public matters. For example, a Gallup poll indicated that whereas 41 percent of the college graduates had read a book in the past month, only 9 percent with a grade-school education had done so. In the past, prior to the development of a permanent Cold War ideology, the scapegoat for lower-class movements seemed to alternate between Catholics and "Wall Street," but in present-day America, the scapegoat for all the evils of the world is communism. A leader like Senator Joseph McCarthy can encapsulate all of these scapegoating tendencies and give them direction.

We are accustomed to associating conservatism with the upper classes, but the configuration of attitudes is not that simple. The poorly educated public may be more "liberal" with respect to economic matters; they favor more welfare measures and more government intervention into economic life than do the upper strata of the society. But the upper strata are much less conservative when conservatism is defined as an emphasis on tradition, order, status hierarchy, duty, obligation, obedience, and authority. Commitment to order and authority is much more a characteristic of poorly educated people.

On the other hand, notice that both leaders and followers have a relatively pro-business attitude. One might assume that the economic

TABLE 5–5.
Democratic
and Anti-democratic
Attitudes among
Elites and Masses
(Percent
Scoring High)

	Leaders	General Public	
		High Education	Low Education
	(N = 3,020)	(N = 787)	(N = 697)
Democratic commitment	49%	36%	13%
Elitism-inequalitarianism	23	31	47
Faith in democracy	40	24	13
Faith in direct action	26	32	53
Faith in freedom	63	53	43
Faith in procedural right	58	32	15
Tolerance	61	55	30
Political cynicism	10	23	41
Sense of political futility	4	22	39
Political suspiciousness	9	20	34
Left wing	7	16	41
Right wing	17	22	46
Populism	13	24	50
Totalitarianism	10	22	47
Authoritarianism	15	21	48
Rigidity	28	33	52
Alienation	17	26	43
Anomie	8	21	51
Cruel, indifferent world	10	16	35
Intellectuality	57	47	23
We-they (general)	23	24	44
We-they (specific)	12	24	49
Chauvinism	13	16	47
Ethnocentrism	17	22	39
Anti-Semitism	28	36	54
Segregation-integration	29	28	49
Pro-business attitudes	50	40	42
Classical conservatism	17	23	53
Economic conservatism	42	23	16
Opposition to government welfare	57	41	25
Support for liberal issues	24	23	22

Source: Adopted from Herbert McClosky, "Personality and Attitude Correlates of Foreign Policy Orientation," in James N. Rosenau (ed.), Domestic Sources of Foreign Policy (New York: Free Press, 1967), pp. 51–110.

liberalism of the poorly educated people would dispose them against the business system; but, actually, there is considerable evidence that the ideology of business is shared by *all* strata of society. The idea of starting a business with one's savings, for instance, is sufficiently alive to prompt literally millions of American workers to establish a business of their own. In the Oakland labor mobility study by Lipset and Bendix, two thirds of the manual workers interviewed had considered going into business for themselves, and about two fifths of them had actually tried to start their own firms. Despite the fact that most of these businesses ultimately fail, self-employment is a career that many Americans regard as desirable. Lipset and Bendix note that "with the exception of the workers at the very bottom of the occupational structure, the majority of Americans are probably related to or know individuals who have become self-employed."[19] It appears, therefore, that the dream of becoming an independent entrepreneur is not restricted to those who have any genuine possibility of achieving this status. However, in spite of the commitment of all sections of the system to a business ideology this ideology is *more* characteristic of the elite than of the masses. Notice, however, that a pro-business attitude is not linked as much with classical conservatism as it is with

[19]Seymour Lipset and Reinhard Bendix, *Social Mobility in Industrial Society* (Berkeley: University of California Press, 1960), p. 103.

economic conservatism. The elite exhibits more congruence of values (consistency of ideology) than poorly educated segments of society (this point will be discussed in the next chapter).

A footnote might be added to the description of the elite as relatively more liberal than the masses. Janowitz describes the military elite as conservative, although his measure of conservatism is limited to the respondent's self-evaluation. He notes that since military elites are well educated, the emphasis they place upon conservatism is especially noteworthy as an exception to the general rule.[20] Indeed, Janowitz describes the ideology of the military elite in terms that make this particular elite more comparable to the masses. Military ideology is concerned with a respect for authority and is characterized by a lack of respect for the compromises inherent in the political process—the same kind of impatience toward democracy and politics that characterizes the poorly educated population.

The rejection of politics and politicians is a basic feature of the rejection of democracy itself. In the minds of the poorly educated, politics in a democracy is "all talk and no action." Moreover, the poorly educated view the government as a manipulating "they." Feelings of helplessness are, of course, not necessarily all in the minds of the poorly educated; indeed, their feeling of helplessness might be a rational and accurate evaluation of the real situation. The poorly educated have no faith in the system because the system has not rewarded them.

Those who feel helpless are not likely to undertake any sort of political activity. However, given the appropriate provocation, those who reject participation in the official procedures of democratic society may initiate more radical types of activities, such as rioting. The Negroes who led the riots in the urban ghettos, for example, were much more inclined than non-rioters to think that the country is not worth fighting for and were substantially less trusting of the city government. Whites of similar social economic status were reacting similarly to their feelings of helplessness when they attacked the Alabama freedom riders. The point is that political behavior of the disadvantaged segments of the society is likely to be violent and illegal rather than to be within the normal framework of democratic decision making.

The potential violence of the under-educated strata is shown by their extreme political beliefs. The appeals of both the left wing and the right wing are more attractive to the masses than to the elite. It is not the content of the ideology that attracts the masses but rather the emotional symbolism that both left and right ideologies offer. As McClosky says:

Both are inspired by chauvinism, both conceive themselves as the nation's defenders against its enemies; both are impatient with or suspicious of the political process, and both regard themselves as dispossessed, pushed aside by men of doubtful patriotism and questionable objectives. The supporters of both political objectives are nostalgic for an era no longer possible; they con-

[20] Morris Janowitz, *The Professional Soldier: A Social and Political Portrait* (New York: Free Press, 1960), p. 238.

tinue to yearn for a return to the simplicity of an earlier period when the nation was invincible and its own master. Xenophobia has characterized both, and their portraits of foreigners and foreign nations have been remarkably alike. Both have been given to jingoism and heroic postures, and both have repudiated the artificial, corrupt, and declining cultures of the Old World. Both are attracted to conspiratorial explanations of human affairs, and both are inclined to attribute American reverses to softness, duplicity, or even treason.[21]

Political Socialization of the Masses*

If education is the key to how commitment to a democratic system is developed, then we need to know something about the quality of the educational experience. The evidence presented so far has suggested, tentatively, that there is a fundamental difference between the college educated and non-college educated population.

This distinction is generally blurred and needs to be sharpened. If one examines the association between education and a variety of attitudes normally attributed to the political elite, it can be discovered that commitment to democratic rules of the game becomes apparent only after substantial exposure to higher (as distinguished from secondary) education. At least through high school, learning how to be a good citizen does not necessarily include respect for the rights of minorities.

Making the usual assumption that racial progress and education are highly related in the South, Matthews and Prothro were surprised to learn that there was a substantial *negative* correlation between median school years completed by whites and black voting registration. As the average education of whites in a county increases, black voter registration decreases. Puzzled by this contradiction to one of the "laws" of political behavior, Matthews and Prothro remarked: "These findings . . . are completely contrary to what we would have expected from earlier studes and 'common sense' interpretations."[22]

However, such findings are not surprising if we regard the social function of the public school as one of the insulation of children from controversial ideas in order to attempt to preserve the *status quo*. As Key puts it: "All national educational systems indoctrinate the oncoming generation with the basic outlooks and values of the political order."[23] Illustrations of these ideas are not hard to find. An early study by Pressey indicated that changes in moral and religious values of society were reflected in shifting beliefs of college students but had no impact upon the ideas of high school students.[24] More recently, Campbell and Schuman's analysis of racial attitudes in 15 cities reaches the conclusion that:

The schools appear to have accepted without question the prevailing culture of race relations. Since World War II, those white students who have

[21]McClosky, "Personality and Attitude Correlates of Foreign Policy Orientation," p. 90.
* This section draws heavily upon Harmon Zeigler and Wayne Peak, "The Political Functions of the Educational System," *Sociology of Education*, 43 (Spring 1970), 115–142.
[22]Donald R. Matthews and James W. Prothro, *Negroes and the New Southern Politics* (New York: Harcourt, Brace and World, 1966), p. 129.
[23]V. O. Key, Jr., *Public Opinion and American Democracy* (New York: Alfred A. Knopf, 1963), p. 316.
[24]S. Pressey, "Changes From 1923 to 1943 in the Attitudes of Public Achool and University Students", *Journal of Psychology*, 21 (1946), 173–188.

gone to college have evidently been exposed to influences which have moved their attitudes away from the traditional pattern. . . . In contrast, the high schools. . . . seem to have been little more involved in the nation's racial problems than they were during the pre-war period. Or, to be more precise, their involvement has been so peripheral that it has had relatively little influence on the racial attitudes of their graduates.[25]

The point is that there is a fundamental qualitative as well as quantitative distinction to be made about education. The liberating effects of free inquiry are, in large measure, reserved for the potential elite who enter college. For those who terminate their education at the level of high school, the learning process is better characterized as "schooling." As Lane and Sears put it: "The home, and, to some extent, early formal education, encapsulate the past; higher education subjects it to scrutiny in the light of different ideas."[26]

Illustrations of the "encapsulation of the past" can be uncovered by looking at the attitudes of those who discontinued their education at high school, compared to those who go to college. The numerous studies of racial attitudes which have appeared since 1964 have been consistent in indicating that whites view America as a land of equal opportunity. To take one illustration, the Gallup Political Index of July 1968 reported that a substantial majority believe that blacks are treated the same as whites and only a minority agrees with the conclusions of the President's Commission on Civil Disorders that our nation is moving toward two societies. In Table 5–6, we can see that the only appreciable impact of education upon attitudes occurs after high school.

One cannot, of course, assume that the lack of exposure to critical thinking is a *sufficient* explanation for the unrealistic attitudes of the masses. For instance, Langton reveals that high school students who *intend* to go to college are more tolerant than those who do not.[27] Nevertheless, it is clear that public education does not provide the opportunity for critical thinking required of decision-makers.

TABLE 5–6.
Attitudes of Various Educational Groups Toward Racial Problems (Percentages)

	Grade School	High School	College
Agree with Kerner Commission	35%	35%	40%
Believe Negroes are treated the same as whites	71	75	71
Believe Negroes are more to blame for present condition than whites	56	58	42
Believe that businesses discriminate against Negroes in hiring	17	19	30
Believe that labor unions discriminate against Negroes in membership practices	15	13	30
Believe that looters should be shot on sight	54	55	45

Source: Gallup Political Index (July 1968): 15–22.

[25] Angus Campbell and Howard Schuman, "Racial Attitudes in Fifteen American Cities," Supplemental Studies for the National Advisory Committee on Civil Disorders (Washington: Government Printing Office, 1968), p. 35.
[26] Robert E. Lane and David O. Sears, *Public Opinion* (Englewood Cliffs, N.J.: Prentice-Hall, Inc., 1964), p. 25.
[27] Kenneth P. Langton, *Political Socialization* (New York: Oxford University Press, 1969), p. 18.

The main thrust of the literature on the school as an agent of political socialization is that the formal instructional process is generally unrelated to changes in the values of students. This is the case primarily because the instructional efforts in public schools are redundant; they are largely symbolic reinforcements of the "democratic creed"—a liturgy heard by most students so many times that sheer boredom would allow for, at the most, slight increments in loyalty, patriotism, and other virtues presumed to be the goal of civics and social studies courses.

We can get some general notion of what students are told in social studies courses from the texts they use and from the attitudes of those who teach. The chief conclusion of such an examination is that controversy is to be avoided. Massialas conducted an exhaustive survey of texts and found them to be of extraordinarily poor quality. Among the more significant of his conclusions are:

> Textbooks generally present an unrealistic picture of American society and government. Many social problems that exist today are not discussed. In statements about democracy and the good life textbooks often do not separate prescriptions from descriptions. Thus the persuasive usage of concepts are not distinguishable from descriptive and explanatory ones. America is presented as the champion of freedom, good will, and rationality, while all other nations are depicted as aggressors or "second raters." . . . Many authors assume naively that the political system functions in accordance with the fundamental laws of the land. . . . Controversial issues are not dealt with in an ethically or intellectually responsible manner. Nowhere do authors outline a defensible model for dealing with social cleavages and value incompatibility.[28]

Some excerpts from texts analyzed by Massialas illustrate his point. Take, for example, the following statement about the American economic system:

> One needs only to look at the great achievements and the standard of living of the American people to see the advantages of our economic system. . . . We believe that a well-regulated capitalism—a free choice, individual incentives, private enterprise system—is the best guarantee of the better life for all mankind.[29]

There is no discussion of any alternative to this economic system, not even in the "some say—others say" style that characterizes some efforts to consider alternatives. Further, a picture accompanying this discussion shows people waiting in line in the rain to be treated by the English National Health Service!

[28] Byron G. Massialas, "American Government: We Are the Greatest!", in C. Benjamin Cox and Byron G. Massialas, *Social Studies in the United States*, (New York: Harcourt, Brace and World, 1967), pp. 191–192.
[29] William A. McClenoghan, *Magruder's American Government* (Boston: Allyn and Bacon, 1966), p. 20. Cited in Massialas, *op. cit.*, p. 179.

Race relations are regarded as a "controversial social issue" and is treated with extreme caution. While there are some texts which are more realistic than others, the following quotation is typical.

In 1954, the United States Supreme Court made a decision stating that separate schools for Negro children were unconstitutional. This decision caused much controversy, but there has been general agreement, however, that some system must be developed to provide equal educational opportunity for all children — regardless of race, nationality, religion or whether they live in cities or rural areas.[30]

Of course, this statement is patently false. There is no discussion of the vigor with which Southern states resisted the order. Presumably, students were given no explanation for the fact that race relations remain America's most divisive problem.

Of the role social classes play in the political process, little can be said because the treatment is so sparse. Consider, for example, the following: .... "Classes in society are more or less inevitable. .... It is important to keep the social classes open."[31] Warner, Hollingshead, the Lynds, Mills, and, in fact, most American sociologists might never have written if this text is to be taken as evidence of their impact below the college level.

Patriotism, which is characteristic of the study of American government in the public schools, may be less jingoistic than it once was. However, texts carefully intersperse discussion of government structure (considered in purely legalistic terms) with appropriate exhortations such as: "No other country has more nearly approached the goals of true democracy as our United States. .... No doubt many of the early settlers were inspired men . . . ,"[32] and, "because the nations of the world have not yet learned to live permanently at peace, the United States today must maintain large defensive forces."[33]

The treatment of the American political process is generally totally unreal. A single example selected from the abundance of current texts should serve to make the point. One text devotes an entire chapter to the electoral process, but fails to mention the twenty-five years of research conducted on elections. As Massialas observed:

The five main ideas of the chapter on voting are: (1) "Voting is a process that makes possible peaceful change," (2) "Voting promotes citizen participation in government," (3) "Voting helps to promote equality," (4) "Voting promotes obedience to government," (5) "Voting promotes the self respect of every individual."[34]

[30] Cited in Mark N. Krug, *History and the Social Sciences* (Waltham, Mass.: Blaisdell Publishing Co., 1967), p. 202.
[31] William E. Cole and Charles S. Montgomery, *High School Sociology* (Boston: Allyn and Bacon, 1963), p. 365. Cited in Emily S. Girault, "Psychology and Sociology " in Massialas and Cox, *op. cit.,* p. 227.
[32] Cole and Montgomery, *op. cit.,* pp. 341–342. Cited in Girault, *op. cit.,* p. 227.
[33] Robert P. Ludlum, *et. al., American Government* (Boston: Houghton, Mifflin, 1965), p. 2. Cited in Massialas, *op. cit.,* p. 180.
[34] Massialas, *op. cit.,* p. 182.

The manner in which texts treat communism is even more astonishing. In both the "Challenge of Communism" courses which have become quite popuar recently and the general civics courses, communism is pictured as a total evil. Most state departments of education are primarily concerned with demonstrating the fallacies of communism rather than encouraging objective comparison. An unswerving, ruthless conspiracy dominated by the Soviet Union (texts have not yet discovered the shift toward China as the source of all evil) is the image that is presented, almost without exception. Texts warn students that they will be "badly fooled" if they "take the Russians at their word"; the "errors" of Marx are listed (no communist sources are cited); and the contrast of good versus evil is made quite explicit. In the event that the students fail to get the message, end-of-chapter assignments, maps, and other visual aids are equally biased. For instance, four projects accompanying one text are: (1) Write a short paper on agreements with other nations broken by the Soviet Union. (2) Draw a chart contrasting the way of life in a democracy and in a totalitarian government. (3) Organize a panel to discuss United States policy toward Cuba (preceded by the statement, "The presence of a Communist dictatorship in Cuba poses a threat to the people of the Western Hemisphere."). (4) Compile a list of Marx's errors.[35]

To provide a sense of geographical continuity, maps frequently are included in social studies texts. One such map divides the world into four camps: The United States, the Communist Bloc, the uncommitted nations, and the Free World—including Spain, Portugal, Formosa, and Haiti (Presumably "free" is a synonym for friendliness with the United States, rather than a description of the internal politics of a country). If, given the boredom which might be expected to accompany class discussions of such simplistic notions, the class still has not figured out how to get a good grade, the final assignment should reduce any remaining ambiguities: "List as many criticisms of Communism as you can."[36]

If it appears, and well it might, that this description draws a caricature of social studies texts, then consider the experience of the Director of the High School Curriculum Center in Government, of Indiana University. The Center has developed a more realistic text in American politics in an effort to correct the obvious flaws in existing texts. The Director of the Center laments:

While the authors know many social studies teachers who are exceptions to the rule and who conduct lively classes that deal intellectually and responsibly with central issues in American society, in general, social studies classes are more like catechism classes than the inquiry-oriented centers of free-wheeling discussion they are supposed to be.[37]

[35] Stuart Gary Brown and Charles L. Pelthier, *Government in Our Republic* (New York: Macmillan, 1964), pp. 20–21. Cited in Massialas, *op. cit.*, p. 183.
[36] McClenoghan, *op. cit.*, pp. 26–27. Cited in Massialas, *op. cit.*, p. 184.
[37] Gerald W. Marker and Howard D. Mehlinger, "Schools, Politics, Rebellion and Other Youthful Interest," in *The School and the Democratic Environment* (New York: Columbia University Press, 1970), p. 51.

There are, surely, some social studies teachers who can contradict the pap of textbooks and produce an element of realism, but they are rare. Most social studies teachers are not trained to distinguish facts from values and, in any case, probably find the anticommunism and ethnocentrism of texts quite compatible with their own values. Therefore, little contrary information filters into the classroom. Further, since such unreal descriptions are reinforced by other sources of information (such as the family), we should expect little attitude change to occur during formal schooling. What probably occurs is attitude *organization*.

The notion of attitude organization, as developed by Jules Henry, consists of grouping and focusing poorly articulated attitudes.[38] Given the conservative goals of the educational system, its success might better be measured in terms of providing order to attitudes and directing them toward larger social goals, such as the maintenance of positive affect toward national symbols. We suggest, moreover, that the crude indoctrination typical of texts is less effective in achieving attitude organization than the more subtle learning experiences manifested by means of teacher-student interaction and the norms of school organization. Teachers, in keeping with the general ethos of public education, are overly concerned about authority. The style of teaching, emphasizing the authority of the teacher, is in contrast to even the symbolic norms of participation presented in texts. The available evidence, such as that in Table 5–7, suggests that teachers are not prepared to engage students in a process of critical exchange of ideas.[39]

Such attitudes provide a strong propensity for creating a rigid classroom situation. Furthermore, in spite of the shibboleths of texts, to which teachers undoubtedly pay lip service, they appear to be as unclear about the application of democratic ideals to concrete situations as is the general population. A minority believe that police should not

TABLE 5–8.
Attitudes of Teachers toward Authority

Item	Percent Agree	Percent Disagree
Children should be given greater freedom in expressing their natural impulses and desires, even if these impulses are frowned upon by people.	42	58
Schools should return to the practice of administering a good spanking when other methods fail.	59	41
A good teacher never lets students address him or her except as Mr., Miss, or Mrs.	75	25
What youth needs most is strict discipline, rugged determination, and the will to work and fight for family and country.	69	31
The main purpose of social studies courses is to teach students to be good citizens.	83	12
Obedience and respect for authority are the most important virtues children should learn.	60	40
Students today don't respect their teachers enough.	57	43

[38] Jules Henry, "Attitude Organization in Elementary School Classrooms," in W. W. Charters, Jr. and N. L. Gage (eds.), *Readings in the Social Psychology of Education* (Boston: Allyn and Bacon, 1963), pp. 254–263.
[39] Zeigler and Peak, *op. cit.*, p. 133.

have the power to censor books and movies; a majority do not wish to provide First Amendment freedoms to social or political nonconformists.

Given the nature of our public education, the lack of commitment to (and understanding of) democracy on the part of the masses is hardly surprising. Most students who do not pursue education beyond high school have really been taught little more than loyalty to symbols. Symbolic loyalty can be deceptive. Merelman's study of education in the Los Angeles area is suggestive of such a result. Although he found teachers to be more open to controversy than is normally the case, he also found students to be poorly equipped to become responsible citizens. He finds that the educational process sustains support for the most obvious democratic symbols, thus enhancing approval for the existing structure of democracy. However, he is cognizant of the conservative implications of symbolic loyalties and remarks that formal education

> . . . seems unable to convey much tolerance for or comprehension of those minorities who would criticize the democratic system. Educational quality, as it presently operates, therefore supports the status quo rather than those who would change the status quo.[40]

Loyalty, rather than tolerance, is the message of public education. An ingenious study by Pock probes beyond the abstract values of "symbolic democrats" among the high school population. Rather than relying upon attitude scales, Pock presented high school seniors with a series of constitutional cases, each raising a separate constitutional issue. Respondents were asked to agree or disagree with the specific actions or decision involved in the case. He concluded,

> confronted by description of situations in which both explicit and implicit civil rights have been violated, a preponderance of students responded approvingly to the use of improperly gathered evidence, secret trials, search without probable cause, setting of excessive bail, and to the use of anonymous witnesses.[41]

We have seen, then, that schools teach loyalty and, to some extent, a belief in the efficacy of individual political participation. However, there is a final irony to the story. Langton & Jennings found that overwhelming majorities of students defined being a "good citizen" in two dimensions: loyalty and participation. However, for Negroes, loyalty rather than participation emerges as the dominant factor.[42] For Negroes, education means that a good citizen is above all loyal rather

[40] Richard M. Merelman, *Political Socialization and Educational Climates* (New York: Holt, Rinehart and Winston, Inc., 1971), p. 129.
[41] John C. Pock, *Attitudes Toward Civil Liberties Among High School Seniors* (Washington: U.S. Department of Health, Education, and Welfare, 1967), p. 134.
[42] Kenneth P. Langton and M. Kent Jennings, "Political Socialization and the High School Civics Curriculum," *American Political Science Review*, 62 (September 1968), 864.

than active. Similar results are found by examining the perceptions of citizenship on the part of lower-class whites. Litt examined the civic education programs in three schools, one serving an upper-middle-class community, one serving a lower-middle-class community, and one serving a working-class community. In all three communities, texts heavily emphasized the "democratic creed." However, in the lower-class school, there were few references to norms that encourage voting. Civic education courses in the lower-class community do not encourage participation. It is only in the upper-class school that politics is viewed as a feasible process for the resolution of conflict.[43] Thus, in the case of both Negroes and lower-class whites, the results of civic education are to encourage obedience and conformity to the beliefs of elites. Both groups are being told to "keep in their place" and to leave the decision-making authority to elites. The college-bound, future elites, are given a somewhat more realistic appraisal of the use of the political process.

Clearly, then, the public educational process operates not to change beliefs, but to reinforce established values; not to encourage diversity, but to demand conformity. Public education serves established elites quite well. It denies political skills and knowledge to the masses. As Lane and Sears aptly put it: "The Platonic Code (only the 'guardians' to be educated for leadership) here, in fact, had its modern incarnation."[44]

How Does Democracy Survive? This portrait of the elite and the masses indicates that survival of a democratic system does not depend upon a consensus that penetrates to every level of society. It is apparently not necessary that most people commit themselves to a democracy; all that is necessary is that they fail to commit themselves actively to an anti-democratic system. One might therefore conclude that American democracy is on shaky foundations. However, it is important to keep in mind that although the masses may have anti-democratic attitudes, they are also inclined to avoid political activity. And those with the most dangerous attitudes are the least involved in politics. As sociologist Herbert Hyman notes, "the normal apathy of the public provided some restraint on violent action against possible victims and also made the public less responsive to appeals to intolerance from national figures."[45] The apathy of the masses acts to counterbalance the radically conservative and potentially irrational nature of their values. It takes an unusual leader, such as George Wallace, to raise them from their apathy. Wallace is a "counter-elite," a clear threat to the values of the established elite. His typical appeal plays upon the fears of the masses:

[43]Edgar Litt, "Civic Education, Community Norms, and Political Indoctrination," *American Sociological Review*, 28 (Feb. 1963), 69–75.
[44]Lane and Sears, *op. cit.*, p. 27.
[45]Herbert H. Hyman, "England and America: Climates of Tolerance and Intolerance, 1962," in Daniel Bell (ed.), *The Radical Right*, (Garden City, N.Y.: Doubleday & Co., 1963), p. 229. Although England went through the same postwar stress as America, English investigations of suspected subversives were more limited. Hyman concludes that "when millions of individuals . . . are brought under official scrutiny as possible security risks, it validates the belief that everyone ought to be regarded with suspicion. . . . It thus encourages in the public at large a climate of intolerance toward those who may exhibit nonconformist opinions."

I think there is a backlash in this country against the theoreticians — some of them in some of our colleges and some of our courts and some of our newspaper editors' offices and some of our pulpits — who look down their nose at the steelworker and the paper worker and the communications worker and the beautician and the barber and the policeman and the fireman and the little businessman and the clerk and the farmer and say that you don't have enough intelligence to decide how to get up in the morning and when to go to bed at night, and people are tired of theorists running their country.[46]

The response of the "little people" to Wallace is indicated by his strength in the lower strata of American society.

Conditions for Mass Activism

Occasionally, mass activism replaces mass apathy. This activism reflects the anti-democratic, extremist, hateful, and violence-prone sentiments of the masses, and constitutes a serious threat to democratic values.

Mass activism tends to occur in crisis situations — defeat or humiliation in war, economic depression and unemployment, or threat to public safety. William Kornhauser correctly observes:

There appears to be a close relation between the severity of crises and the extent of mass movements in Western societies. The more severe the depression in industrial societies, the greater the social atomization, and the more widespread are mass movements (for example, there is a high [inverse] association between level of employment and increase in the extremist electorate). The stronger a country's sense of national humiliation and defeat in war, the greater the social atomization, and the greater the mass action (for example, there is a close association between military defeat and the rise of strong mass movements).[47]

Defeat in war, or even failure to achieve any notable victories in a protracted military effort, reduces mass confidence in established leadership and makes the masses vulnerable to the appeals of counter-elites. Both fascism in Germany and communism in Russia followed on the heels of national humiliation and defeat in war. The current anti-establishment culture in America owes a great deal to the mistakes and failures of the nation's leadership in Vietnam.

Mass anxiety and vulnerability to counter-elites are also increased by economic dislocation — depression, unemployment, or technological change — which threatens financial security. It is not so much poverty itself which breeds anxiety, but change or threatened change in the level of affluence. Another source of anxiety among the masses is their perceived level of personal safety. Crime, street violence, and terrorism can produce disproportionately strong anxieties about personal safety. Historically, when they believe their personal safety is threatened, masses in America have turned to vigilantes, the Ku Klux Klan, and "law and order" movements.

---

[46] *Life* (August 2, 1969), p. 20.
[47] William Kornhauser, *The Politics of Mass Society* (New York: Free Press, 1959), p. 174.

The masses are most vulnerable to extremism when they are alienated from group and community life and when they feel their own lives are without direction or purpose. According to William Kornhauser:

> People become available for mobilization by [counter] elites when they lack or lose an independent group life. The term *masses* applies only where we deal with people who . . . cannot be integrated into any organization based on common interest, into political parties or municipal governments or professional organizations or trade unions. The lack of autonomous relations generates widespread social alienation. Alienation heightens responsiveness to the appeal of mass movements because they provide occasions for expressing resentment against what is, as well as promises of a vitally different world. In short, *people who are atomized readily become mobilized.* Since totalitarianism is a state of total mobilization, mass society is highly vulnerable to totalitarian movements and regimes.[48]

Counter-elites: George C. Wallace as Voice of the People

Threats to established elite values occur periodically, from both left and right. The counter-elite pattern is similar, no matter which ideological direction it moves from. Both left and right counter-elite movements base their appeal upon the desire of those who perceive themselves as powerless to overthrow the established elite. Lipset and Raab refer to this appeal as "anti-elitism,"[49] but counter-elitism is a more appropriate term.

Though "left" counter-elites in America are just as anti-democratic, extremist, intolerant, and violence-prone as "right" counter-elites, their appeal is currently limited to small numbers of alienated blacks, intellectuals, and college students. "Left" counter-elites have no mass following among workers, farmers, or middle-class Americans. In contrast, "right" counter-elites have been more indigenous to American life, and have mobilized broad mass followings. Many changes in American society have contributed to the popular appeal of "right" counter-elites: shifts in power and prestige from the farms to the cities, from agriculture to industry, from the South to the North; shifts away from individual enterprise toward collective action; shifts away from racial segregation toward special emphasis on opportunities for blacks; shifts from old values to new, from religion to secularism, from work to leisure; shifts in scale from small to large, from personal to impersonal, from individual to bureaucratic; increases in crime, racial disorder, and threats to personal safety. Any genuine "people's" revolution in America would undoubtedly take the form of a right-wing nationalist, patriotic, religious-fundamentalist, anti-black, anti-intellectual, anti-student, "law and order" movement.[50]

Counter-elite movements may seem from their rhetoric to be equalitarian but (like all political activity) are well within the control of the articulate few. Rarely, of course, do counter-elites achieve sufficient resources to put any portion of their values into practice. They can,

[48]Kornhauser, p. 33.
[49]Seymour Martin Lipset and Earl Raab, *The Politics of Unreason* (New York: Harper and Row, 1970), p. 348.
[50]Lipset and Raab, p. 3.

however, threaten established elites and prod them into providing symbolic satisfaction, in the hope that the anxieties expressed in the counter-elite movement can be reduced. Nixon's "Southern strategy," for instance is certainly partially generated by his fear of George C. Wallace. Similarly, during the 1930s, Roosevelt's economic policies were partially inspired by a desire to de-fuse the more radically left political movements of the time.

There is perhaps too much significance placed upon the "left" or "right" ideology of counter-elites, and not enough placed upon their deep-seated antagonism toward established elites. For example, granted that Wallace's opposition to integration and his strong support of the Vietnam war are in stark contrast to the professed values of today's radical left, there are some striking similarities in appeal of these two counter-elites. Wallace's economic proposals are appreciably toward the (economically defined) left. For instance, he advocates a federal job-training program, increase in social security, improving Medicare, increases in minimum-wage levels, and other programs quite compatible with the left counter-elite. As one commentator noted:

He is talking about poor people, "ordinary folks," and if you strip him of the southern accent and some of the surrounding rhetoric you might mistake him for a New Left advocate of the poverty program, urging maximum feasible participation of the poor and returning local government to the people, "participatory democracy."[51]

Wallace is typical of many counter-elites in his populism, extremism, anti-elitism and equalitarianism. But Wallace is particularly important because of his mass base: In the 1968 presidential election, 14 percent of the American electorate completely abandoned the two-party system to support Wallace's independent candidacy. Given the historic, institutional role of the two-party system in America, the strength of traditional party loyalties, family ties, and socialization patterns, the fact that so many people would abandon both parties for an independent candidate is truly astounding.

Both North and South, Wallace appeals to *racial sentiments*—a mass characteristic of whites which Wallace successfully exploits.[52] But it is a mistake to dismiss Wallace as merely a racist. He appeals to "little people" throughout the nation by expressing a wide variety of mass sentiments.

Wallace speaks in *populist* terms about the role of "the people":

---

[51] Ward Just, "Discontent Is the Mood of Wallace Audiences," *Washington Post*, October 12, 1967, p. B-4. Cited in Lipset and Raab, *op. cit.*, p. 349.

[52] Whether Wallace is personally a racist is open to question. In his first run for Governor of Alabama in 1958, Wallace shunned KKK support and ran as a Southern "moderate," against strong segregationist John Patterson. Wallace was badly beaten, and was widely quoted as saying "They out-niggered me that time but they'll never do it again." One Wallace observer says, "I would term the Governor a pseudo-demagogue, because he doesn't really believe what he says about the race question. He uses it only as a technique to get the vote of the nonsophisticated white man." But another observer adds, "He used to be anything but a racist, but with all his chattering he managed to talk himself into it." See Robert Sherrill, *Gothic Politics in the Deep South* (New York: Grossman, 1968), p. 283.

The Wallace for President movement is a movement of the people and it doesn't make any difference whether top leading politicians endorse this movement or not. I think that if the politicians get in the way in 1968, a lot of them are gonna get run over by this average man in the steel mill, this barber, this beautician, the policeman on the beat, they're the ones—and the little businessman—I think those are the mass of people that are going to support a change on the domestic scene in this country.[53]

His *anti-intellectualism* and *anti-elitism* hold a great deal of mass appeal:

I think there is a backlash in this country against the theoreticians—some of them in some of our colleges and some of our courts and some of our newspaper editors' offices and some of our pulpits—who look down their nose at the steelworker and the paper worker and the communications worker and the beautician and the barber and the policeman and the fireman and the little businessman and the clerk and the farmer and say that you don't have enough intelligence to decide how to get up in the morning and when to go to bed at night, and people are tired of theorists running their country.[54]

Wallace is *equalitarian* on everything except race. He attacks the "Eastern money interests" and "the over-educated ivory-tower folks with pointed heads looking down their nose at us." He identifies communism with wealth: "I don't believe in all this talk about poor folks turning Communist! It's the damn rich who turn Communist. You ever seen a poor Communist?"[55] Republicans are attacked as "bankers and big money people" who exploit "us ordinary folks." Wallace's welfare and public-works programs, when he was Governor of Alabama, were the most liberal in the state's history, and he was regarded as a threat to conservative business interests in that state.

Mass fears about personal safety are just as influential as racial prejudice in stimulating Wallace support. Wallace frequently referred to demonstrators as "the scum of the earth"; he pledged that if a demonstrator ever tried to lie down in front of a Wallace motorcade "it would be the last car he ever lies down in front of." Wallace's simplistic solution to rioting was "to let the police run this country for a year or two and there wouldn't be any riots."

If we were President today, you wouldn't get stabbed or raped in the shadow of the White House, even if we had to call out 30,000 troops and equip them with 2-foot long bayonets and station them every few feet. . . . That's right, we gonna have a *police* state for folks who burn the cities down. They aren't gonna burn any more cities.[56]

Wallace correctly judged that his mass audience would welcome a police state in order to insure their personal safety. Opinion surveys

[53]Lipset and Raab, *op. cit.* p. 349.
[54]*Life*, August 2, 1969, p. 20.
[55]Lipset and Raab, *op. cit.*. p. 350.
[56]*Newsweek*, September 16, 1968, p. 27.

consistently reported that "crime and violence," "riots," and "law and order" were rated as the most important issues by Wallace's mass following.[57]

Wallace frequently expressed contempt for established institutions and procedures, and an undercurrent of violence is easily detectable in his speeches.

> There is one thing more powerful than the Constitution . . . than any constitution. That's the will of the people. What is a Constitution anyway? They're the products of the people, the people are the first source of power, and the people can abolish a Constitution if they want to.[58]

He symbolized popular resistance to court-decreed desegregation by "standing in the schoolhouse door in person" at the University of Alabama when he personally interposed his body between federal marshals and the entrance to the registrar's office. Wallace expresses very little tolerance of diverse views. Intellectual critics of the Vietnam War are "long-hairs who ought to be treated as traitors, which they are." As for courts and constitutional rights of defendants: "Of course if I did what I'd like to do I'd pick up something and smash one of these federal judges in the head and then burn the courthouse down. But I'm too genteel."

The response of conservative intellectuals (e.g., William Buckley) and conservative politicians (e.g., Barry Goldwater) to Wallace is indicative of their recognition of his status as a counter-elite representative, rather than as a spokesman of the conservative wing of the established elite. He was widely condemned by Buckley's *National Review* as a Populist demagogue. At the same time, he was denounced by the liberal wing of the established elite as a racist. In the 1968 election, the establishment contenders (with Nixon representing the "moderate" wing of the conservative portion and Humphrey representing the "moderate" wing of the liberal portion) were alarmed by Wallace's potential, although each based his fear upon the potential loss of a different constituency. Nixon was afraid of losing the strength in the South established by Goldwater, while Humphrey feared Wallace's erosion of Democratic support among the South. The point is that Wallace is about as popular in the established elite as is Jerry Rubin.

Failure of Elites

Although the masses can usually be counted on to leave politics to the elites, we should not necessarily assume that our freedoms are safe in the hands of the elites. In periods of crisis, support for our civil liberties does not appear to be very great even among those with college educations. For example, a poll taken in Minnesota indicates that the educated citizenry had an unfavorable opinion about those who took part in demonstrations against the war in Vietnam, even though no

---

[57]Lipset and Raab, *op. cit.*, p. 406.
[58]Marshall Frady, *Wallace* (New York: World, 1968), p. 227.

laws were broken. Only 25 percent of the college-educated population had a favorable impression of people who took part in demonstrations.[59] Further, 50 percent of the college-educated population felt that Communists were heavily involved in anti-Vietnam demonstrations. To take another example, the elected leaders of the country, notably President Johnson and Vice-President Humphrey (not to mention Mayor Richard Daley of Chicago), left little doubt that they considered the demonstrations at the 1968 Democratic Convention unpatriotic, and thus provided tacit approval to police attacks on demonstrators.

The failure of the elite to defend the right to demonstrate against the war in Vietnam is not a unique example of the failure of elites to support civil liberties. The career of Senator Joseph McCarthy, and the response of elites to his career, is another example of the failure of elites to respond to a challenge to the system. To be sure, McCarthy's assault upon traditional freedoms was especially popular with those of less education, which is consistent with what we know about the relationship between education and political attitudes. The less-educated were undoubtedly also strongly attracted by McCarthy's anti-intellectual and anti-aristocratic appeals (it is rare that the anti-intellectualism of the masses is provided with articulate leadership). However, for a long period McCarthy's career went virtually unchallenged even by the elites. As David Truman phrases it, "The response in that segment [the elite] during the years 1950–1954 was not reassuring. Though the evidence is not beyond contradiction, it seems clear that among the elites the threat was not generally seen for what it was.[60]

If the masses, acting in accordance with their values, would destroy freedom, then we are left with the elites as the defender of this freedom. Though the elites may be "carriers of the creed" in their attitude, their actions in support of liberty have often been less than adequate. Thus, mass apathy, rather than elite activism, seems to be the key to the survival of democracy.

Elite–Mass Communication

Because of the political apathy of the masses, the elite policy makers generally operate with minimal restriction from the masses. However, they are still constrained by their perception of the opinions of the masses. These perceptions can often be incorrect, unless elites are able to undertake sophisticated analyses of public opinion. For instance, if congressmen pay special attention to their mail, they may reach a conclusion about the opinions of their constituency that is actually quite the reverse of the true structure of opinion.

A study of the opinions of American businessmen about the reduction of tariffs indicates the absence of relationship between actual opinion and communicated opinion. Attitudes toward foreign trade

---

[59] *Gallup Political Index*, June 1967, Report No. 24.
[60] David B. Truman, "The American System in Crisis," *Political Science Quarterly*, 74 (December 1959), 495.

among the public are not well developed, and most people are poorly informed or uninterested in the topic of tariffs.[61] Given the fact that the issue is extremely complex and that information is generally low, interpretations of public opinion are of little value. Nevertheless, the proportion of persons favoring lower tariffs is twice that of persons in favor of raising them. Even among businessmen (those most likely to be affected by a change in tariff policy), protectionist sentiment is slight. The proportion of businessmen favoring the reduction of tariffs is seven times as great as that favoring a raising of tariffs. (It should be noted that tariff policy was not especially important to the business community; businessmen were aware of trade policy but were much more concerned with such problems as taxes and union demands.) The shape of opinion on this issue can thus be summarized in the following manner: In terms of *intensity*, both the masses and the attentive public were relatively unconcerned. In terms of *direction*, sentiment favored a liberalizing of trade policy.

Now let us see what information was transmitted to the congressmen who were responsible for reaching a decision. Protectionists wrote about twice as often as those favoring a reduction of tariff, and the intensity of protectionist letter writing increased as the debate became more heated. Interest in a high tariff was obviously a more effective stimulus to letter writing than was interest in a low tariff, probably because those businessmen concerned with the maintenance of a high tariff system felt most personally threatened by change in the status quo. The authors conclude that "the body of citizens represented by our sample could appear to Congress to be two to one protectionists, when we know they were more nearly three to one liberal traders."

If congressmen had responded to a public defined as those who wrote letters, the decision to reduce tariffs would not have been made. A reduction in tariffs reflected reasonably well the attitudes of both the attentive and the general publics but not the attitudes that were conveyed to Congress. Thus Congress acted in opposition to communicated public opinion but in conformity with unstated opinion. In this case, information flowed between governmental elites and a special portion of the public that had an unusual concern over the issue. Communication from the broader public was virtually nonexistent.

Even within this limited communication system, there was a distortion of messages, in addition to the actual overrepresentation of protectionist sentiment. The image of a congressman in the letter writer's mind tends to control the target of his communication. Protectionists therefore communicated with congressmen perceived to be sympathetic to their position, while liberal traders did likewise.

Congressmen affirm that most of their mail is in agreement with the position that they advocate. The congressman therefore has considerable initiative in organizing the nature of the communications that he

---

[61] Raymond A. Bauer, Ithiel de Sola Pool, and Lewis A. Dexter, *American Business and Public Policy* (New York: Atherton Press, 1963), p. 81.

wishes to receive. By establishing his image in the minds of his constituents, and by establishing relationships with constituency groups whose attitudes are congruent with his own, the congressman can create a world of public opinion that is self-reinforcing: "He makes the world to which he thinks he is responding."[62]

These conclusions suggest that the flow of influence is from the elite to selected sub-elites, rather than the reverse. Elites create pressure to which they respond, if they wish. The phenomenon of elites creating opinions among the masses is sometimes referred to as "the mobilization of bias" or as a "false consensus."[63] Its ramifications for popular democratic theory are great; for elites, by controlling the values and norms of society, can thereby also control the issues upon which governmental decision makers act. Control of this type is subtle and effective. Peter Bachrach and Morton Baratz describe it as follows:

> Of course power is exercised when A participates in the making of decisions that affect B. But power is also exercised when A devotes his energies to creating or reinforcing social and political values and institutional practices that limit the scope of the political process to public consideration of only those issues which are comparatively innocuous to A. To the extent that A succeeds in doing this, B is prevented, for all practical purposes, from bringing to the fore any issues that might in their resolution be seriously detrimental to A's set of preferences.[64]

This same effect can be achieved whether elites covertly control social values or overtly control the mechanism through which wants and demands are transmitted to government. In either case, issues do not receive governmental attention without the approval of the elite. Nor is it obvious to the casual observer that such demands exist, for they remain silent and unarticulated. Since such issues never enter the visible political arena, they arouse no perceptible conflict or debate.

Elite Perception of Mass Attitudes. Given the relative freedom of elites from pressure from below, it should be understood that this freedom varies with the type of issue. In the case of the reduction of tariffs, the low level of public visibility (interest in the issue) undoubtedly contributed to elite freedom. Some evidence for the relationship between issue visibility and congruence of attitude between elites and masses can be gleaned from a study of the interrelations between constituency attitude and congressional attitude in three key areas of public policy: social welfare, foreign affairs, and civil rights. The

---

[62] Bauer, Pool, and Dexter, *American Business and Public Policy.*
[63] E. E. Schattschneider, *The Semisovereign People: A Realist's View of Democracy in America* (New York: Holt, Rinehart, and Winston, 1960), p. 71; and Robert A. Dahl, "A Critique of the Power Elite Model," *American Political Science Review,* 52 (June 1958), 468.
[64] Peter Bachrach and Morton S. Baratz, "Two Faces of Power," in Willis D. Hawley and Frederick M. Wirt (eds.) *The Search for Community Power* (Englewood Cliffs, N. J.: Prentice-Hall, 1968), pp. 241–242. Also see Peter Bachrach, *The Theory of Democratic Elitism: A Critique* (Boston: Little, Brown and Co., 1967). A critical appraisal of this analysis is contained in Richard M. Merelman, "On the Neo-elitist Critique of Community Power," *American Political Science Review,* 62 (June 1968), 451–460.

greatest agreement between the representative and his constituents occurred in the area of civil rights, the next closest in the area of welfare, and the smallest correlation in the area of foreign affairs.[65] Civil rights clearly provokes more interest than social welfare or foreign policy and seems to require that the congressman conform more closely to the wishes of his constituents.

We have already noted that communications between elites and masses are tenuous and that perceptions of mass opinions by elites are distorted. The crucial question, then, is to what extent does the actual voting behavior of the representative reflect the attitudes of constituents, rather than the representative's *perception* of these attitudes? As Figure 5–1 shows, there is generally a stronger correlation between constituency attitude and the representative's *perception* of constituency attitude than there is between constituency attitude and the representative's actual attitude. For example, the association between constituency attitude and the representative's attitude on the question of civil rights is only .39, while the correlation between constituency attitude and the representative's *perception* of constituency attitude is .63. Naturally, since congressmen select the groups with which they wish to communicate, their perception of constituency attitudes is distorted. The greatest correlation occurs between the representative's vote and his perception of his constituents' attitudes, while the weakest correlation occurs between the representative's vote and the actual attitude of his constituents. Thus, perceptual distortions are translated into actual voting behavior. Only on the issue of civil rights are legislators acting in reasonable conformity to the attitudes of the people.

There is no evidence to suggest that a congressman will alter his behavior in accordance with his perceptions of constituents' attitudes. Charles Jones groups members of the House of Representatives into

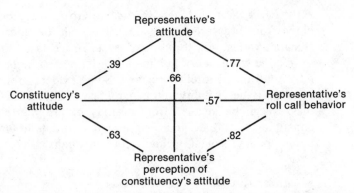

FIGURE 5–1.
Intercorrelations of Variables Pertaining to Civil Rights

Source: Warren E. Miller and Donald E. Stokes, "Constituency Influence in Congress," *American Political Science Review*, 57: 1 (March 1963), 45–56.

[65]Warren E. Miller and Donald E. Stokes, "Constituency Influence in Congress," *American Political Science Review*, 57: 1 (March 1963), 45–56.

three categories: those whose margin of victory from one election to the next was reduced by 5 percent or more, those whose margin was reduced by less than 5 percent, and those who increased their margin of victory. He reasons that if the campaign and election are not issue-oriented events, there should be no difference in changes in voting behavior between these three groups. Alternatively, if the election *is* issue-oriented, the group of congressmen who suffered the greatest decrease in margin of victory should be expected to change their behavior more radically, since they should perceive from the election results that many constituents disapprove of their voting behavior. He finds that there is no appreciable difference between any of the groups, whether the election is issue-oriented or not. Indeed, the representatives who suffered the greatest decline in support exhibited the least change in voting behavior.[66] Thus, even though representatives perceive the outcome of an election to be related directly to their voting behavior, they do not change their behavior because of the results of an election.

The persistence of voting patterns indicates that congressmen do not necessarily respond uncritically to constituent demands. No evidence of the self-perception of congressmen is available, but the self-images of state legislators support this assertion. Wahlke, Eulau, Buchanan, and Ferguson found that the majority of representatives filled the role of the *trustee*; that is, they believed that the representative is a free agent who should follow the dictates of his conscience.[67] The delegate role, an alternative orientation which holds that the representative should act according to the constituency's wishes, was filled by about 25 percent of the legislators. Miller and Stokes, on the other hand, concluded from their research that no single model of representative behavior can be adequate to explain their data. On the issue of civil rights, the representatives behaved more like delegates; on foreign policy, they behaved more like trustees.[68] Although it is unwise to make inferences from these data beyond the setting in which they were gathered, we can at least conclude that elites do not regard effective communication with constituents as a prerequisite for rational decision making.

TV and the Liberal Establishment Bias. It is chiefly by mass media that elites instruct masses about politics. Network television is far more important in elite-to-mass communication than newspapers; the masses watch television hours each day, but seldom do more than glance through newspapers. Television broadcasting in America is overwhelmingly controlled by three private corporations—the American Broadcasting Company (ABC), National Broadcasting Corporation (NBC), and Columbia Broadcasting System (CBS). They deter-

---

[66] Charles O. Jones, "The Role of the Campaign in Congressional Politics," in Zeigler and Jennings (eds.) *The Electoral Process* (Englewood Cliffs, N. J.: Prentice-Hall, 1966), p. 36.
[67] Wahlke, Eulau, Buchanan, and Ferguson, *The Legislative System: Explorations in Legislative Behavior* (New York: John Wiley, 1962), p. 281.
[68] Miller and Stokes, "Constituency Influence in Congress," pp. 45–56.

mine almost all that will be seen by the viewing audience; there is little public regulation of network broadcasting. Individual television stations are privately owned and licensed to use public broadcast channels by the Federal Communication Commission. All but a few of the largest and wealthiest of these stations are forced to receive news and programming from the networks because of the high production costs involved in *producing* news or entertainment at the local station level. The top officials of the networks, particularly those in charge of the news, are indeed "a tiny, enclosed fraternity of privileged men."[69]

This elite permits far *less* diversity of views on television than is in the press, which presents a wide spectrum of views. Conventionally "liberal" and "conservative" news can be found, respectively, in such publications as: *The New York Times* versus *The Chicago Tribune; Time Magazine* versus *U.S. News and World Report; The New York Post* versus *The Wall Street Journal; The New Republic* versus *The National Review; The Village Voice* versus *Barron's Weekly*. One reason for this greater diversity in print than in television is the mass appeal of television versus the specialized appeal of print. The larger the audience, the less the opportunity to satisfy a well-articulated ideological constituency. As the audience for television grows, so does the proportion of people relying upon it primarily for their view of what is happening. Given the general apathy of the masses, the growth of television as an information source was inevitable. Reading about politics is largely the information-gathering device of the educated strata; passively observing the playing out of a political drama is a characteristic of the less educated masses.

Granted that television is truly mass (e.g., unspecialized) communication, and granted that it takes very little effort to flip on the set, networks—and politicians—seem to have overestimated the audience for the major networks' nightly news shows. About 20 percent of the adult population are *regular* news viewers and 80 percent irregular or non-news viewers. Indeed, a slight majority of the population watches *no* network news![70]

Most people watch television to be entertained, not informed. For in-depth information, the half-hour news format is unsatisfactory. So, network news resembles entertainment—but without the audience entertainment has. Norman Nie, drawing upon the extensive research of Gary Steiner, concludes: "When citizens have the opportunity to choose between public information and entertainment, they choose entertainment."[71] These data call into question the popular view of an entire nation waiting breathlessly for the latest *pronunciamentos* from David Brinkley. Once again, elites transfer to masses their own intense

[69] The phraseology is courtesy of Vice President Spiro T. Agnew, who also used the more colorful description of the network top brass—"super-sensitive, self-anointed, supercilious electronic barons of opinion." See *Newsweek* (November 9, 1970), p. 22.
[70] John P. Robinson, "The Audience for National TV News Programs," *Public Opinion Quarterly*, 35 (Fall 1971), 403–404.
[71] Norman Nie, "Communication and Citizen Participation," in Harold Sackman and Norman Nie, *The Information Utility and Social Choice* (Montvale, N.J.: AFIPS Press, 1970), p. 239. See also Gary A. Steiner, *The People Look at Television: A Study of Audience Attitudes* (New York: Knopf, 1963), p. 201.

interest in politics: Because these elites *believe* that news commentators attract huge audiences they tend to treat them as a surrogate public. Even so, 20 percent of the adult population is larger than the readership of the mass-circulation weekly news sources or newspapers.

If the audience for TV news is smaller than most people believe, it is still large and still characterized by a preponderance of less educated persons. That TV news programs have taken on a distinctly moderate-liberal, Eastern-establishment point of view is therefore ironic, because it falls upon the ears of those least likely to find it attractive, *if they perceive overt bias.* Although little empirical evidence for it has yet been gathered, the network news programs, with several conspicuous exceptions, have probably become liberalized on matters of public policy. As Hennessy argues: "The liberalization of the big media has been most noticeable with regard to Vietnam, but apparent too since 1965 on black power, poverty in America, military-industrial complex, environmental pollution, and most of the other quality-of-life issues the new left is seized with."[72]

Such a bias is most likely to appear in the selection of topics to be covered. As David Brinkley explained candidly, "News is what I say it is. It's something worth knowing by my standards."[73] In newspaper reporting, such selection (or "agenda-setting") is possible, but less necessary. On a half-hour news program, *most* of what has happened in the past 24 hours must be excluded. But Brinkley is only part right. The agenda-setting of news broadcasts is partially a function of the entertainment or dramatic potential of the story. There can be very little background analysis; there must be "action." Stories are therefore chosen for their dramatic quality; "people doing something, preferably involving disagreement, conflict, or adventure."[74] Thus, news programs and other media might be significant in telling people *what* they should have opinions about even if they do not sell them an opinion.

Mr. Agnew's protest that TV news showed the bad side of America was correct. The bad side is more interesting and intriguing to watch, and TV is in the business of attracting large audiences who will buy the products offered by its sponsors. A particularly intriguing piece of evidence bears upon the presentation of the "worst" about America (e.g., riots, protests, the Vietnamese War). Comparison of CBS Evening News with the Canadian counterpart, CBC National News, indicates that the American News concentrated much more of its time to violence, protest, and war. Even cancelling out the effects of the Vietnam War, CBS news is bloody compared to CBC (CBC, by arrangement, originates about 20 percent of its news from CBS and NBC). Of course, one can hardly conclude that CBS "distorts reality." One can just as easily argue that since America is considerably more

---

[72] Bernard Hennessy, "Welcome, Spiro Agnew," *The New Republic* (December 13, 1969), p. 14. Edith Efron, *The News Twisters* (Los Angeles: Nash, 1971), makes much the same point. Unfortunately, the content analyses upon which she bases her conclusions are methodologically faulty.

[73] Efron, *op. cit.*, p. 6.

[74] Herbert J. Gans, "How Well Does TV Present the News?", *New York Times Magazine* (January 11, 1970), p. 32.

violent than Canada,[75] CBS is simply telling it like it is. The author of the study concludes that the heavy dose of violence in American television news might be a function of three factors: (1) passive reporting of a violent society, (2) reflections of popular interest in violence, or (3) an emphasis by TV on the more violent aspects of life in America.[76]

Assuming, then, that through a combination of editorial bias in selection, the necessity to entertain the audience, and the responsibility to report (with inevitable bias) the unpleasant facts about life in America, the TV audience is told what to think about — to what extent does the presentation of news induce any appreciable change in attitude?

By most evidence, mass media do not change opinion. For example, media coverage of the 1968 Democratic Convention was biased, according to Efron, for the rioters and against the police.[77] Contrary to the expectations of the newscasters, public opinion samples revealed that the masses remained unsympathetic to anti-war demonstrators, and the networks were flooded with mail protesting the newsmen's interpretation of events. What had happened is quite predictable. People "selectively perceive" reality: What the media present and what people see are often quite different. Selective perception is especially applicable to TV because of the low attention level required to absorb information. The media thought they were presenting a picture of innocent "kids" being brutally assaulted; people saw radical troublemakers getting what they deserved. Previously, when the ghetto riots were in full swing, the Kerner Commission concluded that TV coverage emphasized the control of riots and the activities of police in restoring order rather than actual acts of violence.[78] Yet most of the ghetto dwellers remembered TV as depicting the actual riot, with only a few remembering arrests and crowd control.[79] Finally, there is Vietnam. Presumably, Americans were made more aware of the horrors of death by the uniqueness of the "Living Room War." However, Mueller finds that events reported on TV — the Tet offensive, General Westmoreland's retirement, the emergence of peace candidates, etc. — did not have enough impact to "reduce support for the war below the levels attained by the Korean War, when television was in its infancy, until casualty levels had far surpassed those of the earlier war."[80]

Attitudes — particularly deeply held ones — are not changed easily. The liberal-establishment bias runs into strong resistance: the filtering mechanics of the human perceptual system. Perceptions of reality — as distinguished from attitudes — might be more amenable to manipula-

[75] Ted Robert Gurr, "A Comparative Study of Civil Strife," in Hugh Davis Graham and Ted Robert Gurr, *Violence in America* (New York: Signet, 1969), p. 550.
[76] Benjamin D. Singer, "Violence, Protest, and War in TV News," *Public Opinion Quarterly*, 34 (Winter 1970–71), 612.
[77] Efron, *op. cit.*, p. 178.
[78] Report of the National Advisory Commission on Civil Disorders (New York: Bantam, 1969), p. 369.
[79] Benjamin D. Singer, "Mass Media and Communication Processes in the Detroit Riot of 1967," *Public Opinion Quarterly*, 34 (Summer 1970), 239.
[80] John E. Mueller, "Trends in Popular Support for the Wars in Korea and Vietnam," *American Political Science Review*, 65 (June 1971), 374.

tion. In spite of occasional protests and the support for Agnew's attacks on the media, most people think TV is unbiased. (Those who watch it most, the relatively uneducated, think it is less biased than those who watch it least, the college educated.) Thus, information from a relatively trusted source might gradually change images of reality. For instance, although the majority still supported the government's position in Vietnam, the percentage believing the Americans and South Vietnamese were losing ground rose 15 percent after the 1968 Tet offensive. While attitudes remained firm, the government's assurances that we were winning became suspect as the siege of Saigon unfolded.[81]

It is possible, then, that a *gradual* erosion of confidence, rather than an immediate change in attitude or behavior, can take place.[82] But even if it is indeed occurring, it has little to do with the overt bias of newscasters and much to do with slowly altered images of reality over which the media have little control. We began this section by asserting that elites use media to instruct masses. We can conclude that quite a bit is lost in the translation. Most Americans now believe there is genuine danger of social and political disintegration. The liberal establishment (in this case, television news reporters) believes the causes of disintegration are systemic. The masses, agreeing that "the country is going to hell," do not accept or understand systemic explanations and look for scapegoats.

Mass Perception of Elite Roles. Given the fact that the representative has extremely imperfect information about the preference of his constituency, and given the complementary fact that the constituency is unaware of most of the policy stands of the representative, it seems likely that the delegate role is rarely played by congressmen. The constituency may well believe that this role is appropriate, but they are not able to make it a possibility. For example, one study indicates that only 18 percent of a sample of constituents have a trustee perception of legislators. Twenty-six percent of the respondents supported both delegate and trustee models simultaneously; and by far the largest group, 47 percent, felt that representatives should behave as instructed delegates.[83] In relating these varying perceptions of the proper role of the legislator to certain socioeconomic characteristics of the respondents, the researchers found that the upper socioeconomic groups were more likely to support the trustee perception than were the lower socioeconomic groups. For example, only 3 percent of those with grade school education have trustee orientations, compared to 25 percent of those with college education (Table 5–7). Similarly, professional and managerial occupations provide a high proportion of the support for the trustee role. The greatest commitment to the delegate role occurs among the lower strata of society, those who are least

[81] Richard H. Pride, "Television Network News: Re-thinking the Iceberg Problems," *Western Political Quarterly,* forthcoming.
[82] Pride. *op. cit.*
[83] Carl D. McMurray and Malcolm B. Parsons, "Public Attitudes toward the Representational Roles of Legislators and Judges," *Midwest Journal of Political Science,* 9:2 (May 1965), 167–185.

Education	Instructed Delegate	Trustee	Ambivalent	Politico
Grade school	50%	3%	47%	
High school	49	17	23	11%
College	43	25	22	10

Source: Carl D. McMurray and Malcolm B. Parsons, "Public Attitudes toward the Representational Roles of Legislators and Judges," *Midwest Journal of Political Science*, 9:2 (May 1965), 167–185.

likely to take an active role in the political process. Nearly 60 percent of the nonparticipants in politics support the delegate role, as against 35 percent of the high participants. Ironically, the citizens most jealous of their potential for control over elites are those least likely to try to use that control.

Summary   Most Americans support the norms and ideals of democracy in principle; however, there is a disparity between support in principle and support in practice. Only a fraction of Americans support democracy in practice. It is our contention that the disparity can best be explained in terms of elites and masses, for, in general, elites are more consistent in their support of democracy in both practice and principle than are the masses.

Perhaps the single greatest variable accounting for this phenomenon is education. The active political elites tend to be better educated than their non-active followers. Intellectual and psychological flexibility, levels of information, tolerance, and positive attachment to the social and political environment have all been found to increase with education. Each of these factors contributes to the ability and to the willingness of the well educated—the elites—to actively support the democratic principles in which they believe.

Those lower on the education scale feel politically helpless and have a lower capacity for relating ideology to action. The former characteristic leads to "scapegoating" and prejudice born of frustration; the latter contributes to inconsistency between avowed principles and actual behavior. Indicative of the masses' inability to achieve intellectual consistency is the fact that they highly favor *economic* liberalism but at the same time register a marked preference for authoritarian, classical conservatism. Elites, on the other hand, tend to be liberal in both political and economic dimensions. The single notable exception to elite liberalism is the military elite, who are highly educated but also authoritarian and not committed to the procedural norms or democratic political ideology.

Given the authoritarian, direct-action bias of the masses, it is at first glance improbable that procedural democracy in America should survive. One is tempted to attribute the stability of American democracy to the actions of the elites, who possess the resources, the power, and the inclination to protect it. This conclusion would be inaccurate, however, for in times of crisis, the leadership of the elites has failed to provide a protective bulwark against anti-democratic forces. Ironically, it is to the poorly educated masses—those who are least committed to democratic norms—that the stability of American democracy is to be attributed. Although the poorly educated tend toward authoritarianism, violence, and prejudice, they are also apathetic; they fail to take action on their beliefs. Of course, mass inaction is partially caused by elites, since they can effectively bar the demands of the masses from the political system.

Yet another paradox exists with respect to the differing concepts of the elites and the masses concerning the proper role of legislators. Partially as a result of poor communications, the legislative elite is not responsive to the attitudes of the masses. Yet the masses perceive the role of the legislator to be that of a delegate whose function it is to act on the basis of constituency demands. Moreover, the masses fail to register their demands through the participative channel ostensibly available to them. Conversely, the better-educated, more politically active strata of society perceive legislators as trustees, who should act on their own interpretations of the public interest. The congruence of attitudes between legislators and other elites no doubt goes a long way in explaining such permissiveness among the well educated.

Selected Additional Readings

Bachrach, Peter. *The Theory of Democratic Elitism: A Critique.* Boston: Little, Brown and Co. (Basic Studies in Politics Series), 1967. As the title suggests, this is a theoretical work that recognizes the reality of socio-political elitism. Bachrach presents a concise, readable treatise evaluating the various interpretations of American democracy.

Edelman, Murray. *The Symbolic Uses of Politics.* Chicago: University of Illinois Press (Illini Books edition), 1967. This well written monograph convincingly argues that the masses are frequently pacified in political activity by symbolic rather than actual rewards.

Fromm, Erich. *Escape from Freedom.* New York: Avon Books (paperback), 1965. Fromm presents a stimulating psychological account of forces which may contribute to anti-democratic attitudes among the masses. Originally published in 1941, its insights remain timely today.

Lane, Robert E. *Political Life.* New York: Macmillan Co. (Free Press edition), 1965. Part III of this book is a social-psychological description of the political life of the American citizenry. Part V analyzes the effects of certain social institutions upon that life. Lane's work complements the material presented in *The Irony of Democracy.*

Lipset, Seymour Martin. *Political Man.* Garden City, N.Y.: Doubleday & Co. (Anchor Books edition), 1963. This interpretation of American politics by an eminent political sociologist covers a myriad of factors that affect or are affected by the dynamics of political activity. Parts I and III—respectively entitled "The Conditions of the Democratic Order" and "Political Behavior in American Society"—are particularly germane to the discussion in this chapter.

Schattschneider, E. E. *The Semisovereign People: A Realist's View of Democracy in America.* New York: Holt, Rinehart and Winston (paperback), 1960. This concise, well written book provides empirical evidence supporting our thesis and furnishes additional insights into the relationships between elites and masses.

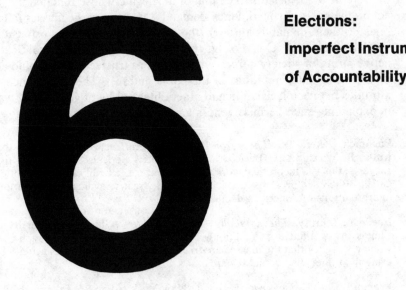

**Elections:
Imperfect Instruments
of Accountability**

Can masses hold elites responsible through elections? Over half a million governmental officials are chosen through the ballot in America, but the extent of popular control of government through elections is undetermined. Although voters help to select the men who occupy prominent positions in government, voters do not order troops to Vietnam, or enact civil rights laws, or write tax legislation; and the effect of elections on these and other actions by governmental elites is unclear. The ballot is widely considered a panacea for social ills, but there is little evidence that voters can directly affect public policy through the exercise of their franchise.

In order for elections to serve as mandates, and for voters to exercise influence over public policy through elections, four conditions would need to be fulfilled: (1) Competing candidates would offer clear policy alternatives; (2) voters would be concerned with policy questions; (3) majority preferences on these questions could be ascertained in election results; (4) elected officials would be bound by the positions they assumed during the campaign.

In this chapter and the next, we shall contend that none of these conditions are fulfilled in American politics and, consequently, that voters cannot exercise direct control over public policy. First of all, the parties do not offer clear policy alternatives. Both parties agree on the major direction of public policy; they disagree only over the *means* of implementing public policy. Therefore, the voters cannot influence public policy by choosing between the parties.

Moreover, voter decisions are not motivated primarily by policy considerations. For a mandate to be valid, the electorate must make informed, *policy-oriented* choices; but traditional party ties and candidate personalities are more influential in most voting decisions than are policy questions. When voters cast their ballot because of traditional party ties, their party loyalty dilutes their influence over policy.

Even if the voters were primarily concerned with policy questions, it would be difficult to ascertain majority preferences on these questions from the election results. Victory for the party of a candidate does not necessarily mean that the voters support that party's programs. For one reason, voters are inconsistent in their policy preferences, and they frequently misinterpret or pay little attention to the policy preferences of a candidate. Generally a candidate's voters include not only advocates of his position but also some who oppose his position, as well as some who vote for him for other reasons. Moreover, a popular majority may really be composed of many policy minorities. How is a candidate to know which of his policy positions resulted in his election? It is unlikely that his election can be interpreted as a mandate for *all* of his policy positions.

Finally, in order for voters to exercise control over public officials through elections, it would be necessary for elected officials to be bound by their campaign pledges. Needless to say, campaign pledges are frequently ignored by elected officials.

The Vietnam War provides an interesting illustration of the difficulties in controlling public officials through elections. In 1964, President Johnson's victory over Barry Goldwater was widely attributed to a popular desire for military restraint and avoidance of escalation. In the campaign, Goldwater presented a more "hawkish" image than President Johnson, who projected an image of restraint and responsibility toward American involvement in Vietnam. Yet detailed examination of voter opinion suggests that hawks and doves among the voters did not divide themselves into supporters of Goldwater and Johnson respectively. Actually, Johnson won the support of a majority of both hawks and doves. While 63 percent of those favoring withdrawal from Vietnam voted for the President, so did 52 percent of those favoring "a stronger stand even if it means invading North Vietnam." Johnson also won 82 percent of those who prefer to keep our soldiers in Vietnam, but try to end the fighting. Thus, opinion surveys suggest that Johnson's victory was *not* a mandate for any particular policy in Vietnam.

Of course, once elected, Johnson violated his implied pledge to avoid escalation of the war. True, it is not clear that Johnson was going against the wishes of the voting majority, since they had given no explicit command on Vietnam, but the President did pursue a policy at variance with his election campaign image. Goldwater could rightly claim that Johnson was pursuing policies that he had earlier criticized Goldwater for proposing.

Thus, the 1964 elections did not provide the voters with an opportunity for influencing the direction of policy in Vietnam. Even though the candidates provided reasonably clear policy alternatives, there is no evidence that the voters were concerned primarily with the question of the Vietnam War in their voting decisions, or that the election of Johnson clearly revealed a majority preference for military restraint. And, in any case, Johnson did not keep his campaign pledges about Vietnam policy.

The Functions of Elections

If elections do not provide a means for voters to exercise direct control over public policy, what is the purpose of elections? Elections are primarily a symbolic exercise for the masses to help tie them to the established order. Political scientist Murray Edelman agrees that voters have little effect on public policy and contends that elections are primarily "symbolic reassurance." According to Edelman, elections serve to "quiet resentments and doubts about particular political acts, reaffirm belief in the fundamental rationality and democratic character of the system, and thus fix conforming habits of future behavior."[1] Even though electoral participation does not permit the masses to determine public policy, it nonetheless gives them a feeling that they play a role in the political system.

The second function of elections is to give the masses an opportunity to express themselves about the conduct of the public officials who have been in power. Elections do not permit the masses to direct *future* events, but they do permit the masses to render judgment about *past* political conduct. For example, in 1968, voters could not choose a specific policy by voting for Nixon. They had no way of knowing what policies Nixon would follow in Vietnam, because Nixon did not set forth any specific proposals regarding that conflict. But the voters *were* able to express their discontent with Johnson's handling of the war by voting against a continuation of the Democratic administration. As Gerald Pomper explains:

> The voters employ their powerful sanction retrospectively. They judge the politician after he has acted, finding personal satisfactions or discontents as the results of these actions. . . . The issue of Viet Nam is illustrative. . . . For their part, critics of the war did not emphasize their own alternative policies, but instead concentrated on retrospective and adverse judgments. . . . Declining public support of the war brought all major candidates to promise its end. The Republican Party, and particularly Richard Nixon, joined in this pledge, but provided no specific programs, instead seeking the support of all voters inclined to criticize past actions.[2]

Pomper also asserts that the voters' retrospective judgment on past administrations may have an impact on the behavior of current and future elected officials. Pomper contends, rather optimistically, that even though the voters have no *power* over government, they nonetheless have an *influence* on government. He accepts Carl Friedrich's definition of influence: "Influence flows into the human relation whenever the influencer's reaction might spell disadvantage and even disaster for the actor, who foresees the effect the action might have and alters more or less in accordance with his foresight."[3] Pomper contends that because "politicians might be affected by the voters in the next election, they regulate their conduct appropriately."[4]

But he fails to say how elected officials are supposed to know the sentiments of voters on policy questions in order to "regulate their

---

[1] Murray Edelman, *The Symbolic Uses of Politics* (Urbana: University of Illinois Press, 1964), p. 17.
[2] Gerald Pomper, *Elections in America: Control and Influence in Democratic Politics* (New York: Dodd, Mead, & Co., 1968), pp. 255–256.
[3] Carl Friedrich, *Man and His Government* (New York: McGraw-Hill Book Co., 1963), pp. 199–201.
[4] Pomper, *Elections in America*, p. 254.

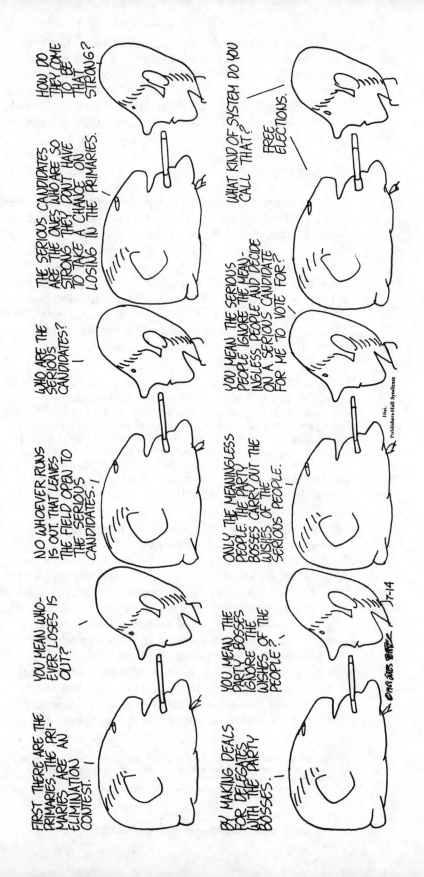

conduct appropriately." As we shall see, most voters do not have an opinion that can be communicated to elected officials; and elected officials have no way of interpreting voters' policy preferences from electoral results. By ousting the Democratic administration from power in 1968, were the voters saying they wanted a military victory in Vietnam? Or were they saying they wanted a negotiated peace and compromise with the Viet Cong?

Perhaps all that we can really say is that the retrospective judgment that voters can render in an election helps to make governing elites sensitive to mass welfare. Elections do not permit masses to decide what should be done in their interests, but they do encourage governing elites to consider the welfare of the masses. Knowing that a day of reckoning will come on election day, elected officials strive to make a good impression on the voters in the meantime.

> The existence of the vote does not make politicians better as individuals; it simply forces them to give greater consideration to demands of enfranchised and sizeable groups, who hold a weapon of potentially great force. . . . The ability to punish politicians is probably the most important weapon available to citizens. It is direct, authoritative, and free from official control.[5]

It has been argued that elections have a third function—that of protecting individuals and groups from official abuse. John Stuart Mill wrote: "Men, as well as women, do not need political rights in order that they might govern, but in order that they not be misgoverned."[6] He went on:

> Rulers in ruling classes are under a necessity of considering the interests of those who have the suffrage; but of those who are excluded, it is in their option whether they will do so or not, and however honestly disposed, they are in general too fully occupied with things they must attend to, to have much room in their thoughts for anything which they can with impunity disregard.[7]

Certainly the long history of efforts to insure Negro voting rights in the South suggests that many concerned Americans believed that if Negroes could secure access to the polls, they could better protect themselves from official discrimination. Some major steps in the struggle for voting rights were the abolishment of the "white primary" in 1944; the Civil Rights Acts of 1957, 1960, 1964, and 1965, all of which contained provisions guaranteeing free access to the polls; and the Twenty-fourth Amendment to the Constitution which eliminated poll taxes. But the high hopes stirred by the development of new law were often followed by frustration and disillusionment when Negroes

---

[5]Pomper, pp. 254–255.
[6]John Stuart Mill, *Considerations on Representative Government* (Chicago: Henry Regnery, Gateway edition, 1962), p. 144.
[7]Mill, pp. 130–131.

realized that their problems could not be solved through the electoral process alone. No doubt William R. Keech is correct when he asserts that the vote is a symbol of full citizenship and equal rights, which may contribute to Negro self-respect.[8] But it is still open to question how much Negroes can gain through the exercise of their vote. In the North, Negroes have voted freely for decades, but conditions in the urban ghettos have not been measurably improved through political action. In signing the Voting Rights Act of 1965, President Johnson said:

> The right to vote is the most basic right, without which all others are meaningless. It gives people—people as individuals—control over their own destinies. . . . The vote is the most powerful instrument ever devised by man for breaking down injustice and destroying the terrible walls which imprison men because they are different from other men.

But the Negro experience in both the North and the South suggests that the ballot cannot eliminate discrimination, much less enable men to "control their own destinies." It is probably true that men can *better* protect themselves from government abuse when they possess and exercise their voting rights, but the right to vote is not a guarantee against discrimination.

The Ignorance of the Electorate If elections are to be a means of popular control over public policy, voters must be reasonably well informed about policy issues and must hold opinions on these issues. Yet available evidence suggests that large numbers of the electorate are politically uninformed and inarticulate.

Some years ago, public-opinion analysts reported what is now a typical finding about the low level of political information among adult Americans (see Table 6–1). Only about one half of the public knew the elementary fact that each state has two United States senators; fewer still knew the length of the terms of congressmen or the number of Supreme Court Justices.[9]

Herbert McClosky discovered that 28 percent of the public was unable (or unwilling) to classify itself as either "liberal," "middle-of-the road," or "conservative."[10] In contrast, only a tiny fraction of the elite was unable to do so. Further, the ordinary voters who did classify themselves showed a poor understanding of the components of an ideology. McClosky and his associates devised a scale of conservatism constructed from the writings of conservative political philosophers. In applying this scale to the mass electorate, he found that the way the respondents classified themselves was unrelated, in many cases, to the objective classification of the respondent on the conservatism scale.

[8]William R. Keech, *The Impact of Negro Voting: The Role of the Vote in the Quest for Equality* (Chicago: Rand McNally, 1968), p.3.
[9]Fred I. Greenstein, *The American Party System and the American People* (Englewood Cliffs, N. J.: Prentice-Hall, 1963), p. 12.
[10]Herbert McClosky, "Consensus and Ideology in American Politics," *American Political Science Review*, 58: 2 (June 1964), 372.

TABLE 6–1.
Proportion of Adult
Americans Informed
about Various
Aspects of the
American
Political System

	Percentage of Correct Responses
How many senators are there in Washington from your state?	55
When a man is elected to the United States House of Representatives, how many years does he serve in one term of office?	47
Do you happen to know whether all United States Senators come up for re-election this fall?	46
Can you tell me how many justices there are normally on the United States Supreme Court, including the Chief Justice?	40
Do you happen to know whether federal or state governments make the laws about who can vote in a presidential election?	33
What do you know about the Bill of Rights? Do you know anything it says?	23

Source: Fred I. Greenstein, *The American Party System and the American People* (Englewood Cliffs, N. J.: Prentice-Hall, 1963).

Typically, elites wage their battles over political issues, while the unconcerned masses occupy themselves with other matters. Even an issue such as the Vietnam War had difficulty in penetrating to a significant degree. In the 1968 Democratic primaries, Senators Eugene McCarthy and Robert Kennedy waged strenuous campaigns based largely upon their opposition to the Vietnam War; yet about two thirds of the voters were unable to identify the position of these candidates on the war.[11]

The failure of voters to identify the position of peace candidates led them, more often than not, to vote for the opposite of their policy preferences. In the New Hampshire primary, McCarthy voters were actually angry with Johnson for not pursuing the war effort more vigorously! McCarthy's good showing against an incumbent president led elites to conclude that there was a sufficiently large "dove" contingent among the electorate to justify serious consideration.[12] Certainly Johnson's decision to attempt de-escalation was influenced by the primary results, as was Robert Kennedy's decision to enter the presidential contest. In a sense, then, though elite behavior is influenced by elections, the influence is a garbled message. Elites assume masses have policy preferences and vote according to them. Elites, who follow news of political affairs extensively, observed the inordinate amount of media coverage given to the McCarthy campaign and probably reasoned that no one could have escaped knowledge of McCarthy's position.

One could legitimately argue that the electorate should not be expected to inform itself about complicated political issues. In general, one could expect that the more complicated the issue, the less information will filter down to the masses. But it can be demonstrated that substantial portions of the mass electorate cannot identify even such clearly symbolic terms as "Cold War," "monopoly," "welfare state," "GOP," and "fallout." Accurate information about political

[11]Public opinion survey in Oregon by Ray Bardsley (not published).
[12]Philip E. Converse, *et al.*, "Continuity and Change in American Politics: Parties and Issues in the 1968 Election," *American Political Science Review*, 69 (December 1969), 1095.

issues is confined to those with superior education. For example, Campbell, Converse, Miller, and Stokes found that 59 percent of those who had attended college were familiar with a variety of domestic and foreign policy issues, compared to 31 percent of those who had attended high school and 21 percent of those who had attended school through the eighth grade.[13] Perhaps it is a truism to observe this relationship; for the purpose of education is, of course, to increase knowledge.

<table>
<tr><td rowspan="2">**TABLE 6–2.**
Education and
Familiarity with
Policy Issues</td><td>Familiarity
with
Issues</td><td>Less Than
8 Years
of School</td><td>High
School</td><td>College</td></tr>
<tr><td>High</td><td>21%</td><td>31%</td><td>50%</td></tr>
<tr><td></td><td>Medium</td><td>37</td><td>47</td><td>44</td></tr>
<tr><td></td><td>Low</td><td>42</td><td>22</td><td>6</td></tr>
<tr><td></td><td>Total</td><td>100</td><td>100</td><td>100</td></tr>
</table>

Source: A. Campbell, P. Converse, W. Miller, and D. Stokes, *The American Voter* (New York: John Wiley, 1960), p. 175.

Contradictions in the Beliefs of Masses

Closely related to the fact that the masses have less information than the elite is the inability of the masses to sort out and relate information that they do possess. We are all familiar with the vagaries of elections and have come to expect that the public will offer simultaneous approval to candidates with fundamentally different outlooks. Such apparent contradictions can be explained partially by low levels of information and low awareness of candidate position. However, it is equally likely that broad segments of the public hold opinions that are contradictory, as a study by Philip Converse shows. Converse uses the word *constraint* to describe the success we might have in predicting a person's attitude in one area if we know his opinion in another. If, for example, we know that a person believes that the federal government should reduce its aid to education, can we assume that this person also wishes the federal government to reduce its spending in other areas? If a person is opposed to expansion of social security, is he also opposed to progressive income tax? Most elite observations of mass behavior assume that constraints are present within the belief systems of the masses. In fact, they are conspicuously *absent*.[14]

Except for those issues which are unusually salient to large numbers of people (such as civil rights), constraints do not characterize the attitude structure of mass publics toward domestic issues. For example, those who support an enlargement of public services do not necessarily support taxes to pay for these services. In fact, many of those persons who support a tax cut also favor federal expansion of welfare measures.

[13]A. Campbell, P. Converse, W. Miller, and D. Stokes, *The American Voter* (New York: John Wiley, 1960), p. 175.
[14]Philip E. Converse, "The Nature of Belief Systems in Mass Publics," in David E. Apter (ed.), *Ideology and Discontent* (New York: Free Press, 1964), p. 210.

Persons who hold inconsistent positions are most likely to come from the lower social strata. These people, although they demand an expansion of federal services and a reduction of the federal budget, hold extremely negative attitudes toward the worth of the services they require. Obviously, self-interest makes simultaneous support for tax reduction and expansion of federal welfare activities quite compatible; one might very well wish to have his tax burden reduced while enjoying the benefits of expanded services. However, for the political system as a whole, the combination of opinions described above is irrational. Even if the elite attempts to interpret and do what the masses want, it cannot satisfy both demands.

A possible reason for these inconsistencies is that the opinions that the masses are supposed to hold are frequently created by public opinion polls. For a substantial portion of the population the questions asked in opinion polls are meaningless; therefore, so are their answers. Many people have never thought about the question before it is asked and will never think about it again; the very absence of consistency in mass opinions is evidence of lack of interest. As one moves down the socioeconomic ladder from elites to masses, consistent political beliefs fade away rapidly. As constraints decline, objects of beliefs shift from abstract principles to simple and concrete goals. As Converse phrases it, the central focus of belief systems shifts from "ideological principles to the more obviously recognized social groups and chauvinistic leaders."[15]

In order to estimate the ability of the electorate to conceptualize, to think abstractly, the Survey Research Center examined the responses of the electorate to questions concerning the good and bad points of the two major parties.[16] The following categorization was derived. *Ideologues* are those respondents who are either "liberal" or "conservative" and are likely to rely upon abstract principles in their evaluation of candidates and issues. *Near ideologues* are those respondents who mentioned an abstract principle, but clearly did not place as much reliance upon it as did the ideologues. With the near ideologues, ideology was peripheral and used in a fashion that raised doubts about the understanding of the terms employed. The next level of respondents, the *group benefits* class, were those who did not exhibit any overriding ideological dimension in their thinking, but were able to evaluate parties and candidates in terms of expected favorable or unfavorable treatment for social groups. A favored candidate was seen as "for" a group with which the subject was identified. Politics, for the *group benefits* portion of the electorate, was perceived as an arena of group conflict. Unless an issue could be linked to the welfare of their own grouping, these respondents could not understand it well enough to respond appropriately to issues and candidates. A fourth level of conceptualization defines respondents whose judgment is

---

[15]Converse, "The Nature of Belief Systems," pp. 213–230.
[16]Campbell *et al., The American Voter*, p. 227.

based upon their perception of the *"goodness" or "badness" of the times*. They blame or praise parties and candidates because of their association with conditions of war or peace, prosperity or depression. This category of respondents also includes those whose only point of reference to public policy is a single issue with which they feel a unique personal identification. The last level includes those respondents whose evaluations of the political scene hold *no relationship whatever to policy*, even in the broadest and most symbolic use of the term. Some of these people profess a loyalty to one of the two parties but have no idea about the positions advocated by that party.

An examination of the entire electorate in terms of the various levels of conceptualization shows quite clearly that ideological commitments are significant in the political decisions of only a tiny fraction (see Table 6–3). Three and one half percent of the electorate are "ideologues," another 12 percent are "near ideologues," and the remainder display no ideological content in their evaluations.

TABLE 6–3. Relation of Education to Levels of Conceptualization, 1956	Grade School	High School	College
Ideologue	0%	2%	10%
Near ideologue	5	8	22
Group benefits	40	49	38
Nature of the times	29	25	20
No issue content	26	16	10
Total	100	100	100

Source: Adapted from Angus Campbell, Philip Converse, Warren Miller, and Donald E. Stokes, *The American Voter* (New York: John Wiley, 1960), p. 250.

It is clear, therefore, that the majority of the public does not conceptualize politics in the manner of the highly educated. Indeed, of the tiny fraction of the electorate classified as ideologues, 65 percent are highly educated. The proportion of highly educated respondents at each level of descending conceptualization drops consistently: 42 percent of the near ideologues are highly educated, but the proportion of highly educated respondents drops precipitously to 18 percent among those who perceive the political process in terms of group benefits. Only 17 percent of those who view candidates and issues in terms of the nature of the times, and a mere 11 percent of those who lack any issue content, are college educated. Thus, except for the small educated portion of the electorate, the ideological debate between the elites has very little meaning. Since the masses lack the interest and level of conceptualization of the educated, they cannot be expected to possess an organized ideology.

Converse has examined the levels of constraint among beliefs on a range of domestic and foreign issues in both an elite and a mass range population. The elite population for his study consisted of candidates for the United States Congress in the year 1958; however, Converse expects that the same properties of an elite would have been discovered if the elite had been any other group of politically active people. Table 6–4 provides the average coefficients of correlation between issues for both the elites and the masses. It can be seen that in every case there is a stronger correlation between beliefs on the part of elites than on the part of the masses. As Converse notes, "The strongest constraint within a domain for the mass public is less than that between domestic and foreign domains for the elite sample."[17]

TABLE 6–4. Summary of Differences in Level of Constraint within and between Domains	Average Coefficients			
	Within Domestic Issues	Between Domestic and Foreign	Within Foreign Issues	Between Issues and Party
Elite	.53	.25	.37	.39
Mass	.23	.11	.23	.11

Source: Adapted from Philip E. Converse, "The Nature of Belief Systems in Mass Publics," in David E. Apter (ed.), *Ideology and Discontent* (New York: Free Press, 1964).

Converse relates the unsophisticated conceptual processes of mass publics with the findings of McClosky, which were discussed in the previous chapter. Those findings showed that there was widespread support for abstract principles of democracy but substantially less support for specific application of these principles. Converse argues that the findings are less a demonstration of cynicism than a demonstration of the inability of the masses to link a specific case to a general principle. That is to say, the inconsistency is simply not recognized.

Another obstacle to mass influence over public policy is the instability of mass opinions. A longitudinal study of the electorate indicated that in responding to a particular controversy only about thirteen out of twenty people took the same side that they had taken four years earlier (ten out of twenty would have done so by chance alone). Indeed, an examination of the correlation between opinions over time indicates that, with the exception of party identification, there is a remarkable instability (Table 6–5). This instability suggests once again that issues and ideology are simply not relevant to the mass electorate. Furthermore, the most consistent attitudes relate to clearly identifiable groups, such as Negroes. Attitudes about school desegregation and federal employment practices commissions are substantially more stable than attitudes toward foreign policy. Evidently, the mass electorate thinks about race relations, but does not think about foreign policy unless someone happens to ask the question. Hence, the answers to questions about foreign policy vary randomly through time. This instability is, of course, also associated with an absence of information.

[17]Converse, "The Nature of Belief Systems," p. 229.

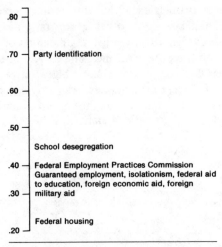

**TABLE 6–5.
Individual Stability
of Different Belief
Elements for
Individuals,
1958–1960**

.80 —

.70 — Party identification

.60 —

.50 —

School desegregation

.40 — Federal Employment Practices Commission
Guaranteed employment, isolationism, federal aid
to education, foreign economic aid, foreign
.30 — military aid

Federal housing
.20 —

Numbers are rank (*tau*ₐ) correlation between individual's
positions in 1958 and 1960 on the same items.

Source: Philip Converse, "The Nature of Belief Systems
in Mass Publics," in David E. Apter (ed.), *Ideology and Discontent* (New York: Free Press, 1964), p. 240.

Looking at the instability of mass attitudes, Converse concludes that "large portions of the electorate do not have meaningful beliefs, even on those issues that have formed the basis for intense political controversy among elites for substantial periods of time."[18] Edelman, reflecting upon the belief systems of masses, concludes that, rather than communicating demands to elites, masses absorb a crude and simplified version of elite attitudes.

The basic thesis is that mass publics respond to currently conspicuous political symbols: not to "facts," and not to moral codes embedded in the character or soul, but to the gestures and speeches that make up the drama of the state . . . The mass public does not study and analyze detailed data about secondary boycotts, provisions for stock ownership and control in a proposed space communications corporation, or missile installations in Cuba . . . It ignores these things until political actions and speeches make them symbolically threatening or reassuring and it then responds to the cues furnished by the actions and speeches, not to direct knowledge of the facts . . . It is therefore political actions that chiefly shape men's political wants and "knowledge," not the other way around. The common assumption that what democratic government does is somehow always a response to the moral codes, desires, and knowledge embedded inside people is as inverted as it is reassuring. This model, avidly taught and ritualistically repeated, cannot explain what happens; but it may persist in our folklore because it so effectively sanctifies prevailing policies and permits us to avoid worrying about them . . . The public is not in touch with the situation, and it "knows" the situation only through the symbols that engage it.[19]

[18]Converse, "The Nature of Belief Systems," p. 245.
[19]Edelman, *The Symbolic Uses of Politics,* p. 172.

Given the ignorance of the masses, one might wonder what is actually decided through elections. In congressional elections, the incumbent is usually re-elected. The tendency of the electorate to return incumbents to office, and the voters' lack of awareness of the policies of the challengers to incumbents, is related to the relatively low-keyed nature of congressional elections, especially in off-years. In presidential elections there is greater awareness of the candidates, but this does not necessarily mean that the issues are more completely discussed. It is somewhat disconcerting to examine the campaigns of presidential aspirants when we realize how little of the issue content of the candidates' efforts penetrates into the mass of the electorate.

The ideal model of democracy requires that the two major parties offer policy alternatives to the electorate and compete for votes on the basis of their contrasting programs. This competition helps keep the elite responsible. Therefore, the masses, although not necessarily completely informed about the explicit nature of the programs advocated by the elites, should at least be aware of the broad outline of a program.

In order for this model to work, the voters must perceive alternatives and determine which alternatives most closely match their own ideological positions. However, the preponderance of evidence suggests that voters are not capable of making choices along the lines suggested by the model. For example, in examining the responses of the electorate in the 1952 and 1956 elections, Campbell, Converse, Miller, and Stokes concluded that only about one third had an opinion, were aware of what the government was doing, and perceived a difference between the parties. This one third is the *maximum* pool of issue-oriented people. While it is true that the nature of the election influences to some extent the size of the issue-oriented portion of the electorate, it is probable that two thirds of the electorate make a choice unrelated to the issues raised by the competing candidates.

It is important to recognize that these blurred perceptions may be caused by the behavior of elites as much as by the ignorance of masses. If the parties do not, in fact, provide clear alternatives, then perhaps those who fail to perceive these alternatives are correct rather than uninformed. Party activists are separated by a wide ideological gulf, but party followers are not. For example, the leaders of the Democratic party are "liberal," and the leaders of the Republican party are "conservative" (when conservatism is measured in terms of economic policy). However, the extent to which these differences are translated into clear statements by either party is questionable, and most Democratic and Republican voters hold fairly similar opinions on most issues. Indeed, Republican voters' opinions are closer to the opinions of Democratic leaders than they are to those of Republican leaders. Thus, although the Republican party traditionally argues for reduced federal expenditures, rank-and-file Democrats are more likely to support cutting taxes than are rank-and-file Republicans. The blurring of the linkage between leader opinions and follower opinions probably occurs in this case because low-income, low-education voters are less willing to support a high level of federal expenditures. These same voters are more likely to identify with the Democratic party.

Since most voters are incapable of making a distinction between the parties and, in any case, do not necessarily share the attitudes of party leaders, it seems that American national elections are not high in their ideological or issue content and that successful candidates are therefore not directed by mass opinion. This is not to suggest that voters are fools who are easily manipulated by clever use of the mass media and other instruments of persuasion. The stability of partisan attitudes and the operation of such screening factors as selective perception reduce the manipulative qualities of campaigns considerably.

Party identification is remarkably stable, while opinions are quite unstable. Ironically, the party is substantially more central to the belief system of mass electorates than are the policies it pursues. Short-term forces, such as a candidate's religion, can deflect voters away from the choice indicated by their party identification, but these short-term forces are, in many cases, unrelated to issues.

Our discussion does not preclude the possibility that *some* voters are issue-oriented and informed. Recall that we described about one-third of the electorate as having an opinion, being aware of what the government was doing, and perceiving a difference between parties. V. O. Key has chosen to characterize the electorate as "responsible," but his conclusion is based solely upon those who switch from one party to another.[20] Depending upon the election, one-fifth to one-eighth of the electorate does this. Since we have described about one-third of the electorate as *potential* switchers, Key's findings and ours are not inconsistent. Indeed, Key's argument indicates that, from the reservoir of potential switchers, relatively few voters actually switch parties. Nevertheless, Key's thesis merits response, because it does tend to portray the electorate in more flattering terms than we have. Key asserts, for instance, that: "From our analyses *the voter* emerges as a person who appraises the actions of the government, who has policy preferences, and who relates his vote to those appraisals and preferences."[21] Granted that in close elections switching voters might be crucial, to describe "the voter" as Key does is to ignore the fact that only a tiny fraction of voters can be properly called "responsible." Even assuming that this fraction has political preferences gives no evidence that they "appraise" the actions of government. A critical problem in Key's work is his failure to explore information levels. As Converse aptly remarked, "opinions, be they ever so fervent, are no proof of information."[22] For instance, on the surface the McCarthy supporters seemed drawn from the ranks of those who opposed Johnson's policy in Vietnam, yet once the surface is broken we discover that such people voted contrary to their policy preference. As Con-

[20] V. O. Key, Jr., *The Responsible Electorate* (Cambridge: Harvard University Press, 1966).
[21] *Ibid.*, pp. 58–59.
[22] Philip E. Converse, review of *The Responsible Electorate*, in *Political Science Quarterly* (December 1966), p. 631.

verse and his colleagues note: ". . . pushing beyond the expression of narrow or superficial attitudes in the mass public to the cognitive nature which underlies the attitudes is a rather disillusioning experience."[23]

We do not wish to suggest that the "responsible electorate" is a complete myth; rather, we suggest that it takes an unusually vigorous assertion of beliefs on the part of a candidate to cause the electorate to link issues with candidates. McCarthy, speaking in his intellectually oriented style, failed. However, George Wallace, whose appeal to his electorate was far less sophisticated, succeeded. The evidence suggests that among Nixon and Humphrey supporters issue positions minimally determined candidate choice. Wallace supporters, by contrast, displayed much stronger issue orientation.[24] Ironically, Key's "responsible electorate" consists largely of the followers of a counter-elite movement using the electoral process to challenge the consensual elite system.

What Factors Win Elections? If most voters are not capable of perceiving the alternative positions of political parties, what do campaigns accomplish? Candidates confer extensively with their advisors, planning elaborate political statements and making public appearances to discuss the issues that they perceive as relevant to the election. While they direct themselves almost exclusively to the issues, the *presentation* of their ideologies apparently produces more voter support than do the ideologies themselves. The medium is the message.

The evidence indicates that about one fifth to one third of the electorate makes up its mind during the campaign. Most of these late deciders are independents and weak partisans who form the potential "floating vote" (those who change their vote from one election to another). In close elections, of course, those who make up their minds during the campaign can be critical. It is very likely that late deciders, if they do play a critical role, are those least qualified to play such a role; they are those least likely to keep themselves informed about the issues and the campaign. Concerning the "floating voters," Converse comments that "susceptibility to party shifting seems higher for some types of voters than for others, and in any given shift between two elections . . . the less involved and less informed voters are disproportionately represented."[25] One should draw a distinction between those who switch their votes during a campaign and those who change their partisan identification on a permanent basis. Those who change their party identification permanently appear to be well organized ideologically; they change because of a desire to achieve congruence between their ideological posture and the perceived policy positions of a political party. These long-term realignments can contribute to the party victory or defeat on an ideological basis. However, those who

[23]Converse, *et al., op. cit.,* p. 1096.
[24]*Ibid.,* pp. 1097–1101.
[25]Philip E. Converse, "Information Flow and the Stability of Partisan Attitudes," *Public Opinion Quarterly,* 26:4 (Winter 1962), 579.

change their party identification constitute only about 10 percent of the electorate. Those who maintain a stable party identification but switch their votes in a particular election are not ideologues. For example, studies of defections away from Democratic identification in 1956 indicate that 18 percent of the ideologues changed their votes; 23 percent of those with "group interest" conceptions of the electoral process switched from Democrat to Republican; 46 percent of those voters with a "nature of the times" orientation did so; and 36 percent of those who exhibited no issue content defected from the Democratic party.[26] Thus, short-term instability in voting is greatest among those who pay little attention to campaigns, ideologies, and issues, simply responding according to broad-gauged perception of whether times are good or bad.

Even though they are not especially well informed, the "floating voters" do provide some mechanism of control. Unfortunately for those seeking political office, the stimulus to which the "nature of the times" voters respond is usually beyond their control. The information level of the "floating voters" is substantially less than that of those who are consistent partisans but is greater than that of those who are infrequent participants in the electoral process. Since their information level is moderate at best and their commitment to partisan symbols unstable, these voters are susceptible to short-term influences. Any new information that reaches them at all is likely to have more effect than the same information that reaches the stable partisans.

Insofar as campaigns serve to heighten short-term factors, they can be viewed as vote deflecting mechanisms. Ironically, candidates campaign more or less on the issues, but the defection occurs most among those to whom the issues are not especially significant. For instance, in 1964, Goldwater lost badly because he "converted into position issues a number of image issues on which a broad consensus had hitherto existed between the parties."[27] In other words, Goldwater's campaign served to strengthen the favorable images of the Democratic party, and gained him nothing in ideological voters. Although he would have lost no matter what he did, he grossly misperceived support for his ideological positions. If there ever was an ideological election, this should have been it; however, the "stay-at-home" conservatives whom Goldwater sought to flush out proved to be nonexistent. In seeking to flush them out, Goldwater strengthened the hand of Johnson, whose personal characteristics were less important to his victory than were the policies with which he was associated. There is a fairly consistent linkage of Democrats with "good" times and Republicans with "bad"; in this election, the "good times" image of the Democrats persisted. There was also a fairly consistent image of the Republicans as the "party of peace," an image that they had held since the election of Eisenhower, but Goldwater's foreign policy positions damaged this image.

[26] Campbell et al., The American Voter, p. 264.
[27] Donald E. Stokes, "Some Dynamic Elements of Contests for the Presidency," American Political Science Review, 60:1 (March 1966), 21.

Given the clearly developed issues of the campaign, the fact that the largest number of voters saw no difference in foreign policy between the two candidates is especially significant. Among those voters who did see a difference, Goldwater succeeded in reversing the image that the Republicans had held under Eisenhower. This was clearly an election in which foreign policy intruded upon the public consciousness more than in any case since 1952.

In 1952, there was anger and frustration with the Democratic administration, and these angry feelings certainly contributed to Eisenhower's victory. Nevertheless, in 1952, as in 1964, it would be an error to attribute the rise and fall of party fortunes to a liberal or conservative shift in the public mood. Eisenhower's victory was not a conservative reaction to the two decades of liberalism, because the surge of voters came from the less well informed. These voters wanted a change in personnel rather than a change in policy. Certainly the Korean conflict contributed to their frustrations, but the desire for a change was not related to anything more than a series of accumulated grievances; voters had no specific policy preferences.

Generally speaking, unless the country is involved in war, domestic issues (to the extent that voters concern themselves with any issues) are more important than is foreign policy. The public typically gives the president a great degree of latitude in making foreign policy (partly because information on foreign policy is more difficult to acquire) and is less capable of maintaining the stability of their opinions in this area. However, a president's persistent perceived failure can, in conjunction with other grievances, take an electoral toll. For instance, the struggle in Korea was initially widely supported by the American population, but as the war dragged on, enthusiasm declined appreciably. In the elections of 1952, the failure of the Democratic administration to end the Korean War was a partial contributor to the partisan surge to the Republican party.[28]

The political situation during the Vietnam War is virtually identical with the situation that faced Truman during the Korean War. The initial enthusiasm for the war in Vietnam diminished and was replaced by gradual lack of support. However, the decline in support could be temporarily arrested by *any* decisive action by President Johnson. If bombing of the North was increased—or if bombing was halted—enthusiasm spurted upward. As Lipset has noted, the president does not follow opinion, he creates it.[29] This is especially the case in foreign policy because the government is the only source of information for the public.

Furthermore, conflicts such as Vietnam blur a distinction between the attitudes of elites and masses as the population unites against the feared and hated communists. In foreign policy, even more than in domestic policy, the information gap between the elite and the masses is enormous. However, when the country is involved in a protracted

---

[28] Angus Campbell, "Voters and Elections: Past and Present," *Journal of Politics*, 26:4 (November 1964), 745–757.
[29] S. M. Lipset, "The President, the Polls, and Vietnam," *Transaction* (September-October 1966), 22.

and controversial conflict, the shape of opinion between elites and masses is not appreciably different. Nevertheless, a leader can adopt any position and find support for it. Given the general instability of opinion on foreign policy, the control that the masses can exercise over governmental elites is minimal.

It is important to note parallels between the Korean War and the Vietnam War in presidential campaign politics. In neither case was there much relationship between campaign statements and policy performance. Warren Miller remarks of Eisenhower's victory:

> Mr. Eisenhower's election was made possible because of dissatisfaction with Democratic foreign policy. He immediately rejected the policy preferences of his supporters and by so doing gained the uncritical gratitude of the same supporters, who forthwith accepted the tenets of the opposition and became more like Mr. Stevenson's supporters than Stevenson supporters themselves.[30]

Specifically, Eisenhower adopted Stevenson's policy toward Korea by easing out of the war. Johnson, who ridiculed Goldwater's position on foreign policy in general and the Vietnam War in particular, received enthusiastic support at the beginning of his Vietnam intervention, even though he was taking the same actions advocated by Goldwater, whom the public tended to regard as "trigger happy." Nixon was elected in 1968 in part because of dissatisfaction over the conduct of the Vietnam War, yet Nixon pledged throughout the campaign to continue the policy position of the Johnson administration. The point of these examples is that the impact of the candidates during an election seems to be greater than the impact of issues. Thus, candidates can operate virtually independently of electoral control over policy making. Voters make their choice on the basis of a candidate's personal style, filtered through partisan commitment, and presidential elections do not necessarily offer a policy choice.

Presidential elections are means for the selection of personnel, not policy. As William Flanigan notes, "It is perfectly appropriate to attribute policy significance to an election on the basis of policy preferences of winning candidates, so long as it is not implied that the voters had these policy implications in mind when they voted."[31] That is, an elected official might interpret election results in a manner unintended by the electorate. In general, the electoral system is not a way of imposing policy standards on elected officials.

One might be tempted to believe that elections at the state and local level are more accurate examples of traditional democratic theory, since they are less complex than national elections. Some state elections are concerned almost exclusively with a single issue. For example, Epstein's study of the 1962 gubernatorial election in Wisconsin indicates that tax policy was the issue that dominated the campaign of both

[30] Warren E. Miller, "Voting and Foreign Policy," in James Rosenau (ed.), *Domestic Sources of Foreign Policy* (New York: Free Press), p. 216.
[31] William H. Flanigan, *The Political Behavior of the American Electorate* (Boston: Allyn and Bacon, 1968), p. 115.

candidates. The question was whether to increase the income tax or to extend the sales tax. Each position developed strong partisans; the Republicans, in keeping with their traditional image, advocated a sales tax extension, while the Democrats, the incumbent party, supported an increase in the income tax. Each candidate took a firm position linked to the ideological perspective of his party.

As is typically the case, the turnout for this election was substantially less than the turnout in presidential elections. Low turnout means an overrepresentation of high-status, well informed people. Given this type of an election, information should have penetrated substantially beyond the better educated voters. However, about one third of the voters could not identify the position of the Democrats. The victory of the Democratic candidate, therefore, can hardly be attributed solely to his position on the sales tax. His majority included a large number of people who disagreed with his tax policy, and many who voted for him for reasons unrelated to the tax issue. Therefore, Epstein concludes that the election, although centered on a single policy, cannot be interpreted as a wish by the majority to extend the income tax.[32]

At the local level, participation in the electoral process is substantially less than at the state or national level. Thirty-five to 45 percent of the eligible population abstain from voting in national elections, but 50 to 90 percent frequently do not vote in local elections. These habitual non-voters are drawn disproportionately from the poor and uneducated, who typically have very little interest in politics. It is difficult for them to become enthusiastic about bond issues and tax referenda, for example, when there are no personalities to relate to the issues. Most voters are not issue-oriented, but rather are attracted to parties and candidates; the relative unimportance of either parties or candidates in local politics contributes substantially to the low turnout. Only citizens who are intensely committed to the community are likely to vote in local elections. These are the interested, committed, high-status citizens who make up the "normal" local electorate. They feel they have a stake in community decision making and therefore participate frequently in local affairs. Also, their better education makes it possible for them to comprehend elections even in the absence of parties and candidates.

Occasionally an abnormal election occurs. People who typically do not vote are stimulated into political activity, perhaps for the first and only time. When local elections generate a substantial increase in turnout, one can infer that the election is a symptom of a deeply felt community conflict. The election has become "heated," and has generated interest among the strata of the population normally unconcerned about local affairs. The added voters are usually from the poorly educated classes of the population, who have few organizational and emotional ties to the community. Abstract issues mean little to

[32] Leon D. Epstein, "Electoral Decision and Policy Mandate: An Empirical Example," *Public Opinion Quarterly*, 28:4 (Winter 1964), 572.

them, and they respond only to campaigns that appeal to the frustrations of an economically inferior position.[33]

Schattschneider wondered what the consequences would be if the 40 million or so people who regularly did not vote in presidential elections suddenly decided to vote. In local politics, there is some evidence that an increase in turnout disrupts the normal governmental process, for a variety of issues—school bonds, parks, and so forth—provides the voter with an opportunity to use the election as an expression of resentment and hostility. Normally the alienation and hostility of the lower strata produce apathy; but if the election turns into a heated community conflict, the lower strata can be drawn into the electoral process, where they often translate their hostility into negative or "no" voting. There is a clear relationship between social status and progressive or "yes" voting at the local level. The better educated, higher income voters are the bedrock of support for school taxes, health facilities, parks, recreation, airports, and other community services. "No" voting for these public services is heavy among lower income, less educated, ethnic group members.

The lower strata are substantially more alienated and suspicious of local politicians than are the upper classes. However, the alienation and suspicion of the lower classes are not necessarily symptoms of a political paranoia; in fact, those in economically powerless positions are realistic in their perceptions of local government. Those without economic power are more likely to lack political power and to have no opportunity for infiltration into the power structure of a community. Their negative vote expresses their desire to "throw a monkey wrench into the machinery," to frustrate the plans of the "establishment." There is a "they" component to negative voting at the local level. For example, in voting for school bonds, the alienated, poorly educated voters translate their unfavorable attitudes into negative votes.[34] Voting against school bonds may be reasonable, since these persons certainly place less value on educational facilities than do the upper classes, but they also vote against fluoridation and practically every other local issue. This means that there is a negative correlation between turnout and positive voting in local referenda, since an increment in turnout is from the lower status, negative voters. For instance, Carter and Savard found that the higher the average turnout in school bond and tax elections, the more likely that the bond issues would be defeated.[35] Coleman presents similar evidence from data in fluoridation referenda. Consequently, local campaigns to "get out and vote" are likely to contribute to policies at variance with the values of those' who initiate such campaigns.[36]

[33]James S. Coleman, *Community Conflict* (New York: Free Press, 1957), p. 19.
[34]Wayne E. Thompson and John Horton, "Political Orientation as a Force in Political Action," *Social Forces*, 38:3 (March 1960), 193.
[35]Richard Carter and William G. Savard, "Influence of Voting Turnout on School Bond and Tax Elections," Cooperative Research Project 5, U.S. Department of Health, Education, and Welfare, 1961.
[36]Coleman, *Community Conflict*, p. 19.

There is an exception to the general rule that the poorly educated strata can be relied upon to contribute negative votes. Negroes, who certainly occupy an objective status in the community substantially inferior to that of the poorer whites, consistently *support* local referenda. In Atlanta, for example, a voter coalition between upper-income whites and Negroes makes it possible for the city to pass bond issues over the opposition of the lower and middle-income whites. Careful negotiation between the mayor and the Negro leaders produces this satisfactory electoral result. The lower and middle-income whites, the Democrats, are traditionally opposed to local spending, just as they are more likely than Republicans to favor budget cuts and tax reductions at the national level.[37]

Electoral Participation and Nonparticipation

Another problem with the theory of popular control over public policy through elections is the fact that over one third of the adult population fails to vote even in presidential elections.

Since the 1960 presidential race between John F. Kennedy and Richard Nixon, voter turnout has steadily slipped from 64 percent of the eligible voters, to 63 percent in the Johnson-Goldwater race in 1964, and to 60 percent in the Nixon-Humphrey-Wallace race in 1968. "Off-year" elections bring out fewer than half of the eligible voters. Yet in these "off-year" contests the nation chooses all of its U.S. representatives, one third of its senators, and about one half of its governors.

Lester Milbrath listed six forms of "legitimate" political participation:[38] Individuals may run for public office, become active in party and campaign work, make financial contributions to political candidates or causes, belong to organizations that support or oppose candidates or take stands on political issues, attempt to influence friends while discussing candidates or issues, and vote in elections. Activities at the top of this list require greater expenditure of time, money, and energy than those activities at the bottom, and they involve only a tiny minority of the population. Less than one percent of the American adult population ever runs for public office. Only about 5 percent are ever active in parties and campaigns, and only about 10 percent make financial contributions. About one third of the population belong to organizations that could be classified as political interest groups, and only a few more ever try to convince their friends to vote a certain way. About 60 to 65 percent of the American people will vote in a hard-fought presidential campaign.

Nonparticipation does not occur uniformly throughout all segments of the population. The Michigan Survey center recorded the percentages (found in Table 6–6) of non-voting for various groups in the 1960 election. Non-voting is associated with lower education levels,

---

[37] M. Kent Jennings and Harmon Zeigler, "Class, Party, and Race in Four Types of Elections: The Case of Atlanta," *Journal of Politics*, 28:2 (May 1966), 391–407.

[38] Lester Milbrath, *Political Participation* (Chicago: Rand McNally, 1965), pp. 23–29.

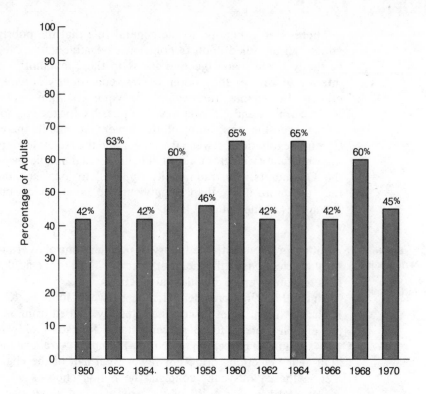

Source: Statistical Abstract of the United States (Washington, D.C.: U.S. Government Printing Office). Composite of data from annual editions.

unskilled occupations, rural living, non-membership in organizations, and the especially deprived status of large numbers of Negroes. Of course, membership in these categories overlaps. High voter turnout is related to college education; to professional, managerial, or other white collar occupations; to metropolitan residence; and to membership in voluntary associations. On the whole, Catholics and Jews (not shown) vote more frequently than Protestants. While these figures pertain only to voting, other forms of participation follow substantially the same pattern. White, middle-class, college educated, white collar, urban Americans participate more in all forms of political activity than non-white, lower-class, grade school educated, unskilled, and rural Americans. Marches and demonstrations, which are special tactics of minority groups, are excepted.

Election turnout figures in the United States are lower than those of several other democracies. The turnout in recent elections has been 74 percent in Japan, 77 percent in Great Britain, 83 percent in Israel, 88 percent in West Germany, and 93 percent in Italy. Of course, the lower turnouts in the United States may be explained by our stricter residence and registration requirements and by the fact that we hold elections more frequently. It may also be that Americans are less "political" than citizens of other democracies, less likely to care about the outcome of elections, and less likely to feel that government makes much of an impact on their lives. This disinterest in politics may be a product of an underlying consensus in America that brings opposing parties and candidates so close to each other on major political issues that it does not matter much which party or candidate wins.[39]

Voter participation is highly valued in American political theory. Popular control of government, control of leaders by followers, is supposed to be effected through the electoral process. The majority of Americans do vote, and by so doing they indicate they have some stake in the outcome of elections, but a sizeable group of Americans never vote or participate in politics in any accepted fashion. It is possible to interpret this non-voting as a reflection of "alienation" from the political system. Political "alienation" involves a feeling that voting and other forms of participation are useless, that nothing is really decided by an election, and that the individual cannot personally influence the outcome of political events. The fact that non-voting occurs most frequently among those at the bottom of the income, occupation, education, and status ladder tends to confirm this view; alienation *should* occur more frequently in groups who have not shared in the general affluence of society. However, this interpretation is discouraging for those who wish well for the democratic ideal, because it suggests that not all groups in society place a high value on democratic institutions.

TABLE 6–6. Non-voters Classified by Group Characteristics, 1960	Group Characteristic	Percentage Not Voting*
	Education	
	Grade school	33
	High school	19
	College	10
	Occupation	
	Professional and managerial	12
	Other white collar	16
	Skilled and semi-skilled	22
	Unskilled	32
	Farm	23
	Community	
	Metropolitan area	18
	Towns and cities	22
	Rural areas	23
	Race	
	White	19
	Negro	46
	Labor	
	Union	23
	Non-union	20
	Religion	
	Protestant	24
	Catholic	15

*The exact percentages may change from one election to another, but the general pattern remains very stable.

Source: Fred I. Greenstein, *The American Party System and the American People* (Englewood Cliffs, N.J.: Prentice-Hall, 1963).

[39]Robert E. Lane, "The Politics of Consensus in an Age of Affluence," *American Political Science Review*, 61:4 (December 1965), 880.

Violence as an Alternative to Elections

There is a strong relationship between status deprivation and political violence. Perhaps this deprivation explains why many Negroes, rather than taking their hostility to the ballot box, have increasingly participated in violence. The rioters in recent disorders were better educated than the non-rioters, but were likely to hold menial jobs, and their intense racial pride was strengthened by the discrepancy between their education and their occupation. For these people, conventional political participation lost its meaning, and violence became a device to communicate intense dissatisfaction. The rioters were not vagrants or criminals; they were long-time residents of the city and were, in fact, cited among the more intellectually oriented and politically sophisticated of the black community.[40]

Furthermore, actions of the militant rioters are supported by substantial portions of blacks who did not participate directly in the riots. Post-riot survey information indicated that roughly 20 percent of the Negroes in the Watts area participated actively in the riot of 1964, and more than half of the residents supported the activities of the rioters. Interviews found that 58 percent of the Watts residents felt that the long-run effects of the riots would be favorable; 84 percent said that whites were now more aware of Negro problems; 62 percent said that the riot was a Negro protest. In summary, the riots are looked upon favorably by a large proportion of the ghetto residents.

Conventional political participation is often deemed hopeless by ghetto dwellers. The election of Negro mayors in Cleveland, Ohio, and Gary, Indiana, in 1967 does not indicate that Negroes elsewhere will find it possible to return to conventional participation as the sole method of influencing political decisions. In Cleveland, more than 90 percent of the white Democrats who voted in the Democratic primary election switched to a Republican candidate in the general election, presumably because the Democratic candidate was a Negro.[41]

Rioting is an alternative to voting, taken when the results of elections provide no tangible rewards, but rioting and political violence are not considered political participation by political scientists. Perhaps this is because we wish to regard political violence as an atypical and temporary aberration. However, the fact that rioters are otherwise typical black citizens and have a strong commitment to the redress of the grievances of the black community suggests that violence may become a common pattern of political participation. Actually, the American political system is not as stable as we like to assume.[42] Although most whites regard the political system as a legitimate one, a substantial proportion of Negroes do not, because they believe that the political system has not provided adequate rewards for their conventional political participation.

[40]*Report of the National Advisory Commission on Civil Disorders* (Washington, D.C., 1968), pp. 111–112; pp. 128–135.

[41]Jeffrey Hadden, Louis H. Masotti, and Victor Thiessen, "The Making of the Negro Mayors, 1967," *Transaction,* 5:3 (January–February 1968), 24.

[42]See Ted Gurr, "Urban Disorder: Perspectives from the Comparative Study of Civil Strife," *American Behavioral Scientist,* 4 (March–April 1968), 50–55; Ivo K. Feierabend and Rosalind L. Feierabend, "Aggressive Behaviors

TABLE 6–7.
Education,
Occupation, and
Participation
in Riots

	Newark		Detroit	
	Rioters	**Non-rioters**	**Rioters**	**Non-rioters**
Education				
Grade school	1.9%	14.3%	7.0%	27.9%
Some high school	63.2	46.8	53.5	33.8
High school graduate	29.2	31.0	23.3	26.1
Some college or college graduate	5.7	7.9	16.2	12.2
Occupation				
Unskilled	50.0	39.6		
Semiskilled or better	50.0	60.4		

Source: *Report of the National Advisory Commission on Civil Disorders* (Washington, D.C., 1968).

Almond and Verba describe Americans as proud of their governmental and political institutions, and further comment that a substantial majority of Americans also expect equal treatment by government officials and police.[43] This description of the American political culture does not apply to blacks; Negroes do not share this opinion of the police. Even though perceptions of unequal treatment by the police are a major precipitating cause of racial violence, whites are unwilling to accept the possibility of brutality and discrimination on the part of police.

In short, middle- and upper-class whites tend to look upon our system of government as extremely satisfactory and find it difficult to understand why a minority group communicates its dissatisfaction violently. In Milbrath's hierarchy of political involvement (discussed on p.187) violence is excluded, because the hierarchy of participation does not apply to behavior "designed to disrupt the normal operation of democratic political processes."[44] But it is quite likely that a new pattern of political participation—violence as a response to both deprivation and resentment—is emerging. To be sure, this form of protest is a criminal one. And it may be irrational and self-defeating, for the great majority of the casualties of the riots—the dead, the injured, and the arrested—were rioters themselves, and much of the property destroyed belonged to ghetto residents. Moreover, the riots may have changed the attitudes of many whites toward the black community and toward the civil rights movement from sympathy or disinterest to opposition. Nonetheless, violence must be recognized as a form of political participation by the masses.

"Politics as usual" is not an apt description of the mood of the nation with regard to the crisis in civil rights. The shattering of consensus produced by violence and reaction to violence has presented the two major political parties with their most severe crisis since the Civil War.

[43] Gabriel A. Almond and Sidney Verba, *The Civic Culture: Political Attitudes and Democracy in Five Nations* (Boston: Little, Brown and Co., 1965), pp. 69–75.
[44] Milbrath, *Political Participation*, p. 18.

TABLE 6–8.
Racial Hostility
and Participation
in Riots in Newark

	Rioters	Non-rioters
Who do you think are nicer?		
Negroes	78.1%	57.3%
Whites	21.9	37.3
About the same	0.0	5.4
Sometimes I hate white people.		
Agree	72.4	50.0
Disagree	27.6	50.0
Political information test		
High score	68.9	51.2
Low score	31.1	48.8
How much did anger with politicians have to do with causing riot?		
Great deal	43.2	19.6
Something	31.8	39.1
Nothing	18.2	24.5
Don't know	6.8	6.6
Is the country worth fighting for?		
Yes	33.0	50.8
No	52.8	27.8
Don't know	14.2	21.4

Source: *Report of the National Advisory Commission on Civil Disorder* (Washington, D.C., 1968).

Summary

In order for elections to function as instruments through which a populace controls public policy, four conditions must be met: (1) Parties, or their candidates, must offer clear policy alternatives to the voters. (2) Voters must be cognizant of and concerned with such policy choices. (3) Majority preferences on issues must be identifiable through elections. (4) And finally, elected officials must be bound by their campaign pledges. In actuality, none of these four conditions are met in the American electoral system; therefore, the masses do not control policy through their votes.

However, American elections do perform other functions with varying degrees of effectiveness. They serve the symbolic function of binding voters to the established order, and they also provide the masses with a means of removing from office those officials whose past performance they judge to be unsatisfactory. In this way, possession of the vote serves as protection against governmental abuse.

In each of the functions mentioned above there is the hidden assumption that possession of the vote is equivalent to the exercise of it. Such an assumption is not warranted. In fact, the lower one's socioeconomic status and level of education are, the less likely one is to vote. Non-voting among the masses is more pronounced in state than in national elections, and more pronounced in local than in state elections.

Another facet of the irony of democracy is that the poorly educated, non-voting masses could not translate their ideology into policy even if they actually did control government. That translation is currently performed by the elite. Lack of information, attachment to symbols, and inconsistency in voting behavior and attitudes characterize the poorly educated; the educated elite, on the other hand, possess significantly more information of a higher quality, in addition to the capacity to conceptualize ideology and to transform it into policy.

The masses, realizing how little political control they have, may simply use elections as a chance to vote "no," to express their hostility against the system. Or, realizing that they can change nothing through elections, they may resort to violence as a means of protest. Violence, as an alternative to elections, seems to be a growing form of political participation.

Selected Additional Readings

Campbell, Angus, *et al. The American Voter: An Abridgement.* New York: John Wiley (paperback), 1964. This is an abridgement of the classic study of voting behavior in the United States conducted by the Survey Research Center at the University of Michigan. Although it is based on 1952 and 1956 surveys, the study remains relevant today.

Flanigan, William H. *The Political Behavior of the American Electorate.* Boston: Allyn and Bacon (paperback), 1968. In this short book, Flanigan draws on a wide range of previous voting studies in explaining American voting behavior. Of particular interest are the discussions in Chapters 3 and 4 of social, economic, and psychological correlates of voting.

Lipset, Seymour Martin. *Political Man.* Garden City, N.Y.: Doubleday & Co. (Anchor Books edition), 1963. Part II contains a discussion of voting behavior in Western democracies and relates empirical findings to democratic theory.

Luttbeg, Norman (ed.). *Public Opinion and Public Policy: Models of Political Linkage.* Homewood, Ill.: Dorsey Press (paperback), 1968. In this reader there are a number of excellent articles that focus on various aspects of the relationships among the attitudes and behavior of American voters and public officials.

Milbrath, Lester. *Political Participation.* Chicago: Rand McNally (paperback), 1965. Milbrath presents a propositional survey of the literature on political participation through the early 1960s. An extensive, though somewhat dated, bibliography is also of value.

Pomper, Gerald. *Elections in America: Control and Influence in Democratic Politics.* New York: Dodd, Mead, & Co. (paperback), 1968. This is an outstanding contemporary study of the American electoral process. In addition to analyzing voting behavior *per se,* Pomper focuses on the impact of that behavior on public policy.

7

The American Party System: A Shrinking Consensus

There is a great deal of truth to the "Tweedledum and Tweedledee" image of American political parties. American parties do, in fact, subscribe to the same fundamental political ideology. Both the Democratic and the Republican parties have reflected prevailing elite consensus on basic democratic values – the sanctity of private property, a free enterprise economy, individual liberty, limited government, majority rule, and due process of law. Moreover, since the 1930s both parties have supported the public-oriented, mass-welfare domestic programs of the "liberal establishment" – social security, fair labor standards, unemployment compensation, a graduated income tax, a national highway program, a federally aided welfare system, counter-cyclical fiscal and monetary policies, and government regulation of public utilities. Finally, both parties have supported the basic outlines of American foreign and military policy since World War II – international involvement, anti-communism, the Cold War, European recovery, NATO, military preparedness, selective service, and even the Korean and Vietnam Wars. Rather than promoting competition over national goals and programs, the parties reinforce societal consensus and limit the area of legitimate political conflict.[1]

The major parties are not, of course, *identical* in ideology; there are nuances of difference. For instance, Republican leaders are "conservative" on domestic policy, while Democratic leaders are "liberal." Moreover, the social bases of the parties are slightly different. Both parties draw their support from all social groups in America, but the Democrats draw disproportionately from labor, urban workers, Jews, Catholics, and Negroes, while the Republicans draw disproportionately from rural, small town, and suburban Protestants, businessmen, and professionals (see Table 7-1). To the extent that the aspirations of these two broad groups of supporters differ, the thrust of party ideology also differs. However, the magnitude of this difference is not very great. Since there are only two parties and a non-ideological electorate, "consumer" demand (as perceived by leadership) requires

---

[1] See Walter Dean Burnham, "The Changing Shape of the American Political Universe," *American Political Science Review*, 59 (March 1965), 28; and Walter Dean Burnham, "Party Systems and the Political Process," in William Nisbet Chambers and Walter Dean Burnham (eds.), *The American Party Systems: Stages of Political Development* (New York: Oxford University Press, 1967), pp. 305-307.

TABLE 7–1.
Who Votes for Each
Party: Differences in
Voter Support Given
the Democratic and
Republican Parties
(by Major
Social Groups)

	1948		1956		1960		1964		1968	
	D	R	D	R	D	R	D	R	D	R
Religion										
Protestant	47%	53%	36%	64%	37%	63%	63%	37%	38%	62%
Catholic	66	34	52	48	83	17	79	21	60	40
Jewish	100	0*	74	26	89	11	89	11	93	7
Race										
White	53	47	40	60	47	53	64	36	41	59
Negro	65	35	82	18	72	28	100	0*	97	3
Education										
Grade school	69	31	49	51	55	45	80	20	62	39†
High school	54	46	43	57	53	47	69	31	48	52
College	24	76	26	74	36	64	54	40	37	63
Age										
34 and younger	63	37	45	55	52	48	72	28	48	52
35 to 44	61	39	45	55	51	49	68	32	52	48
45 to 54	47	53	42	58	55	45	69	31	43	57
55 to 64	43	57	35	65	44	56	70	30	41	59
65 and over	50	50	36	64	38	62	55	45	45	55
Sex										
Male	57	43	43	57	53	47	65	35	45	55
Female	53	47	40	60	46	54	69	31	47	53
Occupation										
Professional and managerial	19	81	32	68	45	55	58	42	38	62
White collar	50	50	35	65	48	52	65	35	45	55
Skilled and semiskilled workers	77	23	48	59	41	77	23	52	48
Unskilled workers	74	26	68	32	59	41	83	17	60	40
Farm operators	64	36	37	63	33	67	64	36	45	55
Union membership										
Labor union families	82	18	56	44	64	36	84	16	43	57
Non-union families	44	56	36	64	44	56	62	38	56	44
Income										
Lower (less than $5000)	65	35	42	58	47	53	74	26	51	49
Lower middle ($5000–$9999)	69	31	46	54	46	54	71	29	45	55
Middle ($10,000–$14,999)	38	62	26	74	46	54	56	44	52	48
Upper middle ($15,000+)	49	51	42	58	55	45	71	29	32	68
Community Size										
Metropolitan areas	60	40	43	57	58	42	72	28	60	40
Cities (over 50,000)	–	–	52	48	50	50	64	33	55	45
Towns (2,500–49,999)	48	52	37	63	40	60	61	39	45	55
Rural (under 2,500)	67	33	39	61	48	52	69	31	37	63

*Fewer than 1 percent of respondents favored the Republican candidate in these instances.
†Rounding error.

Source: Survey Research Center, University of Michigan. (Composite from SRC studies.)

that party ideologies be ambiguous and moderate. Therefore, we cannot expect the parties, who wish to alienate the minimum number of voters and attract the maximum number, to take up a cause supported by only a minority of the population.

Since parties are organizations whose basic motive is to capture political office, strong ideology and innovation are virtually out of the question. Firmer and more precise statements of ideologies by the political parties would probably create new lines of cleavage and eventually fragment the parties. The development of a clear "liberal" or "conservative" ideology by either party would cost the party votes unless the electorate, stimulated by elites, became more ideologically oriented. Even so, it is doubtful that the country could divide itself into two warring camps, one consisting of liberals and the other of conservatives.

The 1964 presidential election is an example of the fact that a strong ideological stance will not win elections in America. In 1964, the Republicans came as close to offering a clear ideological alternative to the majority party as has occurred in recent American political history. Goldwater, the Republican presidential candidate, made a genuine effort to provide the electorate with a "choice, not an echo." He specifically rejected moderation ("moderation in defense of liberty is no virtue") and defended extremism ("extremism on behalf of liberty is no vice"). He rejected the "peace" image of Eisenhower in favor of an aggressive, military-oriented stance on foreign policy.

While most voters did not perceive a *foreign* policy difference between Goldwater and Johnson, they did perceive a *domestic* policy difference. Public opinion data indicate that Johnson's campaign presentation and the general mood of the public were very similar. A Louis Harris poll taken during the campaign revealed that only 1 percent of the respondents considered themselves "radical," but 45 percent considered Goldwater radical. However, 80 percent of the respondents defined themselves as either conservatives or middle-of-the-roaders, and 67 percent identified Johnson as sharing this ideological orientation.[2] Goldwater received 27 million votes, but a Harris poll of January 11, 1965, indicates that 18 million people voted for Goldwater only out of party loyalty; they had doubts about or disagreements with his position on the issues. Also, Goldwater gained 2 million Southern Democratic votes because of his opposition to the Civil Rights Act of 1964. This leaves a total of about 7 million hard-core "conservative" supporters of Senator Goldwater, and this small cadre of ideologues is probably the basic strength of the highly motivated right wing of American politics (at least in 1964).

This overwhelming defeat of the "pure" conservative position is significant, in that it reveals the fallacy of the argument that the non-ideological two-party system suppresses basic ideological cleavages within the masses. The magnitude of Goldwater's defeat indicates that few ideologues will rally to the call. If there *were* strong divisions of opinion within the electorate, the parties, given their "consumer" orientation, would surely reflect them. Parties reflect the consensual, moderate nature of the American public and will continue to do so as long as the majority of voters share the consensus.

Leaders and Followers: Consensus and Conflict

However, the evidence is that the leaders of both parties are much more ideologically divided than their followers. For example, Republican and Democratic Convention delegates differed significantly on 23 of 24 issues presented to them by Herbert McClosky et al.[3] Each group of leaders resembled the popular image of the parties; both Republicans and Democrats mirrored to a considerable extent the

[2]Charles O. Jones, "The 1964 Presidential Election—Further Adventures in Wonderland," in Donald G. Herzberg (ed.), *1965–1966 American Government Annual* (New York: Holt, Rinehart and Winston, 1965), p.17.
[3]Herbert McClosky, Paul J. Hoffman, and Rosemary O'Hara, "Issue Conflict and Consensus among Party Leaders and Followers," *American Political Science Review*, 54 (June 1960), 411.

social group support of each party. Democrats, as we have seen, gain more support from disadvantaged segments and hence subscribe to economic liberalism. Republicans, whose basis of support is the middle and upper classes, advocate an individualistic, laissez-faire philosophy, contained in the "Protestant ethic" described by Max Weber.

Democratic leaders typically display the stronger urge to elevate the low-born, the uneducated, the deprived minorities, and the poor in general; they are also more disposed to employ the nation's collective power to advance humanitarian and social welfare goals (e.g., social security, immigration, racial integration, a higher minimum wage, and public education). They are more critical of wealth and big business and more eager to bring them under regulation. Theirs is the greater faith in the wisdom of using legislation for redistributing the national product and for furnishing social services on a wide scale. Of the two groups of leaders, the Democrats are the more "progressively" oriented toward social reform and experimentation. The Republican leaders, while not uniformly differentiated from their opponents, subscribe in greater measure to the symbols and practices of individualism, laissez faire, and national independence. They prefer to overcome humanity's misfortunes by relying upon personal effort, private incentives, frugality, hard work, responsibility, self-denial (for both men and government), and the strengthening rather than the diminution of the economic and status distinctions that are the "natural" rewards of the differences in human character and fortunes.[4]

Why are parties so non-ideological when the party leaders oppose the philosophies of their opponents? One answer is that the party rank and file does not, as we know, share such highly articulated ideological characteristics. McClosky finds:

Whereas the leaders of the two parties diverge strongly, their followers differ only moderately in their attitudes toward issues. The hypothesis that party beliefs unite adherents and bring them into the party ranks may hold for the more active members of a mass party but not for its rank-and-file supporters. Republican followers, in fact, disagree far more with their own leaders than with the leaders of the Democratic party.[5]

There appears to be, in spite of the low level of political awareness of the American electorate, a reasonably strong consensus in support of the American capitalistic-welfare state combination. The consensus extends to Democratic leaders, Democratic followers, and Republican followers; the Republican leadership is outside this consensus only because they carry the idea to an extreme. McClosky, et al., note:

Whereas Republican leaders hold to the tenets of business ideology and remain faithful to the spirit and intellectual mood of leaders like Robert A. Taft, the rank-and-file Republican supporters have embraced, along with their Democratic brethren, the regulatory and social reform measures of the Roosevelt and Truman administrations.[6]

[4] McClosky et al., p. 426.
[5] McClosky et al., p. 426.
[6] McClosky et al., p. 423.

The explanation for the broad popular consensus in America rests ultimately in the fact that capitalism as an economic system has been extremely successful. The very success of the economic system has helped to smother class differences, which in any case have never been as strong in America as in most other Western democracies. The absence in America of a feudal past and a European-type aristocracy, the vast opportunities provided by the frontier, and relative economic abundance have combined to make Americans a "people of plenty."[7] The mainstream of American life is firmly and irrevocably middle class. Consequently, deeply felt issues that might polarize social classes have not developed. As the working class shares more and more of the benefits of an expanding economy, there is less reason for them to support any serious alteration of the *status quo*. Moreover, the middle class, although it pays allegiance to ideological symbols such as free enterprise and individual initiative, has come to appreciate the stabilities provided by a semi-regulated, welfare-state economy.

How do these facts square with McClosky's evidence about the ideological chasm between the two party elites? One obvious explanation for such an apparent discrepancy is that the issues on which the elites were given the opportunity to differ are actually well within the range of consensus. Elites differ over whether the welfare system should be extended or revised; none favor a guaranteed annual income. They differ about the extent of regulation needed for industry; none favor nationalization of industry. None of the issues presented to the elite by McClosky involved radical economic innovation; rather, they involved tinkering with the existing system.

Party leaders reinforce consensus by selecting the issues for public debate. Those who set the agenda for public debate are more powerful than those who compete in the resolution of a particular conflict once it has been placed upon the agenda. As Schattschneider observes, "The best point at which to manage conflict is before it starts."[8] For example, neither the Democratic nor the Republican elite includes many individuals who score high on a left-wing scale.

Political Parties as Organizations Any comparison of leaders and followers among the Democratic and Republican parties should take into account the uniquely decentralized and informal characteristics of the American party system. Unlike European mass-membership parties, American parties are not "organizations" in the sense normally understood by that term. To be a "Democrat" or a "Republican" involves no greater commitment to the organization than supporting, occasionally, the nominees of that party.

There is, of course, a party organization, consisting of the formally chosen leadership, informal power-holders (who do not hold government or party office), and the party activists who contribute their time

[7]David M. Potter, *People of Plenty: Economic Abundance and the American Character* (Chicago: The University of Chicago Press, 1954).
[8]E. E. Schattschneider, *The Semisovereign People: A Realist's View of Democracy in America* (New York: Holt, Rinehart and Winston, 1960), p. 15.

and money and consequently acquire the right to make decisions in the name of the party. However, neither political party is structurally hierarchical. Both are decentralized to the extent that no chain of command from national through state to local levels can be said to exist. But the structure of power within the activist group in each party is not especially relevant to our concern. Rather, we are interested in interaction *between* this group and the overwhelming majority of Democrats and Republicans, who do not involve themselves in formulation of party objectives or the selection of candidates (except in primaries) but merely accept or reject the product offered to them by the party activists. For all but a tiny portion of the participants in the political system, the major political act is that of a consumer. The association with the party is entirely passive.

It is somewhat of an irony that the parties, as the agents of democratic decision making, are not themselves democratic in their structures. One of the most sweeping indictments of political parties on this count comes from Roberto Michels, whose "iron law of oligarchy" leads him to conclude that "every party . . . becomes divided into a minority of directors and a majority of directed."[9] However, the organizational characteristics of American parties supply few relevant data to either support or refute Michels' assertion. There is, indeed, an active minority, but there is no passive majority because the party in the electorate, the masses, are not really members of the party. The party as an organization is composed of those persons who exercise varied degrees of influence within the activists' cadre. Sorauf describes American parties in this way:

> Despite recent trends, the American parties remain largely skeletal, "cadre" party organizations, manned generally by small numbers of activists and involving the great masses of their supporters scarcely at all. . . . By the standards of the parties of much of the rest of the world, American party organization continues to be characterized by its unusual fluidity and evanescence, by its failure to generate activity at non-election times, and by the ease by which a handful of activists and public officeholders dominate it.[10]

The evidence suggests that American parties, within the activists' cadre, are not a perfect fit for Michels' model, for party activists are neither as homogeneous nor as numerically small as his model requires. A more appropriate analytic construct would appear to be one developed by Harold Lasswell and Abraham Kaplan, and most recently employed by Samuel Eldersveld—the "stratarchy."[11] A stratarchy is a hierarchical structure best described as a flat-topped pyramid, in which power resides at the top level (just as it does with conical-shaped hierarchies), but in which there are a number of persons occupying that

[9]Roberto Michels, *Political Parties: A Sociological Study of the Oligarchical Tendencies of Modern Democracy* (New York: Dover Publications, 1959; originally published in English in 1915), p. 32.
[10]Frank J. Sorauf, *Party Politics in America* (Boston: Little, Brown and Co., 1968), pp. 79–80.
[11]Harold D. Lasswell and Abraham Kaplan, *Power and Society* (New Haven, Conn.: Yale University Press, 1950), pp. 219–220; and Samuel J. Eldersveld, *Political Parties: A Behavioral Analysis* (Chicago: Rand McNally, 1964), pp. 9, 98–117.

level. In the case of American party stratarchies, those who are at the top level — the activists — are both numerous and heterogeneous. Power is diffused among them rather than centralized. The exception to this rule is a few large city political machines, such as those found in Chicago, Pittsburgh, and Philadelphia; these political machines are tightly and hierarchically controlled.

Although the other extreme — virtual disorganization — is more typical of both parties, big city machines play a more pivotal role in the organization of the party than would be suggested by their numbers alone. Their influence is more evident in the Democratic party and is particularly manifest during the nomination of the presidential candidate. The power of the political machines is largely a consequence of the fact that there is no national party organization, and thus the national party is no more than a coalition of state and local parties that assembles every four years to nominate a presidential candidate. In such a bargaining process, a cohesive local political organization can play a key role. For instance, Mayor Richard Daley of Chicago can deliver almost all the votes of the Illinois delegation.

In essence, power in American parties tends to rest in the hands of those who have the time and the money to make it a full-time, or nearly full-time, occupation. Party activists — consisting of no more than 3 or 4 percent of the adult population — can decide what product is to be offered to political consumers (the party in the electorate). Beyond this, there is little interaction between the party in the electorate and the party activists. The crucial question is, therefore, who are the party activists? We know, from research cited in previous chapters, that the activists are strongly ideological and committed to the norms of the democratic decision-making process. Since these characteristics describe the upper socioeconomic groups, it is not surprising to discover that party activists are of relatively high socioeconomic status, and come from families with a history of party activity. The highest socioeconomic levels are found in the highest echelons of the party organization. As Sorauf notes, "the parties . . . attract men and women with the time and financial resources to be able to afford politics, with the information and knowledge to understand it, and with the skills to be useful in it."[12]

It is, of course, true that — reflecting the basis of support among the party in the electorate — Democratic activists are of somewhat lower socioeconomic status than their Republican counterparts. The activists of both parties are somewhat representative of their clientele. Nevertheless, the socioeconomic status of both Democratic and Republican activists is above the average for the area they represent. This distinction between elite and mass, then, is especially characteristic of American political parties.

But what does it matter whether or not the parties are democratic in structure? If the competition between parties is similar to the com-

[12] Sorauf, *Party Politics in America*, p. 94.

petition between businesses, the structural characteristics of each group of producers are not very important. Each competitor, democratic or not, has the primary function of satisfying his customers. For instance, it is of no concern to the average consumer that he does not have a voice in determining the type of electric toaster manufactured by the General Electric Corporation. If he does not like this toaster, he can always buy one from Sunbeam or Westinghouse or any one of a number of competitors.

Unfortunately, this analogy is not especially apt for American political parties. The political alternatives offered by parties are much more constricted than are the alternatives offered in business. The voter cannot choose from a number of competing products, but is limited to a choice between two. If the voter finds the product of one competitor unsatisfactory, he must either accept the single alternative or decline to become a consumer. Given the consensual nature of American parties, the range of alternatives is quite narrow.[13]

Further, it is difficult for consumers to force the producers to change their product. At first glance, it would seem easy to become an activist in a party and change the agenda-setting personnel. At most levels of political participation, this is superficially quite simple. State legislatures generally require that the party machinery be "open," so anyone can become an activist. Indeed, thousands of party positions are unfilled. However, gaining control of the political party apparatus takes longer than the normally short-term commitment that even more active portions of the citizenry are willing to make. Also, challenges to the dominant group of activists are generally focused around a candidate such as Eugene McCarthy, and such a strategy is futile, since the majority of delegates to the national conventions are not selected in primaries but are chosen by party organizations. Thus, a relatively small number of party leaders can control the decisions of a large proportion of the delegates to the national conventions. The choice of a nominating convention will be, therefore, the choice of the party activists who have long-term commitments to the party, rather than the choice of those activists who are occasionally mobilized by a particular candidate. Only on the rare occasions when temporarily mobilized activists encounter the power of the permanent activists are we able to see the extent to which the parties are the property of the small cadre willing to commit themselves to politics as an avocation.

| The Development of Party Consensus | Although the beginnings of the welfare-capitalism consensus can be traced to the very origin of the country, the consensus was considerably broadened in the years after the Civil War. Both parties, caught up in the industrial expansion of the era, came under the control of those favoring maximization of private enterprise. Since both parties |

[13] See the consideration of the party-voter-as-business-firm-customer relationship in Robert A. Dahl, *Pluralist Democracy in the United States: Conflict and Consent* (Chicago: Rand McNally, 1967), pp. 247–252.

espoused a virtually identical ideology, neither was able to represent adequately certain disadvantaged segments of the population, especially farmers and urban workers, who were not sharing in the prosperity. These groups became progressively alienated from the established order. The result of this alienation was the mass Populist movement, agrarian rebels who gained control of the Democratic party and nominated William Jennings Bryan in 1896. This rebellion did not develop within elite circles; it was clearly from the "outsiders." But it was a disaster—for the agrarians, for the Democrats, and for participatory democracy in the United States. Probably because an alliance of agrarian farmers and urban workers is unrealistic, the Democratic party was crushed in urban areas of the North, while conservative Democrats completed their hegemony in the South. Consequently, both parties became even more conservative. The triumph of the business system, accomplished by a nonviolent expulsion from the political arena of the disadvantaged segments, was total.

A severe decline in voting participation occurred after the election of 1896, and the decline has not been reversed since then. Many of the masses who had supported Bryan simply dropped out of the electoral system. Turnout decreased from 85 percent in 1896 to 68 percent in the period 1952–1960. The destruction of political competition, with the crushing of the Populist rebellion in 1896, is largely responsible for the marked decline in the active voting population. As Burnham concludes:

> This revolutionary contraction in the size and diffusions in the shape of the voting universe was almost certainly the fruit of the heavily sectional party realignment which was inaugurated in 1896. . . . It is difficult to avoid the impression that while all the forms of political democracy were more or less scrupulously preserved, the functional result of the "system of 1896" was a conversion of a fairly democratic regime into a rather broadly based oligarchy.[14]

The party system of 1896 was modified by the Great Depression and the election of 1932, which established a liberal elite and replaced the Republicans as the majority party. As result of this realigning election, the consensus shifted gradually from "rugged individualism" to a more public-oriented philosophy under Franklin D. Roosevelt. The Republican party clung to the philosophy of rugged individualism in the 1936 election with the candidacy of the "Kansas Sunflower," Alf Landon, but the prevailing mood of both elites and masses favored economic reform and social welfare. By 1940, the GOP candidate, Wendell Willkie, president of a giant public utilities empire, was expressing support for social security, fair labor standards, unemployment compensation, public welfare, and most other New Deal programs. The Republican party found itself promising to administer

[14] Walter Dean Burnham, "The Changing Shape of the American Political Universe," p. 23.

reform programs more efficiently and more effectively than the Democrats! The Republican party, as a part of the shifting consensus, came to accept most of the innovations introduced by the Democrats. The Eisenhower administration was conservative rather than reactionary, and the Eisenhower years illustrated the extent to which the consensus had become solid.

This apparent resolution of the conflicts of the 1930s had led some observers to proclaim an "end to ideology."[15] Some viewed the alleged end to ideology with contentment, others with dissatisfaction. Perhaps the most explicit statement of the consequences of an "end to ideology" comes from Barrington Moore, Jr.:

> Once the ideal has been achieved, or is even close to realization, the driving force of discontent disappears, and a society settles down for a time to a stolid acceptance of things as they are. Something of this sort seems to have happened to the United States.[16]

In such a situation, political parties cannot produce genuine alternatives. Evidence of consensus politics is found in patterns of partisanship and attitudes toward political parties. Lane notes that, as increasing proportions of the working class achieve security and adopt middle-class values, they nevertheless remain Democrats.[17] Also, members of the middle class now associate their own well-being with the welfare state. Nominally Republicans, they recognize the stability of economic planning and retain only their symbolic identification with laissez-faire capitalism. Thus values are not necessarily stable or related to party affiliation, which in contrast is extremely stable. Since both classes are generally satisfied, and neither party proposes a serious modification of the status quo, there is a low sense of electoral crisis. Campaigns tend to be moderate and calm. Surveys show that only 3 percent of Americans think that Democrats would endanger their country's welfare; in contrast, 17 percent of the English think that the Labour Party would do so. Two thirds of the American population do not think that they would be personally any better or any worse under either party.[18] The level of tension is low among members of the consensual majority because personal stakes in electoral outcomes are not very great. However, when marginal individuals and groups that are not members of the majority are considered in conjunction with those who embrace middle-class values, tension is very high.

The durability of the American consensus is illustrated by the Goldwater election. Goldwater symbolized an attack upon this consensus, and his candidacy caused a massive electoral shift in all strata of the

[15] Daniel Bell, *The End of Ideology: On the Exhaustion of Political Ideas in the Fifties* (New York: Collier Books, 1961).

[16] Barrington Moore, Jr., *Political Power and Social Theory* (Cambridge, Mass.: Harvard University Press, 1958), p. 183.

[17] Robert E. Lane, "The Politics of Consensus in an Age of Affluence," *American Political Science Review*, 59 (March 1965), 880.

[18] Lane, p. 883.

society. Outside the South, Republican losses were excessive in all social classes. The Republican party, identified as the "party of business," usually receives large donations from the legendary "fat cats." However, the 1964 election produced a radical shift in the financial contributions to political parties (Table 7–2). In 1964, only about 20 percent of the Republican contributions were $500 or more. This indicates a massive defection from Goldwater on the part of normal Republican contributors.

Johnson, therefore, benefited from the Goldwater candidacy. His support among businessmen was considerably greater than John Kennedy's in 1960. In 1964, contributions to the Democrats by members of the Business Advisory Council—the elite group of business and industry—exceeded contributions to the Republicans for the first time (Table 7–3). Further, in 1968 businessmen indicated that they preferred George Romney over either Richard Nixon or Ronald Reagan; thus businessmen have indicated their preference for "moderate Republicanism" in the Eisenhower tradition rather than "conservative Republicanism" in the Taft tradition. The pattern of giving in the 1964 election indicates dramatically the extent to which the consensus has penetrated all strata of the society. Big business, once considered an implacable foe of welfare capitalism, emphatically

TABLE 7–2. Percentage of Contributions of $500 or More

	1948	1952	1956	1960	1964
Democrats	69%	63%	44%	59%	69%
Republicans	74	68	74	58	28

Source: Herbert E. Alexander, *Financing the 1964 Election* (Princeton, N.J.: Citizens' Research Foundation, 1966) p. 86.

TABLE 7–3. Contributions by Members of the Business Advisory Council

	Republicans	Democrats
1956	$268,499	$ 4,000
1960	241,060	35,140
1964	87,100	135,450

Source: Herbert E. Alexander, *Financing the 1964 Election* (Princeton, N.J.: Citizens' Research Foundation, 1966), p. 94.

rejected a candidate who espoused an individualistic economic philosophy.

In spite of the bureaucratization of the economy, people are able to maintain symbolic values that buttress the individualistic consensus. For instance, most people believe that personal achievement can produce economic success, and that environmental handicaps are easily overcome. In a recent Gallup survey[19] the question was asked:

[19] *Gallup Opinion Index*, Report No. 25 (July 1967), p. 17.

"In your opinion, what is more to blame if a person is poor: lack of effort on his part, or circumstances beyond his control?" Notice that the largest proportion of respondents in 1967 indicated that a lack of effort rather than circumstances produced poverty (see Table 7–4). Apparently, however, commitment to the individualistic ethic is flexible. The proportion of respondents giving this answer has increased since 1964, perhaps partly as a negative reaction to the increased visibility of poverty, produced by riots and poor people's marches. The strength of the symbolic attachment to the Protestant ethic is shown by the fact that only 36 percent of the population favored a guaranteed annual income of at least $3,200, but 78 percent favored guarantee of enough *work* so that $3,200 a year could be *earned*. The

Table 7–4. Reasons for Poverty	1964	1967
Lack of Effort	33%	42%
Circumstances	29	19
Both	32	36
No opinion	6	3

Source: *Gallup Opinion Index,* Report No. 25 (July 1967), p. 17.

lesson that emerges from these data is that it is possible to accept federal intervention in the economy while maintaining an attachment to the symbols of laissez-faire capitalism.

When a candidate or a party seriously threatens the continuation of government intervention in the economy, he is soundly defeated. In general, therefore, candidates of the major parties do not propose radical alternatives to the economic status quo; the party system in the United States strengthens the national consensus. The consensus is also strengthened by other institutions of society, such as public schools and the mass media. Education in this country indoctrinates the youth with the basic values of the political order; teachers' political values are moderate to conservative, and they tend to avoid the introduction of controversy into the classroom. The mass media also avoid serious criticism of the political system. A few minor publications, such as *Ramparts,* have leveled fundamental criticisms, but mass circulation newspapers and magazines limit themselves to mild scoldings of specific policies. In short, the entire environment of the United States reinforces a commitment to the status quo. Most people are, therefore, immersed in an established political system and are totally unaware of radical alternatives.

Strains on Party Consensus The economic and political assimilation of labor into the middle class has produced the age of consensus that settled the question of the welfare state. However, the benefits of the welfare state have not been evenly distributed in this country. Major pockets of poverty exist, and hard-core poverty groups remain untouched by the general affluence of the society. Although income in this country is undoubtedly more equitably distributed than in many others, the level of poverty remains quite stable. In the 1930s, the lowest fifth of the income scale received 4.1 percent of the total personal income of the country. This percentage has increased only to about 4.7 percent.[20] The fact that the poverty issue is linked to the racial question makes it doubly difficult for the parties to resolve. However, the inability of the parties to assimilate the lowest classes has meant that about 40 million Americans are outside of the political, economic, and social system. Consequently, they are not socialized to the consensus.

The level of participation in American politics has never returned to the level of the nineteenth century. This means that socially and economically disadvantaged groups are under-represented in the active electorate. The 40 percent or so of American adults who are excluded from the political, economic, and social system of the consensual society pose a threat to the existence of the consensus, since they have the potential to be mobilized by counter-elites. A major crisis or an authoritarian movement might pull the outsiders into the political system, with the possible effect of destroying that system.

But this conclusion does not mean that widespread participation is in and of itself bad for democracy. After all, in the nineteenth century America enjoyed participation rates as great as those of the industrial democracies of today. However, increased participation must be structured by the parties so that the newly mobilized voters will not be captured by the radicalism of the left or right. The failure of the parties to mobilize these voters leaves the danger of rapid mobilization unchecked. This failure, argues Burnham, is due primarily to the unwillingness of the American political system to accept the legitimacy of non-middle-class values. Thus, we have constructed a political system that has achieved stability by keeping out dissidents, and, within the walls of the political community, the politics of consensus is appropriate. However, by narrowing the political community, we have created a total system that is potentially unstable.

This conflict between middle-class consensus and the demands for change by those excluded from the consensus has produced a crisis for the American two-party system in the 1960s. This crisis has been brought about in part by the willingness of today's outsiders (the poor, the youth, and blacks, and the opponents of war) to resort to methods other than those provided by the established political system. These methods have included peaceful demonstrations, nonviolent confrontations, planned disruptions of normal institutional activity, civil disobedience, and — in the case of urban ghetto blacks — riots. And the crisis has been deepened by the reaction of the insiders (the majority who profit by the consensus) to the methods of the outsiders (the minority who do not). This reaction has produced the strong third-party movement of George C. Wallace and, perhaps more importantly,

[20] Michael Harrington, *The Other America: Poverty in the United States* (Baltimore: Penguin Books, 1963), p. 179.

led both major parties to pledge themselves to use greater force to end dissent and enforce consensus (see Table 7–5).

TABLE 7–5.
Wallace Support,
1968

	April	November vote
National	9%	13.6%
Republicans	2	5
Democrats	9	14
Independents	16	25
College	5	9
High school	10	15
Grade school	12	15
Professional and business	6	10
Clerical and sales	8	12
Manual labor	12	15
Farmers	15	20

Sources: April attitudes are from *Gallup Opinion Index*, Report No. 38 (August 1968), p. 7. November vote data are from *Gallup Opinion Index*, Report No. 42 (December 1968), p. 5.

But even as both parties struggle to insure consensus, their efforts appear to be unsuccessful, for larger numbers of people on both the Left and Right in American politics are deserting the Democratic and Republican parties. To be sure, there is substantial evidence that the poor and the blacks were never wholly within the two-party system in the first place. Figures on non-voting indicate that a majority of Negroes and a majority of the poor (families earning less than $3,000 per year) do not participate in American party politics. It is true, of course, that the Civil Rights Act of 1964, the most sweeping civil rights act in American history, and the Economic Opportunity Act of 1964, an outgrowth of the "War on Poverty," represented attempts to incorporate the black and the poor communities into the national consensus. But the actual impact of these acts seemed to be one of raising expectation levels without really bringing about any noticeable changes in the lives of most black and poor people. The effect of these efforts seemed to increase alienation from the political systems rather than reduce it, as promises went unfulfilled and expectations unmet. In the words of the Commission on Civil Disorders, "The expectations aroused by the great judicial and legislative victories of the civil rights movement have led to frustration, hostility, and cynicism in the face of the persistent gap between promise and fulfillment."[21]

The third-party candidacy of George Wallace in 1968 was a serious threat to the two-party system. The Wallace movement was a mass movement, and it was opposed by established elites in both parties. Essentially, the Wallace movement represented a reaction of the lower-class white masses to the demands of black masses and the attempts of elites to incorporate blacks into the political system. In 1968, a

[21] *Report of the National Advisory Commission on Civil Disorders* (Washington, D.C., 1968), p. 204.

majority of the American people did not vote for *either* the Republican or Democratic candidates. The non-votes, together with the third-party votes for George Wallace, outnumbered Democratic and Republican votes, combined.

Summary   The American political party system, as it exists today, is admirably suited to the segment of the public that it serves – those who identify with middle-class values. The two major parties are essentially similar in their ideological bases and in the content of the policies they espouse; the few differences that exist between them are only marginal. Those who do not embrace the values of the middle class are functionally excluded from participation in the system. The substance of ideological agreement has shifted somewhat over time; however, party ideologies have been substantially alike since 1896, when "rugged individualism" held sway. With the inception of the New Deal following the 1932 election, an ideological transition to welfare capitalism took place.

Leadership in each of the major parties is diffused among those who are active in the party. Leaders tend to have a somewhat higher socioeconomic status than do members of the rank and file; the socioeconomic status of both rank and file and leadership are a little higher for Republicans than for Democrats. In neither party does the non-active party identifier have much of a voice in determining party policy or in selecting party candidates. Both of these functions are performed by leaders who possess power as a result of prior party activity. This is not a tension-producing situation within the confines of the party system, however, for the values of the leaders are substantially similar to those held by the passive rank and file.

But the party system does not encompass the entire populace. Between one fourth and one third of the citizenry have not been socialized to middle-class standards. This mass of "marginals" or "outsiders" is composed primarily of the poor and of ethnic and racial minorities. The party system does not exist to serve their interests, nor is it responsive to their needs. Therefore, such "outsiders" fail to engage in even a minimum of participatory behavior, and they have no chance of achieving leadership positions within the parties from which to alter party ideologies and policy positions. Any attempts at forcing change in the party system by "outsiders" must be external to the existing party structure – that is, such attempts must take place through third-party activity, or they must be extra-political.

As long as the majority consensus obtains, such attempts have little chance of success. However, action breeds reaction, and the growing external activity by "outsiders" seems to be causing a breakdown in the middle-class consensus. Those on the right are breaking away to form their own reactionary splinter groups outside of the two-party system, which they perceive to be no longer effective in dealing with minority "dissidents" and "deviants."

Downs, Anthony. *An Economic Theory of Democracy.* New York: Harper & Row (paperback), 1957. Downs develops an abstract model of party politics based upon traditional democratic political theory. The relationships among voters, parties, and governmental policy according to the democratic model are clearly presented, and empirical propositions are deduced therefrom.

Key, V. O., Jr. *Politics, Parties, and Pressure Groups,* 5th edition. New York: Thomas Y. Crowell Co., 1967. This work is a classic in the area of American party politics. Key traces the historical development of our present parties and discusses their role in the political system.

Luttbeg, Norman (ed.). *Public Opinion and Public Policy: Models of Political Linkage.* Homewood, Ill.: Dorsey Press (paperback), 1968. Several articles describing American parties and their relationship to voters and to the political system in general are offered in this collection of readings.

Pomper, Gerald. *Elections in America: Control and Influence in Democratic Politics.* New York: Dodd, Mead Co. (paperback), 1968. In focusing on the linkage between electoral behavior and public policy, Pomper discusses at some length the role of political parties, historically and within the contemporary context. Chapters 5, 7, and 8 are most useful in this regard.

Sorauf, Frank J. *Party Politics in America.* Boston: Little, Brown and Co. (Basic Studies in Politics Series), 1968. Sorauf employs the organizing concept of the political system in this theoretical work. He focuses on the parties within the American political system—their structure and the functions they perform.

The Organized Interests: Defenders of the Status Quo

Interest groups, private non-governmental organizations, should be a more effective method of political participation than individual voting. Presumably, a combination of voices is more effective than a single one. The "interests" with their better organization achieve more tangible benefits than do the unorganized "people" (voters). In fact, serious studies of the policy-making process indicate that cohesion and organization *do* contribute disproportionately to political success. The myth that interest groups are the "real" influence behind policy making contains just enough truth to make the study of them worthwhile.

What are the functions of interest groups? Why are some groups powerful and others not? Why are some issues vulnerable to group influence and others not? Do some political systems contribute to interest group strength?

The Premises of Interest Group Theory Some contemporary writers contend that interest groups perform important functions for their members and for the total society. First, the organized group is said to serve as a link between the individual and his government:

> Voluntary associations are the prime means by which the function of mediating between the individual and the state is performed. Through them the individual is able to relate himself effectively and meaningfully to the political system.[1]

Actually, the extent to which this particular function is served is open to question, as is the extent of the power of groups. Is the organization, operating as a mediating link between the individual and the government, any more efficient than a direct citizen-government interaction? Why do we need a "middleman"?

It is also said that interest groups contribute to individual well being. In a mass society, with primary associations (small groups, such as

[1] Gabriel A. Almond and Sidney Verba, *The Civic Culture: Political Attitudes and Democracy in Five Nations* (Boston: Little, Brown and Co., 1965), p. 245.

the family) diminishing in importance, secondary associations may help the individual overcome the sense of powerlessness characteristic of mass societies. Groups may integrate the individual with society.

Finally, interest groups are said to help reduce potentially divisive conflicts. At first glance, it might be assumed that interest groups intensify conflict. In America, political parties are deliberately devoid of firm ideologies. Interest groups, so the argument runs, since they represent narrower sets of values, can afford to sharpen conflict. An individual who is a Republican might also be a member of the National Association of Manufacturers. While his party membership does not encourage competition, his NAM membership might. Thus, while parties moderate conflict, groups—in working for a favorable allocation of resources or for some symbolic point—increase conflict.

However, one can also argue that groups can *mute* conflict because of overlapping affiliations. The theory of overlapping memberships suggests that all citizens are members of groups (unorganized and organized).[2] Each person can be summed up as a product of his group affiliations. A person may be, for example, a lawyer, a Southerner, and a Protestant, each of these affiliations imposing contradictory values upon him. A person who was raised in a Southern conservative family might begin a teaching career in a Northern university with a predominately liberal environment. Under these circumstances, neither group affiliation would be able to claim the total loyalty of the individual, and thus full mobilization of group resources is impossible, given divided loyalties. If an organization that attempts to represent a value imposes demands that conflict with the wishes of a substantial proportion of its members, it faces a loss of cohesion and thus a reduction in bargaining position. Hence, group demands are modified and societal conflict reduced. A problem with this theory is that the conflict management function of interest groups is difficult to test, because of the difficulty of measuring affiliation with unorganized groups.

To sum up, interest groups are now considered "good" because they provide for a more effective voice for citizens competing for the allocation of resources. They reduce the anxiety produced by a feeling of powerlessness, and they provide an element of stability for the society. The "old theory" that interest groups are "bad" because they are opposed to the "public interest" has been replaced.

In replacing it, political scientists have performed a subtle but significant transformation on pluralism by making interest group theory part and parcel of pluralist thinking. Organized group activity is considered to be a means whereby individuals who want something from a government can pool their resources and get it. Indeed, there are thousands of organizations making their demands on Congress—various administrative agencies, state legislatures, city councils, and even school boards. A glance at the list of registered lobbyists in Washington and in the various state capitals gives superficial credence to the argument. Each group, or potential group, is free to organize.

[2] David B. Truman, *The Governmental Process* (New York: Alfred A. Knopf, 1951).

Consequently, organization produces counter-organization. In the process of resolving group demands, each interest is given a voice, and public policy is formed in response to these competitive demands. Interest groups, then, serve pluralistic democracy well by insuring that governmental decision makers respond to the claims of the various publics. It is in the *competition* among the varieties of competitive groups that pluralism finds its most frequently stated defense. Pluralistic interest-group theory does not deny the existence of elites, but rather contends that each elite is specialized, representative of a set of mass demands, and counter-balanced by a set of opposing demands. As Arnold Rose puts it:

[the multi-influence hypothesis] conceives of society as consisting of many elites, each relatively small numerically and operating in different spheres of life, and of the bulk of the population classifiable into organized groups and publics as well as masses. Among the elites are several that have their power through economic controls, several others that have power through political controls, and still others that have power through military, associational, and other controls. While it is true that there are inert masses of undifferentiated individuals without access to each other (except in the most trivial respects) and therefore without influence, the bulk of the population consists not of the mass, but of integrated groups and publics, stratified with varying degrees of power.[3]

As described by Rose, a typical exponent, interest group theory contains a series of assumptions which must be verified if the theory is to be judged correct. The assumptions are: (1) Membership in organizations is widespread and thus broadly representative of *all* the relevant publics. (2) People join organizations to secure political representation. Although not themselves interested in taking their time to engage in political bargaining, they expect the leadership of the organization to reflect their demands. (3) Organized groups efficiently translate membership expectation into political demands. Nothing is lost in the translation, but a great deal is gained by the presentation of demands from a representative association. (4) Although representation by an interest group is not uniformly successful (some groups win and some lose), each group has equal access to the political resources necessary for success, irrespective of the nature of its demands. (5) By their representative functions, organizations contribute to a feeling of political efficacy among their members; they strengthen the social fabric.

We contend that the first four of these assumptions are incorrect; and we will present evidence to refute them. And though we concede that the final assumption has empirical evidence in its behalf, we will argue that *because* of their integrative function, organizations help to guide their members toward an acceptance of the *status quo*. We suggest that interest groups, rather than articulating the demands of masses, serve to protect the values of established elites.

[3] Arnold Rose, *The Power Structure* (New York: Oxford University Press, 1967), p. 6.

It is popularly assumed that "Americans are joiners." It appears that a majority of the population belong to at least one formal organization. However, membership in voluntary associations is clearly linked to socioeconomic status (see Table 8–1). A variety of evidence has demonstrated that membership is greatest among the professional and managerial classes, among college trained people, and among people with high incomes. Voluntary association membership is primarily an upper-middle-class to upper-class phenomenon. For instance, 80 percent of the respondents in the Almond-Verba study with "some college" are members of associations, compared to 46 percent of those respondents with a primary education or less.[4]

The upper-class bias of voluntary associations varies, of course, with the nature of the organization. Unions (which frequently are *not* voluntary) recruit from the lower strata, as do civil rights organizations and the Ku Klux Klan. However, even within the civil rights movement, the masses of blacks are uninvolved. Civil rights organizations are lower class in comparison to white organizations, but within the black community, participation and social status are still related. For example, the National Association for the Advancement of Colored People represents the moderate Negro "establishment," not the blacks in urban ghettos who take direct and violent action. At any rate, the social bias in voluntary association membership,

TABLE 8–1.
Percentage of
Respondents Who
Belong to
Some Organization
by Nation and
Education

	Total (%) (no.)*	Primary or Less (%) (no.)	Some Secondary (%) (no.)	Some University (%) (no.)
United States	57 (970)	46 (339)	55 (443)	80 (188)
Great Britain	47 (963)	41 (593)	55 (322)	92 (24)
Germany	44 (955)	41 (792)	63 (124)	62 (26)
Italy	30 (995)	25 (692)	37 (245)	46 (54)
Mexico	24 (1,007)	21 (877)	39 (103)	68 (24)

*Numbers in parentheses refer to the bases upon which percentages are calculated.

Source: Gabriel A. Almond and Sidney Verba, *The Civic Culture: Political Attitudes and Democracy in Five Nations* (Boston: Little, Brown and Co. 1965) p. 249.

whether or not the association is "political," is complemented by the high social origins of lobbyists and the predominance of business organizations in *effective* lobbying.

This bias has obvious implications for the ascribed functions of interest groups. Whatever they do, they do it mostly for the upper-middle and upper classes, not for the total population. As Schattschneider observes, "The notion that the pressure system is automatically representative of the whole community is a myth fostered

[4] Almond and Verba, *The Civic Culture*, p. 249.

by the universalizing tendencies of modern group theory."[5] For one thing, even if interest groups are an effective link between the citizen and his government, many citizens do not avail themselves of this benefit. For example, 87 percent of the farm laborers do not belong to an organization, compared to 58 percent of the farm owners. Even if the voluntary association does reduce anxiety or increase feelings of power, it does not serve the very people whose alienation from the society is the greatest and whose need for such services is most extreme.

Further, among those who are members of associations, active participation — and the holding of formal organizational office — is directly related to social status. Whereas membership in associations is characteristic of the majority of Americans, *active* participation is characteristic of a minority of members. All organizations are typically controlled by a small elite. Michels' "iron law of oligarchy" describes the fact that even the most democratically inclined organizations gradually evolve into oligarchies. The oligarchs, who help to shape the goals of the organization, are drawn disproportionately from the upper social classes.[6]

Participation in organizations is also related to satisfaction with one's life situation. The more satisfied one is with his job, for example, the more likely he is to participate in union affairs. Hence, those who have the least to complain about are most likely to guide the affairs of formal organizations. Naturally, the higher one's social status, the less one has to complain about.

Thus, our first empirical test of contemporary interest group theory fails to corroborate an important assumption upon which such theory is based. Those who are active in interest groups constitute only a small portion of the populace; moreover, they tend to be from a higher socioeconomic status than those who are not active. In short, it is the elites who are the most active in interest groups in America.

Given the class bias in organizational membership, it is not surprising that business associations are the single largest lobbying group at the state and national levels. In Washington, of the 25 top spenders among lobbying groups, nine are business (see Table 8–2). Further, of the 269 organizations that reported any lobbying expenditures, 143 are business organizations. At the state level, the domination of business associations is equally apparent. In a survey of interest groups represented in the states, it was found that business lobbyists were clearly the most visible and most numerous. No matter what kind of economy a state has, business dominates its lobbying. Even in a state such as South Dakota, which has 30 percent of its population employed

[5] E. E. Schattschneider, *The Semisovereign People: A Realist's View of Democracy in America* (New York: Holt, Rinehart and Winston, 1960), p. 35.
[6] Roberto Michels, *Political Parties: A Sociological Study of the Oligarchical Tendencies of Modern Democracy* (New York: Dover, 1959; originally published in English in 1915), esp. p. 248.

in non-industrial occupations, two-thirds of the registered lobbyists represent business.[7] As Schattschneider concludes:

> The business or upper-class bias of the pressure system shows up everywhere. . . . The data raise a serious question about the validity of the proposition that special interest groups are a universal form of political organization reflecting *all* interests.[8]

Interest group conflict, then, reflects merely the most visible disputes between factions within the established elite. Business and labor may contest over the raising of the minimum wage, but both unite to keep demands for radical reform out of the pressure system. The game of pressure-group politics has rules which exclude the masses.

TABLE 8–2.
The 25 top spenders of 1969, of the 269 organizations that filed lobby spending reports

Organization	1969	1968
National Association of Letter Carriers (AFL-CIO)	$295,970	$ 63,797
United Federation of Postal Clerks (AFL-CIO)	250,827	170,784
Realty Committee on Taxation	229,223	–
AFL-CIO (headquarters)	184,938	154,466
American Farm Bureau Federation	146,337	147,379
National Committee for the Recording Arts	139,726	25,949
National Association of Home Builders of the United States	138,472	70,095
United States Savings and Loan League	126,421	119,784
Record Industry Association of America Inc.	115,334	111,394
American Legion	114,609	141,134
Council for a Livable World	112,603	154,022
National Education Association, Office of Government Relations and Citizenship	97,537	84,146
National Housing Conference Inc.	95,562	96,935
American Medical Association	91,355	56,374
Railway Labor Executives Association	86,286	–
National Association of Theatre Owners	84,049	–
Citizens Committee for Postal Reform	83,951	–
Brotherhood of Railway, Airline & Steamship Clerks, Freight Handlers, Express and Station Employees (AFL-CIO)	80,985	93,456
American Trucking Associations Inc.	80,896	121,399
Liberty Lobby Inc.	79,927	75,807
National Federation of Independent Business Inc.	75,528	102,455
National Farmers Union	73,264	95,639
National Association of Postal Supervisors	68,365	35,694
National Council of Farmer Cooperatives	62,496	57,832
National Federation of Federal Employees	61,269	57,148

Source: Congressional Quarterly Weekly Report, July 31, 1970.

Why Do People Join Organizations?

Why do people join associations? To answer this question, we need to know something about the various kinds of organizational opportunities. Since motivations for joining are related to the goals of the organization, the aims of groups are significant because they indicate the type of member that will initially be recruited.

Occasionally a distinction is made between "political" and "nonpolitical" organizations. This distinction is unsatisfactory. It is true

---

[7]Harmon Zeigler, "Interest Groups in the States," in Herbert Jacob and Kenneth N. Vines, eds., *Politics in the American States* (Boston: Little, Brown and Co., 1965), p. 109.
[8]Schattschneider, pp. 31–34.

that some groups—such as the National Committee for an Effective Congress and the Americans for Democratic Action—are primarily political, while others—such as historical clubs and mountain-climbing associations—are not. However, organizations can become more or less political as the environment increases or decreases its hostility. Groups that are political at inception may become essentially nonpolitical. For example, the Grange began as a vigorously political movement but gradually abandoned politics for more comfortable economic and social functions. Groups that are nonpolitical at their inception may become political. The National Rifle Association originally devoted itself to membership programs, hunter safety, and the like. But the outbreak of political assassinations—and the growing demand for gun control legislation—has transformed the NRA into an active lobbying group.

Further, organizations provide a multitude of services, only a fraction of which are political. The American Legion employs lobbyists and develops legislative programs; yet, at the local level, the American Legion is primarily a social club. The National Education Association, in addition to its political activities, also provides insurance and other benefits for its members. Unions are certainly political, but one could hardly maintain that motivations for joining them are related solely to this particular function.

About 40 percent of the members of American associations think that their particular organization is engaged in political activities. Only 50 percent of the members of labor unions are of this opinion, yet we know that unions make political contributions to campaigns and conduct extensive lobbying efforts. Members may be quite unaware of the political activity of their organizations and maintain membership for nonpolitical reasons.[9] For these reasons, the simple categorization of groups according to the degree of their political involvement is misleading.

What classification, then, can we use to guide us to an understanding of motivations for joining groups? We can classify them according to the kinds of objectives they pursue. Terms for this classification are suggested by Edelman, who refers to some goals as "tangible" and others as "non-tangible" or "symbolic."[10] Some groups concern themselves with the allocation of economic (tangible) resources. Trade associations, for example, dedicate most of their energies toward the solution of the problems of economic competition, and unions concern themselves predominately with labor-management issues. Other organizations are ideological; the goals they seek are intangible. For example, anti-Communist groups, such as the John Birch Society or the Americans for Constitutional Action, address themselves to problems unrelated to the distribution of economic resources. Of course, it is important to understand that this classification is an "ideal type," suggestive

[9]Harmon Zeigler, "Interest Groups in the States," in Herbert Jacob and Kenneth N. Vines (eds.) *Politics in the American States: A Comparative Analysis* (Boston: Little, Brown and Co., 1965), p. 105.
[10]Murray Edelman, *The Symbolic Uses of Politics* (Urbana: University of Illinois Press, 1964).

of *tendencies* in organizational goals. Obviously, most organizations concern themselves with a mix of tangible and intangible goals.

A distinction must be made between the stated goals and actual accomplishments of groups. For instance, an organization may seek tangible benefits but settle for intangible ones; the passage of a law may result in no reallocation of tangible resources but may provide a group with a symbolic victory. Froman points out that group leaders are less likely than followers to be satisfied with symbolic rewards. However, when they realize that their victory is a hollow one, they exaggerate their accomplishments to their followers. Followers are not likely to be knowledgeable enough to make a critical judgment:

> Hence influencing followers involves appeals to emotion. Not being interested or knowledgeable about the specific issues affecting the group, followers are more swayed by broad appeals for the attainment of some nonspecific goal such as "better" working conditions or "lower" interest rates.[11]

On the other hand, some organizations are *overtly* symbolic in their aspirations. Both leaders and followers in this type of organization are potentially satisfied by the same kinds of rewards. A law, whether or not it reallocates tangible resources, can express values about a group. Right-to-work laws tell the society that unions are not "legitimate"; anti-trust laws do the same thing to big business. Gusfield designates issues in which the stakes are prestige as "status" issues.[12] Deference to status can be satisfied in a purely symbolic fashion; all that is necessary is that a gesture be made.

However, an extreme form of status anxiety, in which the organization seeks a declaration from society that the fundamental social structure is wrong, cannot be satisfied. For example, the domestic communism issue, and the behavior of the advocates of the anti-Communist position, can be understood as the clash between two cultural subgroups: the "traditional" and the "modern." There is no possibility of satisfying the demands of the traditional subculture. The *expression* of the demands of the group, not its success in its stated goals, is the justification for its existence. Action for its own sake can be gratifying, no matter what actual decisions are reached by the government. Hence, the decisions of government cannot cause any modification in the demands of such groups. An examination of the statements of extremist groups shows the remarkable stability of their ideology. International and domestic crises come and go, but these organizations operate unaffected in a different world.

As we noted, most group political activity mixes tangible and intangible goals. Nevertheless, groups generally can be fitted into one category. But it should be understood that achieving tangible success is difficult, and few groups can claim such victories. Hence, many of the

[11] Lewis A. Froman, Jr., *People and Politics: An Analysis of the American Political System* (Englewood Cliffs, N.J.: Prentice-Hall, 1962), p. 47.
[12] Joseph R. Gusfield, *Symbolic Crusade: Status Politics and the American Temperance Movement* (Urbana: University of Illinois Press, 1963).

rewards of the group struggle are symbolic. The predominance of symbolic rewards is fortunate for the survival of organizations, since survival depends upon the recruitment and maintenance of members. Because large numbers of people tend to view government in stereotypic, symbolic terms, they can be satisfied rather easily. Membership in voluntary associations is probably quite volatile outside the active elite, and symbolic rewards—as a substitute for tangible ones—help to maintain some degree of membership stability.

However, in most cases (with the exception of extreme ideologues), symbolic satisfactions in themselves are not a sufficient inducement to membership. As we know, most people are not very interested in politics. Other than voting occasionally, they do not take an active political role. Why then should they join a political organization? Economist Mancur Olson addresses himself to this question. Theoretically, it is not rational for a person to join a group in order to support lobbying and other political activities that result in benefits for non-members as well as members. A group may work for collective benefits (minimum wages, price supports, etc.), but all farmers or workers will benefit, whether or not they are members of the organization. Balancing costs against benefits, there is no reason for an individual to join or continue membership.

To explain why people are willing to establish and maintain membership, Olson argues that there is a distinction between *collective* benefits—those that benefit an entire category of people—and *selective* benefits—those that are available only to members of the association.[13] In studying groups, political scientists usually neglect selective benefits, because they are likely to be part of the nonpolitical aspects of an organization. Since many organizations devote at least a portion of their energies to politics, and since political scientists are usually interested only in political behavior, they study a small fraction of organizational activity and neglect the rest. For example, political scientists concern themselves with the American Medical Association or the National Education Association as lobbying groups, which they certainly are. But the American Medical Association also provides, for the price of membership, a variety of useful services. It offers the doctor

. . . the social and professional contacts indispensable to the growth of his practice—contacts which may lead to patient referrals and consultations. Additionally, there is the all-important factor of association with men engaged in his own science, with opportunities for exchange of knowledge and acquisition of professional status. The medical societies disseminate the latest scientific information through professional journals which are available to members either at no cost, or at reduced rates, and through lectures, exhibits, and medical libraries which the societies support. In addition to these professional services, the local and state societies aid members by providing group malpractice insurance and by offering legal advice. Many of the larger societies maintain

[13] Mancur Olson, Jr., *The Logic of Collective Action: Public Goods and the Theory of Groups* (Cambridge, Mass.: Harvard University Press, 1965).

bill collection agencies. There may also be direct economic benefits incidental to membership. Since the societies often contract to furnish medical aid to indigents and veterans, participating physicians have supplementary sources of income from these programs. Membership can also be a conduit to such professional advancements as hospital staff appointments, teaching positions, and specialty ratings.[14]

AMA lobbying against the various medical care bills (collective benefits) is possible because the AMA provides other services. Most doctors do not have the time for medical politics and are content to leave this aspect of the profession to the staff of the AMA.

Similarly, the National Education Association and its state affiliates are active lobbying groups. State legislators regularly list education associations as active and influential organizations, yet most teachers join for reasons unrelated to politics. Some join to gain access to professional literature and ideas; others join because of administrative pressure to do so. About 10 percent join for "political" reasons.[15] Thus, only a few teachers join because they support the education associations' lobbying activities, or because they think it will provide them with defense against political attack in the event that they become embroiled in a community controversy. If the only services provided by the NEA were lobbying and protective benefits, it would fold immediately. This is not to suggest that the members of the NEA *object* to political activities, only that most members are likely to be unconcerned and uninformed about the organization's goals in the legislature.

Ideological groups, on the other hand, do not try to offer selective benefits, because they attract a different kind of member. The National Committee for an Effective Congress, which is an unusual organization consisting of a small group of politically active financial contributors, provides no service to its members other than the opportunity to contribute to a candidate whose ideology is comparable to that of the contributor. The contributors, however, are drawn from the minority of the electorate that conceptualizes campaigns in ideological dimensions. They are wealthy, educated, and politically aware. For them, the function of the organization in channeling funds is in itself a sufficient motivation for continued participation.[16]

Organizations like the John Birch Society attract a different kind of ideologue and promise a different kind of benefit: an expressive reward that is satisfying psychologically rather than tangibly. Such organizations bear little relation to an objective reality, and therefore need not concern themselves with selective benefits. Membership in the Ku Klux Klan, another expressive organization, is drawn primarily from the upper working and lower middle classes. The marginal economic situation of Klansmen is accompanied by insecurity about status and

[14]Frank R. Kennedy, "The American Medical Association: Power, Purpose, and Politics in Organized Medicine," *Yale Law Journal*, 63 (May 1954), 939–940.
[15]Harmon Zeigler, *The Political Life of American Teachers* (Englewood Cliffs, N.J.: Prentice-Hall, 1967), pp. 59–60.
[16]Harry M. Scoble, *Ideology and Electoral Action: A Comparative Case Study of the National Committee for an Effective Congress* (San Francisco: Chandler Publishing Co., 1967).

anxiety about personal power. The members need to feel they are important. They accept the validity of the American success story, but are thwarted in their efforts to live according to the plot of this story. They do not *reject* the rags to riches ideology, but *overidentify* with "100 percent Americanism." Secrecy, exaggerated symbolism, elaborate regalia, and weird titles set the Klansman apart and give him an identification that reduces the anxiety of his economic marginality. Even so, the rewards of membership are not sufficient to insure a stable organization. The Klan is characterized by splinter groups and unstable membership.

Such groups advocate programs that have no possibility of success. If the Communists are in control of every institution, what chance is there for improvement of society? As the John Birch Society phrases it, the Communists are winning in "the press, the pulpit, the radio, the television media, the labor unions, the schools, the courts, and the legislative halls of America." Membership in such an organization is entirely expressive and cannot be satisfied even symbolically; these groups have a history of organizational turmoil.

The answer to the question "Why do people join organizations?" is many-faceted. Motives vary over a wide range of anticipated rewards. Some seek material rewards but settle for symbolic ones; others settle for tangible, selective benefits; some seek and receive nothing other than psychological, symbolic payoffs. Only a few seek and *receive* tangible rewards from governmental action as a result of organized activity.

Thus the second assumption of pluralistic group theory receives scant evidential support. Even within the elite organizations of the pressure system, the articulation of political demands remains the function of the few. The members of such organizations are less concerned with politics than are the leaders, and exercise little restraint upon their behavior.

How Well Do Groups Mediate? The next test of group theory concerns the function of transmitting member demands into political action. Since we have seen in the previous section that membership demands are rarely made, we can hardly expect that organizational leadership is merely a middleman. Still, group leaders *do* lobby and, to the extent that they are successful, protect their membership (even though the membership may not know or care) in most cases.

The size of the group is an important variable in its leadership's effectiveness as a middleman. Access to legislators is enhanced by a large membership, since elected officials are sensitive to numbers. However, large groups find it difficult to commit themselves to an explicit position, since their membership is so heterogeneous. The policy positions of mass membership organizations must be vague and broad, devoid of specific content, and thus harmless. The Chamber of Commerce, for example, seeks to represent "businessmen," without regard for the nature of the business. Since intra-business disputes are often as bitter as labor-management disputes, the Chamber cannot take a position on many of the minute legislative and administrative details that involve the economic health of various portions of the business community.

Generally, mass membership groups achieve symbolic success, while smaller, more cohesive groups are able to persist in the pursuit of limited objectives and gradually exhaust their enemy. Edelman makes the point that tangible benefits are rarely redistributed by legislatures, the arena of the large groups. Rather, they are redistributed in the *administration* of legislation, an activity in which small groups have the advantage. Numbers are not as important to administrators, who are only indirectly concerned with election results, as they are to legislators. When administrative action reverses legislative intent, "deprived groups often display little tendency to protest or to assert their awareness of the deprivation. . . . The most intensive dissemination of symbols commonly attends the enactment of legislation, which is most meaningless in its effects upon resource allocation."[17]

Groups seeking symbolic achievement exhibit the following characteristics: (1) shared interest in the improvement of status through protest activity, (2) an unfavorably perceived strategic position with respect to reference groups, (3) stereotyped, inexact information and perception, (4) response to symbols connoting suppression of threats, (5) relative ineffectiveness in achieving tangible rewards as a result of political activity, (6) little organization for purposive action, (7) quiescence (inactivity), and (8) relatively large numbers.

Most of the groups active in the legislative process display many, but not all, of these characteristics. Labor unions, for example, are large and well organized. Still, many of their achievements are symbolic. Much the same can be said of those civil rights organizations that seek to achieve political results through established democratic procedures. In spite of the turmoil since the 1954 decision outlawing segregation in public schools, the economic condition of Negroes has changed very little, the law itself has not been enforced by government sanctions. Indeed, for the first decade after the desegregation decision, many of the demands of Negro organizations were symbolic. What, for instance, is the significance of forcing Woolworth's to integrate their lunch counter? Clearly, nothing other than the conferring of legitimacy upon the goals of the movement was achieved. Gusfield notes the symbolic value of desegregation efforts:

Desegregation is a status issue par excellence. Its symbolic characteristics lie in the deference which the norm of integration implies. The acceptance of token integration, which is what has occurred in the North, is itself prestige-conferring because it establishes the public character of the norm supporting integration. It indicates what side is publicly legitimate and dominant. Without understanding this symbolic quality of the desegregation issue the fierceness of the struggle would appear absurd. Since so little actual change in concerted

[17]Edelman, *The Symbolic Uses of Politics*, pp. 24–26.

behavior ensues, the question would be moot if it were not for this characteristic as an act of deference toward Negroes and of degradation toward whites.[18]

However, it may be that symbolic victories are needed as a prelude to the achievement of tangible ones. The civil rights movement, as leadership is wrested away from the moderate elements, is directing itself more toward equality of economic opportunity.

In contrast to these groups, organizations enjoying tangible benefits are small and highly organized, with rational procedures related to realistic goals. Their members have precise information. The group has an effective interest in a specifically identified, tangible resource. Members have a favorably perceived strategic position with respect to reference groups. Small groups, based upon narrow interests, can achieve cohesion more readily and concentrate their resources upon a limited objective. They can act decisively and persistently. Such organizations are most frequently business or industrial; the business groups employ the majority of lobbyists at the state and national level. Many businessmen are organized into trade associations representing varieties of industrial and commercial activity. Their membership is limited to a specific form of business activity, for example, insurance, so the trade associations are frequently quite small, some with as few as 25 members. Trade associations also provide non-collective benefits, but they can provide tangible, collective benefits that the larger groups cannot offer. They have disproportionate power with regard to the *specific* values they advocate, while the business community *as a whole* fights symbolic battles.

The "businessmen in politics" movement, in which the United States Chamber of Commerce distributed a "practical politics" package to companies to be used in classes for junior executives, exhibits the symbolic nature of the struggles of the larger, undifferentiated business community. A similar, widely distributed package was offered by the Manufacturers Association of Syracuse. Executives were provided with a text. Recordings (by Richard Nixon) and pamphlets (including homework assignments) were included in the package, and training courses, designed to activate businessmen as a force to combat the alleged domination of American politics by organized labor, were conducted. Executives spoke of labor's "domination of Congress," alleging business to be "powerless."[19]

The practical politics seminars were profitable for those who organized and staffed them and were perhaps symbolically meaningful. Tangibly, however, they were valueless. Business is *not* powerless with regard to the allocation of tangible rewards to specific kinds of business, and it is symbolically powerful as a whole. How often does one turn from the business section of a newspaper to a "union section"? The symbol of success in America *is* the businessman. Does the American success story include the image of a union organizer? Do the mass

[18] Gusfield, *Symbolic Crusade*, p. 173.
[19] Andrew Hacker and Joel D. Aberbach, "Businessmen in Politics," *Law and Contemporary Problems*, 27 (Spring

media of communication concern themselves with unions? For example, in television situation comedies, how many families are working class? Lindblom has presented an appropriate summary of the dominance of business values:

> The bias in policy making is of course not limited to interest-group participation. Elected and appointed proximate policy makers are overwhelmingly from the more favored classes; in the federal government 60 percent of them come from business and professional families. They will therefore seek out and listen to interest-group leaders with whose desires they are already sympathetic. To be sure, officials do not see themselves as representing the interests of some classes against others; rather it is that they see the general interest in the light of their own group affiliations, a phenomenon conspicuous in small-town politics in which, in any easy relation between business and public officials, both see the public interest as equivalent to what they agree on. Every man is, of course, a product of early and continuing indoctrinations reflecting family and group socioeconomic status. What is more, the prestige of middle-class attitudes and political preferences is so overwhelming in some countries, the United States included, that many of the disadvantaged themselves subscribe to them, thus endorsing and perpetuating the very bias in policy making against which they might be expected to protest.[20]

Lobbying. Lobbying is defined as any communication directed at a public official with the hope of influencing his decision. The lobbyist plays a very functional role in the legislative process. He provides an important communication link between non-governmental elites and their congressmen; communications flow both ways as a congressman learns about the interest of non-governmental elites, and these elites are influenced to support the congressman. The lobbyist presents demands on the legislative system from organized interests, participates in negotiations leading to resolution of conflicts, and helps to facilitate elite support for public policy through his involvement in these decisions.

The Federal Regulation of Lobbying Act of 1946 requires the registration of names and spending reports of anyone who "solicits, collects or receives money or any other thing of value to be used principally to aid in . . . the passage and defeat of any legislation by the Congress of the United States." However, enforcement of this law is quite lax, and many of the larger lobby groups—for example, the National Association of Manufacturers, the National Bankers Association, the Americans for Constitutional Action—have never registered as lobbyists. Only about 300 groups register as lobbyists each year, and only about $4 million per year is reported as having been spent for lobbying activities. But these figures grossly underestimate the extent of lobbying activity in Congress. The law only requires reports on money spent on direct lobbying before Congress, not money spent for public relations or for campaign contributions. Further, many hundreds of lobby-

---

[20]Charles E. Lindblom, *The Policy-Making Process* (Englewood Cliffs, N.J.: Prentice-Hall, 1968), p. 68.

ists do not register on the pretext that they are not really lobbyists, but lawyers, researchers, or educational people. However, more restrictive legislation on lobbying might violate the First Amendment freedom to "petition the government for a redress of grievances."

Political scientists examining the political activity of a group's elite tend to infer the values of the group's followers from the group's lobbying actions, when in fact lobbyists and other organization leaders have much the same function in relation to members as do societal elites to masses in general. They make opinions more often than they follow them.

Whatever the nature of the goals of the group, an organization is dominated by its active minority. An organization is composed of formal leaders, active followers, and passive followers, the latter group consisting of the majority of members. A "realistic" theory would have leaders (including lobbyists) representing "virtually"—by means of shared values—the aspirations of their followers. Actually, leaders accommodate only those factions represented by active members, whose values are not necessarily reflective of the values,of most members. Since in most cases the followers are not especially interested in political activities, lack of accurate representation is not crucial to their continued membership. Only when the leaders go beyond the limits of acceptable behavior, and thus become highly visible, will they encounter much opposition.

The discrepancy between leaders' and followers' beliefs is greater than leaders perceive it to be. Interest group leaders pride themselves on their ability to sense intuitively the feelings of followers. However, like all elites, they are inclined to attribute to followers ideologies which the followers do not possess.

For example, the fact that labor union leaders support civil rights legislation does not mean that union members support it. Civil rights are not likely to receive much support among the clientele of unions. However, in spite of the absence of a clear chain of communication between leaders and followers, leaders can still exert lobbying pressure based on the number of their followers. Legislators may operate upon the *assumption* that these numbers are convertible into a deliverable vote. In Oregon, for example, the Oregon Education Association is regarded as powerful by legislators primarily because it has a large membership. The inference is that these members can be turned out to vote in a block; actually, few of the members can correctly identify the position of the organization, and fewer still are likely to follow the advice of group leaders. Therefore, power is not necessarily a function of *actual* resources but rather of *perceived* resources.

However, the surest way to dissipate such a resource is to allow it to be put to the test. An inexperienced lobbyist might threaten to defeat a legislator at the polls, but most skilled lobbyists never mention electoral defeat, because they know that the threat is an empty one. Threats are ineffective in influencing behavior, in any case; fear-arousing communications produce negative reactions. If directly threatened, a legislator may take an adamant position to prove that he is independent. Independence is a highly valued trait in American political lore, and legislators are reluctant to contradict their image of themselves. Unless the threat is capable of being enforced immediately, it is usually ineffective.[21] However, if the threat is only implied, and thus no one has seen evidence that the threat is ineffective, it retains its influence.

The general lack of a one-to-one relationship between the policy statements of the lobbyist and the voting preferences of the members of the organization is most conspicuous when the lobbyist advocates positions unrelated to the immediate self-interest of the members. For example, Edelman notes:

> The officers of the AFL-CIO, in lobbying for a civil rights bill and liberal tariff policies, get some immediate status benefit from posing as statesmen influential in the general affairs of state. The rank-and-file members, who do not share in this benefit, are likely to find the objectives of such legislation remote from their experience and sometimes find that they clash with perceptions of immediate interests: economic or status rivalry with Negroes or employment in an industry losing its market to foreign goods. Congressmen who ignore the official labor position on civil rights or foreign trade can accordingly be fairly confident that the votes and the lofty rhetoric will often be found in different places.[22]

The political resources of the lobbyists are not immediately convertible into power. The legislator, however, possesses a resource that is highly valued by the lobbyist: his vote. Therefore, the lobbyist seeks to create goods desired by the legislator so that the legislator's resource will be used to the benefit of the lobbyist's organization. The key resource that a lobbyist may develop is *information*. Information may be technical, dealing with the details of legislation; or it may be political, concerning the impact of legislation upon the attitudes and behavior of a public. The degree to which a lobbyist can use information as a resource depends upon the existence of competing sources of information. In state legislatures, the informational role of the lobbyist is more important because legislators do not have personal or committee staffs. National legislators, on the other hand, are difficult for lobbyists to see, because their other sources of information are usually adequate for their tasks. Thus, recent estimates of the effects of lobbying in Congress indicate that the efforts of lobbyists have been highly exaggerated by popular commentators.[23]

Also, lobbyists can occasionally be more effective in state politics because of the absence of professionalism among state legislators. State legislators are comparative amateurs. The turnover in state legislatures is very high; in any given session, a substantial proportion of the legislators are "freshmen." This inexperience makes it difficult for them to acquire an "in group" identification with their colleagues.

[21] Harmon Zeigler and Michael A. Baer, *Lobbying: Interaction and Influence in American State Legislatures* (Belmont, Calif.: Wadsworth Publishing Co., 1969), pp. 120–121.
[22] Edelman, *The Symbolic Uses of Politics*, p. 124.
[23] See, for example, Lester W. Milbrath, *The Washington Lobbyists* (Chicago: Rand McNally, 1963).

The institutional life of the state legislature is consequently more permeable by outside forces.

Successful lobbying has little to do with "pressure." In fact, successful lobbying is *negatively* related to the application of pressure techniques. Groups that are perceived by legislators to be the most pressure-oriented are least likely to achieve satisfactory results. The smaller, persistent groups that concern themselves with tangible rewards have no resources for the application of pressure; yet they are successful, especially at the administrative level, because their personnel gradually identify with the day-to-day problems of a particular industry. This identification results in the desire to protect the clientele from non-industry attackers. Agencies originally designed by legislation (in victories won by larger groups) to regulate an industry in the "public interest" frequently are converted to agencies defending the industry against its competition. The members of the agency come to share the values of the regulated industry. This type of interest group's success, while less visible than symbolic victories, is more meaningful in terms of the allocation of tangible resources.

A good example of the success of interest groups in the administrative process occurs, ironically, with the passage of the Economic Opportunity Act in 1964. This Act, the pride of the war on poverty, provided clear symbolic satisfaction to the "have-nots." The Job Corps, VISTA, and the Office of Economic Opportunity had a firm legislative mandate to uplift the poverty-stricken.

It is in the administration of the Act, however, that the real allocation processes can be discovered. The rhetoric surrounding the Community Action Program takes direct aim on the local power structures; it indicates a desire to shake up the establishment:

The local organization applying for a Community Action Program must satisfy only one basic criterion: It must be broadly representative of the interests of the community. It may be a public agency. . . . *Or it may be* a private non-profit agency which has the support *of the relevant elements* of the community. . . .[24]

The law and the rhetoric were intended to delegate decision-making authority to interest groups, in accordance with the pluralist belief that such groups are "broadly representative." As these groups stepped forward, or were newly created, in response to the availability of large sums of money, they became officially recognized by the governmental bureaucracy. Once recognized, they used their official recognition as a resource to prevent the emergence of still newer groups. The political conflict within the war on poverty consists largely of a struggle for control of the administration, with the result that a new establishment is created—those groups with the greatest stake

[24]U.S. House of Representatives, *To Mobilize the Human and Financial Resources of the Nation to Combat Poverty in the United States,* 88th Congress, 2nd sess., 1964, H.R. 10440, pp. 17–18. Cited in Theodore J. Lowi, *The End of Liberalism* (New York: W. W. Norton & Co., 1969), p. 236.

in the program: ". . . . the organizations newly organized had such narrow constituencies that their demands were usually narrow . . . rather than calls for broad reform which would improve education for all those in their class or ethnic group."[25]

Thus the war on poverty, as administered, satisfies the restricted needs of specialized groups, not the needs of the poor. Those portions of the population not specifically organized around immediate, tangible goals are excluded. Who, for example, benefits, when group demands result in the appointment of a black principal of a ghetto school?

The creation of a new, privileged set of interest groups has been the only appreciable impact of the war on poverty. Small groups of elites, blessed with official recognition, have gained the authority to spend federal money. Leaders of such groups, appropriately coöpted, become protective of the new *status quo*. Their struggle is largely over control of resources. They do battle with previously established welfare groups, and the poor are forgotten. The argument is not, "how can we eliminate poverty?" but rather, "which set of elites shall rule?"[26]

Studies of participation by "the poor" in various poverty programs are consistent in their findings that the more affluent segments of the lower strata are more likely to be incorporated into administrative positions. Through prior involvement in welfare activities, these people are more organizationally adept. Program officials, anxious to produce visible evidence of program integrity, facilitate the participation of the more skilled "nearly poor." Hence, those with knowledge of opportunities, learned from previous exposure to other service agencies, are recruited. Thus,

Similar types of affiliation patterns have been found to exist among the poor as for the total range of socioeconomic groups: the participants are more likely to come from the relatively affluent segments of the population. One consequence is that these programs are not reaching those persons with the greatest needs.[27]

Thus, the groups most effective as mediators between their members and government are small, cohesive groups that represent finite but well articulated interests. These elite groups are best able to concentrate their resources and activities where they can attain tangible rewards for their members. Governmental administrators tend to be the targets for groups of this type. Large groups are characterized by broad, hazily defined goals, and their activities tend to be directed at legislators rather than at administrators. What rewards such groups receive tend to be symbolic.

[25] Paul E. Peterson, *City Politics and Community Action* (doctoral dissertation, University of Chicago, 1967), pp. 14–15. Cited in Lowi, *op. cit.*, p. 246.
[26] For an excellent elaboration of this idea, see Lowi, *op. cit.*, ch. 8.
[27] Russell L. Curtis, Jr. and Louis A. Zurcher, Jr., "Voluntary Associations and the Social Integration of the Poor," *Social Problems*, 18 (Winter 1971), 353.

We have argued that much of the energy of pressure groups is dissipated by the receipt of symbolic rewards. Such rewards create the *illusion* of pluralist competition and equal access to political resources. In fact, political resources are *not* equally available to all groups seeking to influence public policy. Conspicuously absent from the successful group process are those organizations seeking to articulate the demands of various powerless strata in society: "protest" groups. By the very nature of their demands and their constituency, such groups are doomed to a short life and political failure.

As an illustration of such a failure, consider the example of the Newark Community Union Project.[28] Organized in 1964 by members of the Students for a Democratic Society and some residents of Newark's South Ward, the NCUP was meant to mobilize ghetto residents into a social protest movement. However, rather than seek the broad and symbolic rewards typical of such movements, NCUP organizers concentrated on specific, tangible problems within the ghetto. During the period from 1964 to 1968, three issues were focused upon.

The first issue was housing. Ghetto residents were paying exorbitant rents for inadequate housing. After months of presenting the problem to the attention of various local agencies had brought no success, a rent strike was begun. In response the tenants were evicted and, in some cases, arrested, and the strike ended. The strikers learned the hard way that laws dealing with rent collection and eviction are swiftly enforced, while those dealing with violations of building codes were unenforceable. In short, the rent strike was a failure.

The next NCUP effort concerned the apparently trivial matter of a traffic light at a dangerous intersection. The issue was, however, especially salient to residents of the ghetto because of deaths and injuries to children from speeding cars. In this case, after rallies, petitions, and letter writing campaigns, the mayor granted an audience and agreed to install the light. Thus a "victory" had apparently been achieved. However, nothing happened. After more protests, demonstrations, and delays, the matter was finally referred to the State Bureau of Motor Vehicles, which declared that traffic lights could be installed only after a survey of traffic conditions — a survey which was never made. Soon after, residents of a white middle-class community were able to get a traffic light installed 28 days after they submitted a petition containing 50 signatures. The light in the ghetto was never installed.

The next effort by NCUP was an attempt to challenge the dominant Democratic leadership electorally. In 1965, the United Freedom Ticket, a coalition of various minority groups, asked NCUP to support an insurgent black Democrat in his fight to challenge the regular Democratic nominee to the state legislature. Against the organization and influence of the regular Democratic organization, defeat was inevitable. Less than half the blacks (as compared to two thirds of the

---

[28]This discussion is taken from Michael Parenti, "Power and Pluralism: A View from the Bottom," *Journal of Politics*, 32 (August 1970), 501–530.

whites) voted, and the United Freedom Ticket candidate drew less than five percent of the vote.

Thus in every attempt to win even a minor victory the protest group was defeated. Not only did NCUP lose every issue it contested, but the organization was subject to harrassment (wire-taps, arrests on trumped-up charges, evictions, etc.) by city officials. After about three years NCUP ceased to exist.

The lessons are clear. Although pluralist interest-group theory argues that effective organizations and use of political resources gives everybody an equal opportunity to win, this opportunity is in fact restricted to established, relatively conservative interests. In Newark, there may have been a plurality of interests, but these interests coalesced to defend themselves against an assault from an organization viewed as a threat. Clearly, then, organization is no guarantee of even the opportunity to contest issues legitimately. If a protest group is to survive, it must produce results. Since established elites can effectively deny even the most trivial victory, the protest group is doomed. It cannot compete, and thus is not a participant in the "normal" interest group process. In order to convert potential power into actual power, an organization must have some political resources with which to begin the process. But protest groups have none. They have no money; their constituency—although numerically impressive—is apathetic, and their values are a direct challenge to the established structure of authority. Withholding rent payments, temporary disruption of traffic, and unsuccessful electoral challenges are regarded by the established elites as minor threats to be nipped in the bud, rather than as bargaining resources. Parenti points out the closed nature of the interest group system:

Those who are most needful of substantial reallocations are by that very fact usually farthest removed from the resources necessary to command such reallocations and least able to make effective use of whatever limited resources they possess.[29]

How Well Do Groups Integrate the Individual? There remains the question of the meaning of group membership for the individual and for the society. Belonging to an organization has beneficial consequences for the individual, and through him for the society, *if we assume that stability is a desirable societal attribute.* Although membership in voluntary groups is highly related to social status (which, as we know, contributes to feelings of efficacy), membership in a group contributes to an individual's efficacy no matter what his social status. In measuring "subjective competence" (feelings of personal power toward government), Almond and Verba found that members of political organizations believed themselves to be more competent than members of nonpolitical organizations, who in turn felt more competent than people who did not belong to an organi-

---

[29]Parenti, p. 530.

zation.[30] These consequences of group membership on the attitude of the individual are not necessarily related to an objective measurement of the ability of the organization to mediate for the individual. Indeed, most people do not regard organized group activity as the most efficient method of influencing governmental decisions. Thus, integrative functions, to the extent they are performed at all, are performed by voluntary associations because they provide the *opportunity* for influence, not necessarily because they provide evidence of influence.

Members of organizations, whatever the nature of the organization, are more active and interested in political affairs, and they are more committed to, and satisfied with, "the system." For instance, members of organizations are more in accord than are non-members with community preferences. Community influences are mediated through organizations, contributing to a general commitment on the part of members to the concept of the community. For instance, community preferences can be defined in terms of partisan division of the vote. The votes of members of two or more associations are more closely correlated with community preferences than the votes of members of one organization, and the votes of members of one organization are more clearly related to community preferences than the votes of non-members. Group members in Democratic communities are more likely to vote Democratic than non-members.[31] Coleman has speculated that the reason for the relationship between high turnout and defeat of local referenda (e.g., school bonds and fluoridation) is that a high turnout indicates that people unattached to the community (through voluntary associations) are stimulated to vote negatively. In "normal" elections only a small core of community identifiers vote, thus insuring the success of the referenda.[32] In the high turnout election the participation of unaffiliated individuals is much greater, while the participation of members of associations remains constant.

As was mentioned at the beginning of the chapter, many political scientists believe that groups have a stabilizing influence on the individual because overlapping memberships create conflicting demands, and thus modify the effects of each single group on the individual. But membership in voluntary associations is stabilizing in itself, not because of overlapping membership. Few people belong to more than one organization. Even among those who do, memberships are likely to be cumulative rather than conflicting. People associate with reinforcing groups; most political discussion takes place among partisans rather than among adversaries. If a member encounters conflict in a group, a natural response is to reduce his activity. If activity is reduced, the leadership of the organization acquires *more* discretion rather than less.

Further, due to the ability of people to compartmentalize conflicting values, and also because of the desire to avoid dissonance, people

---

[30] Almond and Verba, *The Civic Culture*, p. 253.
[31] Robert D. Putnam, "Political Attitudes and the Local Community," *American Political Science Review*, 60 (September 1966), 646–648.
[32] James S. Coleman, *Community Conflict* (New York: Free Press, 1957), p. 19.

can have loyalty to two sets of values (and to the organizations that reflect these values), even though they are in conflict. As we noted earlier, beliefs do not have to be constraining. Presumably, a Catholic member of a labor union dominated by Communists would have a difficult conflict to resolve, provided there was a strong commitment to both ideologies. A study of just such a conflict reached the following conclusions: "Perhaps the most important finding in this study of cross pressures is the small number of individuals who evidenced awareness of conflicting influences."[33]

The Conservative Influence of Organizations

Organizations perform a conservative, stabilizing function for the society. Formal associations do not cause social change. Of course, the goals of associations vary, some being more radical than others. But in general, organizations that survive, even if they began as radical, become moderate as organizational perpetuation and maintenance of bureaucracy displace the original goals:

> Phillip Selznick's theory of bureaucracy states that the running of an organization creates problems not related to original goals. These goals of internal relevance assume an increasing proportion of time and may gradually be substituted for externally directed goals. The day-to-day behavior of the permanent staff and active participants (a minority of the membership) becomes centered around proximate goals of primarily internal importance, modifying or "displacing" the stated goals of the organization.[34]

Messinger has described this development as a shift from the implementation of the values of the organization to maintaining the structure as such, even if this means the loss of the organization's central mission.[35] Organizations thus come to be dominated by those who have the greatest stake in the existing social system. This is not to suggest that organizations seek no change, but that the extent of change they seek is minimal. If they achieve even a portion of what they wish to achieve, then they have established a stake in the ongoing system and have a rational basis for moderate politics. Social stability is apparently a product of the organizational system, not necessarily because of overlapping affiliations, but because of the inevitable nature of organizations. Associations that begin with a radical ideology must modify their views to attract the sustained membership necessary for organizational health. Organized labor, for example, is not as radical a force as it once was, even though business executives treat it as such. Lipset's study of the Cooperative Commonwealth Federation contains an example of the changes that occur in an organization when its self-perceived competitive position alters:

[33] Martin Kriesberg, "Cross-Pressures and Attitudes: A Study of the Influence of Conflicting Propaganda on Opinions Regarding American-Soviet Relations," *Public Opinion Quarterly,* 13 (Spring 1949), 8.
[34] Harmon Zeigler, *Interest Groups in American Society* (Englewood Cliffs, N.J.: Prentice-Hall, 1964), p. 81.
[35] Sheldon L. Messinger, "Organizational Transformation: A Case Study of a Declining Social Movement," *American Sociological Review,* 20 (February 1955), 10.

Most of the C.C.F. leaders assume that if farmers are given economic security and increased social services they will continue to support the movement in its effort to socialize the rest of the economy. Experiences in other countries do not lend weight to this assumption. In fact, the contrary seems to be true—farmers tend to become conservative when they achieve their economic goals. The farmer is radical vis-à-vis the larger society when his economic security and land tenure are threatened. He may join other exploited groups, such as the workers, to win his own economic demands. However, once the farmer achieves these immediate goals and becomes a member of the secure property holders of society, he resents government controls and labor or tax legislation that interfere with the expansion of his business.[36]

Pressure for substantial social change (as distinguished from incremental or moderate change) comes from forces outside the associational structure. Even leaders of "radical conservative" groups (for example, the Daughters of the American Revolution and the American Legion) display more commitment to the system than does the general population. Most liberals are accustomed to thinking of the American Legion as an instrument of the radical right, without concern for civil rights and freedom of speech. Yet studies show that the leaders of the American Legion are more committed to democratic rules than are unaffiliated citizens.[37] Since all organizations develop bureaucracies that resist change, groups serve to stabilize the social system, irrespective of the official ideology of the organizations.

Since groups serve society by cementing their members to the established social system, those who seek an alteration in this system find organizations an unsatisfactory mechanism. It is true that some groups are created with radical change in mind, but the process of bureaucratization and the evolution of the position of the membership from "have-nots" to "haves" gradually reduces the commitment of any organization to substantial change. Impoverished people and Negroes have gained little from groups because the group structure is dominated by people with a favored position in society. Violent protest is the most effective method of entry into the political process for segments of society effectively barred from other forms of participation. Ironically, if deprived peoples succeed in organizing and achieving a more equitable distribution of rewards, violence will probably decline, to be replaced by organizational activity. In time, the new organizations (for example, the "new left" groups) will develop their own commitment to the status quo, thus making likely the development of more radical groups.

As agents of integration, then, groups function quite effectively. Not only do group members tend to feel efficacious, but they are also more active and interested in political affairs, are more satisfied with the political system, and identify more readily with the community. Because they contribute to the social integration of their members,

---

[36]Seymour Martin Lipset, *Agrarian Socialism* (Toronto: Oxford University Press, 1950), p. 229.
[37]Samuel A. Stouffer, *Communism, Conformity, and Civil Liberties* (New York: John Wiley, 1966), p. 31.

organized interest groups have a conservative, stabilizing influence on society.

Summary We have attempted to assess the empirical validity of pluralist group theory, which asserts that groups are broadly representative of all segments of society; that people seek political action through organizations; that groups translate membership demands efficiently; that all groups have equal access to political resources; and that groups contribute to social stability.

We have found that active group membership is not as widespread as pluralist group theory requires. The active members of organizations tend to be of a higher social status than passive members or non-members. That interest groups are therefore elitist organizations is reflected in the business dominance of the pressure system.

People join organizations for many and varied reasons. It cannot be said that a majority, or even a sizable minority, of members join in order to pursue tangible goals. Moreover, those who do and who are successful in achieving their goals are a small minority—an elite minority. Likewise, groups mediate between their members and the public with varying effectiveness. But here again it has been found that small elitist groups function best. Resources, not equally available to *all* organizations, are more available to those who already have resources. The interest group system leaves the masses untouched.

Finally, group members do tend to be better integrated—more socialized than non-members. Given the elite nature of groups, this is not surprising, for one would expect that those who have the greatest stake in a system would identify with and be supportive of that system. Thus we find that, as instruments of the elites, interest groups defend the *status quo*.

Selected Additional Readings

Edelman, Murray. *The Symbolic Uses of Politics*. Chicago: University of Illinois Press (Illini Books edition), 1967. In this analysis of the symbolic functions of political activity, Edelman discusses differences in perception and behavior between interest group leaders and followers and assesses the roles of such groups in American politics.

Key, V. O., Jr. *Politics, Parties, and Pressure Groups*. 5th edition. New York: Thomas Y. Crowell Co., 1967. Part I of this classic is devoted to the study of interest groups representing diverse segments of the population.

Luttbeg, Norman (ed.). *Public Opinion and Public Policy: Models of Political Linkage*. Homewood, Ill.: Dorsey Press (paperback), 1968. Section III of this reader contains articles relevant to the study of interest groups.

Olson, Mancur, Jr. *The Logic of Collective Action: Public Goods and the Theory of Groups*. New York: Schocken Books (paperback), 1968. This work is a well written monograph dealing with the rational basis for interest group activity. Individuals are the units of analysis, and Olson constructs a model of individual motivation for collective behavior based upon the assumption of rationality.

Schattschneider, E. E. *The Semisovereign People: A Realist's View of Democracy in America.* New York: Holt, Rinehart and Winston (paperback), 1960. *The Semisovereign People* views democratic politics as a means whereby social conflict can be peacefully resolved. Interest groups are not only parties to such conflict, but they are integral parts of the reduction mechanism. Their structure and the functions are explored in Chapter 2, entitled "The Scope and Bias of the Pressure System."

Scoble, Harry M. *Ideology and Electoral Action: A Comparative Case Study of the National Committee for an Effective Congress.* San Francisco: Chandler, 1967. A single interest group, the National Committee for an Effective Congress, is subjected to intensive study in this book. Scoble describes its history, its ideology, its organization, and its activities. Additionally, he relates his observations to interest group theory and compares the NCEC to other types of interest groups.

Zeigler, Harmon. *Interest Groups In American Society.* Englewood Cliffs, N.J.: Prentice-Hall, 1964. This comprehensive study of the composition and roles of interest groups in the political system of the United States discusses the development of interest group theory, the relationship of such theory to broader aspects of democratic political thought, and empirical data concerning group phenomena.

The Presidency and the Executives

Authority and Power Government consists of the structures and processes by which rules and decisions are *authoritatively* determined by society. By "authoritative," we mean *enforcible* through the legitimate use of physical compulsion. Of course, other organizations in society—the Blackstone rangers or the Mafia, for example—may use physical force to enforce their decisions; but only government may do so *legitimately*. By "legitimate," we mean the general acceptance by people that government can use physical force, if need be, to implement its decisions.

Governments do not always make the most important decisions for society. The decision of steel companies to increase prices, the decision of electrical manufacturers to market color television sets, or the decision of a religious leader to ban birth control pills may have more profound effects upon American life than anything the government does. Moreover, governmental elites generally do not initiate and decide policy questions themselves; rather, they merely ratify and give legitimacy to the decisions made by non-governmental elites—business leaders, interest group leaders, party influentials, or other prominent individuals or groups. Thus, governmental decision making is not necessarily more important than private decision making.

But government does possess the ability to make and enforce decisions for the *whole* society, for governmental decision making includes the principal responsibility for maintaining order and for resolving the differences that arise between segments of society. Governmental elites regulate conflict by establishing and enforcing general rules by which conflict is to be carried on, by arranging compromises and balancing interests, and by imposing settlements that the parties in dispute must accept. In other words, governmental elites lay down the "rules of the game" in political activity. Governmental elites make decisions that allocate values for other elites, as well as for the masses, and see to it that these decisions are carried out. Thus, governmental elites are distinguished by (1) the fact that they may legitimately enforce their decisions with physical compulsion, and (2) the fact that their decisions extend to the whole of society and enable them to resolve conflicts between segments of society.

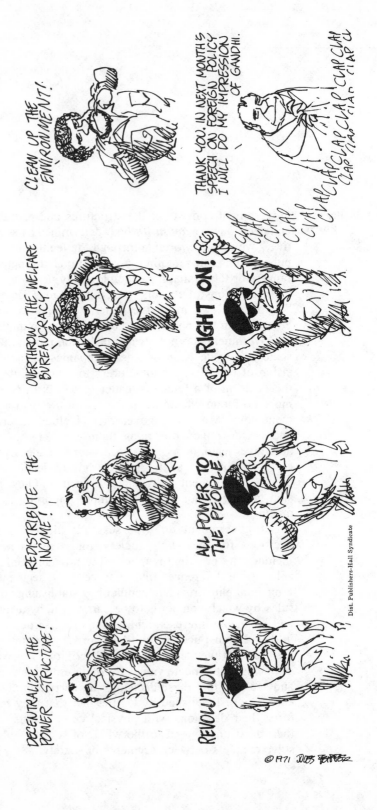

Dist. Publishers-Hall Syndicate

© 1971 Jules Feiffer

Obviously, the potential power of governmental elites is very great. This potential for power worried the Founding Fathers. They were not so much concerned with the possibility of a *minority* seizing control of the national government as with the possibility that the *majority* of people might gain access to the legitimate use of force and threaten the established men of principle and property. There was a real fear that, even under the republican and federal structure of the American government, a majority might still be able to "outnumber and oppress the rest." The Founding Fathers, therefore, sought to place additional obstacles in the way of "an unjust and interested majority."

Separation of Powers— Ambition to Counteract Ambition

To provide some "auxiliary precautions" against mass movements that might threaten the rights of property, the Founding Fathers devised two different but related arrangements—separation of powers and checks and balances. These arrangements had two goals: first, to make it more difficult for the masses to capture control of the government; and second, to prevent governmental elites from abusing their power and threatening the interests of non-governmental elites.

The idea of a separation of powers—that is, the dividing of power among the three branches of national government—was derived from the writings of an early French political scientist, Baron Montesquieu, whose two volumes on *The Spirit of the Laws* appeared about 1748. Montesquieu wrote:

> In every government there are three sources of power: the legislative, the executive and the judiciary power. . . . When the legislative and executive powers are united in the same person, or in the same body of magistrates, there can be no liberty. . . . Again, there is not liberty if the judiciary be not separated from the legislative and executive.[1]

Montesquieu's doctrine was widely accepted by American elites in 1787. In *The Federalist* No. 47, James Madison echoed Montesquieu:

> No political truth is certainly of greater intrinsic value or is stamped with the authority of more enlightened patrons of liberty, than that the accumulation of all powers, legislative, executive, and judiciary in the same hands, whether of one, a few, or many, and whether hereditary, self-appointed, or elective, may justly be pronounced the definition of tyranny.[2]

The separation of powers concept is expressed in the opening sentence of the first three articles of the Constitution, which establishes separate legislative, executive, and judicial branches of government. To further separate these powers, each of the major decision-making bodies in the national government is chosen by a different constituency—the House by voters in the several legislative districts, the

[1] Baron de Montesquieu, *The Spirit of the Laws.*
[2] James Madison, Alexander Hamilton, and John Jay, *The Federalist* No. 47 (New York: Modern Library, 1937).

Senate by the state legislatures and later by the voters of whole states, the president by "electors" chosen by the voters in whole states, and the judiciary by the president with the consent of the Senate. A sharp differentiation is also made in the terms of office of each of these decision-making bodies, so that a complete renewal of government by popular majority at one stroke is impossible. The House is chosen for two years, and the Senate for six; but the entire Senate is not chosen in one election, for one third of the senators go out every two years. The president is chosen every four years, and the judges of the Supreme Court hold office for life. Thus the people are restrained from bringing about immediate changes in government policy.

Dividing power in itself was not enough; "ambition must be made to counteract ambition." Not only did the Founding Fathers want separate branches of government to be responsive to different constituencies, they also wanted to give each branch of the national government some opportunity to control the operations of the others. The separate branches of the American government are not independent but, rather, interdependent. There is really a sharing of power among the branches of the national government, not a separating of power; for each branch participates in the activities of every other branch.

The great security against the gradual concentration of the several powers in the same department consists in giving to those who administer to each department the necessary constitutional means and personal motives to resist encroachment upon the others. . . . Ambition must be made to counteract ambition.[3]

Thus, an elaborate system of overlapping powers and responsibilities was established. The president shares the legislative powers through his veto and through his responsibility to make recommendations to Congress about legislation he believes to be necessary and expedient. He can also convene special sessions of Congress. But the appointing power of the president is shared by the Senate, as is his treaty-making power; and Congress can override effective presidential vetoes. The president must execute the laws; but in order to do so he must rely upon executive departments, and these must be created by Congress. Moreover, the executive branch cannot spend money that has not been appropriated by Congress. The president appoints judges of the Supreme Court, but only with the consent of the Senate. And the Supreme Court can determine when the president has acted outside the Constitution or the laws of Congress and can even invalidate laws of Congress which are contrary to the Constitution.

Those who criticize the United States government for its slow, unwieldy processes should realize that this characteristic was deliberately built into the government by its founders. These cumbersome arrangements—the checks and balances and the fragmentation of authority that make it difficult for government to realize its potential

[3]Madison, Hamilton, and Jay, *The Federalist* No. 51.

power over private interests (business, industry, banks, and labor) — were designed by the Founding Fathers to protect the private interests from governmental interference and to shield the government from an unjust and self-seeking majority. If the system handcuffs government and makes it easy for established groups to oppose change, then the system is working as the Founding Fathers intended.

The Founding Fathers planned well. The system of intermingled powers and conflicting loyalties that they established is still alive today. Of course, some things have changed: senators are now directly elected by the voters, and the president is more directly responsible to the voters than was originally envisioned. But the basic arrangement of checks and balances endures. Presidents, senators, representatives, and judges are chosen by different constituencies; their terms of offices vary, and their responsibilities and loyalties differ. This system makes direct majority rule impossible. If, for example, the majority of the voters should elect the president, he would face powerful minorities entrenched in Congress, the Supreme Court, and even the executive bureaucracy.

Decision Making among Governmental Elites

If the majority does not rule, who does? It is clear that the government can act only with the consent of the leaders of the major interests in American society. Decision making by governmental elites is a process of bargaining, accommodation, and compromise among the dominant interests in American society. Governmental elites act essentially as go-betweens, mediating between major interest groups and seeking policies that are mutually beneficial to the major interests — industrial, financial, labor, farm, military, bureaucratic, and so on. Governmental elites in America do not command; they seek consensus.

Bargaining, accommodation, and compromise, as the prevailing style of American politics, are made possible by the consensus existing among elite groups in the nation — a consensus that includes fundamental agreement among the elites on the worth of the system itself. Bargaining is possible because elites do not perceive their interests as irreconcilable. If elite differences in America were fundamental, it would be difficult to find acceptable accommodations, bargains, or compromises.

On the other hand, if governmental elites acted on behalf of a firm, united majority of citizens with a well defined popular program, it would be unnecessary for the elites to constantly engage in bargaining and compromise. Occasionally it is urged that majorities be permitted to govern through a system of disciplined and responsible parties. Reformers have argued that the American political parties should be more representative of the people and less responsive to the pressures of organized interests. They believe that the parties should develop clear-cut policies reflecting popular attitudes. Competitive parties would then present alternative policies to voters in elections, and the winning party would be responsible for enacting the policies by which it won the election. The party should be required to discipline its members in office—especially those in Congress—so that they would not desert the party program.

This system of responsible, well disciplined, programmatic, and competitive parties would better enable majorities to rule in America; for it would help to overcome the separation of powers and the checks and balances that make it so difficult for majority opinion to become law. Party reformers argue that decision making by competitive, responsible parties should replace bargaining among elites as the prevailing style of decision making in American politics. They believe that responsible parties would forge a stronger link between the people and the government. The men in power would be the leaders in the majority party; they would be bound by the wishes of the majority of people, who expressed their policy views by electing the party with a clear-cut programmatic platform. If party leaders ignored this platform, they would risk losing the support of the people at the next election. Advocates of party reform stress this accountability to the popular majority.

But elites in America have generally opposed strict majority rule. Like the Founding Fathers, they believe that the majority contains the seeds of tyranny, that majority rule might very well destroy the nation. An unrestrained majority, under no obligation to bargain or compromise with important interests, may act rashly and threaten the stability of the system. Majority rule could overrun important minority interests—economic, sectional, religious, and so on. The present governmental system, with all of its hesitations and delays, protects governmental elites and minority interests from the whims of popular majorities. Majority rule might result in violent changes in public policy when first one party and then the other came to power; for a responsible party system would place all of the conservatives in one party and all of the liberals in the other. The result would be a degree of extremism unknown in American politics today. In contrast, decision making by elite bargaining avoids the uncompromising extremism of majority rule and insures the stability of the American system. No powerful interest ever loses completely in the American game of politics; therefore, there is no incentive for any powerful interest to oppose or convulse the system. Government by elite bargaining protects the diverse interests in America; it gives dominant elites a stake in the government and, by so doing, insures their loyalty to it. Brokerage politics is the price of unity.[4] Governmental elites serve as unifying agents, not as representives of majorities. As Professors Robert Dahl and Charles Lindblom acknowledge, "No unified, cohesive, acknowledged, and legitimate representative-leaders of the 'national majority' exist in the United States."[5] And in the absence of a unified and effective majority, elites rule through a process of bargaining, accommodation, and compromise.

[4] See Herbert Aggar, *The Price of Union* (New York: Houghton Mifflin Co., 1950), pp. 689–690.
[5] Robert Dahl and Charles Lindblom, *Politics, Economics, and Welfare* (New York: Harper & Row, 1963), p. 306.

Governmental elites are free to act as brokers among America's elites because they are relatively free from mass influence in their decision making. On most policy questions, governmental elites have no idea what might be the preferences of the masses for the good reason that, on most policy questions, the masses have no opinion. In fact, the political elites must supply the masses with opinions. Given the apathy and the inattention of most Americans to policy matters, the failure of governmental elites to be aware of and act upon mass opinion is hardly unexpected.

Bargaining among elites does not have to be explicit; direct communication is not always necessary when elites already understand the interests of other elites. Of course, explicit contracts, by formalizing agreements among elites, minimize the chance of misunderstanding. In international politics, these contracts appear in the form of treaties; in domestic politics, they appear in the form of wage contracts, government defense contracts, and so on. (Probably the most famous example of an explicit agreement or contract among the elites is the Constitution of the United States itself.) But most bargaining assumes the form of implicit or tacit understandings, in which elites agree to render support for each other in exchange for "good will" and expectations of future support. "You scratch my back and I'll scratch yours" is the traditional style of policy making in America.

Everyone is familiar with the kind of implicit understanding in which Congressman A agrees to "go along" with the legislation proposed by Congressmen B in exchange for Congressman B's tacit agreement to support proposals of Congressman A at some future time. But more important implicit understandings occur when major interests tacitly agree to support each other in their respective spheres of influence. For example, the U. S. Chamber of Commerce supports the American Medical Association on health legislation; Lockheed Aircraft participates in the work-study program of the War on Poverty; and so on.

Incrementalism in Decision Making

If there is really such a consensus among American elites, why do we observe so many political struggles between parties, interest groups, president and Congress, and other political actors? If American elites are really in fundamental agreement with each other, why do they fight as hard as they do over public policy? The answer is that most public policies are *not* the subject of political controversy. Controversy captures our attention, but the largest proportion of public policy is made in the absence of controversy. Research in the legislative process in Congress has shown that the vast majority of bills are passed by unanimous or near-unanimous votes.[6] Research in the budgetary process has indicated that only marginal increases in the budget are ever the subject of political controversy; both the president

---

[6] See Malcolm E. Jewell and Samuel C. Patterson, *The Legislative Process in the United States* (New York: Random House, 1966), p. 415.

and the congressmen accept the great bulk of any budget as given by budget officers.[7]

Political struggle is usually found when *changes* in public policy are proposed. But because decision making by governmental elites is a very conservative process, dramatic changes in process are very rare. Policy innovation normally occurs by gradual, or incremental, changes in policies extending over decades; in other words, by evolution rather than revolution.

"Incrementalism" is a style of decision making in which governmental elites limit their consideration of policy alternatives to those that differ only slightly from the pattern of existing policy. Elites accept previous policy decisions mainly without review, focusing their attention upon a limited number of minor policy changes. Incrementalism simplifies some of the complexities of policy making, and it contributes to the stability of the political system.

Incremental decision making stands in contrast to what is known as "rational decision making." Ideally, public policy in a democracy would be formulated only after a thorough debate and an examination of all policy alternatives; no policy would be taken for granted. The choice of policies would then be the result of a rational calculation of means and ends. Rational decision making involves: (1) a clear understanding of the goals of society; (2) an examination of the means of achieving society's goals; (3) a careful weighing of the costs of alternative means to the desired ends; (4) a careful choice among all available policies to determine the most efficient means to the desired end. But decision making by the governmental elites is rarely, if ever, "rational" in this ideal sense. Congress may debate the details of military spending—particularly new projects, such as the C5-A, that call for marginal increases in appropriations—but it never seriously debates whether the entire military establishment should be dismantled or whether the nation should consider unilateral disarmament. These latter notions are outside the prevailing elite consensus.

**The Presidency—
Energy for the
Elite System**

In the words of Alexander Hamilton in *The Federalist* No. 70:

Energy in the executive is a leading character in the definition of good government . . . a feeble executive implies a feeble execution of the government. A feeble execution is but another phrase for a bad execution; and a government ill-executed, whatever it may be in theory, must be, in practice, a bad government.[8]

The president's real power does not depend upon his formal authority, but upon his abilities at persuasion. He does not stand above America's elites but rather among them; he does not command, he

[7]See Aaron Wildavsky, *The Politics of the Budgetary Process* (Boston: Little, Brown and Co., 1964), pp. 125–126.
[8]James Madison, Alexander Hamilton, and John Jay, *The Federalist* No. 70.

persuades. Richard Neustadt reports that, in 1952, President Truman felt that President-elect Eisenhower would not understand how executive power in government is dependent upon persuasion. Neustadt quotes Truman: "He'll [Eisenhower] sit here . . . and he'll say, 'Do this! Do that!' and nothing will happen. Poor Ike—it won't be a bit like the army. He'll find it very frustrating." Neustadt further reports that Eisenhower indeed found it frustrating; he quotes an Eisenhower aide in 1958: "The President still feels . . . that when he has decided something, that ought to be the end of it . . . and when it bounces back undone or done wrong, he tends to react with shocked surprise." Neustadt also quotes Truman as saying: "I sit here all day trying to persuade people to do things they ought to have sense enough to do without my persuading them . . . that's all the powers of a president amount to."[9]

The president does not command American elites, but he stands in a central position in the elite structure. The responsibility for the initiation of public policy falls principally upon the president and his staff and executive departments. He has a strong incentive to fulfill this responsibility; for in the eyes of a large segment of the American public, the president is responsible for everything that happens in the nation during his term of office, regardless of whether he has the authority or the capacity to do anything about it. At the very least, there is a general public expectation that every president, even a president committed to a "caretaker" role, will put forth some sort of policy program.

Through the power of policy initiation alone, the president's impact on American elites is considerable. The president sets the agenda for public decision making. The president's programs are presented to Congress in various presidential messages and in his budget, and the president thereby largely determines what the business of Congress will be in any session. Few major undertakings ever get off the ground without presidential initiation; the president frames the issues, determines their context, and decides their timing.

The powers of the presidency and the importance of this office in the American political system vary with political circumstances and with the personalities of the men who occupy the office. In debates about the real extent of executive power, the contrasting views of Presidents William Howard Taft and Theodore Roosevelt are often quoted as examples of the different approaches individuals take to the presidency. Taft once said:

The true view of the executive function is, as I conceive it, that the president can exercise no power which cannot be fairly and reasonably traced to some specific grant of power or justly implied and included within such express grant as proper and necessary to its exercise. Such specific grants must be either in the federal constitution or in the pursuance thereof. There is no

[9] Richard Neustadt, *Presidential Power* (New York: John Wiley, 1960), pp. 9–11.

undefined residuum of power which can be exercised which seems to him to be in the public interest.[10]

The alternative view was held by Theodore Roosevelt:

I decline to adopt the view that what was imperatively necessary for the nation could not be done by the president unless he could find some specific authorization to do it. My belief was that it was not only his right but his duty to do anything that the needs of the nation demanded, unless such action was forbidden by the Constitution or by the laws. Under this interpretation of executive power I did and caused to be done many things not previously done by the president and the heads of departments. I did not usurp the power, but I did greatly broaden the use of executive power.[11]

On the whole, evaluations of a presidential performance are likely to weigh favorably the more activist approach to the office. Taft, Herbert Hoover, and Dwight Eisenhower, who took more restricted views of the presidency, are usually downgraded in comparison with Woodrow Wilson, Theodore and Franklin Roosevelt, and Harry Truman, who were much more active presidents.

It is sometimes argued that the presidency has grown more powerful in the twentieth century, but few presidents have been more powerful than Abraham Lincoln, as Wilfred Binkley comments:

Unquestionably, the highwater mark of the exercise of the executive power in the United States is found in the administration of Abraham Lincoln. No President before or since has pushed about the degrees of executive power so far into the legislative sphere . . . Under the war power he proclaimed the slaves of those in rebellion emancipated. He devised and put into execution his peculiar plan of reconstruction. With disregard of law he increased the army and navy beyond the limits set by statute. The privilege of the writ of habeas corpus was suspended wholesale and martial law declared. Public money in the sum of millions was deliberately spent without Congressional appropriation. Nor was any of this done innocently. Lincoln understood his constitution. He knew, in many cases, just how he was transgressing, and his infractions were consequently deliberate. It is all the more astonishing that this audacity was the work of a minority president performed in the presence of a bitter congressional opposition even in his own party.[12]

Yet, on the whole, presidents of the twentieth century have exercised greater power and initiative than those of the nineteenth century, partly because of America's greater involvement in world affairs and the constant increase in the importance of military and foreign policy. The Constitution gives the president unmistakable and far-reaching powers in foreign and military affairs: the president is given

---

[10] William Howard Taft, *Our Chief Magistrate and His Powers* (New York: Columbia University Press, 1938), p. 138. Reprinted in John P. Roche and L. W. Levy (eds.), *The Presidency* (New York: Harcourt, Brace & World, 1964), p. 23.
[11] From Arthur B. Tourtellot, *Presidents on the Presidency* (Garden City, N.Y.: Doubleday & Co., 1964), pp. 55–56.
[12] Wilfred E. Binkley, *President and Congress* (New York: Alfred A. Knopf, 1947), p. 127.

the power to send and receive ambassadors and to make treaties (with the advice and consent of the Senate), and is made commander-in-chief of the armed forces. In effect, these powers give him almost exclusive authority over foreign and military policy in the nation.

A second factor contributing to the power of the president in the twentieth century has been the growth of the executive branch which he heads. The federal bureaucracy has grown into a giant elite structure, and the president's constitutional powers as chief executive place him at the top of this structure. The Constitution gives the president broad, albeit vague, powers to "take care that the laws be faithfully executed" and to "require the opinion in writing of the principal officer of each of the executive departments upon any subject relating to the duties of their respective offices." This clause gives the president general executive authority over the 2.5 million civilian employees of the federal bureaucracy. Moreover, the president has the right to appoint (and generally the right to remove) the principal officers of the executive branch of government (the Senate consenting). A major addition to the president's constitutional authority over the executive branch came in the Budget and Accounting Act of 1921, in which Congress vested in the president the control of the initiation and execution of the federal budget. Budgetary control is a major weapon in the hands of the president, for it can mean the life or death of an administrative agency. While it is true that Congress must appropriate all monies spent by executive departments, nonetheless, the president has responsibility for formulating the budget. Congress may cut a presidential budget request and even appropriate more than the president asks for a particular agency or program, but by far the greatest portion of the president's budget is accepted by Congress.

The third reason for the importance of the presidency in the twentieth century can be traced to technological improvements in the mass media and the strengthening of the role of the president as party leader and molder of mass opinion. Television brings the president directly in contact with the masses, and the masses have an attachment to the president which is unlike their attachment to any other public official or symbol of government. Fred I. Greenstein has classified the "psychological functions of the presidency"[13]: First, the president "simplifies perception of government and politics" by serving as "the main cognitive 'handle' for providing busy citizens with some sense of what their government is doing." Second, the president provides "an outlet for emotional expression" through public interest in his and his family's private and public life. Third, the president is a "symbol of unity" and of nationhood (as the national shock and grief over the death of a president clearly reveals). Fourth, the president provides the masses with a "vicarious means of taking political action," in the sense that he can act decisively and effectively while they cannot do so. Finally,

[13]Fred I. Greenstein. "The Psychological Functions of the Presidency for Citizens," in Elmer E. Cornwell (ed.), *The American Presidency: Vital Center* (Chicago: Scott, Foresman and Co., 1966), pp. 30–36.

the president is a "symbol of social stability," in that he provides the masses with a feeling of security and guidance. Thus, for the masses, the president is the most visible elite member. The masses clearly identify with the president.

The president has many sources of formal power (see Table 9–1); he is chief administrator, chief diplomat, commander-in-chief, chief of state, party leader, and voice of the people. But despite the great powers of the office, no president can monopolize policy making. The

TABLE 9–1.
Formal Presidential Powers

Chief administrator
Implement policy—"Take care that laws be faithfully executed."
Supervise executive branch of government.
Appoint and remove policy officials.
Prepare executive budget.

Chief legislator
Initiate policy—"Give to the Congress information of the State of the Union and recommend to their consideration such measures as he shall judge necessary and expedient."
Veto legislation passed by Congress.
Convene special sessions of Congress "On extraordinary occasions."

Party leader
Control national party organization.
Control federal patronage.
Influence (not control) state and local parties through prestige.

Chief diplomat
Make treaties ("with the advice and consent of Senate").
Make executive agreements.
Power of diplomatic recognition—"to send and receive ambassadors."
Represent the nation as chief of state.

Commander-in-chief
Command U.S. Armed Forces—"the President shall be Commander-in-chief of the army and the navy."
Appoint military officials.
Initiate war.
Broad war powers.

president functions within an established elite system, and he can only exercise power within the framework of the elite system. The choices available to the president are limited to those alternatives for which he can mobilize elite support. He cannot act outside existing elite consensus, outside of the "rules of the game." The president must be sensitive to the interests of major elites—business, agriculture, military, education, bureaucratic, and so on.

Of course, on some issues the president may have greater opportunity for mobility and a larger number of alternatives for which he can find elite support. But on many questions of domestic and foreign policy, the president is hedged in by other governmental elites—Congress (see Table 9–2), the Supreme Court, and party leaders—and by the demands of influential business, financial, agricultural, and military elites. The Congress can clearly frustrate the president when it chooses to do so, particularly on budgetary questions. For example, most presidential requests for foreign aid have been cut by Congress, despite the best efforts of the White House; and for years, Congress rejected the presidential proposals on civil rights and medical care. Similarly, the Supreme Court may restrict presidential actions. For example, in 1952, within three months after President Truman ordered the government to seize the steel industry to end a strike during the

TABLE 9–2.
Presidential Success
in Congress,
1954–1970

Year	Proposals Submitted	Approved by Congress	Approval Score
1954 Eisenhower	232	150	64.7%
1955 "	207	96	46.3
1956 "	225	103	45.7
1957 "	206	76	36.9
1958 "	234	110	47.0
1959 "	228	93	40.8
1960 "	183	56	30.6
1961 Kennedy	355	172	48.4
1962 "	298	133	44.6
1963 "	401	109	27.2
1964 Johnson	217	125	57.2
1965 "	469	323	68.9
1966 "	371	207	55.8
1967 "	431	205	47.6
1968 "	414	227	55.0
1969 Nixon	171	55	32.2
1970 "	210	97	46.2

Source: Congressional Quarterly figures.

Korean War, the Supreme Court held his action unconstitutional, and the steel mills were returned at once to the owners. President Truman also encountered strong opposition from governmental, military, and private elites when he dismissed General Douglas MacArthur from his command in Korea for failure to carry out presidential orders. This action nearly led to the President's censure by Congress, owing to the great following that the distinguished general had in Washington and the country. Many presidents have been forced to discard or modify policies because of negative responses from industry, farmers, doctors, union leaders, and so on.

The president must rely on bargaining and incrementalism as much as other governmental elites. President Johnson's invitation to public and private elites to "come reason together" reflects the emphasis on bargaining and persuasion as the principal method of exerting presidential policy leadership. It also suggests that elite differences in America are not so great that they cannot be resolved by accommodation, bargain, and compromise.

Other Executive Elites

The presidency is not one man, but more than a thousand permanent employees in the executive office of the president (see Figure 9–1), which is composed of the White House Office, the Bureau of the Budget, the Council of Economic Advisers, the National Security Council, the National Aeronautics and Space Council, the Office of Emergency Planning, and the Office of Science and Technology. In addition, there is the presidential Cabinet, consisting of heads of twelve major executive departments. Finally, there are more than forty independent agencies that function outside of the regular departmental organization of the executive branch, including the Interstate Commerce Commission, the Federal Reserve Board, the Federal Trade Commission, the Federal Power Commission, the Federal Communications Commission, the Securities and Exchange Commission, the National Labor

Relations Board, the Civil Aeronautics Board, and the Atomic Energy Commission.

Closest to the president is a group of aides and assistants who work with him in the White House Office. These aides and assistants perform whatever duties the president assigns them, and the president organizes the White House Office as he sees fit. There is usually a press secretary, an appointment secretary, and one or more special assistants for liaison with Congress. Some of the president's assistants have ad hoc assignments, while others have a particular specialty. Theodore Sorensen, Special Assistant to President Kennedy, defined the role of the White House staff as the auxiliary eyes and ears of the president, with responsibilities as broad as those of the president.[14]

The Bureau of the Budget is the largest agency in the executive office of the president. The function of the bureau is to prepare the budget of the United States for the president to submit to Congress. No money may be spent by the federal government without appropriations by Congress, and all requests for congressional appropriations must be cleared through the Bureau of the Budget. This gives the Bureau of the Budget great power over the executive branch of government. Since all agencies request more money than they can receive, the primary responsibility for reducing budget requests rests with the bureau. The bureau reviews, reduces, and approves estimates submitted by departments and agencies (subject, of course, to their appeal to the president), and it also continuously scrutinizes the organization and operations of executive agencies in order to recommend changes that would promote efficiency and economy. Like members of the White House staff, the top officials of the Bureau of the Budget are solely responsible to the president, and they are supposed to reflect the president's goals and priorities in their decision making.

The Council of Economic Advisers, created by the Employment Act of 1946, is composed of three professional economists of high standing, appointed by the president with the consent of the Senate. The functions of the council are to analyze trends in the economy and to recommend to the president the fiscal and monetary policies necessary to avoid both depression and inflation. In addition, the council prepares the Economic Report which the Employment Act of 1946 requires the President to submit to Congress each year. The Economic Report, together with the annual budget message to Congress, give the president the opportunity to assess broadly the major policies of his administration.

The National Security Council resembles a cabinet; it is composed of the president as chairman, the vice-president, the Secretary of State, the Secretary of Defense, and the director of the Office of Emergency Planning (a minor unit in the executive office). The chairman of the Joint Chiefs of Staff and the director of the Central Intelligence Agency are advisors to the Security Council. The staff of the council is headed by a special assistant to the president for national security affairs. The

[14] See Theodore C. Sorensen, *Decision Making in the White House* (New York: Columbia University Press, 1963).

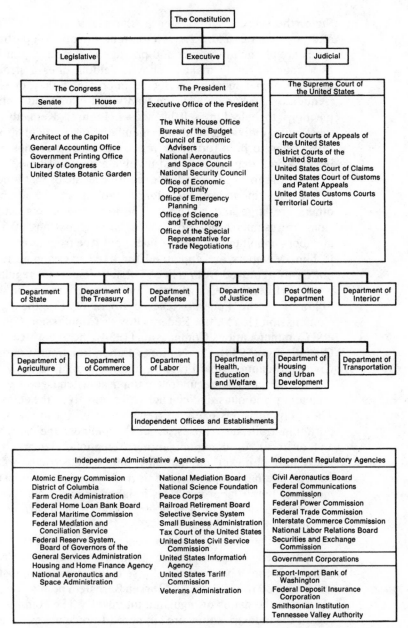

**FIGURE 9–1.
Governmental
Organization of the
United States**

The Constitution

Legislative | Executive | Judicial

The Congress

Senate | House

Architect of the Capitol
General Accounting Office
Government Printing Office
Library of Congress
United States Botanic Garden

The President

Executive Office of the President

The White House Office
Bureau of the Budget
Council of Economic
  Advisers
National Aeronautics
  and Space Council
National Security Council
Office of Economic
  Opportunity
Office of Emergency
  Planning
Office of Science
  and Technology
Office of the Special
  Representative for
  Trade Negotiations

**The Supreme Court of
the United States**

Circuit Courts of Appeals of
  the United States
District Courts of the
  United States
United States Court of Claims
United States Court of Customs
  and Patent Appeals
United States Customs Courts
Territorial Courts

Department of State | Department of the Treasury | Department of Defense | Department of Justice | Post Office Department | Department of Interior

Department of Agriculture | Department of Commerce | Department of Labor | Department of Health, Education and Welfare | Department of Housing and Urban Development | Department of Transportation

Independent Offices and Establishments

Independent Administrative Agencies

Atomic Energy Commission
District of Columbia
Farm Credit Administration
Federal Home Loan Bank Board
Federal Maritime Commission
Federal Mediation and
  Conciliation Service
Federal Reserve System,
  Board of Governors of the
General Services Administration
Housing and Home Finance Agency
National Aeronautics and
  Space Administration

National Mediation Board
National Science Foundation
Peace Corps
Railroad Retirement Board
Selective Service System
Small Business Administration
Tax Court of the United States
United States Civil Service
  Commission
United States Information
  Agency
United States Tariff
  Commission
Veterans Administration

Independent Regulatory Agencies

Civil Aeronautics Board
Federal Communications
  Commission
Federal Power Commission
Federal Trade Commission
Interstate Commerce Commission
National Labor Relations Board
Securities and Exchange
  Commission

Government Corporations

Export-Import Bank of
  Washington
Federal Deposit Insurance
  Corporation
Smithsonian Institution
Tennessee Valley Authority

Source: Adapted from *United States Government Organization Manual, 1965–1966*, Washington, D.C. Government Printing Office, 1965.

purposes of the National Security Council are to advise the president on security policy and to coordinate foreign, military, and domestic policies. However, presidents do not rely exclusively on the National Security Council for direction in major foreign and military decisions.

Cabinet officers in the United States are powerful because they sit at the heads of giant administrative organizations. The secretary of

State, the secretary of Defense, the secretary of the Treasury, the attorney general, and, to a lesser extent, the other departmental secretaries are all men of power and prestige in America. But the Cabinet, as a council, rarely makes policy.[15] Seldom does a strong president hold a Cabinet meeting to decide important policy questions. More frequently, he knows what he wants and is inclined to hold Cabinet meetings to help him sell his views. John F. Kennedy preferred to meet with individual Cabinet members on particular policy issues rather than to hold formal or regular Cabinet meetings, which he believed were "unnecessary and involve a waste of time."

There are forty independent executive agencies that function outside of the departmental organization. Some are small and obscure, while others are large and powerful. The independent regulatory commissions are usually headed by boards or commissions of five to eleven members appointed by the president but free from direct responsibility to him. Members are appointed for fixed overlapping terms and are not easily removed from office. The first important regulatory agency was the Interstate Commerce Commission, created in 1887; it was followed by the Federal Reserve Board (1913), the Federal Trade Commission (1915), the Federal Power Commission (1920), the Federal Communications Commission (1934), the Securities and Exchange Commission (1934), the National Labor Relations Board (1935), the Civil Aeronautics Board (1938), and the Atomic Energy Commission (1946). All of these regulatory commissions engage in policy making, regulation, and quasi-judicial activities, mostly in the economic sphere. These commissions exercise tremendous power in the fields of transportation (railroads, buses, trucks, pipelines, the merchant marine, and airlines), of communications (telephone, telegraph, radio, and television), of power and natural resources (electricity, water and flood control, and natural gas), of unfair trade practices in industry and commerce, of unfair labor practices in labor-management relations, and of banking practices, credit policies, issuance of securities, and trading in national stock markets.

The regulatory commissions generally represent the industry they are supposed to regulate, rather than "the people." One reason is that commission members are usually selected from the industry that they are supposed to regulate. As Marven Bernstein points out, "Expertness plays into the hands of regulated interest."[16] The commissions usually regard the industries they are supposed to regulate as clients who need to be promoted and protected. While the commissions may act against wayward members of an industry, they seldom do anything that is not clearly acceptable to industry leaders. This point is well illustrated in the operation of the Federal Reserve System. The Federal Reserve Board (FRB) is composed of seven men appointed by the president with the consent of the Senate for staggered terms of fourteen years; a

[15] See Richard F. Fenno, Jr., *The President's Cabinet* (Cambridge, Mass.: Harvard University Press, 1959).

[16] Marven H. Bernstein, *Regulating Business by Independent Commissions* (Princeton, N.J.: Princeton University Press, 1965), p. 118.

chairman is designated by the president from among its members. The Federal Reserve Board is essentially the governing board of the nation's banking system. However, Federal Reserve Board members are generally bankers themselves, and financial support for the Federal Reserve System comes from payments made by banks that are members of the system (while only half of the nation's banks are members of the Federal Reserve System, this half possesses over 85 percent of all deposits). The policies of the FRB toward the supply of money and credit in the nation, which profoundly affect the state of the economy, generally reflect the views of bankers in economic matters. Neither the president nor Congress has direct control over the activities of the FRB.

President Johnson and the Paris Peace Talks

An interesting example of the operation of governmental elites is the process of President Johnson's decision to reduce the bombing of North Vietnam and ask for peace negotiations with the Democratic Republic of Vietnam in Hanoi. While the records of this decision are still highly classified, the following account was pieced together from newspaper reports.

On March 18, 1968, President Johnson invited eight prominent hawks and one dove—all from outside the government—to gather in the White House for a night and a day, meeting with governmental officials and discussing the progress of the Vietnam War. The non-official elites were former Under Secretary of State George Ball; Arthur Dean, a Republican Wall Street lawyer who was a Korean War negotiator during the Eisenhower administration; Dean Acheson, President Truman's Secretary of State; General Matthew B. Ridgway, retired commander of the nation's troops in Korea; General Maxwell B. Taylor, former Chairman of the Joint Chiefs of Staff; Cyrus Vance, former Deputy Defense Secretary and a key troubleshooter for the Johnson administration; McGeorge Bundy, Ford Foundation president and formerly the Special Assistant to the President for national security affairs under President Kennedy; former Treasury Secretary C. Douglas Dillon; and General Omar Bradley, a leading supporter of the president's war policies. This group met with Secretary of State Dean Rusk; Defense Secretary Clark M. Clifford; Ambassador Averell Harriman; Walt W. Rostow, Special Assistant to the President for national security affairs; General Earl G. Wheeler, chairman of the Joint Chiefs of Staff; Richard Helms, Director of the Central Intelligence Agency; Paul Nitze, Deputy Defense Secretary; Nicholas Katzenbach, former Attorney General and at the time Under-Secretary of State; and William P. Bundy, Assistant Secretary of State for Pacific Affairs and brother of McGeorge Bundy.

The whole group heard lectures by Phillip C. Habib, a top career diplomat in Vietnam; Major General William E. Depuy, Special Assistant to the Joint Chiefs of Staff for counter-insurgency activities; and George Carver, a CIA analyst for Vietnam affairs. Under heavy questioning by both official and unofficial advisers, these officials admitted that the Saigon government was generally weaker than the previous reports had indicated, that reports of casualties inflicted upon the enemy had been greatly exaggerated, that the enemy still had substantial military capability, and that the bombing of North Vietnam had little identifiable military value. Much to the surprise of President Johnson, this group of official and unofficial military advisers, although overwhelmingly hawkish in composition, recommended that the President curtail bombing and intensify his efforts to seek political solutions at the negotiating table.

The President ordered Habib, Depuy, and Carver to give him direct briefings on affairs in Vietnam, since many of their comments were inconsistent with those that the President was receiving from the State Department and the Defense Department. At the same time, Clark Clifford, who had come to the same conclusion as his predecessor, Robert S. McNamara, that the bombing in Vietnam was not achieving any military objective, directly contacted the President himself. As a result of these recommendations by top governmental, military, and private elites, President Johnson decided to reduce bombing and seek negotiations. These decisions were announced in his famous speech of March 31, 1968. (His decision not to seek re-election, which was announced in the same speech, was largely a personal decision of President Johnson's, for which he did not seek advice from others.)

It is interesting to note that because the President's elite advisors shared a broad consensus about the importance of maintaining American military ascendancy and generally supported U.S. involvement in Asian affairs, this decision reflected only marginal change in U.S. policy — a reduction in bombing that had already been judged ineffective and a commitment to talk to the other side, without changing our basic objectives. There was no effort to completely reconsider the role of the United States in Asia.

President Nixon and the Vietnam War

When President Richard M. Nixon came into office in January 1969, elite opinion in the nation had already shifted against the Vietnam War effort. It would not have been possible for the President to continue to strive for military victory in Vietnam even if he had desired to do so. The President does not command America's elite — his power is not his formal authority but his ability to mobilize other elites. And by 1969, elite opinion favored withdrawal from Vietnam.

Public policy accords with elite preferences rather than mass demands. This fact is clear when we examine elite and mass opinion on the Vietnam war. At the outset of the war, elites gave greater support than did the masses. Figure 9–2 reveals that in 1966 a greater proportion of poorly educated people believed the war was a "mistake" than did well-educated people. Reflecting elite opinion about the wisdom of the war, President Johnson proceeded with a policy of military escalation — gradually increasing U.S. combat forces in South Vietnam and stepping up the bombing of North Vietnam.

By 1968, elite opinion was divided on the wisdom of the war, and in the 1968 elections both Democratic and Republican presidential candidates gave only guarded support for the policy of the Johnson Administration. By 1969, elite opinion had shifted dramatically; nearly two out of three well-educated Americans had come to believe that U.S. involvement in Vietnam was a "mistake." Mass opposition to the war had also grown, but mass opinion did not shift as dramatically as elite opinion.

The masses, once more dovish than the elite, were now more hawkish. It was at this point that the policy of escalation was reversed, and President Nixon inaugurated his policy of gradual U.S. combat troop withdrawal and "Vietnamization" of the war.

It is important to note that this shift in presidential policy in Vietnam correlated with a major shift in *elite* opinion. Changes in presidential policy were not a product of mass demands or the activities (marches, demonstrations, riots, etc.) of counter-elites. Note also that President Nixon chose a *gradual* (incremental) withdrawal from Vietnam rather than an immediate cessation of the war. And the President continued to stress that "Vietnamization" did not mean U.S. withdrawal from Asia or an end to American efforts to halt the spread of communism.

FIGURE 9–2. Agreement That U.S. Involvement in Vietnam Was a Mistake, by Education Levels

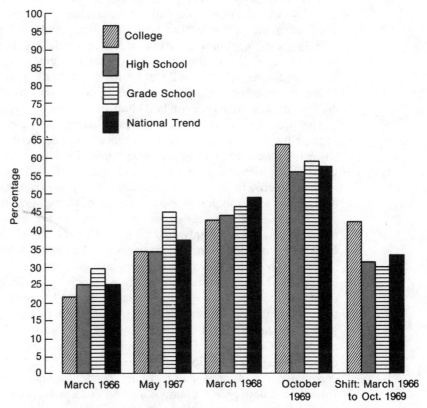

Source: Gallup Opinion Weekly (October 1969), p. 15.

The policy change on Vietnam represents a redefinition by elites of American interests, but it does not represent any fundamental change in American purposes or involvements in world affairs.

Summary The government is distinguished from the rest of the elite structure by its authority, or ability to use force legitimately in enforcing its decisions; and by the fact that governmental elites may make decisions for the whole society, which enables them to resolve conflicts between segments of society. The structure of the government of the United States was deliberately planned to prevent the possibility of majority rule or the possibility of governmental elites gaining undue control over private elites; the complicated system of separation of powers and checks and balances, although admittedly inefficient, was intended to work that way.

Governmental elites in the United States do not rule by command; their chief function is to arbitrate conflicts among the dominant interest groups of the country, achieving accommodation among the elites. The political process in the United States is one of bargain and compromise, made possible by the basic consensus of American elites. Some political reformers have argued that if majority rule could be achieved by party reform, policy decisions in accord with the will of the majority could be made without bargaining or compromise. However, it seems probable that such a system would ignore powerful elite interests, encourage extremism, and eventually split the country apart. As it is, the willingness of governmental elites to compromise and bargain makes the political process generally very peaceable. Political struggles usually occur over minor issues; most policy decisions involve only very gradual change.

The president of the United States is central to the elite structure of the country, and the power of his office has been increasing steadily since the nineteenth century, although it varies somewhat from president to president. The increasing importance of military and foreign affairs, the growth of the executive branch, and the growth of the president's role as a molder of mass opinion have all contributed to the greater power of the presidency. However, the president, like other elites, can make policy only through his powers of persuasion—through bargain, accommodation, and compromise. His policy alternatives are limited to those for which he can mobilize elite support.

Besides the president, the executive branch of the federal government includes the White House Office (aides and special assistants to the president), the Bureau of the Budget, the Council of Economic Advisors, the National Security Council, the National Aeronautics and Space Council, the Office of Emergency Planning, and the Office of Science and Technology; the presidential Cabinet, with its twelve departments; and more than forty independent agencies, including the Interstate Commerce Commission, the Federal Reserve Board, and the Federal Communications Commission.

Important presidential decisions are generally made in consultation with key elite members from inside and outside of government; such decisions reflect elite consensus, and are, moreover, incremental— they involve marginal shifts in public policy rather than fundamental changes in American purposes or objectives. Both President Johnson's decision to end the bombing of North Vietnam and open the Paris peace talks and President Nixon's decision to begin the withdrawal of American troops from the war reflect the consensual and incremental character of elite decision making.

Selected Additional Readings

Hamilton, Alexander, John Jay, and James Madison. *The Federalist.* New York: Modern Library, 1937. The description of constitutional provisions pertaining to the executive branch of the federal government contained in this collection of essays is excellent. The relationship of these provisions to democratic theory and to the important issues at the time of the nation's founding is made evident.

Lindblom, Charles E. *The Intelligence of Democracy.* New York: Free Press, 1965. Lindblom analyzes the democratic decision-making process and prescribes the "best" way of making decisions. He discusses in depth the implications of incremental decision making.

Neustadt, Richard. *Presidential Power.* New York: John Wiley, 1960. In this fascinating study of the presidency, Neustadt focuses on the exercise of presidential power by Eisenhower and Truman.

Schlesinger, Arthur. *A Thousand Days.* New York: Houghton Mifflin, 1965. This entertaining and instructive chronicle of the Kennedy administration is devoted mostly to historical accounts of executive decision making, primarily in the area of foreign policy.

10

**Congress and
the Federal Courts**

Congressmen and Their Constituents

Congress was established to represent the "people" in policy making. But how does Congress "represent" the people, and who are "the people" that Congress represents? It is our contention that because of the way congressmen are elected, Congress tends to represent local elites in America and thereby injects a strong parochial influence into national decision making. Congressmen are part of local elite structures; they retain their local businesses, club memberships, and religious affiliations. Also, congressmen are recruited by local elites rather than national elites. They are not responsible to national political leaders but rather to leaders within their home constituency. Thus, congressmen represent many small segments of the nation, rather than the nation as a whole.

A congressman must concern himself with the interests of local elites; he is not as free as the president or the executive elites to direct himself to national problems or concerns. Moreover, a congressman represents a more homogeneous constituency than the president; a congressman's constituency is usually well defined — rural or urban, mining or manufacturing or agricultural, defense-oriented or cotton-producing or citrus-growing. A president, on the other hand, must please a much wider and more heterogeneous constituency. No single interest need dominate his judgment; he is freer to seek bargains, accommodations, and compromises among separate elites. He is freer to be concerned about the general welfare, and he can take a more cosmopolitan view of national affairs. Similarly, senators, who represent larger constituencies than representatives, are somewhat less parochial and are freer to be concerned about the general public welfare. Lewis A. Froman presents evidence that senators support "liberal" measures more often than do representatives, and he suggests that this difference in political behavior may result from the narrower constituencies of representatives and the localism of their political orientation.[1]

Who *are* the constituents of a congressman? The relevant political constituency of a congressman is not the general population of his

---

[1]Lewis A. Froman, *Congressmen and Their Constituencies* (Chicago: Rand McNally, 1963).

district but its local elite. Less than half of the general population of his district even knows his name, and fewer still have any idea of how he voted on any major issue. No more than 10 percent of the population ever writes or talks to a congressman to give him their views on a public issue. On the basis of a national survey, Miller and Stokes report:

Of constituents living in congressional districts where there was a contest between a Republican and a Democrat in 1958, less than one in five said they had read or heard something about both candidates, . . . of detailed information about policy stands not a chemical trace was found. Among the comments about the candidates given in response to an extended series of free-answer questions, . . . only about three comments in every hundred had to do with legislative issues of any description. . . . [However] congressmen feel that their individual legislative actions may have considerable impact on the electorate, yet some simple facts about the representative's salience to his constituents imply that this could hardly be true. . . . The communication most congressmen have with their districts inevitably puts them in touch with organized groups and individuals who are relatively well-informed about politics. The representative knows his constituents mostly from dealing with people who *do* write letters, who *will* attend meetings, who *have* an interest in his legislative stands. As a result, his sample of contacts with a constituency of several hundred thousand people is heavily biased.[2]

The relevant constituents of a congressman, then, are the active, interested, and resourceful elites of his home district. Usually these are the key economic elites of his district. In an agricultural district, they are the leaders of the American Farm Bureau Federation and the major agricultural producers—cotton producers, wheat growers, dairymen, tobacco growers, peanut producers, or others. In the Southwest, a congressman's key constituents may be oil producers or cattlemen; in the mountain states, the copper, lead, and silver mining interests; in upper New England, the lumber, granite, and fishing interests; in central Pennsylvania and West Virginia, the coal interests and leaders of the United Mine Workers. In more heterogeneous urban constituencies, there may be a variety of influential constituents—bankers and financial leaders, real estate owners and developers, owners and managers of large industrial and commercial enterprises, top labor leaders, and the owners and editors of newspapers and radio and television facilities. In certain big city districts with strong, disciplined party organizations, the key constituents of a congressman may be the city's political and governmental elites—the city or country party chairmen or the mayor. And, of course, anyone who makes major financial contributions to a congressman's campaign is always considered an important constituent, for many congressmen are hard put to find enough money to finance the increasingly expensive costs of campaigning.

[2]Warren Miller and Donald Stokes, "Constituency Influence in Congress," *American Political Science Review,* 57 (March 1963), 55.

Defense industries and military bases are especially important constituents in a large number of congressional districts, because of the very visible economic benefits that derive from them for the district. Fewer than 75 of the 435 members of the House of Representatives do *not* have a major defense plant or a military installation in their district. The opening, expansion, cut back, or closing of military bases is of vital interest to the congressman whose district is concerned, as is the awarding of prime military contracts.

Congressmen work very hard to secure military bases or contracts for their district. An often-cited example of the congressional quest for military-industrial constituents is the state of Georgia, which is represented by the chairman of the Senate Armed Services Committee, Richard B. Russell, and until his retirement in 1965, by the chairman of the House Armed Services Committee, Carl M. Vinson. A general once remarked regarding military installations in Georgia, "One more base would sink the state." Georgia, hardly an industrial state, ranked tenth in prime military contracts. When the first C5-A cargo plane was completed, President Johnson warmly complimented the Georgia delegation for landing the contract for their state: "I would have you good folks of Georgia know that there are a lot of Marietta, Georgias scattered throughout the fifty states . . . all of them would like to have the pride that comes from this production . . . but all of them don't have the Georgia delegation.[3]

On the whole, congressmen do *not* appear to respond in their voting records to the preferences of the masses in their district. In a most careful study of the relationship between mass opinion and congressional voting, Warren E. Miller and Donald Stokes found very low correlations between congressmen's voting records and the attitudes of their constituents on social welfare issues and even lower correlations on foreign policy issues.[4] Only in the area of civil rights did congressmen appear to vote according to the views of a majority of their constituents. In general, "The representative has very imperfect information about the issue preferences of his constituency, and constituency's awareness of the policy stands of the representative is ordinarily slight." With the possible exception of civil rights questions, most congressmen are free from the influence of popular preferences in their legislative voting.

This is not to say that a congressman is free from local influences. On the contrary, the voting behavior of congressmen on roll-call votes correlates very closely with district characteristics. Districts of different social and economic makeup have different kinds of elite structures and produce different political orientations and voting records for congressmen. For example, congressmen from urban-industrial districts are more likely to vote "liberal" than are congressmen from

---

[3] See *Congressional Quarterly*, Special Report, "The Military Industrial Complex," May 24, 1968.
[4] Miller and Stokes, "Constituency Influence in Congress;" see also Charles F. Cnudde and Donald J. McCrone, "The Linkage Between Constituency Attitudes and Congressional Voting Behavior," *American Political Science Review*, 60 (March 1966), 66–72.

rural, agricultural districts, regardless of party affiliation. Congressmen from suburban, high-income, white-collar districts have different voting records than congressmen from big city, low-income, political machine-dominated districts.

Since congressmen are products of the social system in their constituency, they share its dominant goals and values. They have deep roots in the social system of their constituency — many organizational memberships, many overlapping leadership positions, lifetime residency, close ties with social and economic elites, shared religious affiliations, and so on. A congressman is so much "of" his constituency that he needs little direct prompting or supervision from local elites, and conflicts seldom occur between his own views and the dominant views in his constituency.

Thus English political philosopher Edmund Burke's classic question about representation — Should the legislator be guided by his party, his constituents, or his personal judgment? — is an artificial one for the Congress. A majority of legislators in America *say* they follow their conscience in decision making, because this reflects the popular image of the congressman as an independently courageous defender of the public interest, who acts out of his own personal virtue and conviction, regardless of the consequences. But most congressmen do not perceive many conflicts between the wishes of their constituents, their party, and their own judgment. Even where conflict is perceived, congressmen usually attempt to balance conflicting demands rather than represent a party, constituency, or self exclusively. One state legislator whisked away the whole Burkean question in a single sentence: "A representative's judgment should arise from knowing the needs and wants of his district and state."[5]

The Functions of Congress   What is the difference between the role of Congress and the role of other elites? Policy proposals are initiated outside Congress; Congress's role is to respond to proposals from the president, executive and military elites, and interested non-governmental elites. Congress does not merely ratify or "rubber stamp" decisions, it plays an independent role in the policy-making process. But this role is essentially a deliberative one, in which Congress accepts, modifies, or rejects the policies initiated by others. For example, the national budget, perhaps the single most important policy document, is written by executive and military elites and modified by the president before it is submitted to Congress. Congress may make further modifications, but it does not formulate the budget. Of course, Congress is a critical obstacle through which appropriations and revenue measures must pass. But sophisticated lawmakers are aware that they function as arbiters rather than initiators of public policy. As Robert Dahl explains:

[5]Frank Sorauf, *Party and Representation* (New York: Atherton, 1963), p. 147.

The Congress no longer expects to originate measures but to pass, veto, or modify laws proposed by the Chief Executive. It is the President, not the Congress, who determines the content and substance of the legislation with which Congress deals. The President is now the motor of the system; the Congress applies the brakes. The President gives what forward movement there is in the system; his is the force of thrust and innovation. The Congress is the force of inertia—a force, it should be said, that means not only restraint, but stability in politics.[6]

From a constitutional point of view, of course, the potential for power in Congress is very great. Article I empowers Congress to levy taxes, borrow and spend money, regulate interstate and foreign commerce, coin money, declare war, maintain armies and navies, and a number of other important functions, including the passing of all laws "necessary and proper" to carry out these powers. Congress may also propose amendments to the Constitution or call a convention to do so. Congress admits new states. In the event that no candidate receives a majority of votes in the electoral college, the House of Representatives may select the president. The Senate "advises and consents" to treaties and approves presidential nominations to executive and judicial posts. The House has the power to impeach, and the Senate to try, any officer of the United States government, including the president. Congress may also conduct investigations, discipline its own members, and regulate its internal affairs.

Yet despite these extensive formal powers, Congress is only one component of America's elite system. Many important decisions, particularly in foreign and military affairs, are made without the direct participation of Congress. The president may commit Congress and the nation to a foreign policy or military action that Congress cannot prevent or reverse. For example, Congress could do little more than appropriate the necessary funds for the Korean War and the Vietnam War. Often congressional leaders are told of a major foreign policy decision only moments before it is announced on national television.

Congress is more influential in domestic than in foreign and military affairs. It is much freer to reject presidential proposals in business, labor, agriculture, education, welfare, urban affairs, civil rights, taxations, and appropriations. Congressional committees share with the president control over executive agencies dealing with domestic affairs. Executive agencies—for example, the Office of Education, the Social Security Administration, the Housing Assistance Administration, the Department of Agriculture, the Office of Economic Opportunity—must go to Congress for needed legislation and appropriations. Congressional committees can exercise power in domestic affairs by giving or withholding the appropriations and the legislation wanted by these executive agencies.

Finally, congressional committees are an important communication link between governmental and non-governmental elites; they serve as

[6]Robert Dahl, *Pluralist Democracy in the United States* (Chicago: Rand McNally, 1967), p. 136.

a bridge between the executive and military bureaucracies and the major non-governmental elites in American society. Congressional committees bring department and agency heads together with leading industrial representatives — bankers, cotton producers, labor leaders, citrus growers, government contractors.

The Elaborate Procedures of Legislative Elites

The rules and procedures of Congress are elaborate but important to the functioning of legislative elites. A great deal of legislative debate concerns rules and procedures; and many policy questions turn on the question of proper procedure. Legislative procedures and rules make the legislative process fair and orderly; without established customs, rules, and procedures, it would be impossible for 435 men to arrive at collective decisions about the thousands of items submitted to them during a congressional session. Yet the same rules also delay or obstruct proposed changes in the status quo; they strengthen Congress's conservative role in policy making. Congressional procedures offer many opportunities to defeat legislation and many obstacles to the passage of legislation. Of course, it is not surprising that an elite that functions as an arbiter of public policy should operate under rules and procedures that maximize deliberation and grant advantages to those who oppose change.

Congress follows a fairly standard pattern in the formal process of making laws. Table 10–1 describes briefly some of the more important procedural steps in bill passage. Bills are generally drafted in the president's office, in executive departments, or in the offices of interested elites, but they must be formally introduced into Congress by members of the House or Senate. A bill may be introduced in either the House or the Senate, except that bills for raising revenue are required by the Constitution to begin in the House. Upon introduction, a bill is referred to one of the standing committees of the House or the Senate, which may: (1) recommend it for adoption with only minor changes; (2) virtually rewrite the bill into a new policy proposal; (3) ignore the bill and prevent its passage through inaction; (4) kill it by majority vote. The full House or Senate *may* overrule the decision of its committees, but this is a rare occurrence. Most members of Congress are reluctant to upset the prerogatives of the committees and the desires of recognized leaders. Therefore, committees virtually have the power of life or death over every legislative measure.

Committee work is essential to the legislative process; Congress as a body could never hope to review all the measures put before it. As early as 1885, Woodrow Wilson described the American political process as "government by the standing committees of Congress." But in the process of reducing legislative work to manageable proportions, the committees exercise considerable influence over the outcome of legislation. A minority of the legislators, sometimes by a single committee chairman, can delay and obstruct the legislative process.

In the Senate, the most prestigious committees are Foreign Relations, Appropriations, and Finance. In the House, the most power-

TABLE 10–1.
How a Bill
Becomes a Law

1. *Introduction.* Most bills can be introduced in either house. (In this table, the bill is first introduced in the Senate.) It is given a number and referred to the proper committee.

2. *Hearings.* The committee may hold public hearings on the bill.

3. *Committee action.* The full committee meets in executive (closed) session. It may kill the bill, approve it with or without amendments, or draft a new bill.

4. *Calendar.* If the committee recommends the bill for passage, it is listed on the calendar.

5. *Debate, amendment, vote.* The bill goes to the floor for debate. Amendments may be added. The bill is voted on.

6. *Introduction to the second house.* If the bill passes, it goes to the House of Representatives, where it is referred to the proper committee.

7. *Hearings.* Hearings may be held again.

8. *Committee action.* The committee rejects the bill, prepares a new one, or accepts the bill with or without amendments.

9. *Rules Committee consideration.* If the committee recommends the bill, it is listed on the calendar and sent to the Rules Committee. The Rules Committee can block a bill or clear it for debate before the entire House.

10. *Debate, amendment, vote.* The bill goes before the entire body, is debated and voted upon.

11. *Conference Committee.* If the bill as passed by the second house contains major changes, either house may request a conference committee. The conferees—five persons from each house, representing both parties—meet and try to reconcile their differences.

12. *Vote on conference report.* When they reach an agreement, they report back to their respective houses. Their report is accepted or rejected.

13. *Submission to the president.* If the report is accepted by both houses, the bill is signed by the speaker of the House and the president of the Senate and is sent to the president of the United States.

14. *Presidential action.* The president may sign or veto the bill within ten days. If he does not sign and Congress is still in session, the bill automatically becomes a law. If Congress adjourns before the ten days have elapsed, it does not become a law. (This is called the "pocket veto.") If the president returns the bill with a veto message, it may still become a law if passed by a two-thirds majority in each house.

ful committees are the Rules Committee, Appropriations, and Ways and Means. (The 20 standing committees of the House and the 15 of the Senate are listed in Table 10–2 below.) To expedite business, most standing committees create subcommittees to handle particular matters falling within their jurisdiction. This practice further concentrates power over particular subject matter in the hands of a small number of congressmen. A great deal of power lies in the hands of subcommittee

TABLE 10–2.
Standing
Committees
of the House
and Senate,
Ranked in Estimated
Order of Prestige

Senate	House
1. Foreign Relations	1. Rules
2. Appropriations	2. Appropriations
3. Finance	3. Ways and Means
4. Agriculture	4. Armed Services
5. Armed Services	5. Banking and Currency
6. Judiciary	6. Agriculture
7. Commerce	7. Education and Labor
8. Banking	8. Government Operations
9. Rules	9. Public Works
10. Interim	10. Judiciary
11. Post Office	11. Interstate and Foreign Commerce
12. Public Works	12. Foreign Affairs
13. Government Operations	13. Interior and Insular Affairs
14. District of Columbia	14. Science and Astronautics
15. Labor	15. Post Office and Civil Service
	16. Merchant Marine and Fisheries
	17. Veteran Affairs
	18. Un-American Activities
	19. District of Columbia
	20. House Administration

members, especially the chairmen; interested elites cultivate the favor of powerful subcommittee chairmen as well as committee chairmen.

In examining legislation, a committee or subcommittee generally holds public hearings on bills deemed worthy by the chairman or, in some cases, by the majority of the committee. Influenced by the legal profession, from which a majority of Congressmen are drawn, the committees tend to look upon public hearings as trials in which contestants present their side of the argument to the committee members, the judges. Presumably, during this trial the skillful judges will sift facts on which to base their decisions. In practice, however, committees use public hearings primarily to influence public opinion, influence executive action, or, occasionally, to discover the position of major elite groups on the measure under consideration. Major decisions are made in executive session in secret.

The membership of the standing committees on agriculture, labor, interior, insular affairs, and judiciary generally reflects the interest of particular elite groups in the nation. Farm interests are represented on the agricultural committees; land, water, and natural resource interests are represented on interior and insular affairs; congressmen with labor ties and urban industrial constituencies gravitate toward the labor committee; and lawyers dominate the judicial committees of both houses.

In view of the power of congressional committees, the assignment of congressmen to committees is one of the most significant activities of Congress. In the House of Representatives, the Republicans assign their members to committees through a Committee on Committees that consists of one representative from each state sending a Republican to Congress. Each representative votes with the strength of his state delegation. But the real business of this committee is conducted by a subcommittee appointed by the Republican party leader. The subcommittee fills committee vacancies with freshman congressmen and members who are requesting transfer from other committees. The Committee on Committees considers the career backgrounds of congressmen, their seniority, and their reputation for "soundness,"which usually means adherence to conservative policy positions. Often, the chairman of a standing committee tells the Committee on Committees whom he prefers to have on his committee. Democrats in the House are assigned by a Committee on Committees composed exclusively of Democrats on the prestigious Ways and Means Committee. In the Senate, Republican committee positions are filled by a Committee on Committees, and Democratic committee positions are selected by a steering committee appointed by the Democratic floor leader. Usually, only senators with seniority are eligible for major committee positions in the Senate, such as Foreign Relations, Armed Services, and Appropriations.

Committee chairmen are very powerful. They usually determine which bills will be considered by the committee, whether or not public hearings will be held, and what the agenda of the committee will be. The chairman of the committee is officially consulted on all questions relating to his committee; this procedure gives him status with the executive branch and with interested non-governmental elites. Only occasionally is the chairman's decision about a committee matter overruled by a majority within the committee.

The practice of awarding chairmanships according to seniority is another guarantee of conservatism in the legislative process. The member of the majority party having the longest continuous service on the committee becomes chairman; the member of the minority party with the longest continuous service on the committee is the ranking minority member. Therefore chairmen are not chosen by their own committees, by their own party, or by the House and Senate as a whole. They are chosen by the voters of non-competitive congressional districts, for the congressmen from these districts are likely to stay in office the longest. Thus, the major decisions in Congress are made by men from areas where party competition and voter participation is low; in the past, these areas have been southern and rural constituencies and big city machine constituencies. In both chambers, the seniority system works against the competitive urban and suburban districts.

In the House of Representatives, after a standing committee reports a bill that it has considered favorably, a special rule or order must be issued by the Rules Committee before the bill can be considered by the membership of the House. This means that in the House of Representatives bills must be approved by the Rules Committee as well as the standing committee. (The only exceptions are bills reported by the House Appropriations and the Ways and Means Committees; their bills may be considered at any time as "privileged motions.") The Rules Committee can kill a bill by shelving it indefinitely. It can insist that the bill be amended as the price of permitting it on the floor and can even substitute a new bill for the one framed by another committee. The Rules Committee determines the extent of the debate that will be permitted on the floor of the House on any bill and the number and kind of amendments that may be offered from the floor. The only formal limits on Rules Committee authority are the "discharge petition" (which is rarely used and hardly ever successful) and "calendar Wednesday," a cumbersome procedure that permits standing committees to call up bills that have been blocked by the Rules Committee. The Rules Committee, clearly the most powerful single committee in Congress, is dominated by senior members elected from non-competitive districts.

In the Senate, control of floor debate rests with the majority leader. But the majority leader does not have the power to limit debate; once a senator has the floor, he may talk as long as he pleases, and he may yield the floor to whomever he chooses. If enough senators wish to talk a bill to death in a filibuster, they may do so. This device permits a small minority to tie up the business of the Senate and prevent it from voting on a bill. Under Rule 22 of the Senate, debate can be limited only by cloture. When 16 members sign a petition for a cloture, cloture must be voted upon, and a two-thirds vote of the senators present ends the filibuster. But cloture has been successful only six times in the history of the Senate. It has been a major weapon in civil rights legislation; the Civil Rights Act of 1964 passed the Senate through a cloture petition. But generally senators agree to protect each other's right of unlimited debate. Like the Rules Committee in the House, the filibuster is a means by which a small elite can defend itself against majority preferences.

Of the 10,000 bills introduced into Congress every year only about 1,000 or one in ten, becomes law. After a bill has been approved by the standing committee in the Senate or by the standing committee and the Rules Committee in the House, it is reported to the floor for a vote. Usually the most crucial votes come on the amendments to the bill that are offered to the floor (however, amendments may be prevented in the House by the Rules Committee). Once major amendments have either been defeated or incorporated into the bill, the bill usually picks up broad support, and the vote on final passage is usually a lopsided one in favor of the bill.

One of the most conservative features of American government is its bicameralism; the complicated path that a bill follows in one house must be repeated in the other. A bill must pass both branches of Congress in identical form before it can be sent to the president for his signature. However, the Senate often amends a House bill, and the House usually amends Senate bills. This means that even after a bill has passed both houses, it must be resubmitted to the originating house to see if it will concur with the changes made by the other. If either house declines to accept changes in the bill, specific differences must be ironed out by an ad hoc joint committee, called a conference committee. Disagreements between the houses are so frequent that from one third to one half of all public bills, including virtually all important ones, must be referred to conference committees after passage by both houses.

Members of conference committees are appointed by the presiding officers of each house, but are usually drawn from the two standing committees that handled the bill in each house. Since the final bill produced by the conference committee is generally accepted by both houses, conference committees have tremendous power in determining the final form of legislation. Reports of conference committees must be accepted or rejected as a whole; they cannot be further amended. Conference committees are held in secret and are unrecorded; they hold no hearings and listen to no outside testimony. The bill that emerges from their deliberations may not represent the view of either house and may contain items never considered by either house. Conference committees have sometimes been characterized as a "third house" of Congress, whose members are not elected by the people, keep no record of their work, and perform entirely in secret—and there can be no debate about their product.

Elites within Elites—The Congressional Establishment

In 1964 Congressman Everett G. Burkhalter of California announced, after his first term in Congress, that he would not seek re-election. "I could see I was not going to get any place. Nobody listens to what you have to say until you've been here ten or twelve years. These old men have everything so tied down you can't do anything. There are only about forty out of the 435 members who call the shots. They're the committee chairmen and the ranking members and they're all around seventy or eighty." Congressman Burkhalter realized that, as a 67-year-old freshman in the House, he was unlikely ever to exercise any power over public policy.

There is a power hierarchy among federal governmental elites. This power hierarchy is supported by protocol, by the distribution of formal constitutional powers, by the powers associated with party office, by the committee and seniority systems of Congress, and by the "informal folkways" of Washington. According to the protocol of Washington society, the highest social rank is held by the president, followed by former presidents and their widows, the vice-president, the Speaker of the House, members of the Supreme Court, foreign ambassadors and ministers, the Cabinet, United States senators, governors of states, former vice-presidents, and finally congressmen.

The Constitution grants greater formal powers to senators than to representatives. There are only 100 senators; therefore, each senator is more visible than a representative in the social and political life of Washington, as well as in his home state. Also, senators have a special authority in foreign affairs not accorded to Representatives, for the Senate must advise and consent by a two-thirds vote to all treaties entered into by the United States. The threat of Senate repudiation of a treaty makes it desirable for the president to solicit Senate views on foreign affairs; generally the Secretary of State works closely with the Foreign Relations Committee of the Senate. Influential senators undertake personal missions abroad and serve on delegations to international bodies. Another constitutional power afforded senators is to advise and consent on executive appointments, including Supreme Court members, Cabinet members, federal judges, ambassadors, and other high executive officials. Even though the Senate generally approves the presidential nominations, the added potential for power contributes to the difference between the influence of senators and of House members. Finally, senators are elected for a six-year term and from a broader and more heterogeneous constituency. Thus, they have a longer guaranteed tenure in Washington, more prestige, and greater freedom from minor shifts in opinion among non-governmental elites in their home states.

Senators can also acquire additional power through their political roles; they often wield great power in state parties and can usually control federal patronage dispensed in their state. The power of the Senate to confirm nominations has given rise to the important political custom of "senatorial courtesy." Senatorial courtesy gives individual senators who are of the same party as the president a virtual veto power over major appointments—federal judges, postmasters, customs collectors, and so on—in their state. When presidential nominations are received in the Senate, they are referred to the senator or senators from the state involved. If the senator declares the nominee "personally obnoxious" to him, the Senate usually respects this declaration and rejects the appointment. Thus, before the president submits a nomination to the Senate, he usually makes sure that the nominee will be acceptable to his party's senator or senators from the state involved.

Party leadership roles in the House and the Senate are major sources of power in Washington. (See Table 10–3 for a list of Senate and House leaders for the 91st Congress.) The Speaker of the House of Representatives, who is elected by the majority party of the House, exercises more power over public policy than any other member of the House or Senate. Before 1910 the Speaker appointed all standing committees and their chairmen, possessed unlimited discretion to recognize members on the floor, and served as chairman of the Rules Committee. But in 1910, a group of progressives, led by George Norris, severely curtailed the authority of the Speaker. Today he shares power over the appointment of committees with the Committee on Committees; committee chairmen are selected by seniority, not by the Speaker; and the Speaker no longer serves as chairman of the Rules Committee. However, the Speaker retains considerable authority. He refers bills to committees, appoints all conference committees, rules on all matters of House procedure, recognizes those who wish to speak, and generally

TABLE 10–3.
The Congressional Establishment for the 91st Congress, 1969–1971

Senate Leadership

President pro tempore—Richard B. Russell (D-Ga.)
Majority Leader—Mike Mansfield (D-Mont.)
Majority Whip—Edward M. Kennedy (D-Mass.)
Democratic Conference Secretary—Robert C. Byrd (D-W.Va.)
Minority Leader—Everett McKinley Dirksen (R-Ill.)
Minority Whip—Hugh Scott (R-Pa.)
Republican Policy Committee Chairman—Gordon Allott (R-Colo.)
Republican Conference Chairman—Margaret Chase Smith (R-Maine)
Republican Conference Secretary—Milton R. Young (R-N.D.)

House Leadership

Speaker—John W. McCormack (D-Mass.)
Majority Leader—Carl Albert (D-Okla.)
Majority Whip—Hale Boggs (D-La.)
Minority Leader—Gerald R. Ford (R-Mich.)
Minority Whip—Leslie C. Arends (R-Ill.)
Republican Policy Committee Chairman—John J. Rhodes (R-Ariz.)
Republican Conference Chairman—John B. Anderson (R-Ill.)

Senate Committee Chairmen

Appropriations—Richard B. Russell (D-Ga.)
Armed Services—John Stennis (D-Miss.)
Labor and Public Welfare—Ralph Yarborough (D-Texas)
Banking and Currency—John J. Sparkman (D-Ala.)
Foreign Relations—J. W. Fulbright (D-Ark.)
Government Operations—John L. McClellan (D-Ark.)
Judiciary—James O. Eastland (D-Miss.)
Finance—Russell B. Long (D-La.)
Agriculture—Allen J. Ellender (D-La.)

House Committee Chairmen

Rules—William D. Colmer (D-Miss.)
Ways and Means—Wilbur D. Mills (D-Ark.)
Interstate Commerce—Harley O. Staggers (D-W.Va.)
Judiciary—Emanuel Celler (D-N.Y.)
Government Operations—William L. Dawson (D-Ill.)
Foreign Affairs—Thomas E. Morgan (D-Pa.)
Banking and Currency—Wright Patman (D-Tex.)
Armed Services—L. Mendel Rivers (D-S.C.)
Appropriations—George H. Mahon (D-Tex.)
Agriculture—W. R. Poage (D-Tex.)

directs the business of the floor. More importantly, he is the principal figure in House policy formulation, leadership, and responsibility; although he shares these tasks with standing committee chairmen, he is generally "first among equals" in his relationship with them.

Next to the Speaker, the most influential party leaders in the House are the majority and minority floor leaders and the party whips. These party leaders are chosen by their respective party caucuses, which are held at the beginning of each congressional session. The party caucus, composed of all the party's members in the House, usually does little more than elect these officers; it makes no major policy decisions. The floor leaders and whips have little formal authority; their role is to influence legislation through persuasion. Party floor leaders are supposed to combine parliamentary skill with persuasion, good personal relationships with party members, and close ties with the president and administration. They cannot deny party renomination to congressmen who are disloyal to the party, but they can control committee assignments and many small favors in Washington so a maverick congressman will have a difficult time becoming an effective legislator. The whips, or assistant floor leaders, keep members informed about legislative business, see that members are present for important floor votes, and communicate party strategy and position on particular issues. They also serve as the eyes and ears of the leadership, counting noses before important votes are taken. Party whips should know how many votes a particular measure has, and they should be able to get the votes to the floor when the roll is called.

The vice-president of the United States, who serves as president of the Senate, has less control over Senate affairs than the Speaker of the House has over House affairs. The vice-president votes only in case of a tie, and he must recognize senators in the order in which they rise. The majority party in the Senate also elects from its membership a president pro tempore who presides in the absence of the vice-president.

The key power figures in the Senate are the majority and minority leaders. The majority leader usually has great personal influence within the Senate and is a powerful figure in national affairs. The majority leader, when he is of the same party as the president, is in charge of getting the president's legislative program through the Senate. He has somewhat less formal authority than the Speaker of the House, but he has the right to be the first senator to be heard on the floor; and, with the minority floor leader, he determines the Senate's agenda. He can greatly influence committee assignments for members of his own party. But on the whole, his influence rests upon his powers of persuasion. It is widely recognized that the most effective majority leader in recent times was Lyndon Johnson, Senate majority leader from 1953 to 1960.

The committee system and the seniority rule also create powerful congressional figures, the chairmen of the most powerful standing committees—particularly the Senate Foreign Relations, Appropriations, and Finance Committees, and the House Rules, Appropriations, and Ways and Means Committees. Chairmen of the standing committees acquire their power because the members of each house respect the authority of their committees. The standing committee system is self-sustaining, because each committee and committee chairman tends to regard an attack upon the authority of one committee or committee chairman as a threat to all. If one committee or committee chairman can be bypassed on a particular measure, other committees and committee chairmen can be bypassed on other measures. Hence, committee chairmen and ranking committee members tend to stand by each other and support each other's authority over legislation assigned to their respective committees. Committee chairmen or ranking committee members are also respected because of their seniority and experience in the legislative process. Committee chairmen are often experts in parliamentary process as well as in the substantive area covered by their committees. Finally, and perhaps most importantly, committee chairmen and ranking committee members acquire power through their relationships with executive and private elites who are involved in the policy area within the jurisdiction of the committee. "Policy clusters" — alliances of leaders from executive agencies, congressional committees, and private business and industry — tend to emerge in Washington. Committee chairmen, owing to their control over legislation in Congress, are key members of these policy clusters. One policy cluster might include the chairmen of the House and Senate committees on agriculture, the Secretary of Agriculture and other key officials of the Department of Agriculture, and the leaders of the American Farm Bureau Federation. Another vital policy cluster would include the chairmen of the House and Senate Armed Services Committees; the Secretary and Under-Secretaries of Defense; key military leaders, including the Joint Chiefs of Staff; and the leadership of defense industries such as Lockheed and General Dynamics. These alliances of congressional, executive, and private elites determine most public policy within their area of concern.

Power also accrues to key senators and congressmen by virtue of custom and informal folkways. Professor David B. Truman writes that Congress "has its standards and conventions, its largely unwritten system of obligations and privileges. . . . The neophyte must conform, at least in some measure, if he hopes to make effective use of his position."[7] A new member of Congress should expect to "go along" with the customs of Congress if he wishes to "get along." These informal folkways appear more important in the Senate, where there are fewer formal controls over members than in the House. Donald Matthews has described some of the folkways of the Senate as: respect for the seniority system; good behavior in floor debate; humility in freshmen senators; a willingness to perform cheerfully many thankless tasks, such as presiding over floor debate; deference to senior members; making speeches only on subjects on which you are expert or which

[7]David B. Truman, *The Governmental Process* (New York: Alfred A. Knopf, 1955), p. 344.

concern your committee assignment or your state; doing favors for other senators; keeping your word when you make an agreement; remaining friendly toward your colleagues, whether you are in political agreement with them or not; and speaking well of the Senate as an institution.[8]

Ralph K. Huitt describes the Senate type as:

> . . . a prudent man, who serves a long apprenticeship before trying to assert himself, and talks infrequently even then. He is courteous to a fault in his relations with his colleagues, not allowing political disagreements to affect his personal feelings. He is always ready to help another Senator when he can, and he expects to be repaid in kind. More than anything else he is a Senate man, proud of the institution and ready to defend its traditions and prerequisites against all outsiders. He is a legislative workhorse who specializes in one or two policy areas. . . . He is a man of accommodation who knows that "You have to go along to get along;" he is a conservative, institutional man, slow to change what he has mastered at the expense of so much time and patience.[9]

Senators and prominent reporters have described the Senate "establishment" as the "inner club" where power in the Senate and in Washington is concentrated. The establishment is composed primarily of conservative senators from both parties who have acquired great seniority and control key committee chairmanships. The establishment consists of those senators who have learned the folkways of the Senate over a long period of time and who now appear to be running the Senate. In 1963, United States Senator Joseph S. Clark of Pennsylvania attacked the Senate "establishment" as "the antithesis of democracy."[10] He charged that it was composed of political conservatives from the Democratic South and the Republican Midwest who had acquired seniority and who controlled appointment to committees and other important posts. William S. White also talks of the "inner club" in the Senate, composed of men who "express consciously or unconsciously the deepest instincts and prejudices of 'the Senate type.'" For White, a Senate type is one who displays "tolerance toward fellows, intolerance toward any who would in any real way change the Senate," and commitment toward the Senate as "a career in itself, a life in itself, and an end in itself."[11]

In summary, it seems clear that there are elites within elites. There are elites within the House, the Senate, and the executive branch who exercise disproportionate control over government and who are not representative even of the majority of governmental elites. Power within the House and Senate appears to flow downward from senior party leaders and influential committee chairmen, whose dominance in congressional affairs is seldom challenged by the rank-and-file

---

[8] Donald R. Matthews, "The Folkways of the United States Senate: Conformity to Group Norms and Legislative Effectiveness," *American Political Science Review*, 53 (December 1959), 1064–1089.

[9] William S. White, *The Citadel: The Story of the U.S. Senate* (New York: Harper & Row, 1956), Chapter VII.

[10] Joseph S. Clark, *The Senate Establishment* (New York: Hill & Wang, 1963).

[11] White, *The Citadel*, p. 84.

congressmen. Senator Clark writes: "The trouble with Congress today is that it exercises negative and unjust powers to which the governed, the people of the United States, have never consented. . . . The heart of the trouble is that power is exercised by minority, not majority, rule."[12]

Conflict and Consensus: Party Voting in Congress

Studies of roll-call voting in Congress show that political parties play an important role in legislative conflict.[13] *Party* votes, those roll-call votes in which a majority of voting Democrats oppose a majority of voting Republicans, occur on about *half* of all the roll-call votes taken in Congress. Roll-call voting follows party lines more often than it follows sectional, urban-rural, or any other divisions that have been studied. How much cohesion exists within the parties? Table 10–4 shows the number of party votes that have been taken in Congress in recent years and the average support Democratic and Republican congressmen have given to their parties. Democrats and Republicans appear equally cohesive, with members of both parties voting with their party majority more than two thirds of the time. Party voting appears more frequent in the House than in the Senate.

Bipartisan votes, those roll calls in which divisions are not along party lines, occur most frequently in the areas of foreign policy and defense matters. Bipartisan agreement also appears on appropriation bills and roll calls where there is little dispute. Recently bipartisan voting has settled issues of federal aid to education, highway beautification, water pollution, voting rights, presidential continuity, and increases in federal employees' pay and veterans' benefits.

Conflict between parties occurs most frequently over issues involving social welfare programs, housing and urban development, economic opportunity, medical care, anti-poverty programs, health and welfare, and the regulation of business and labor. Party conflict is particularly apparent in the budget, the most important policy document of the national government. The budget is identified as the product of the president and carries the label of his party. On some issues, such as civil rights and appropriations, voting will follow party lines during roll calls on preliminary motions, amendments, and other preliminary matters, but swing to a bipartisan vote on passage of the final legislation. This means that the parties have disagreed on certain aspects of the bill, but compromised on its final passage.

Many of the issues that cause conflict between the Democratic and Republican parties are related to the conflict of government and private initiative. In general, Democrats have favored: lower tariffs; federal subsidies for agriculture; federal action to assist labor and low income groups through social security, relief, housing, and wage hour regulation; and generally a larger role for the federal government in

[12] Joseph S. Clark, *Congress: The Sapless Branch* (New York: Harper & Row, 1964), pp. 22–23.
[13] See Malcolm E. Jewell and Samuel C. Patterson, *The Legislative Process in the United States* (New York: Random House, 1966); William J. Keefe and Morris Ogul, *The American Legislative Process* (Englewood Cliffs, N.J.: Prentice-Hall, 1964).

TABLE 10–4.
Party Voting
in Congress

	Party Votes as Percentage of Total Votes	Party Support* Democrats	Party Support* Republicans
1955–1960			
Senate	41%	69%	70%
House	48	70	69
1961–1964			
Senate	44	65	66
House	49	71	72
1965			
Senate	42	63	68
House	52	70	71
1966			
Senate	50	57	63
House	41	62	68
1967			
Senate	35	61	60
House	36	67	74
1968			
Senate	32	51	60
House	35	59	64

*Party support: Average percentage of times a congressman voted with his party majority in disagreement with the other party's majority.

Source: Compiled from Congressional Quarterly Almanac, Vols. XI–XXIV (Washington: Congressional Quarterly Service, 1955–1968).

TABLE 10–5.
Democratic and
Republican Party
Positions in
Congress,
1965–1968

	All Democrats				All Republicans			
	'65	'66	'67	'68	'65	'66	'67	'68
Overall Support for President								
Support								
Senate	64%	57%	61%	48%	48%	43%	53%	47%
House	74	63	69	64	41	37	46	51
Opposition								
Senate	21	23	22	27	39	38	31	35
House	15	15	17	19	48	45	44	35
Johnson Foreign Policy								
Support								
Senate	60	63	64	50	58	61	61	51
House	77	60	66	66	41	33	40	49
Opposition								
Senate	22	20	21	21	25	21	24	24
House	13	15	18	17	49	47	48	37
Johnson Domestic Policy								
Support								
Senate	65	54	60	48	45	37	49	46
House	73	64	70	64	41	38	47	52
Opposition								
Senate	20	24	22	28	44	43	34	38
House	16	14	17	19	48	44	43	34
Federal Role								
Larger								
Senate	82	74	69	66	46	48	52	55
House	79	69	73	69	33	39	39	48
Smaller								
Senate	15	22	26	23	52	51	46	39
House	18	26	24	27	63	56	58	48

Source: Data compiled from Congressional Quarterly Almanac, Vols, XXI–XXIV (Washington: Congressional Quarterly Service, 1965–1968).

launching new projects to remedy domestic problems. Republicans, on the other hand, have favored higher tariffs, free competition in agriculture, less government involvement in labor and welfare matters, and reliance on private action.

Further, each party supports the president to a different degree. The president generally receives greater support from his own party than from the opposition party in Congress. The figures in Table 10–5 show that President Johnson received the support of 64 percent of all Senate Democrats and 74 percent of the House Democrats on the 274 roll calls in 1965 presenting clear-cut tests for support for his views. In contrast, the Republicans in both houses supported President Johnson on less than half of these presidential support votes. Democrats rarely opposed the President's program, while Republicans frequently did. However, Republicans were much more critical of the President's domestic programs than of his foreign policy programs.

Party lines are hazy when it comes to issues involving veterans, civil service, public works, and states' rights; and differences between the parties on foreign policy are practically non-existent. Before World War II, Democrats tended to support United States international involvement, while the Republicans were heavily committed to neutrality and "isolationism." Now, only the question of foreign aid divides the parties significantly in foreign affairs; Democrats generally give greater support to foreign aid than Republicans.

The Conservative Coalition

Although party voting appears more important than regional alignments, one regional voting block can be identified on a significant number of issues in Congress. As David Truman explains, "the evidence is clear that there [is] a solid and sharply identifiable die-hard element among the Southern Democrats, whose opposition extend[s] well beyond the issues of intense regional loyalty to almost a whole range of questions growing out of the strains and stresses to which the American society has been subjected in the mid-twentieth century." On the civil rights votes, this block of Southern Democrats votes in opposition to a majority of both Northern Democrats and Republicans.

More significant, however, is the "conservative coalition" of Southern Democrats and Republicans who oppose the Northern Democrats. In recent years this coalition has occurred on about 20 percent of all congressional roll calls (see Table 10–6). The coalition votes together on such issues as aid to depressed areas, minimum wage laws, federal aid to education, public housing, urban renewal, medical care for the aged, taxation, and other domestic welfare questions. Not all Southern Democrats or Republicans vote with the coalition; a roll-call coalition is defined as any roll call in which a majority of voting Southern Democrats and a majority of voting Republicans oppose a majority of Northern Democrats. The coalition generally has less concern for the public than the president or the Northern Democrats do, and it has resisted the expansion of federal power and the increase of federal spending programs.

TABLE 10–6. The Conservative Coalition in Congress, 1958–1968	Percentage of Coalition Roll Calls to Total	Percentage of Coalition Victories on Coalition Roll Calls
1958		
Senate	19%	86%
House	15	64
1959		
Senate	13	65
House	13	91
1960		
Senate	22	67
House	20	35
1961		
Senate	32	48
House	20	74
1962		
Senate	15	71
House	13	44
1963		
Senate	19	44
House	13	67
1964		
Senate	17	47
House	11	67
1965		
Senate	24	39
House	24	25
1966		
Senate	30	51
House	19	32
1967		
Senate	18	54
House	22	73
1968		
Senate	25	80
House	23	63

Source: Compiled from the *Congressional Quarterly Almanac,* Vols. XVIII–XXIV (Washington: Congressional Quarterly Service, 1962–1968).

The coalition was highly successful during the Eisenhower administration and, to some extent, during the Kennedy years. But when Johnson won an overwhelming victory in the presidential election of 1964, he carried into office enough Northern Democratic congressmen to help him break the back of the conservative coalition in the 1965 session of Congress. The coalition lost almost two thirds of the coalition roll calls in 1965. However, the Republican victories in the mid-term congressional elections of 1966 strengthened the coalition. Even though the coalition emerged on nearly 20 percent of the roll-call votes in recent years, it should be remembered that the coalition takes second place to the importance of parties as voting blocks.

Elites in Black Robes

The Founding Fathers viewed the federal courts as the final bulwark against mass threats to principle and property. In *The Federalist* No. 78, Hamilton wrote:

By a limited Constitution I understand one which contains certain specified exceptions to the legislative authority; such, for instance, as that it shall pass no bills of attainder, no ex post facto laws, and the like. Limitations of this kind can be preserved in practice no other way than through the medium of courts of justice, whose duty it is to declare all acts contrary to the manifest tenor of the Constitution void. Without this, all the reservations of particular rights or privileges would amount to nothing.[14]

In *Marbury* v. *Madison,* John Marshall argued persuasively that: (1) The Constitution is the supreme law of the land, and the laws of the United States and of the States must be made in pursuit thereof; (2) Article III of the Constitution gives to the Supreme Court the judicial power, which includes the power to interpret the meanings of laws, and, in case of conflict between laws, decide which law shall prevail; (3) the courts are sworn to uphold the Constitution; therefore, they must declare void a law that conflicts with the Constitution.[15]

Since 1803, the federal courts have struck down more than eighty laws of Congress and uncounted state laws that they believed conflicted with the Constitution. Judicial review and the power to interpret the meaning and decide the application of law are great sources of power for judges. Some of the nation's most important policy decisions have been made by courts rather than by executive or legislative bodies. In recent years, federal courts have taken the lead in eliminating segregation in public life, insuring the separation of church and state, defining relationships between individuals and law enforcers, and guaranteeing individual voters equal voice in government. Courts are an integral component of America's governmental elite system, for sooner or later most important policy questions are brought before the courts.

The undemocratic nature of judicial power has long been recognized in American politics. Nine Supreme Court justices—who are not elected to office, whose terms are for life, and who can be removed only for "high crimes and misdemeanors"—possess the power to void the acts of popularly elected presidents, congresses, governors, and state legislators.

The decision of the Founding Fathers to grant federal courts the power of judicial review of *state* decisions—as stated in Article VI, that the Constitution and the laws and treaties of the national government are the supreme law of the land, "anything in the Constitution or laws of any state to the contrary notwithstanding"—is easy to understand. Federal court power over state decisions is probably essential in maintaining national unity, for fifty different state interpretations of the meaning of the United States Constitution or of the laws and treaties of Congress would create unimaginable confusion. Thus, the power of federal judicial review over state constitutions, laws, and court decisions is seldom questioned.

---

[14]James Madison, Alexander Hamilton, John Jay, *The Federalist* No. 78 (New York: Modern Library, 1937).
[15]*Marbury* v. *Madison,* 1 Cranch 137 (1803).

However, at the national level, why should the views of an appointed court about the meaning of the Constitution prevail over the views of an elected Congress and president? Congressmen and presidents are sworn to uphold the Constitution, and it can reasonably be assumed that they do not pass laws that they believe could be unconstitutional. Since laws must be approved by majorities of those voting in both houses and must have the president's formal approval, why should the Founding Fathers have allowed the decisions of these bodies to be set aside by the federal courts?

The answer appears to be that the Founding Fathers distrusted both popular majorities and elected officials who might be influenced by popular majorities. They believed that government should be limited so that it could not attack principle and property, whether to do so was the will of the majority or not. So the courts were deliberately insulated against popular majorities; to insure their independence, judges were not to be elected, but appointed for life terms. Originally, it was expected that they would be appointed by a president who was not even directly elected himself and confirmed by a Senate that was not directly elected. Only in this way, the writers of the Constitution believed, would they be sufficiently protected from the masses to permit them to judge courageously and responsibly.

The Supreme Court is best understood as an elitist institution, rather than as a "conservative" or "liberal" institution in American government. During the 1930s, the Supreme Court was a bastion of conservatism; it attacked the economic programs of the New Deal and clung to the earlier elite philosophy of rugged individualism. In recent years, the Court has been criticized as too liberal in its orientations toward equality of the law, church-state relations, and individual rights before the law. The apparent paradox can be understood if we view the Court as an exponent of the dominant elite philosophy, rather than as a constant liberal or conservative element in national politics. When the dominant elite philosophy was rugged individualism, the Court reflected this fact, just as it reflects a liberal philosophy today. Of course, owing to the insulation of the Court even from other elites, through life terms and independence from the executive and legislative branches, there is a time lag between changes in elite philosophy and the Court decisions reflecting these changes. For example, Franklin D. Roosevelt came to power in 1933, but the Supreme Court did not generally approve New Deal legislation until after 1937.

Before the Civil War, the Supreme Court was spokesman first for the Federalists under John Marshall and later for Southern planters and slaveholders under Roger Taney. Marshall, who served as Chief Justice for 34 years, helped to elevate the Supreme Court to a position of importance in American government corresponding to that of Congress and the president. Rulings by his court helped establish the authority of the national government over the states and protect the rights of property. Taney, Marshall's successor, retreated from Marshall's nationalism and defended property rights in land and slaves. In

Dred Scott v. *Sanford*,[16] Taney declared that slavery was constitutionally protected and invalidated the Missouri Compromise by declaring that Congress did not have the power to exclude slavery from any of the territories.

Following the emergence of industrial capitalism in the second half of the nineteenth century, the Supreme Court became the spokesman for the prevailing elite philosophy of social Darwinism. The Court struck down the federal income tax; prevented prosecutions of corporations under the Sherman Antitrust Act, while applying this Act against labor unions; and struck down child labor laws and laws limiting the workweek. The Court gave such a restrictive interpretation of the interstate commerce clause that it prevented federal regulation of the economy. It interpreted the "due process" clause of the Fifth and Fourteenth Amendments and the contract clause of Article II, Section 10, in such a way as to protect business enterprise from almost any form of government regulation. Justice Oliver Wendell Holmes lamented, "the Fourteenth Amendment does not enact Mr. Herbert Spencer's social statistics. . . . A constitution is not intended to embody a particular economic theory whether of paternalism . . . or of laissez faire."[17] But Holmes was writing a minority opinion. The majority impulse of the Court was indeed to read social Darwinism into the Constitution itself and to give it constitutional protection.

The Supreme Court's greatest crisis occurred when it failed to respond swiftly to changes in elite philosophy. When Franklin D. Roosevelt became president in 1933, the Supreme Court was committed to the philosophy of rugged individualism. In a four-year period, 1933–1937, the Court made the most active use of the power of judicial review over congressional legislation in its history, in a vain attempt to curtail the economic recovery programs of the New Deal. It invalidated the National Industrial Recovery Administration, nullified the Railroad Retirement Act, invalidated the National Farm Mortgage Act, and threw out the Agricultural Adjustment Act. Having denied the federal government the power to regulate manufacturing, petroleum, mining, agriculture, and labor conditions, the Court reaffirmed the notion that the states could not regulate hours and wages. By 1936, it appeared certain that the Court would declare the Social Security Act and the National Labor Relations Act unconstitutional.

After Roosevelt's unsuccessful but traumatic attempt to pack the Court by expanding its size and adding new liberal members, the Court changed its attitude, with Chief Justice Hughes and Justice Roberts making timely changes in their position. In *National Labor Relations Board* v. *Jones & Laughlin Steel Corporation*,[18] the Court expanded the definition of interstate commerce to remove constitutional barriers to government regulation of the economy. The power of the federal government to establish a social security system was upheld in a series

[16] *Dred Scott* v. *Sanford*, 19 Howard 393 (1857).
[17] *Lochner* v. *New York*, 198 U.S. 45 (1905).
[18] *National Labor Relations Board* v. *Jones & Laughlin Steel Corp.*, 301 U.S. 1 (1937).

of decisions that struck down the "due process" objections to social legislation. And the contract clause was reinterpreted to permit states to regulate wages, hours, and conditions of work.

A liberal concern for the underprivileged in America was reflected in the development of civil rights law by the Supreme Court under the leadership of Chief Justice Earl Warren. The Court firmly insisted that no person in America should be denied equal protection of the law. It defended the right of Negroes to vote, to attend integrated schools, and to receive equal justice in the courts; it upheld the power of Congress to protect Negroes from discrimination in public accommodations, employment, voting, and housing. It ruled that discrimination against any group of voters by state legislatures in the apportioning of election districts was unconstitutional. It protected religious minorities (and the nonreligious) from laws establishing official prayers and religious ceremonies in public schools. It protected defendants in criminal cases from self-incrimination through ignorance of their rights, through the subtlety of law enforcement officials in extracting confessions, or through lack of legal counsel.

It is interesting, however, that the Court was noticeably less concerned with civil liberty when the cold war ideology of the liberal establishment was involved. In *Dennis* v. *United States*,[19] the Court permitted the prosecution of Communists for merely "advocating" the overthrow of the government, and in *Communist Party, U.S.A.* v. *Subversive Activities Control Board*,[20] it upheld the right of government to require the registration of "subversive" organizations. It permitted congressional committees to interrogate citizens about their political views and upheld loyalty oaths and loyalty-security programs. Only recently has it undertaken to protect "Communists" and "subversives" from some of the harsher provisions of federal law.

As an elitist institution reflecting prevailing elite values, the Court has seldom been popular with the masses. Consequently, the Court is frequently the object of attack by counter-elites. In 1968, George C. Wallace made the Court a major political issue.

The social backgrounds of judges are not unlike those of other governmental elites, reflecting close ties with the upper social strata of society. John R. Schmidhauser reports that over 90 percent of the 94 Supreme Court justices serving on the Court between 1789 and 1962 were from socially prominent, politically influential, upper-class families.[21] No Negroes served on the Supreme Court until the appointment of Associate Justice Thurgood Marshall in 1967. Henry Abraham depicts the typical Supreme Court justice: "White; generally Protestant. . . ; fifty to fifty-five years of age at the time of his appointment; Anglo-Saxon ethnic stock. . . ; high social status; reared in an urban environment; member of a civic-minded, politically active, economically comfortable family; legal training; some type of public office;

[19] *Dennis* v *U.S.*, 341 U.S. 494 (1951).
[20] *Communist Party, U.S.A.* v. *Subversive Activities Control Board*, 367 U.S. 1 (1961).
[21] John R. Schmidhauser, *The Supreme Court* (New York: Holt, Rinehart and Winston, 1960).

generally well educated."[22] Of course, social background does not necessarily determine judicial philosophy. But as Schmidhauser observes, if the Court is the "keeper of the American conscience, it is essentially the conscience of the American upper middle class," conditioned by the "conservative impact of legal training and professional legal attitudes and associations" and motivated by "individual social responsibility and political activism."[23]

Summary Congressmen, each of whom represents the local elites of his constituency, inject a strong parochial influence into national decision making. Senators are less parochial than representatives, but more so than federal executives or judges. In spite of their local orientation, congressmen are relatively free from the influence of mass preferences in their legislative voting; it is the preferences of their local elites that is reflected in congressional votes.

Congress' function is not to initiate policy, but to respond to policy proposals initiated by the president, executive and military elites, and interested non-governmental elites. Thus, Congress plays a conservative role, deliberating on and accepting or rejecting policy changes proposed by other elites. Another important function of Congress is to link governmental with non-governmental elites through congressional committees.

The function of the elaborate rules and procedures of Congress is to delay and obstruct proposed changes in the status quo. The process through which a bill becomes a law is a difficult one, offering many opportunities to defeat the legislation, and many obstacles to its passage.

The committee system places effective control over legislation in the hands of a relatively few members; and, because of the seniority rule, these powerful members are usually conservative. Committee chairmen and ranking committee members, along with the Speaker of the House, the floor leaders, the party whips in the House, and the majority and minority leaders in the Senate, make up the elite establishment within Congress.

What conflict exists in Congress tends to follow party lines more often than it follows any other factional divisions. Conflict occurs most often over the implementation of domestic and foreign policy; there is seldom conflict over the major directions of policy.

Courts are a major component of the federal elite system; some of the nation's most important policy decisions have been made by the Supreme Court. The power of federal court review over the laws of Congress and of state legislatures was intended by the writers of the Constitution as an additional safeguard against majority attacks on liberty and property. The Court is better understood as an elite insti-

[22] Henry Abraham, *The Judicial Process* (New York: Oxford University Press, 1962), p. 58.
[23] Schmidhauser, *The Supreme Court*, p. 59.

tution, rather than a permanently conservative one; its decisions generally reflect the prevailing elite philosophy.

Selected Additional Readings

Clark, Joseph S., *et al. The Senate Establishment.* New York: Hill & Wang, 1963. Clark's book contains speeches made on the Senate floor that deal with power relationships in the Senate, especially the disproportionate power of the conservative coalition.

Hamilton, Alexander, John Jay, and James Madison. *The Federalist.* New York: Modern Library, 1937. The general quality of this collection has been mentioned in previous chapters. Essays concerning the legislature and judiciary are relevant to the present chapter.

Schmidhauser, John. *The Supreme Court.* New York: Holt, Rinehart and Winston, 1960. *The Supreme Court,* written as a supplement to American government texts, traces the development of the Court as an institution and investigates the judicial behavior of its members.

White, William S. *The Citadel: The Story of the U.S. Senate.* New York: Houghton Mifflin Co., 1956. Though White's attitude toward the Senate is reverential when compared to Clark's critical view, *The Citadel* contains much information in an easy, enjoyable, though somewhat dated, book.

Elites in States
and Communities

Sub-Elites in the American Political System

There are more than 90 thousand state and local governments in America—states, counties, cities, towns, boroughs, villages, special districts, school districts, and public authorities. Legally, states are the important units of government in America; they are endowed with all governmental powers not vested specifically in the national government or reserved to the people by the U.S. Constitution. All other governmental jurisdictions are subdivisions of states; states may create, alter, or abolish these other units of government by amending state laws or constitutions. Over time, the number of local governments in America has been decreasing, mostly because of the consolidation of small school districts. Even so, the multiplicity of governments in America is still impressive.[1]

Decentralization—decision making by sub-elites—reduces strain on the national political system and on national elites by keeping many issues out of the national arena. Conflict between sub-elites is resolved by allowing each to pursue its own policies within the separate states and communities and not battling over a single national policy to be applied uniformly throughout the land. For example, sub-elites who wish to raise taxes and spend more money for public schools can do so in their own states and communities, and sub-elites who wish to reduce taxes and eliminate educational "frills" can also do so within *their* own states and communities. As Robert Dahl explains:

> Their local governments permit Americans to take or to keep many questions out of the great arena of national politics, and therefore out of a strictly either-or kind of conflict; they make it possible for Americans to deal with many problems in different ways, ways presumably more in harmony with local tastes and values than any national solution could possibly be. To this extent, presence of a vast network of local government with a good deal of autonomy has probably reduced by a considerable margin the severity of conflict that a wholly national system would run into. By denationalizing many conflicts, local governments can reduce the strain on national political institutions. Importance of denationalizing conflicts can hardly be overestimated, particularly in a large country like the United States where there is a great diversity in resources and local problems.[2]

---

[1] For a comprehensive survey of government and politics in American states and communities, see Thomas R. Dye, *Politics in States and Communities* (Englewood Cliffs, N.J.: Prentice-Hall, 1969).
[2] Robert Dahl, *Pluralist Democracy in the United States* (Chicago: Rand McNally, 1967), p. 181.

The masses look upon their local governments as more manageable, more accessible, and more responsive to individual desires than national elites. (See Table 11-1.) In a national survey, the number of people who said they understood "local issues in this town or part

TABLE 11-1.
Public Attitudes
toward Local
and National
Government

Estimated degree of impact of national and local government on daily life	National Government	Local Government
Estimated degree of impact of national and local government on daily life		
Great effect	41%	35%
Some effect	44	53
No effect	11	10
Other, don't know, etc.	4	2
	100	100
"On the whole, do the activities of the national (local) government tend to improve conditions in this area or would we be better off without them?"		
Yes, tend to improve	74%	69%
Sometimes improve, sometimes not	18	23
Better off without them	3	4
Other, don't know, etc.	5	4
	100	100
Sense of understanding of issues		
Very well	7%	21%
Moderately well	38	44
Not so well	37	23
Not at all	14	10
Depends, other, don't know, etc.	4	2
	100	100
"If you made an effort to change a proposed law or regulation you considered very unjust or harmful, how likely is it that you would succeed?"		
Very likely or moderately likely	11%	28%
Somewhat unlikely	18	15
Not at all likely, impossible	36	25
Likely only if others joined in	24	25
Other, don't know	9	6
	100	100

Source: Original unpublished data from survey by Gabriel A. Almond and Sidney Verba, The Civic Culture (Boston: Little, Brown and Co., 1963); table from analysis by Robert A. Dahl, Pluralist Democracy in the United States (Chicago: Rand McNally, 1967), pp. 198–201.

of the country" "very well" was three times as large as the number who said they understood "the important national and international issues facing the country." Over half the public say they do not understand national and international issues, but only a third felt this way about local issues. Moreover, when asked whether they felt they could change a proposed law or regulation that they considered "very unjust or harmful," 28 percent felt that their efforts were likely to succeed at the local level, but only 11 percent felt this way at the national level. It is interesting to note, however, that a majority of persons felt it was "unlikely" that they would be successful in changing any unjust law. But Americans feel significantly more capable of understanding and affecting local issues than national issues.

This feeling that local elites are responsive to local needs is to some extent justified. Sub-elites do tend to reflect local environmental conditions in their decision making. Economic development appears to be the most influential environmental variable.[3] For example, among the states per pupil expenditures for public schools vary widely, according to the state wealth; some states spend over two and one-half times more than other states on the education of each child. (See Figure 11–1.) Also, public welfare benefits per recipient vary among the states by as much as 200 percent; these variations are closely related to income levels in the states. (See Figure 11–2.) Per capita highway expenditures vary more than 300 percent from the lowest to the highest state. These variations are related to urbanization and industrialization in states; per capita highway expenditures are significantly higher in the rural, agricultural states. And, most important, the ability of the states to raise revenue is a function of their level of economic development. Tax revenues in the states are closely related to income levels.

Public confidence in state and local government is high. Most Americans believe that the state governments spend taxpayers' dollars "more

**FIGURE 11–1.
The Fifty States
Arranged
According to Median
Family Income and
Per Pupil
Expenditures, 1962**

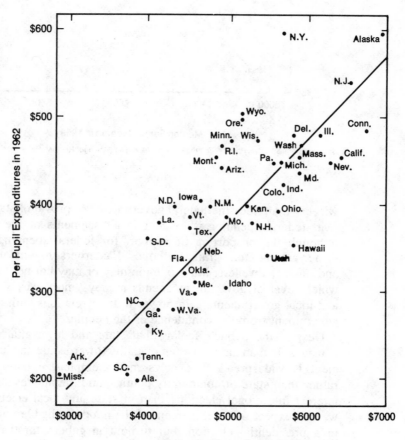

Source: Thomas R. Dye, *Politics, Economics, and the Public* (Chicago: Rand McNally, 1966).

[3]See Thomas R. Dye, *Politics, Economics, and the Public* (Chicago: Rand McNally, 1966).

FIGURE 11–2.
The Fifty States
Arranged
According to
Median Family
Income and
Average Old Age
Assistance
Payments, 1962

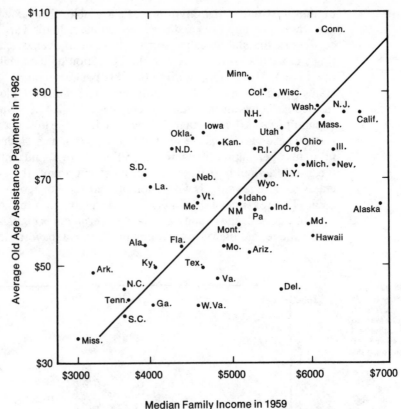

Median Family Income in 1959

Source: Thomas R. Dye, *Politics, Economics, and the Public* (Chicago: Rand McNally, 1966).

wisely" than does the federal government. Approval of state spending over federal spending is evident in all segments of the population, although the proportion of support for federal spending is slightly higher among Democrats, Catholics, Easterners, low-income earners, and big-city dwellers. Mass opinion may or may not be "right" about which level of government spends money "more wisely," but state and local governments gain power in their relations with the national government from the confidence of the people.

Despite the public's feeling that state and local affairs are more manageable than national affairs, apathy toward state and local government is widespread. The news media emphasize national politics rather than state or community politics, and the masses show greater interest in national elections than in state and local elections. Thus, we can expect 60 to 65 percent of the nation's eligible voters to vote in a presidential election, but turnout in gubernatorial elections in non-presidential years averages closer to 50 percent. Municipal elections often attract fewer than one third of the eligible voters. In short, masses participate less in state and local politics than they do in national politics.

States' Rights: Who Controls Local Governments? Debate over state versus national power can never be removed from the political context in which it takes place. Interests that are dominant in national politics assert the supremacy of the national government and extol the virtues of national regulation. In contrast, interests that are weak in national politics, but dominate politics in one or more states or communities, emphasize the preservation of the rights of states and communities and the merits of decision making by sub-elites. For example, states' rights have been so vigorously defended in recent years by Southern sub-elites seeking to preserve the segregation of the races that states' rights has become almost synonymous with prejudice. In contrast, civil rights groups appeal to the national elites for support in their fight against local and regional elites, and in several important instances — *Brown* v. *The Board of Education of Topeka* in 1954, the Civil Rights Act of 1964, the Voting Rights Act of 1965, and the Fair Housing Act of 1968 — have moved national elites to overrule the segregationist position of dominant local and regional elites. (For further discussion, see Chapter 12.)

States' rights have also been argued by conservative and rural political interests that oppose big government and big spending and do not feel the necessity of extensive public education, health, welfare, housing, transportation, or urban renewal services. Some economic interests that argue for states' rights may merely be attempting to avoid effective regulation, since the states are incapable of effectively regulating national economic enterprise. For example, in the early 1950s, when the issue of national versus state authority over offshore oil wells was raised, the nation's major oil companies objected strenuously to national control of offshore oil deposits. They argued vigorously on behalf of the right of states to regulate the use of these important natural resources. Professor Robert J. Harris describes the controversy as follows:

The solicitude of the oil companies for states' rights is hardly based on convictions derived from political theory but rather from fears that federal ownership may result in the cancellation or modification of state leases favorable to their interests, their knowledge that they can successfully cope with state regulatory agencies, and uncertainty concerning their ability to control the federal agency.[4]

The tidelands oil controversy ended in victory for the states' rights advocates; that is, for the oil companies.

Generally, in domestic affairs, American business interests have opposed centralization in Washington and have consistently defended state and local powers. This fact may help to explain the continued reliance of the nation upon state and local governments for the management of most domestic programs. But states and communities are not in a good position to regulate businesses and industries with national

[4]Robert J. Harris, "States' Rights and Vested Interest," *Journal of Politics*, 15 (November 1954), pp. 457–471.

organization and scope, since states and communities compete with one another to attract business and industry. The success of the states' efforts often depends on whether they can offer a "favorable climate" for business. This means that in addition to the availability of transportation, land and a skilled labor force, states and communities attempt to provide a favorable tax structure for business and industry. This factor explains in part why state and local tax structures are not as progressive as the federal government's tax system. In short, the states and communities, as smaller political units, are more easily divided and ruled by economic interests than is the federal government.

National Power in States and Communities

In the American federal union, the Constitution divides power between two separate authorities, the nation and the states, each of which can directly enforce their own laws on individuals through their own courts. In a disputed area, only the Constitution can determine whose authority is legitimate. American federalism differs from a "unitary" political system in that the central government has no legal authority to determine, alter, or abolish the power of the states. At the same time, American federalism differs from a confederation of states, in which the national government is dependent upon its states for power. The American system shares authority and power constitutionally and practically. National and state power are sometimes considered as the opposite ends of a seesaw—if national powers are increased, then state power must decline. But, although national power has expanded over the years, so has the power of states and communities. States and communities perform more services, employ more people, spend more money, and have a greater impact on the lives of their citizens than they have ever had in the past. The scope of their activities is expanding at a much faster rate than national government activities. Between 1956 and 1966, the expenditures of state and local governments increased by 118 percent; during the same period federal expenditures rose by only 88 percent.

The Constitution, in the Tenth Amendment, "reserves" to the states the power to protect and advance the public health, safety, welfare, or morals. This means that the national government may enact no laws dealing directly with housing, streets, zoning, schools, health, police protection, crime, and so on. However, the national government may *tax* or *borrow* or *spend money* to contribute to the general welfare. Thus, Congress cannot outlaw billboards on highways, because billboard regulation is not among the enumerated powers of Congress in the Constitution. But the national government, through its power to tax and spend, can provide financial grants-in-aid to the states to build highways, and then pass a law threatening to withdraw financial aid if the states do not outlaw billboards themselves. Thus, the federal government can indirectly enforce its decisions in such areas as highways and billboard regulation, even though these fields are "reserved" to the states.

The federal government is expanding its power in states and communities by the use of grants-in-aid. During the Great Depression of the 1930s the national government used its taxing and spending powers in a wide variety of areas formerly reserved to states and communities. Grant-in-aid programs to states and communities were initiated for public assistance, unemployment compensation, employment services, child welfare, public housing, urban renewal, highway construction, and vocational education and rehabilitation. The inadequacy of state and local revenue systems contributed significantly to the increase of national power in states and communities. Federal grants-in-aid to state and local governments have expanded rapidly in recent years (see Table 11–2 for the record of federal grants from 1932 and 1968), not only in terms of dollar amounts, but also in terms of the percentage of the total revenue of states and communities that comes from the federal government.

TABLE 11–2. Federal Grants to States and Communities, 1932–1968

Year	Total Federal Grants (in millions of dollars)	Federal Grants as Percent of State-Local Revenue
1932	232	2.9%
1938	800	7.2
1942	858	6.5
1950	2,486	9.7
1955	3,131	8.3
1960	6,974	11.6
1962	7,871	11.3
1965	11,029	12.5
1967	15,366	14.0
1968	17,439	15.0

Source: Bureau of the Census, *Statistical Abstract of the United States.*

Whenever the national government contributes financially to state or local programs, the state or local officials are left with less discretion than they would have otherwise. Federal grants-in-aid are invariably accompanied by congressional standards or "guidelines" that must be adhered to if states and communities are to receive their federal money. Often Congress delegates to federal agencies the power to establish the conditions attached to grants. Federal standards are designed to insure compliance with national minimum standards, but they are bound to annoy state and local leaders. Sometimes protests from state and local leaders are loud enough to induce Congress to yield to the views of sub-elites.

State or communities can reject federal grant-in-aids if they do not wish to meet federal standards, and some have done so. But it is difficult to resist the pressure to accept federal money. They are "bribed" by the temptation of much-needed federal money; and they are "blackmailed" by the thought that other states and communities will get the federal money if they do not, although the money was contributed in part by federal taxation of their own citizens.

In short, through the power to tax and spend for the general welfare and through the conditions attached to federal grants-in-aid, the national government can exercise important powers in areas originally "reserved" to the states. Of course, federal grants-in-aid have enabled many states and communities to provide necessary and desirable services that they could not have afforded without federal aid, and federal guidelines have often improved standards of administration, personnel policies, and fiscal practices in states and communities. Further, federal guidelines have helped to insure that states and communities will not engage in racial discrimination in federally aided programs. However, many commentators are genuinely apprehensive that states and communities have surrendered many of their powers to the national government in return for federal money. They argue that the role of states and communities in the American federal system has been weakened considerably by federal grant-in-aid programs and the conditions which are attached to them, because the centralization of power in Washington and the increased role of the national government in state and community affairs limits the individuality of state and local elites.

Elite Structures in the States

Elite structures vary among the fifty states, but observers generally agree that economic elites are the most influential. The authors of *The Legislative System* interviewed state legislators in four states, asking them which interests were perceived as most powerful.[5] In all four states, business interests were named the "most powerful groups" more often than any other interests; educational and labor interests, although important, were ranked below business interests in perceived influence. Agricultural interests, government interests (associations of city, county, and township governments, and government employee associations), ethnic interests, and religious, charitable, and civic interests were given only minor mention by state legislators.

It is difficult to measure the relative strength of economic interests in all fifty states. The strength of any interest group is a function of many factors, including resources, organization, leadership, prestige, "cohesion" (unity), and "access" (contacts) to decision makers. Some years ago, the American Political Science Association questioned social scientists in the several states, asking them to judge whether interest groups in their state were strong, moderately strong, or weak.[6] Their judgments are open to challenge, but they are probably the best testimony of interest group strength in the states. This classification of the states in terms of the strength of their interest groups does not focus exclusively upon economic interests; but it is reasonable to

[5]John Wahlke, *et al.*, *The Legislative System* (New York: John Wiley, 1964).
[6]See Belle Zeller, *American State Legislatures* (New York: Thomas Y. Crowell Co., 1954), pp. 190–191.

assume that the judgments of these observers were heavily influenced by economic factors.

Table 11–3 shows the relationship between the perceived strength of interest groups in the states, the level of inter-party competition, the degree of party cohesion, and the socioeconomic environments in the states. States with stronger interest groups are more likely to be (1) one-party states, rather than competitive two-party states; (2) states in which parties in the legislatures show little cohesion and unity; (3) states which are poor, rural, and agricultural. Wealthy, urban, industrial states may have *more* interest groups, but it is difficult for a single interest to dominate the political scene. In contrast, the poorer, rural, agricultural states with relatively backward economies may have fewer interest groups, but the interest groups are stronger and may exercise considerable power over public policy.[7] These findings lend some empirical support to James Madison's belief that "the smaller the society, the fewer the number of interests, and the greater the likelihood that a single interest will dominate."[8] Madison believed

TABLE 11–3.
The Strength of Pressure Groups in Varying Political and Economic Situations

Social Conditions	Types of Pressure System*		
	Strong (24 states)†	Moderate (14 states)‡	Weak (7 states)§
Party competition			
One-party	33.3%	0.0%	0.0%
Modified one-party	37.5%	42.8%	0.0%
Two-party	29.1%	57.1%	100.0%
Cohesion of parties in legislature			
Weak cohesion	75.0%	14.2%	0.0%
Moderate cohesion	12.5%	35.7%	14.2%
Strong cohesion	12.5%	50.0%	85.7%
Socioeconomic variables			
Urban	58.6%	65.1%	73.3%
Per capita income	$1,900.	$2,335.	$2,450.
Industrialization index	88.8	92.8	94.0

*Alaska, Hawaii, Idaho, New Hampshire, and North Dakota are not classified or included.
†Alabama, Arizona, Arkansas, California, Florida, Georgia, Iowa, Kentucky, Louisiana, Maine, Michigan, Minnesota, Mississippi, Montana, Nebraska, New Mexico, North Carolina, Oklahoma, Oregon, South Carolina, Tennessee, Texas, Washington, Wisconsin.
‡Delaware, Illinois, Kansas, Maryland, Massachusetts, Nevada, New York, Ohio, Pennsylvania, South Dakota, Utah, Vermont, Virginia, West Virginia.
§Colorado, Connecticut, Indiana, Missouri, New Jersey, Rhode Island, Wyoming.

Source: Harmon Zeigler, "Interest Groups in the States," in Herbert Jacob and Kenneth Vines (eds.), *Politics in the American States* (Boston: Little, Brown and Co., 1965), p. 116.

that the larger the political society, the less likely a single elite was to dominate its politics.

Let us divide the state elite systems into types to facilitate the identification of elite patterns in state politics. First, in the *single unified elite* system, usually found in a state with a non-diversified

[7]Harmon Zeigler, "Interest Groups in the States," in Herbert Jacob and Kenneth A. Vines (eds.), *Politics in the American States* (Boston: Little, Brown and Co., 1965), p. 114.
[8]James Madison, Alexander Hamilton, John Jay, *The Federalist* No. 10 (New York: Modern Library, 1937).

economy and weak, non-competitive parties, a cohesive group of economic interests dominates state politics. A good example of this type of elite system is Maine, of which Duane Lockard writes: "In few American states are the reins of government more openly, more completely in the hands of a few leaders of economic interest groups than in Maine."[9] Specifically, power, timber, and manufacturing — "the big three" — have combined into a cohesive economic elite, due to their key position in the economy of the state. Over three fourths of the state is woodland, and most of this land is owned by a handful of timber companies and paper manufacturers. The timber interests, combined with power companies and textile and shoe manufacturers, "control" Maine politics to protect their own economic well being. The "predominant authority" of the big three is rarely challenged with a significant degree of organization or sustained effort.

The deep South states also display the cultural homogeneity and unified elites characteristic of non-diversified or agricultural economies. In addition, Southern elites have traditionally benefitted from the general consensus among the white masses that the Negro must be kept "in his place, and that any efforts by national elites to rearrange racial patterns must be met by a unified white community."[10] Competition among Southern elites is considered particularly dangerous, since a split might contribute to Negro political influence. Occasionally, "populist" candidates have arisen from the masses to temporarily challenge the dominance of the planting, landowning, and financial elites in Southern states. But once in power, the demagogues have seldom implemented populist programs; more frequently they have become instruments of the established elites whom they castigated in campaign oratory.

A second type of elite structure we shall label *a dominant elite among lesser elites*. This structure is also found in states with a non-diversified economy, although the states may display a reasonably competitive party system, with moderate party cohesion in the legislature. The distinctive feature of the dominant elite among lesser elites structure is the prevailing influence of a single company or industry. A classic example of this elite structure is Montana, where the Anaconda Company has exercised unparalleled influence for almost a century. In a state in which the extraction of minerals is the major non-agricultural source of personal income, Anaconda is the largest employer. In Montana politics, Anaconda is known simply as "the company." The immensity of the Anaconda empire is described by Thomas Paine:

Its strength rests not only in its wealth and resources but also in its elaborate network of relationships with key citizens, banks, legal firms and business organizations throughout the state. Rare is that unit of local government—

[9]Duane Lockard, *New England State Politics* (Princeton, N. J.: Princeton University Press, 1959), p. 79.
[10]See V. O. Key, Jr., *Southern Politics* (New York: Alfred A. Knopf, 1948).

county, city, or school district—that does not have among its official family an associate, in some capacity, of the Anaconda Company.[11]

However, some leaders, such as Burton K. Wheeler, have built a political career out of opposition to the company, and the company has been forced to accept defeat on certain occasions when faced with a strong combination of lesser elites. In 1959, Anaconda sold its chain of newspapers in the state and assumed a somewhat less visible role in electoral politics. In recent years, Anaconda has remained as quiet as possible, confining itself to legislation directly affecting its economic interests.

The position of Anaconda in Montana is roughly parallel to the position of single dominant economic interests in other states, such as oil in Texas, or DuPont in Delaware. Doubtless the reputation of these interests for absolute control of a state far exceeds their actual exercise of control over public policy; there are many issues in Delaware, for instance, in which the DuPont Corporation and the DuPont family do not become actively involved. Yet it is unlikely that the state of Delaware would ever enact legislation adversely affecting the DuPont Corporation. Likewise, the reputation for oil control of Texas politics is exaggerated. The chairman of the Texas Democratic Executive Committee once said: "It may not be a wholesome thing to say, but the oil industry today is in complete control of state politics and state government."[12] This is an overstatement that one frequently hears in political circles; many issues in state politics are of little concern to the oil interests. However, it is unlikely that Texas politicians will ever oppose the oil depletion allowance in the federal tax structure, for this is a matter of direct and vital concern to the oil producers.

A *bipolar elite* structure is most likely to be found in an industrial, urban, competitive state with strong and cohesive political parties. Michigan is the prototype of this form of elite structure. While Michigan's economy is industrial rather than agricultural, it is non-diversified and heavily dependent upon the automotive industry; the automobile manufacturers are the largest single employer. But automobile manufacturers do not dominate Michigan politics, because organized labor has emerged as an effective counter-elite to the automobile manufacturers. Walter Reuther, president of the United Automobile Workers, and George Romney, former president of American Motors, are both influential members of Michigan's bipolar elite system. Joseph La Palombara concludes that "no major issues of policy (taxation, social legislation, labor legislation, etc.) are likely to be decided in Michigan without the intervention, within their respective parties and before agencies of government, of automotive labor and automotive management."[13] Labor and management elites in Michigan each

[11]Thomas Paine, "Under the Copper Dome: Politics in Montana," in Frank H. Jonas (ed.), *Western Politics* (Salt Lake City: University of Utah Press, 1961), pp. 197–198.
[12]Robert Engler, *The Politics of Oil* (New York: Macmillan Co., 1961), p. 354.
[13]Joseph La Palombara, *Guide to Michigan Politics* (East Lansing: Michigan University, Bureau of Social and Political Research, 1960), p. 104.

have "their own" political party, and polarization in the elite system is accompanied by strong competition between well-organized, cohesive, and disciplined Democratic (labor) and Republican (management) party organizations.

A *plural elite* structure is typical of a state with a highly diversified economy. California may have the most diversified economy of any state in the nation, with thriving agricultural interests, timber and mining resources, and manufacturing enterprises that run the gamut from cement to motion pictures. The railroads, the brewers, the race tracks, the motion pictures, the citrus growers, the airplane manufacturers, the insurance companies, the utilities, the defense contractors, and a host of other economic interests co-exist in this state. No one economic interest or combination of interests dominates California politics. Instead, a variety of elites govern within specific issue areas; each elite concentrates its attention on matters directly affecting its own economic interest. Occasionally, the economic interests of elites may clash, but on the whole co-existence, rather than competition, characterizes the relationships among elites. Political parties are somewhat less cohesive and disciplined in the plural elite system. Economic elites, hesitating to become too closely identified with a single party, even make financial contributions to opposing candidates to insure that their interests will be protected regardless of which party or candidate wins office.

Single Elites in American Communities   One of the earliest studies of community elites was the classic study of Middletown, conducted by Robert and Helen Lynd in the middle 1920s, and again in the mid-1930s.[14] In Muncie, Indiana, the Lynds found a monolithic power structure dominated by the owners of the town's largest industry, the "X" family. Community power was firmly entrenched in the hands of the business class, which controlled the economic life in the city, particularly through its ability to control the extension of credit. The city was run by a "small top group" of "wealthy local manufacturers, bankers, the local head managers of . . . national corporations with units in Middletown, and . . . one or two outstanding lawyers." Democratic procedures and governmental institutions were window dressing for business control. The Lynds described the typical city official as a "man of meager caliber" and as a "man whom the inner business control group ignores economically and socially and uses politically." Perhaps the most famous passage from the Lynds' study was a comment by a Middletown man made in 1935:

If I'm out of work, I go to the X plant; if I need money I go to the X bank, and if they don't like me I don't get it; my children go to the X college; when I get sick I go to the X hospital; I buy a building lot or house in the X subdivision; my wife goes downtown to buy X milk; I drink X beer, vote for X po-

---

[14]Robert S. and Helen M. Lynd, *Middletown* (New York: Harcourt, Brace, & World, 1929); and *Middletown in Transition* (New York: Harcourt, Brace & World, 1937).

litical parties, and get help from X charities; my boy goes to the X YMCA and my girl to their YWCA; I listen to the word of God in a X subsidized church; if I'm a Mason, I go to the X Masonic temple; I read the news from the X morning paper; and, if I'm rich enough, I travel via the X airport.[15]

W. Lloyd Warner, who studied Morris, Illinois, in the 1940s, describes a power structure somewhat similar to that encountered by the Lynds in Muncie. About one third of all of the city's workers had jobs in "The Mill," which Warner says dominated the town:

> The economic and social force of the mill affects every part of the life of the community. Everyone recognizes its power. Politicians, hat in hand, wait upon Mr. Waddell, manager of The Mill, to find out what he thinks on such important questions as "Shall the tax rate be increased to improve the education our young people are getting?" — "Should the city support various civic and world enterprises?" — "Should new industries enter the town and possibly compete with The Mill for the town's available labor supply?" They want to know what Mr. Waddell thinks. Mr. Waddell usually lets them know.[16]

Hollingshead studied the same town (sociologists seem to prefer to disguise the names of towns they are studying: Warner called the town Jonesville, Hollingshead called it Elmtown), and his findings substantially confirmed Warner's.[17] And in sociologist Floyd Hunter's influential study of Atlanta, Georgia[18] (presented in Chapter 1 of this book as a prototype of the "ruling elite" model of power), community policy is described as originating in a group composed primarily of business, financial, religious, and education leaders rather than from the people of the community.

Business approval of community projects is considered essential, especially on proposals involving great change in the community — metropolitan area government, urban renewal, public housing, freeway construction, and other massive public works requiring bond issues, condemnation of properties, and increased tax burdens. Business support bestows great prestige on a proposal, and the low prestige of municipal officials helps to explain why businessmen are needed to help promote any major community project. Moreover, middle-class people, whose vote is important in local politics, tend to respect the views of businessmen more than the views of city officials. Peter B. Clark quotes a Chicago attorney who has long been involved in civic affairs:

> By and large, those with strong business backgrounds command greater respect . . . than those with the same skills who don't have that background. And the same is true of a lawyer versus the president of General Motors. They both could say the same thing . . . but the president would be listened

[15] Lynd and Lynd, *Middletown in Transition*, p. 74.
[16] W. Lloyd Warner, *Democracy in Jonesville* (New York: Harper & Row, 1949), p. 10.
[17] August B. Hollingshead, *Elmtown's Youth* (New York: John Wiley, 1949).
[18] Floyd Hunter, *Community Power Structure* (Chapel Hill: University of North Carolina Press, 1953).

to more. They transfer part of their business achievement into their public life.[19]

The views of businessmen are also respected because the community's economic growth and prosperity are linked to business firms and the men who head them. A community that depends upon the businessmen for employment must seriously consider the suggestion that a particular proposal might "hurt business" or "slow down the economy." Only occasionally is a firm required to threaten to close down and move elsewhere in order to get its way in policy matters. Business support lends a "conservative" image to community proposals. Businessmen are expected to be sound guardians of the status quo, who oppose "radical" sweeping changes in governmental structure, tax programs, and public services. Thus, the endorsement by these conservatives of any new program helps to assure the community that the program does not represent a radical break with the past.

In addition to the respect and prestige it lends, business support is also sought because so many community projects—public works, urban renewal, schools, streets, auditoriums, and hospitals—require financial investment; and banks and investment firms must underwrite the bond issues. Businessmen also have technical information that local governments, normally operating without a large professional staff, cannot themselves provide. Finally, business support often disarms potentially influential businessmen who might oppose a proposal if they were not consulted about it in its earliest stages.

The influence of businessmen can be felt even in matters in which they are not directly involved. Many government officials and civic organization workers admit that they anticipate the views of big businessmen in policy decisions, even when the businessmen are not directly consulted. Peter Clark quotes a civic staff man who explained why a particular community project failed: "This thing wasn't done right. It was just announced. The power structure and the newspaper people weren't checked out. All hell broke loose." Another staff man revealed both his style and his motives when he said: "My method of operation is to touch base early before I raise a question. I do my homework thoroughly to get the controversy out of it. Either revise it or throw it out. I have never proposed anything that hasn't been accepted. I don't want to propose anything that would fail."[20]

Plural Elites in American Communities Pluralist models of community power stress the fragmentation of authority, the influence of elected public officials, the importance of organized group activity, and the roles of public opinion and elections in determining public policy. Who, then, rules in the pluralist community? "Different small groups of interested and active citizens [rule] in different issue areas with some overlap, if any, by public

[19] Peter B. Clark, *The Businessman as a Civic Leader* (New York: Free Press, 1964), p. 6.
[20] Clark, p. 11.

officials, and occasional intervention by a larger number of people at the polls."[21] Citizens' influence is felt not only through organized group activity, but also through elites anticipating the reactions of citizens and endeavoring to satisfy their demands. Leadership in community affairs is exercised not only by elected public officials, but also by interested individuals and groups who confine their participation to one or two issue areas. The pluralist model regards interest and activity, rather than economic resources, as the key to elite membership. Competition, fluidity, access, and equality characterize community politics.

Perhaps the most influential of the pluralist community studies was Robert Dahl's *Who Governs?*, a detailed analysis of decision making in New Haven, Connecticut. Dahl's description of New Haven is presented in Chapter 1 as an example of a polycentric and dispersed system of elites. But Aaron Wildavsky's study of Oberlin, Ohio, revealed, if anything, an even more pluralistic structure of decision making than Dahl found in New Haven. Oberlin was a reaffirmation of small-town democracy, where "the roads to influence . . . are more than one; elites and non-elites can travel them, and the toll can be paid with energy and initiative as well as wealth."[22]

Wildavsky studied eleven community decisions in Oberlin, including such diverse issues and events as the determination of municipal water rates, the passage of the fair housing ordinance, the division of United Appeal Funds, and a municipal election. He found "that the number of citizens and outside participants who exercise leadership in most cases is an infinitesimal part of the community,"[23] but that no person or group exerted leadership on *all* issue areas. To the extent that overlap among leaders in issue areas existed, the overlap involved public officials—the city manager, the mayor, and city councilmen—who owed their positions directly or indirectly to "expressions of the democratic process through a free ballot with universal suffrage." Leaders often competed among themselves and did not appear united by any common interest. Persons exercising leadership were of somewhat higher social status than the rest of the community, but it was not status or wealth that distinguished leaders from non-leaders; it was their degree of interest and activity in public affairs.

Edward Banfield's excellent description of decision making in Chicago also fails to reveal a single "ruling elite," although the structure of influence is centralized. Banfield finds that Mayor Daley's political organization, rather than a business or financial elite, is the center of Chicago's influence structure. According to Banfield:

Civic controversies in Chicago are not generated by the efforts of politicians to win votes, by differences about ideology or group interest, or by the behind-the-scenes efforts of a power elite. They arise, instead, out of the maintenance and enhancement needs of large formal organizations. The heads of

[21]Aaron Wildavsky, *Leadership in a Small Town* (Totowa, N.J.: Bedminister Press, 1964), p. 8.
[22]Wildavsky, p. 214.
[23]Wildavsky, p. 265.

an organization see some advantage to be gained by changing the situation. They propose changes. Other large organizations are threatened. They oppose, and a civic controversy takes place.[24]

It is not usually business organizations that propose changes in Chicago; "in most of the cases described here the effective organizations are public ones, and their chief executives are career civil servants." Though business and financial leaders played an important role in Chicago politics, they did not constitute a single elite.

After studying seven major decisions in Chicago, Banfield concluded that political heads such as Mayor Daley, public agencies, and civic associations employed top business leaders to lend prestige and legitimacy to policy proposals. The "top leaders" of Chicago—the Fields, McCormacks, Ryersons, Swifts, and Armours—and the large corporations—Inland Steel, Sears Roebuck, Field's Department Store, and the Chicago Title and Trust Company—were criticized less for interfering in public affairs than for "failing to assume their civic responsibilities." Few top leaders participated directly in the decisions studied by Banfield. Banfield admits that this fact is not proof that the top business leadership did not influence decisions behind the scenes; and he acknowledges the widespread belief in the existence of a ruling elite in Chicago. He quotes the head of a Negro civic association as saying: "There are a dozen men in this town who could go into City Hall and order an end to racial violence just like you or I could go into a grocery store and order a loaf of bread. All they would have to do is say what they wanted and they would get it."[25] Banfield states that top business leaders in Chicago have great "potential for power"—"Indeed, if influence is defined as the *ability* to modify behavior in accordance with one's intentions, there can be little doubt that there exist 'top leaders' with aggregate influence sufficient to run the city"[26]— but he maintains that these top leaders do not, in fact, run the city. Business leaders, divided by fundamental conflicts of interest and opinion, do not have sufficient unity of purpose in community politics to decide controversial questions. They have no effective communication system that would enable them to act in concord; and they lack the organization to carry out their plans, even if they could agree on what should be done.

Sub-Elites: A Comparative View

Differing descriptions of the structures of power in American communities may be a product of the differences among social scientists in theory and methods of research. It is likely, however, that community power structures in the United States range from monolithic elites to very dispersed pluralistic elites. Unfortunately, we do not yet know enough about community power structures across the nation to estimate the frequency of different structures.

[24] Edward Banfield, *Political Influence* (New York: Free Press, 1961), p. 263.
[25] Banfield, p. 289.
[26] Banfield, p. 290.

The key to understanding community power is relating the types of power structure to local social, economic, and political conditions. For example, we may find that large communities with a great deal of social and economic diversity, a competitive party system, and a variety of well-organized, competing interest groups have pluralist elite systems. On the other hand, small communities with a homogeneous population, a single dominant industry, non-partisan elections, and few competing organizations may be governed by a single cohesive elite.

One of the most important comparative studies of community power was made by Agger, Goldrich, and Swanson, an intensive study of "power and impotence" in four American communities during a fifteen-year period.[27] These scholars identified four types of power structure, based upon the degree of citizen participation and influence and the degree of competition and conflict among political leaders (Table 11–4). If many citizens shared political influence and two or more leadership groups competed with each other, the community was said to have a "competitive mass" power structure. If many citizens shared political influence, but little disagreement or conflict occurred among leaders, the community's power structure was termed "consensual mass." If few citizens shared political influence and leaders rarely disagreed among themselves, the power structure was said to be "consensual elite." If few citizens shared political influence but leaders divided into competing groups, the community was said to have a "competitive elite" structure.

TABLE 11–4.
Types of Power Structures

Political Leadership	Distributions of Political Power among Citizens	
	Broad	Narrow
Convergent	Consensual mass	Consensual elite
Divergent	Competitive mass	Competitive elite

Source: Robert Agger, Daniel Goldrich, and Bert Swanson, The Rulers and the Ruled (New York: John Wiley, 1964), p. 73.

The "consensual elite" structure most closely resembles the monolithic or single elite model described earlier, because citizen influence is limited and leaders share a single ideology. The "competitive mass" structure most closely resembles our pluralist model, inasmuch as many citizens share power and competition occurs among leadership groups. The "ideal" community is probably the "consensual mass" type, in which influence is widely shared among the citizens and little conflict occurs among leaders. The municipal reform movement en-

[27] Robert Agger, Daniel Goldrich, and Bert Swanson, The Rulers and the Ruled (New York: John Wiley, 1964).

visions such a community, in which democracy prevails and "reasonable men" agree to govern in "the public interest."

The authors also proposed a typology of community "regimes" based upon the recognized "rules of the game" in community politics and the degree to which people believe that citizens can be politically effective (Table 11–5). When the "rules of the game" are followed by political leaders, the regime is labeled a "developed democracy" if citizens believe they can influence policy, and an "undeveloped democracy" if they believe they cannot. If leaders frequently resort to il-

TABLE 11–5.
Types of Regimes

Sense of Political Effectiveness	Probability of Illegitimate Sanctions Being Used	
	Low	High
High	Developed democracy	Guided democracy
Low	Undeveloped democracy	Oligarchy

Source: Robert Agger, Daniel Goldrich, and Bert Swanson, *The Rulers and the Ruled* (New York: John Wiley, 1964), p. 183.

legitimate means—including loss of employment, discrimination, or severe social ostracism—to curtail political participation or free expression, the regime is labeled either a "guided democracy," if public confidence remains high, or an "oligarchy," if people no longer feel they can affect policy.

The Rulers and the Ruled study produced many interesting findings about community power. The "competitive mass" type of power structure (pluralist) is related to a "developed democracy" regime. A sense of political effectiveness among citizens and adherence to the rules of games by leaders is essential for the development of broad citizen participation in community affairs and the emergence of competitive leadership groups. A lack of political confidence among residents and a widespread belief that political activity is useless often result in a monopoly of political leadership and a "consensual elite" (monolithic) power structure.

If leadership changes from competitive to consensual, the distribution of power changes from mass to elite. In other words, with the disappearance of competition among leadership factions, citizen participation declines, fewer issues are submitted to popular referenda, and the power distribution becomes more elitist. Conversely, when the distribution of power changes from elite to mass—that is, when an increasing number of people begin to "crack" the power structure—political competition is likely to increase.

A "competitive mass" (pluralist) type of power structure will be more stable through time if the competing leadership groups represent high and low socioeconomic classes than if the competitors represent the same socioeconomic class. Pluralism depends in part upon socioeconomic cleavages in the community being represented by separate leadership groups. When competitive leaders represent the same socio-economic class, competition can easily disappear over time, and the power structure can become "consensual" rather than "competitive."

Agger, Goldrich, and Swanson also find that "developed democracy" regimes and "competitive mass" power structures are less likely to occur in communities in which the major industries are home-owned. Economic leaders of home-owned industries tend to be members of a single group of political leaders that discourage competition. The prominence of these people influences some groups in their communities to refrain from political activity because they fear illegitimate political sanctions, even though the actual use of these sanctions is relatively infrequent. Interestingly, Agger, Goldrich, and Swanson found no relationship between community size or growth rate and either the type of regime or the nature of the power structure in the four communities they studied.

Summary   The importance of sub-elites in the larger American political system can be seen in the fact that states and communities spend twice as much money for domestic government as the federal government does. Sub-elites take a great deal of pressure for decision making off of the federal government. Moreover, the existence of the sub-elites allows for a diversity in state and local government policies, and thus reduces conflicts that would inevitably occur if the national government attempted to administer uniform policies in all sectors of the country. Although the masses participate more frequently in national elections, they have a more positive attitude toward their local and state governments.

States' rights have traditionally been supported by Southern segregationists, by industries trying to avoid effective regulation, and by conservatives ideologically opposed to big government. Both the states and the federal government have increased their influence in American life over the years. On the other hand, even though the federal government has no constitutional power in the control of welfare, highways, and natural resources development, it is able to wield considerable influence in states and communities through the conditions attached to the federal grant-in-aid.

The elite structures of the states may be divided into four main types: the single unified elite, in states with non-diversified economies and weak political parties; the dominant elite among lesser elites, in states where the economy is non-diversified, but the main industry is not completely in control; the bipolar elite, in industrial states with strong, competitive parties; and the plural elite, in states with highly diversified economies, where parties are less disciplined.

Elite structures in communities are also widely diversified, ranging from a monolithic ruling elite, in which business and economic interests dominate the community, to a pluralistic elite, in which a broad base of interested citizens and their elected officials run the community. Small communities with a homogeneous population, a single dominant industry, a weak party structure, and few competing organizations are more likely to be governed by a monolithic elite. Larger communities with a great deal of social and economic diversity, a competitive party system, and a variety of well organized, competing interest groups are more likely to have pluralist elite systems. Monolithic power structures are also associated with a lack of political confidence among residents and a widespread belief that political activity is useless. A plural elite system is associated with a sense of political effectiveness among citizens and adherence to "the rules of the game" by leaders.

Selected Additional Readings

Agger, Robert, Daniel Goldrich, and Bert Swanson. *The Rulers and the Ruled*. New York: John Wiley, 1964. This book presents an in-depth study of "power and impotence" in four American communities over a fifteen-year period.

Robert A. Dahl, *Who Governs?* New Haven: Yale University Press, 1961. Dahl's work is a classical study of a polyarchial elite in New Haven, Connecticut.

Dye, Thomas R. *Politics, Economics, and the Public.* Chicago: Rand McNally, 1966. This book is an analysis of policy outcomes in education, health and welfare, highways, taxation, and correction in the American states and reveals the impact of economic development on public policy.

Hunter, Floyd. *Community Power Structure*. Chapel Hill: University of North Carolina Press, 1953. Hunter's study of a hierarchical elite system in Atlanta, Georgia, could usefully be compared to Dahl's study (listed above).

12

**Civil Rights:
Challenge to
Dominant Elites**

Two overriding facts emerge from our study of American democracy: (1) It is a political system controlled by elites, who govern according to the tenets of a welfare-capitalistic ideology. (2) The survival of the American political system depends on how well and how wisely these elites are able to cope with the internal tensions that develop in American society. At the time of this writing, the wisdom of the elite is being put to a severe test; for the tensions engendered by long-standing racial inequalities have reached critical proportions. The success with which our elitist democracy deals with the civil rights problem will determine whether this governmental form will survive or whether it will become a historic anachronism. In this chapter we shall examine the historical and social roots of the continuing tensions and the current crisis in the civil rights problem, and we shall assess the prospects for the survival of elitist democracy in America.

The place of the Negro in American society has been a central domestic issue of American politics since the first Negro slaves were brought to the United States in 1619. The American nation as a whole, with its developing (if ambiguous) democratic tradition, has felt strong sentiments against slavery, segregation, and discrimination. But white America has also harbored an ambivalence toward the Negro—a recognition of the evils of inequality but a reluctance to take steps to eliminate it. Gunnar Myrdal, writing in 1944, captured the essence of the American racial dilemma:

The "American dilemma" . . . is the ever-raging conflict between, on the one hand, the valuations preserved on the general plane which we shall call the "American creed," where the American thinks, talks, and acts under the influence of high national and Christian precepts, and, on the other hand, the valuation on specific planes of individual and group living, where personal and local interests; economic, and social, and sexual jealousies; considerations of community prestige and conformity; group prejudices against particular persons or types of people; all sorts of miscellaneous wants, impulses, and habits dominate his outlook.[1]

[1]Gunnar Myrdal, *An American Dilemma*, Vol. I (New York: McGraw-Hill Book Co., 1964), p. lxxi.

Mydral's formulation of the American dilemma has much in common with the more general attitudes of the American masses toward democracy: commitment to abstract ideals, but substantially less commitment to the behavior that follows from these ideals. As it was pointed out earlier, elites need pay little attention to mass opinion in making most policy decisions; for the most part, the masses are ignorant of and apathetic about policy issues. But the attitudes of white masses toward Negroes are important for two reasons: (1) Civil rights is so visible an issue that elite behavior is more circumscribed by mass opinion than is normally the case; and (2) since Negroes constitute only a small portion of the total population, they are largely dependent upon the benevolence of the white majority.

The struggle of the Negroes for full citizenship can be viewed as a dialogue—sometimes violent, sometimes peaceful—between the demands of black counter-elites and the response of dominant white elites. Although the dialogue receives its most complete articulation in the behavior of elites, its base is in the attitudinal structure of the masses. Each group of elites interprets (and consequently distorts) the aspirations of the masses whom they pretend to represent. And each group interprets and distorts the aspirations of the opposing group as well.

That there should be such a struggle at all in the United States is a demonstration of the extent to which racial feelings take precedence over moral and constitutional requirements. The language of the Fourteenth Amendment leaves little doubt that the original purpose of this amendment was to achieve full citizenship and equality for American Negroes.

All persons born or naturalized in the United States, and subject to the jurisdiction thereof, are citizens of the United States and of the state wherein they reside. No state shall make or enforce any law which shall abridge the privileges or immunities of citizens of the United States; nor shall any state deprive any person of life, liberty, or property without due process of law; nor deny to any person within its jurisdiction the equal protection of the law.

However, 100 years after the ratification of this amendment, the National Advisory Commission on Civil Disorders wrote: "Our nation is moving toward two societies, one black, one white—separate and unequal."[2] The commission strongly implicated whites in the failure of Negroes to share equally in the affluence of American society.

What white Americans have never fully understood—but what the Negro can never forget—is that white society is deeply implicated in the ghetto. White institutions created it, white institutions maintain it, and white society condones it.[3]

[2] *Report of the National Advisory Commission on Civil Disorders* (Washington, D.C., 1968), p. 1.
[3] *Report of the National Advisory Commission on Civil Disorders*, p. 2.

The commission thus assumed that whites must solve the problem that they created. This assumption is a radical reversal of the American consensus that each *individual* can achieve anything he wishes in this open society. The generally negative reaction of governmental elites and of the masses to the report of the Commission on Civil Disorders indicates how radical is the idea that environmental rather than individual circumstances are the reason for ghetto life and violence.

In recent years, the civil rights movement has undergone a substantial shift in goals and in techniques. Beginning with efforts to remove legal discrimination, principally in the South, the civil rights movement has lately turned its attention toward economic inequalities in the North. Although the legal foundations of segregation have gradually eroded, the economic conditions of the Negro have failed to improve. As Bayard Rustin observes: "The very decade which has witnessed the decline of legal Jim Crow has also seen the rise of *de facto* segregation in our most fundamental socioeconomic institutions."[4] Americans can understand legal discrimination; and the majority—even a strong minority in the South—agree that such discrimination is inconsistent with the norms of a democratic society. However, the idea that society as a whole has a responsibility to reduce economic inequalities is alien to the myths and symbols that cement white society together.

The Historical Background of Black Subjugation

The period of slavery is of more than historical interest; we are still feeling the impact of the brutality of this period. The scars of the rigidly enforced obedience system and the matriarchal family structure characteristic of slavery are still present today. Elkins has compared Southern slavery to Nazi concentration camps in its effects upon personality.[5] Both institutions were closed and highly authoritarian; both produced, for the most part, total obedience to the authority figure. In concentration camps, for example, guards were frequently viewed as father figures. Correspondingly, among slaves, the master often represented a father figure. Slavery, by rewarding obedience and compliance, negatively sanctioned individual effort and achievement. Even today, Southern Negroes are, in comparison to those of Northern origin, passive and non-militant. The relative acquiescence of those Negroes whose backgrounds are closest to slavery is a remnant of the dependent position of the slave upon his master.

Another factor with consequences that Negroes are still struggling to overcome is the "deculturation" of the slaves. That is, blacks from many different cultures were thrown together, and there was no common cultural buffer to make it possible for them to resist the psychological effects of the economic and social conditions of slavery. The condition of slavery became their dominant institution—an institution

---

[4] Bayard Rustin, "From Protest to Coalition Politics," in Marvin E. Gettleman and David Mermelstein (eds.), *The Great Society Reader* (New York: Vintage Books, 1967), p. 265. A short discussion of *de facto* segregation appears later in this chapter.
[5] Stanley M. Elkins, *Slavery: A Problem in American Institutional and Intellectual Life* (New York: Universal Library, 1963).

that molded the personality of the blacks. For example, slaves, in order to survive within the system, developed child-rearing practices that emphasized obedience rather than achievement; and the descendants of these slaves still show the effects of this training.

McClelland, who has developed devices to measure need for achievement, found that lower-class Negroes, who are the group least removed from the effects of slavery, have the lowest need for achievement of any minority group. McClelland found, on the other hand, that middle-class Negroes are uniformly higher in the need for achievement than are middle-class whites. This illustrates, first, that it is not being Negro that reduces the need for achievement and, second, that achieving members of the minority groups need to be more motivated than achieving members of majority groups. Since most Negroes are lower class, however, they are unable to break out of the pathology of the ghetto. Ghetto norms reinforce the traditions of the past.[6]

Slavery also hindered the development of a strong family life. Since many slave-owners separated families on the auction block, the slave household developed a matri-focal pattern. After slavery was abolished, poverty in the ghetto strengthened the mother-centered tradition. Even now, about one fourth of the non-white families, compared to only 9 percent of the white families, have female heads.[7] The percentage of Negro families with female heads is increasing even as the economic position of blacks improves slightly.

In 1865, the Thirteenth Amendment abolished slavery everywhere in the United States. The Fourteenth Amendment, which was passed in 1867 by a Republican Congress that intended to reconstruct Southern society after the Civil War, made "equal protection of the laws" a command for every state to obey. The Fifteenth Amendment, passed in 1869, provided that the right to vote could not be abridged by either federal or state governments "on account of race, color, or previous condition of servitude." In addition, Congress passed a series of civil rights statutes in the 1860s and 1870s guaranteeing the new Negro freedman protection in the exercise of his constitutional rights. The Civil Rights Act of 1875 specifically outlawed segregation by owners of public accommodation facilities. Between 1865 and the early 1880s, the success of the civil rights movement was reflected in widespread Negro voting throughout the South, the presence of many Negroes in federal and state offices, and the almost equal treatment afforded Negroes in theaters, restaurants, hotels, and public transportation.

But by 1877, support for reconstruction policies began to crumble. In what has been described as the Compromise of 1877, the national government agreed to end military occupation of the South, give up its efforts to rearrange Southern society, and lend tacit approval to white supremacy in that region. In return, the Southern states pledged their

[6] David C. McClelland, *The Achieving Society* (Princeton, N.J.: D. Van Nostrand Co., 1961), pp. 376–377.
[7] U.S. Department of Commerce, Bureau of the Census, *Current Population Reports*, P-20, No. 125, 116, 106, 100, 88, 83, 75, 67, 53, 44, 33, and 26.

support for the Union, accepted national supremacy, and agreed to permit the Republican candidate, Hayes, to assume the presidency, although the Democratic candidate, Tilden, had received a majority of the popular vote in the disputed election of 1876. The Supreme Court adhered to the terms of this compromise. In the famous Civil Rights Cases of 1883, the Supreme Court declared unconstitutional those federal civil rights laws preventing discrimination by private individuals. By denying Congress the power to protect Negroes from discrimination, the Court paved the way for the imposition of segregation as the prevailing social system of the South. In the 1880s and 1890s, segregation was imposed in public accommodations, housing, education, employment, and almost every other sector of private and public life. By 1895 most southern states had passed laws *requiring* segregation of the races in education and in public accommodations.

In 1896, in the famous case of *Plessy* v. *Ferguson,*[8] the Supreme Court upheld state laws requiring segregation of the races. Even though segregation laws involved state action, the Court held that segregating the races did not violate the equal protection clause of the Fourteenth Amendment so long as the persons in each of the separated races were treated equally. Schools and other public facilities that were "separate but equal" won constitutional approval.

The violence that occurred during this period was almost entirely one-sided and consisted of attacks by whites upon Negroes. Grimshaw refers to this type of racial violence as "Southern style."[9] The pattern of race relations at the turn of the century was clearly one of violent repression, the exclusion of Negroes from jobs and labor unions, and rigid segregation. Negroes had lost most of what they had gained during Reconstruction.

Twentieth-Century Responses

As a result of the repressive pattern of the late nineteenth century, the first Negro organizations emerged. The National Association for the Advancement of Colored People (NAACP) and the National Urban League were formed in 1909 and 1910, respectively. Both of these organizations reacted against Booker T. Washington's acceptance of the inferior status of the Negro, and both worked closely with white liberals. These organizations, depending as they did upon the goodwill of whites, chose a strategy of seeking Negro equality through court action and other legal means. They were (and still are) moderates, dominated by middle-class Negroes and upper-class whites. They accepted the premise that meaningful change can be obtained within the framework of the American legal system. They were (and are) conservative in the sense that their techniques require commitment to the institutional *status quo*. They specifically disavowed any attempt to change or overthrow the basic political and economic structure of the society, for the changes they sought were limited to the inclusion

[8] *Plessy* v. *Ferguson,* 163 U.S. 537 (1896).
[9] Allen D. Grimshaw, "Lawlessness and Violence in America and Their Special Manifestations in Changing Negro-White Relationships," *Journal of Negro History,* 44, 1 (January 1959), 67.

of the Negro in the existing society. In other words, they took literally the ideology and premises of the American democratic system.

When the concentration of Negroes in Northern cities increased the potential for mass action, a new style of violence began to emerge. A series of grievances, such as discrimination in housing and transportation, is expressed by the Negro community. As grievances build and expression becomes more aggressive, a precipitating incident occurs; and blacks respond by attacking whites or their property. The Northern style riot differs substantially from the Southern style violence; Negroes no longer remain passive victims but become active participants. The "Northern style" riot made its first appearance in Springfield, Illinois, in 1908.

Perhaps the first important black counter-elite was Marcus Garvey. Since the NAACP was an avowedly elitist organization both in membership and appeal, the Universal Negro Improvement Association was organized by Garvey, a West Indian, to articulate the feelings of a latent black nationalism. Garvey's programs for a separate Negro nation in Africa held considerable appeal for impoverished blacks, especially as white bigotry, in the form of the Ku Klux Klan, spread north in the wake of Negro economic advance. Garvey's appeal was essentially similar to that of the Black Muslims of the 1950s and 1960s and the more radical black nationalists of the late 1960s. Like the Muslims, Garvey urged his followers to practice personal frugality and establish a high level of morality. Like the nationalists, he sought to teach Negroes that "black" is a color of which one could be proud rather than ashamed. At one time, Garvey had a following estimated at three million, but his movement collapsed in the middle 1920s. However, the response from the black masses was very important, for Garvey's appeal rested on the assertion that Negroes would never achieve what the NAACP insisted that they could achieve—an equal share in the American economic system. As Myrdal observes, the Garvey movement "tells of the dissatisfaction so deep that it mounts to hopelessness of ever enjoying a full life in America."[10]

The period following the Korean War, marked by enormous legal and symbolic victories, was crucial in the development of the relationship between blacks and whites. The long labors of the NAACP paid off in the historic *Brown* v. *Board of Education of Topeka*[11] decision in which the Court reversed the *Plessy* v. *Ferguson* doctrine of "separate but equal." This decision symbolized the beginning of a new era of high expectations among Negroes. While elected elites had remained silent on civil rights and, in fact, exhibited substantial hostility, an appointed elite, the Supreme Court, declared that Negroes and whites were equal in the eyes of the law.

However, the hostility of *elected* elites continued throughout the 1950s. With World War II over, the Fair Employment Practices Commission—symbolic though it was—was destroyed, and no civil rights legislation could pass through the gauntlet of Congress. In 1948, for example, attempts to re-establish the Fair Employment Practices

[10] Myrdal, *An American Dilemma*, Vol. II, p. 749.
[11] *Brown* v. *Board of Education of Topeka*, 347 U.S. 483 (1954).

Commission, to outlaw poll taxes, to eliminate segregation in public transportation, and to pass a federal anti-lynching law were all unsuccessful. The Dixiecrat Revolt of 1948, led by Strom Thurmond, was in direct response to the increasing commitment of the Democratic party to civil rights and indicated the strength of the "conservative coalition" in the Senate and House. This coalition of Southern Democrats and Northern Republicans was able to block civil rights legislation regularly, and it held firm through the 1950s.

Brown v. *Board of Education of Topeka* marked the beginning, not the end, of the political battle over segregation. Segregation would not be abolished merely because the Supreme Court had declared it unconstitutional. Unless the political power of the white majority in the South were successfully challenged by another political elite with equal resources, the pattern of segregation would remain unchanged. Segregation was widespread and deeply ingrained. Seventeen states required segregation, and the Congress of the United States required segregation in Washington, D.C. Four other states (Arizona, Kansas, New Mexico, and Wyoming) authorized segregation at local option.

The Supreme Court, in not ordering immediate desegregation, snatched the tangible portion of the victory away from Negroes. The Court placed primary responsibility for enforcing this decision upon local officials and school boards, thus in effect returning power to the white sub-elites in the South. As a result, during the 1950s the white South developed a wide variety of schemes to resist integration. Ten years after *Brown* v. *Board of Education of Topeka,* only about 2 percent of the Negroes in the South had actually been integrated; the other 98 percent remained in segregated schools. In short, the decision meant nothing to the overwhelming majority of Negroes, whose frustrations were intensified by the discrepancy between the declarations of the Supreme Court and the behavior of the local officials. Legally they were victorious, but politically they were impotent, since the South stubbornly refused to abide by the decision of the Court.

While Southern elites overtly resisted integration, *de facto* segregation in the North was totally unaffected by the Brown decision. Thus, the period after the Korean War was one of retrogression. Not only were Southern elites remaining intransigent and Northern elites indifferent, but the economic position of the Negroes in comparison to the whites was slipping. From a high of 60 percent in 1952, the Negro percentage of white income had declined to 56 percent by 1962. Unemployment among blacks was growing at an alarming rate. In 1952, 5.4 percent of the blacks and 3.1 percent of the whites were unemployed, giving a ratio of non-white to white unemployment of 1.7. Negro unemployment began an upturn in 1952, peaking in 1964 at 11 percent, while white unemployment had increased only to 4.6 percent. Thus the ratio of non-white to white unemployment had expanded to 2.1. While unemployment among blacks had doubled, unemployment among whites had increased only about one third.[12]

---

[12]"Recent Trends in Social and Economic Conditions of Negroes in the United States," Department of Commerce, Bureau of the Census, Current Population Series, P-23, No. 26, BLS Report No. 347, July 1968, p. 11.

The continuation of this symbolic victory and tangible defeat re-oriented the civil rights movement away from the removal of legal restrictions and toward the removal of *de facto* segregation and unequal socioeconomic institutions.

That this phase of the civil rights movement is strongly elitist should be carefully noted. The bargaining and exchanges took place largely between the NAACP and the Supreme Court, both of which were insulated from both white and black masses. The elite orientation of the NAACP, as previously noted, meant that its leadership accepted the prevailing values of white elites. Its attraction was to the "talented tenth"—the minority of upper class, educated blacks. Its strategy was the "rules of the game"—litigation, not protest. White elites, especially those most removed from mass sanction, found NAACP values quite compatible with their own. The educated blacks of the NAACP sought only the removal of legal barriers in order to provide equality of opportunity. Being educated, they regarded education as the key to success. NAACP leadership, being economically successful on the whole, gained a relatively higher degree of acceptance by white elites. Thus, they were culturally at the periphery of the black community. The success of the NAACP depended largely upon the maintenance of "good connections" with white elites, and the organizational leadership did not intend to risk its favored position by identifying with those sections of the black community unacceptable to the white elites.

Creative Disorder and Hostile Outbursts. The first stage in the re-orientation of the civil rights movement toward creative disorder began in 1955, immediately after the *Brown* v. *Board of Education of Topeka* decision. Certainly the symbolic importance of this decision cannot be overestimated; and despite the fact that tangible benefits were minimal, the decision undoubtedly stimulated the escalation of Negro expectations and demands. Additional elite sanctions, such as President Eisenhower's sending troops to Little Rock, Arkansas, in support of the 1954 decision (in spite of the fact that he disapproved of the Court's decision), gave further support to the rising expectations of Negroes. Now the executive branch, in addition to the judiciary, had committed itself to the legal equality of Negroes. Kenneth Clark assesses the importance of official sanction as follows:

> ... This [civil rights] movement would probably not have existed at all were it not for the 1954 Supreme Court school desegregation decision which provided a tremendous boost to the morale of Negroes by its clear affirmation that color is irrelevant to the rights of American citizens. Until this time the Southern Negro generally had accommodated to the separation of the black from the white society.[13]

Dramatic support for Clark's hypothesis can be found in the 1955 refusal of a Negro to ride in the back of a bus in Montgomery, Alabama.

[13]Kenneth B. Clark, "The Civil Rights Movement: Momentum and Organization," in Talcott Parsons and Kenneth B. Clark (eds.), *The Negro American* (Boston: Beacon Press, 1966), p. 610.

AS A MATTER OF RACIAL PRIDE WE WANT TO BE CALLED "BLACKS."

WHICH HAS REPLACED THE TERM "AFRO-AMERICAN."

WHICH REPLACED "NEGROES"—

WHICH REPLACED "COLORED PEOPLE"—

WHICH REPLACED "DARKIES"—

WHICH REPLACED "BLACKS."

© 1960 JULES FEIFFER

Her act resulted in the Montgomery boycott and the first significant evidence of a shift away from the legalism of the NAACP. Ironically, the shift of the civil rights movement away from the NAACP occurred at least partially because of the legal successes of the older organization.

The Montgomery bus boycott illustrated the general relationship between elites and masses. The work of the NAACP was conducted exclusively by black elites. Their work stimulated mass behavior, which in turn required mass-oriented leadership. The need for mass-oriented leadership was filled initially by Martin Luther King, who was catapulted into prominence by the bus boycott. The Southern Christian Leadership Conference (SCLC) emerged in 1957 as the first Southern-originated civil rights group. Although substantially more militant than the older Negro organizations, it was nevertheless explicitly nonviolent. Mass demonstrations were to be used to challenge the legality of both legal and *de facto* segregation and to prick the consciences of white elites.

The tactics of the SCLC were expanded upon by the Student Nonviolent Coordinating Committee (SNCC), which was created from the next phase of direct action, the sit-in demonstrations and freedom rides of the 1960s. In February 1960, at Greensboro, North Carolina, the first sit-ins were conducted by North Carolina Agricultural and Technical College students. These sit-ins were followed by others, and SNCC was organized in order to coordinate this new student protest. SNCC, unlike the SCLC, encouraged Negroes to feel proud of being black. The Congress on Racial Equality, which had been created in the 1940s, emerged from limbo to lead the freedom rides, which challenged the Jim Crow laws of transportation facilities. Many thousands of students participated in these extremely dangerous freedom rides.

The vigor with which the freedom rides and sit-ins were pursued indicated that the civil rights movement was committed to direct action. However, even this new phase of the civil rights movement was not a mass movement; the participants were still relatively privileged in comparison to the black masses. The most frequent participants in the confrontations of the early 1960s were urban students, who were substantially less prejudiced and bitter against whites than were later leaders. These students had a very tolerant and optimistic attitude toward the white community. The freedom riders were not despair-driven anarchists but optimistic young people. The relatively privileged youths were disappointed in the unwillingness of the white society to recognize their merit. According to Matthews and Prothro:

This resulted in a sense of relative deprivation when they compared their chances with those of middle-class whites and the values professed by the white community. Thus the active protestors felt deprived by "white" or general American standards of judgment at the same time they felt relatively advantaged by Negro standards.[14]

[14] Donald R. Matthews and James W. Prothro, *Negroes and the New Southern Politics* (New York: Harcourt, Brace, & World, 1966), p. 424.

This phase of the Negro civil rights movement can thus best be explained by the relative-deprivation hypothesis advanced by Crane Brinton. He argues that revolutions are most likely to be led *not* by those at the bottom of the status pyramid, but by those who are more privileged than the masses they lead.[15]

In 1963, in Birmingham, Alabama, prolonged demonstrations were conducted on the broadest front yet conceived by civil rights leaders. Demands to end discrimination in public accommodations, employment, and housing were presented to the white elite of Birmingham. Under the leadership of Martin Luther King, these demonstrations were committed to nonviolence. Probably because of the broad nature of the demands, participation in these demonstrations reached the grass roots of the black community for the first time. All strata of the black community were involved.

Birmingham was, as we have mentioned, the beginning of a new militancy on the part of all classes of Negroes. But it was also the signal for an escalation of violence on the part of whites. In Mississippi, Medgar Evers was shot; in Alabama, a white postman, participating in the civil rights march, was ambushed and killed. Violence was sanctioned by Southern elites, as was their custom. No one was punished for the murder of Medgar Evers, and Alabama Governor George Wallace stood at the door of the University of Alabama to prevent a Negro from entering. In Birmingham, a bomb killed four Negro girls who were attending Sunday school; and this was the twenty-first bombing and the twenty-first time that the bombers were never apprehended. These incidents gave evidence of the increasing tension between the races.

The Birmingham demonstrations were another landmark in the civil rights movements. As a partial consequence of the repressive behavior of Southern elites toward these peaceful demonstrations, the Kennedy administration was moved to propose significant civil rights legislation. The Birmingham demonstration of 1963 began what was to become the Civil Rights Act of 1964 and the first significant entry of Congress into the civil rights field.

The Civil Rights Act of 1964 passed both houses of Congress by more than a two-thirds favorable vote; it won the overwhelming support of both Republican and Democratic congressmen. It ranks with the Emancipation Proclamation, the Fourteenth Amendment, and *Brown* v. *Board of Education of Topeka* as one of the most important steps toward full equality for the Negro in America. The act provides:

I. That it is unlawful to apply unequal standards in voter registration procedures or to deny registration for irrelevant errors or omissions on records or applications.

II. That it is unlawful to discriminate or segregate persons on the grounds of race, color, religion, or national origin in any place of public accom-

[15] Crane Brinton, *The Anatomy of Revolution* (New York: Vintage Books, 1965), pp. 100–105.

modation, including hotels, motels, restaurants, movies, theatres, sports areas, entertainment houses, and other places which offer to serve the public. This prohibition extends to all establishments whose operations affect interstate commerce or whose discriminatory practices are supported by state action.

III. That the Attorney General shall undertake civil action on behalf of any person denied equal access to a public accommodation to obtain a federal district court order to secure compliance with the act. If the owner or manager of a public accommodation continues to discriminate, he shall be in contempt of court and subject to preemptory fines and imprisonment without trial by jury. [This mode of enforcement gave establishments a chance to mend their ways without punishment, and it also avoided the possibility that Southern juries would refuse to convict persons for violations of the act.]

IV. That the Attorney General shall undertake civil actions on behalf of persons attempting orderly desegregation of public schools.

V. That the Commission on Civil Rights, first established in the Civil Rights Act of 1957, shall be empowered to investigate deprivations of the right to vote, to study and collect information regarding discrimination in America, and to make reports to the president and Congress.

VI. That each federal department and agency shall take action to end discrimination in all programs or activities receiving federal financial assistance in any form. This action shall include termination of financial assistance.

VII. That it shall be unlawful for any employer or labor union with 25 or more persons after 1965 to discriminate against any individual in any fashion in employment, because of his race, color, religion, sex, or national origin, and that an Equal Employment Opportunity Commission shall be established to enforce this provision by investigation, conference, conciliation, persuasion, and, if need be, civil action in federal court.

The Civil Rights Act of 1964, while largely symbolic, did result in some tangible gains for Southern Negroes. The withdrawal of federal grant-in-aid money as a sanction was a remarkable innovation in federal enforcement of civil rights. When the United States Office of Education began to apply pressure in the South, progress was impressive in comparison with the previous ten years. Two years after the passage of the Civil Rights Act in 1964, the percentage of Negroes in integrated schools increased from 2 percent to 16 percent. The lessons of this astonishing increase are quite clear: in order to convert symbolic into tangible victories, a tangible sanction must be utilized. However, the Civil Rights Act of 1964 contained an amendment that forbade government agencies to issue any orders achieving racial balance in areas that did not have legally segregated schools in the past. Thus, the United States Office of Education could not issue desegregation guidelines outside the South, and the act, therefore, had no effect on the plight of Negroes in the ghettos.

Nevertheless, the 1964 Civil Rights Act was a symbolic victory nearly equal to that of the 1954 *Brown* v. *Board of Education of Topeka* decision. One hundred years after the end of the Civil War, the three branches of the federal government had declared themselves to be in sympathy with black Americans.

In this phase of the civil rights movement, the dominance of the NAACP was broken, and more militant action was undertaken. Black elites, even those who successfully challenged NAACP hegemony, were still largely of middle-class origin. By appealing to the conscience of white elites they were able to extend symbolic victories to the legislative process. Though resulting in minimal tangible reallocations, such victories contributed to a loss of control by black elites of the black masses. The masses, activated by symbolic victories, began to rebel against black elites.

Economics: The Real Issue. The 1964 Civil Rights Act was oriented toward conditions in the South, and it dealt with the legal, rather than the economic, status of Negroes. However, the violence in American cities in the 1960s is *national* in scope and socioeconomic in origin. On June 4, 1965, President Johnson delivered an address at Howard University emphasizing not legal efforts to remove segregation but rather financial efforts to end the squalid social and economic conditions of the ghettos. This speech marked the first time that an official response to any needs other than legal ones had been articulated. President Johnson was heavily influenced by a report by Daniel Moynihan that emphasized the family instability of the ghetto. Moynihan, in turn, was greatly influenced by psychologists such as Kenneth Clark, who had written extensively about the pathological conditions existing in the Negro areas of Northern cities. During the previous year, a "War on Poverty" had been declared, indicating that the executive branch was re-orienting itself away from the South and toward the nation with respect to the economic and social conditions of the Negro.

Unfortunately, the President's speech occurred at a time when the established civil rights leaders were losing influence over the course of events in the ghettos. A basic problem at this phase of the Negro-white dialogue was the fact that the established civil rights leadership could not be certain of their control over the volatile black masses. The Negroes who were most violent were those who had no representation in the civil rights establishment.

The Watts riots in the summer of 1965 confounded both the established Negro leadership and the governmental elites. It became clear, moreover, that the President's Howard University speech and the "War on Poverty" were to become no more than a symbolic gesture; the Johnson administration turned away from quelling domestic violence toward instigating its own foreign violence. The preoccupation with Vietnam sapped the administration's energies, making it impossible to devote either psychological or financial resources to the domestic crisis:

The demands of Vietnam, both external and internal, distracted the White House from any central involvement with the new civil rights programs on the order suggested by the Howard University speech. There was first a diversion of intellectual resources and Presidential attention. Beyond this, there would certainly have been a disinclination to invest time and energy working at the new multi-billion dollar racial and economic program so clearly suggested by the Howard University speech at a time when new multi-billion dollar Vietnam commitments were being made.[16]

Shortly after Johnson's Howard University speech in June 1965, a conference with established civil rights leaders was announced. This conference was to direct itself to the conditions described by Johnson and Moynihan.

When the conference between the administration and civil rights organizations was finally held in June 1966, it was supported only by the NAACP. It was boycotted by some of the more militant Negro groups and severely criticized by others. Significantly, Martin Luther King, who apparently had inspired some confidence in the Negro masses, was not in attendance. The conference, which accomplished nothing with respect to civil rights, revealed an absence of linkages between the White House and civil rights leaders *and* between the established civil rights leaders and the ghetto dwellers. Several weeks after the conference had concluded, representatives of the conference met with Johnson to discuss possible implementation. The President spoke with them for one hour. According to Rainwater and Yancey:

Approximately four minutes of the time was devoted to the subject of civil rights, and for 56 minutes the President harangued his council about Vietnam, the importance of the war, and the stupidity of domestic "doves," and of foreign diplomats who run off to Hanoi and Washington trying to make peace through compromises.

It appears, therefore, that by 1966, the governmental elites had directed their attention away from the civil rights movement and toward Vietnam. Also, the civil rights movement itself was splintered.

The situation in the summer of 1966, which resulted in the polarization of black leadership, was symbolized by the new slogan of the militants, "Black Power." This slogan had its origins in the Mississippi march led by James Meredith. The marchers began chanting it, and the theme gradually came to dominate the march as white hostility against the marchers increased. In the heat and intensity of the Mississippi summer, the slogan "Black Power" seemed ominous indeed. Stokely Carmichael expressed it this way:

The only way we gonna stop the white man from whippin' us is to take over. We been saying "Freedom" for six years and we ain't got nothin'. What

---

[16]Lee Rainwater and William L. Yancey, *The Moynihan Report and the Politics of Controversy* (Cambridge, Mass.: MIT Press, 1967), p. 205.

we gonna start saying now is "Black Power.". . . Ain't nothin' wrong with anything all black, because I'm all black, and I'm all good. . . . From now on when they ask you what you want, you know what to tell them: Black Power, Black Power, Black Power![17]

Carmichael's speech was roundly condemned by the NAACP and even by King. White elites joined the established black leadership in a strongly negative reaction against this overt rejection of the strategy of coalition with whites.

By 1966, white backlash was an operative fact in American politics; for 1966 was a threatening year. There were riots in 44 cities, and television screens were filled nightly with Negroes chanting "Black Power." Public opinion polls indicated an increasing white hostility to Negro demands, and this hostility was reflected in the 1966 elections. Republicans gained 47 seats in the House, and conservative Republican Ronald Reagan became the governor of California. Two years prior to the election that catapulted Reagan into prominence, the voters of California had approved a proposition voiding the state's open housing law. The vote for Reagan and the vote against open housing were closely correlated.[18]

The angry mood of the public was also reflected in Congress, where President Johnson's proposal of a federal open housing law was killed by a Senate filibuster. In the same session, limits were imposed upon the authority of the Department of Health, Education, and Welfare to divert funds from schools failing to desegregate. While preventing the passage of civil rights legislation, Congress also began a trend toward repressive legislation directed against those who were responsible, in the eyes of Congress, for the urban violence. A law prohibiting the distribution of anti-poverty funds to persons convicted of promoting a riot that resulted in property damage was typical of the congressional mood. The conservative coalition of Congress demonstrated substantial strength and, for the first time in two years, was able to deny legal sanction to the aspirations of civil rights groups.

Backlash continued unabated through 1968. The passage of the Open Housing Law in 1968 would probably have not occurred without the assassination of Martin Luther King. Moreover, this measure, as passed, is another example of symbolic legislation. The original proposal gave enforcement power to the Department of Housing and Urban Development, which was to issue cease and desist orders and fine those who did not comply. But in the final version of the bill, a person who believes that he has been discriminated against in the sale or rental of housing files a complaint with the Housing and Urban Development Department, but the Department can merely investigate and attempt to conciliate the dispute. If conciliation fails, the person

[17]Joel D. Aberbach and Jack L. Walker, "The Meanings of Black Power: A Comparison of White and Black Interpretations of a Political Slogan," a paper prepared for delivery at the annual meeting of the American Political Science Association, Washington, D.C., September 2–7, 1968, p. 1.
[18]Seymour M. Lipset, *Revolution and Counter-Revolution: Change and Persistence in Social Structures* (New York: Basic Books, 1968), p. 328.

discriminated against has the responsibility of bringing legal action in federal court to seek an injunction. Therefore, the burden of proof and the burden of action rest upon the person who alleges discrimination. The loss of effective enforcement power made the 1968 Open Housing Law roughly comparable in results to the 1954 *Brown* v. *Board of Education of Topeka* decision.

The presidential election of 1968 accurately reflected backlash in the white elites and white masses. Republican candidate Richard Nixon was not in sympathy with the Department of Health, Education, and Welfare's strongly worded and enforced guidelines for school desegregation, nor was he in sympathy with the open housing legislation. Both he and Hubert Humphrey shifted their campaign rhetoric in the direction of third-party candidate George Wallace, consistently emphasizing "law and order." While only Wallace was overtly racist, the other candidates still made highly emotional demands for the preservation of the *status quo* in the "law and order" slogan. The candidates of the two major parties also consistently deemphasized inequities in the economic and social structure. The masses, as reflected in public opinion polls, ranked the law and order issue second only to Vietnam and substantially more important than racial inequalities in their hierarchy of concerns.

Life in the Ghetto
The ghettos were initially created when Negroes migrated into, and whites out of, slum areas. This migration has gradually been declining, but the ghettos are well established. Only about one half of the American Negro population lives in the South; the other half lives in the central cities of the North. Fully 98 percent of the Negro population increase in recent years has taken place in the central cities, while 77 percent of the white population increase has occurred in the suburbs.[19] Thus, the central cities are becoming black and the suburbs white.

All major American cities are characterized by a high degree of residential segregation. In 1960, the segregation index for the 707 largest cities was 86.2, meaning that 86 percent of all Negroes lived in essentially all-black areas in the cities. In the larger cities outside of the South, those containing over two thirds of the Negro population, segregation indexes are unusually high. For example, the segregation index of Chicago was 92.6; that of New York, 79.3; that of Los Angeles, 81.8; that of Detroit, 84.5; and that of Philadelphia, 87.1. These figures have remained quite stable and in many cases have actually increased since 1960. Consequently, Tauber and Tauber conclude:

In the urban United States there is a very high degree of segregation of the residences of whites and Negroes. This is true for cities in all regions of the country and for all types of cities — large and small; industrial and com-

---

[19] Report of the National Advisory Commission on Civil Disorders, p. 390.

mercial, metropolitan and suburban. It is true whether there are hundreds of thousands of Negro residents or only a few thousand. Residential segregation prevails regardless of the relative economic status of the white and Negro residents. It occurs regardless of the character of local law and policies and regardless of the extent of other forms of segregation or discrimination.[20]

The physically crowded conditions in ghettos are pathological and conducive to violent collective behavior. Some of the more overt manifestations of the pathology of ghetto life can be observed in the remarkably high crime rate. Table 12–1 indicates the remarkable persistence of criminal activity within the ghetto. Crimes against persons are extremely high, and the presence of police seems to make little difference. Police departments apparently tolerate substantially more violence among blacks, even though they assign more patrolmen to ghettos areas.

TABLE 12–1. Incidence of Crime and Patrolmen Assignments per 100,000 Residents in Four Chicago Police Districts, 1965

Economic Makeup of Districts	Crimes against Persons	Crimes against Property	Patrolmen Assignments
High income white	80	1,038	93
Low-middle income white	440	1,750	133
Mixed high-low income white	338	2,080	115
Low income Negro	1,618	2,508	243

Source: Report of the National Advisory Commission on Civil Disorders (Washington, D.C., 1968), p. 267.

Lawlessness in the ghetto is seemingly sanctioned by both whites and blacks and has become a way of life. For example, until the riots, there were no "law and order" protests against crime and violence in the ghetto. So long as the victims of black violence were blacks, the white society remained complacent. Similarly, although the probability of being a victim of a violent crime is 78 percent higher for non-whites than it is for whites, it is the whites who now express concern about the maintenance of "law and order."

The poverty of the ghetto undoubtedly contributes to the high incidence of crime. While there has been substantial improvement in the economic position of blacks in recent years, this improvement is not bringing the ghetto population appreciably closer to the white standard of living. It is customary to compare the relation of white to non-white income to ascertain the extent of the progress; and it is true that black income, as a proportion of white income, has been increasing. However, the dollar difference between the white and the black median family incomes has actually been increasing. In 1952, the difference in per capita income between the two races was $1,415; in 1966, it was $2,908.

[20]Karl E. Tauber and Alma F. Tauber, Negroes in Cities (Chicago: Aldine Publishing Co., 1965), pp. 35–36.

At the same time that the actual dollar gap between black and white income widens, the discrepancy between educational levels narrows. Education is supposed to be the key to success, but a significant discrepancy exists in the lifetime earnings of whites and blacks at identical educational levels. Moreover, the discrepancy between black and white incomes increases as education increases. That is, the more education a Negro achieves, the less is the dollar value of the education to him (see Table 12–2). Given two equally motivated people—one white and one black—it is worth $309,000 to the white to get as much education as he can, but it is only worth $151,000 to the black to do likewise. Since the income gap widens as education increases, a non-white college graduate earns less in a lifetime than a white with only an eighth-grade education. In a lifetime, a black truck driver earns $97,000; a white truck driver earns $162,000.

TABLE 12–2.
Education
and Lifetime
Earnings,
White Men versus
Non-white Men*

	White	Non-white	Non-white as Percent of White
Elementary school:			
less than 8 years	$157,000	$ 95,000	61%
8 years	191,000	123,000	64
High school:			
1 to 3 years	221,000	132,000	60
4 years	253,000	151,000	60
College:			
1 to 3 years	301,000	162,000	54
4 years	395,000	185,000	47
5 years or more	466,000	246,000	53

*Earnings for men aged 18 to 64, based on 1960 census figures.

Source: U.S. Senate, 88th Congress, 1st Session, hearings before the Committee on Labor and Public Welfare on bills relating to equal employment opportunities, July and August 1963.

To measure the net effect of this kind of frustration, we have constructed an index of satisfaction by dividing the average family income by years of schooling for the total population and for the non-white population (see Table 12–3). The index is a ratio of non-white want satisfaction to the want satisfaction of the white population. Although it does not reflect the absolute level of satisfaction for either group, the index does reflect the inequality of satisfaction between the two. For example, a score of 50 indicates that non-whites enjoy only half the want satisfaction that whites enjoy, whereas a score of 100 means that the two groups are equally satisfied (or dissatisfied, as the case may be).

The index indicates that economic rewards have been sporadic. Rising to its peak in 1952, the relative satisfaction of Negroes then declined consistently until the 1960s. In the 1960s a new increase in the index of satisfaction corresponded with the increase in violence in the cities.

TABLE 12–3.
Index of Want
Satisfaction,
1940–1967

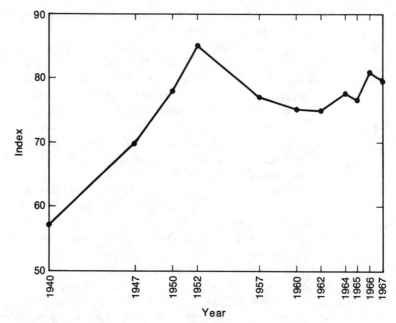

Source: Figures from *The Statistical Abstract of the United States.*

Such statistics should not make the mistake of failing to distinguish between ghetto blacks and those living in other areas, for economic conditions are always worse in the ghetto than they are outside. Unemployment is also substantially higher in the ghettos. In 1968, for example, the unemployment rate of blacks was 6.6 percent, roughly twice that of whites. But in the Hough district of Cleveland, the unemployment rate of blacks was 15.6 percent.[21] These figures indicate a strong temptation on the part of ghetto blacks to drop out of the employment market. Consequently, unemployment rates are even higher for non-white high school graduates than for white drop-outs. Even though the education of the black population improves, therefore, the ratio of white to non-white unemployment remains unchanged; life in the ghetto brings unemployment even with improved education. For Negroes, getting an education is simply not as important as it is for whites; the costs are greater and the rewards are fewer.

Inequality *among* Negroes is much greater than *among* whites. The Negro social class structure resembles a pyramid. Most of the Negro population is at the bottom of the pyramid, with only a few Negroes at the top.[22] The white social class structure, on the other hand, is diamond-shaped; there are a few whites at both the top and the bottom, and most whites are in the middle. This is proved economically.

---

[21] Carl T. Rowan, "Is the Negro Going Too Fast?" Eugene *Register Guard,* October 16, 1968.
[22] St. Clair Drake, "The Social and Economic Status of the Negro in the United States," in Parsons and Clark, *The Negro American,* p. 17.

The inequality of income distribution is greater among blacks than among whites and is not improving.

This persisting inequality of income among blacks is evidence of the politics of tokenism. A few Negroes attain middle-class economic status, but in so doing they lose contact with the ghetto. These Negroes, who are at the top of the pyramid, are looked upon by whites as examples of what can be accomplished in an egalitarian society. Actually, the relationship of these few middle-class Negroes to the black masses is so remote as to make them useful primarily as symbolic rewards for white liberal elites. They are certainly not useful as practical or even symbolic leaders for the ghetto blacks.

Ironically, income inequalities between middle-class and lower-class Negroes operate to strip the Negro population of many potential leaders. For example, efforts in Northern cities to speed up residential integration at the middle-class level skim off those Negroes whose life styles are middle class and co-opt them into the white society in limited numbers. Those who remain behind—the overwhelming majority of Negroes—cannot accept the leadership of those who leave the ghetto; for upwardly mobile blacks often try to outdo middle-class whites in conformity and achievement. It is noteworthy that demands for integration are made largely from the upwardly mobile segments of the black population who want to get out of the ghetto and are frequently critical of lower-class blacks. The fact that some black property has been attacked in recent riots attests to the hostility which exists among blacks. As Kenneth Clark observes: "The ghetto develops a sinister power to perpetuate its own pathology, to demand conformity to its norms; it ridicules, drives out, or isolates those who seek to resist these norms or even transform them."[23]

The psychology of the ghetto, argues Clark, produces cynicism, suspicion, and fear of the outside world. The ghetto psychology consequently prevents the development of potentially effective leaders, thus contributing to the cycle of pathology. The pathology of the ghetto also manifests itself in the attitudes and life patterns of Negroes. Basically, ghetto life encourages both severe alienation and extreme mental illness. Self-identity problems of Negroes are especially acute. Since about one fourth of the families in the ghetto have female heads, Negro boys are deprived of the benefits of socialization into manhood by a male model. Consequently, their problems of sexual identification are intense. Matriarchal traditions, begun by slavery and enhanced by poverty, also lower the self-esteem of black males. Lowered self-esteem, as we have seen, reduces achievement motivations; and reduced achievement motivations often result in economic failure and, occasionally, individual violence, in order to compensate for the loss of self-esteem.

Discrimination is also substantially harder on males than females. The Negro male was most humiliated by segregation; keeping the

[23] Kenneth B. Clark, *Dark Ghetto: Dilemmas of Social Power* (New York: Harper & Row, 1965), p. 62.

Negro "in his place" usually meant keeping the Negro *male* in his place. The submissiveness that segregation implies is more destructive to the male than to the female personality. The popularity of Africana among Negroes may be linked to problems of self-esteem. However, the popularity of African music, styles of dress, and hair styles should not be confused with a genuine desire for separatism or a return to Africa. No more than one fourth of the black population is genuinely separatist; and separatism is no more than an extreme desire to develop a more favorable self-image. There is a substantial yearning by American Negroes for some sort of cultural identity.

Among the Negro masses, there is the persistent belief that whites are not in sympathy with them. Only one third see whites as well intentioned, while two thirds see them as either hostile or indifferent.[24] The white masses feel that this suspicion is unjustified, since they are willing to express a verbal commitment to civil rights. But most whites, denying the existence of discrimination, avoid any responsibility for the conditions in the ghetto. Only one fifth of the whites, compared to two fifths of the Negroes, believe that Negroes are discriminated against in employment. Denying the existence of discrimination makes it possible for whites to blame Negro problems on Negroes themselves, specifically upon their lack of ambition and industriousness.[25] Since we have seen that ghetto life does lower aspiration levels, there is some surface truth to these white beliefs. Actually, however, lower aspiration levels and lower actual achievement are environmentally induced; they are not inherent characteristics of Negroes. As we noted earlier, middle-class Negroes have higher achievement levels than middle-class whites.

Police in the Ghetto.   To many ghetto dwellers, the police are the symbol of white oppression. "Police brutality" has become a theme with enormous emotional impact among Negroes. James Baldwin's description of the attitude of ghetto dwellers toward police cannot be improved upon. He notes that:

. . . their very presence is an insult, and it would be, even if they spent their entire day feeding gumdrops to children. They represent the force of the white world, and that world's real intentions are, simply, for that world's profit and ease, to keep the black man corralled here in his place. The badge, the gun and the holster, and the swinging club make vivid what will happen should this revolution become overt. . . . He moves through Harlem, therefore, like an occupying soldier in a bitterly hostile country; which is precisely what, and where, he is, and is the reason they walk in twos and threes.[26]

[24] William Brink and Louis Harris, *The Negro Revolution in America* (New York: Simon and Schuster, 1964), p. 126; see also "Racial Views of Racial Issues," in *Supplementary Studies for the National Advisory Commission on Civil Disorders* (Washington, D.C., July 1968), p. 25.
[25] Brink and Harris, pp. 138–153; see also "White Beliefs about Negroes," in *Supplementary Studies for the National Advisory Commission on Civil Disorders,* July 1968.
[26] James Baldwin, *Nobody Knows My Name* (New York: Dell, 1961), p. 62.

Since the policeman's role in the ghetto is that of a symbol of white authority and repression, even the most exemplary behavior on his part would risk offense to the ghetto dwellers. And, of course, the behavior of many policemen is far from exemplary. The white masses strongly reject the idea that police behavior in the ghettos has been brutal or even discriminatory; only a small proportion of whites accept without reservation the possibility that Negroes might be subject to rough treatment and disrespect by police. Seventy-two percent of the whites believe that Negroes are treated the same as whites.[27] Of course, dissatisfaction with the police among the Negro masses runs very deep; Table 12–4 shows the extent of this hostility.

TABLE 12–4. Black and White Mass Perceptions of the Police: Percentage Agreeing with Various Statements		Black	White
	The police do not come quickly when called.	51%	27%
	The police do not show respect and use insulting language.	38	16
	The police frisk and search without good reason.	36	11
	The police are too rough when arresting.	35	10

Source: Supplementary Studies for The National Advisory Commission on Civil Disorders (Washington, D.C., July 1968), p. 44.

Given this state of high tension between police and ghetto residents, it is almost invariable that a police action is the precipitating event immediately preceding a riot. A routine arrest made in an atmosphere of increasing tensions and black exasperation by previous perceptions of police hostility is usually the trigger for large-scale rioting. Negroes feel by a two to one margin that police brutality is a major cause of disorder, an idea that is rejected by whites by an eight to one margin.

Studies of police attitudes have uncovered a substantial reservoir of anti-Negro bias. For instance, Albert Reiss reported the following information to the Kerner Commission:

In predominantly Negro precincts, over three fourths of the policemen expressed prejudice or highly prejudiced attitudes towards Negroes. . . . What do I mean by extreme prejudice? I mean that they describe Negroes in terms that are not people terms. They describe them in terms of the animal kingdom. . . .[28]

Peter Rossi also studied the police in the cities that suffered violence. He finds that policemen feel that Negroes are pushing too hard. Sev-

[27] "White Beliefs about Negroes," in Supplementary Studies for the National Advisory Commission on Civil Disorders, p. 30.
[28] Report of the National Advisory Commission on Civil Disorders, p. 306.

enty-nine percent of the police do not believe that Negroes are treated worse than the whites; and, like most whites, the policemen cannot see the need for any further push toward equality. They exhibit fairly strong anti-Negro attitudes; for example, 49 percent do not approve of the idea of whites and Negroes socializing, and 56 percent are disturbed at Negroes moving into white neighborhoods.[29] In an accurate estimate of Negro opinion, the police believe that only a small minority of Negroes regard them as their friends, whereas a substantial majority of the whites do so. However, policemen cannot understand why Negroes resent them. Still, it is interesting that the police view themselves in much the same terms as Negroes view them as to their status in the ghetto: The policemen feel alone in a strange and hostile land.

Table 12–5 compares the attitudes of police and educator about the causes of riots. We can see that the police perceive riots as acts of criminal irresponsibility, whereas educators view the riots as produced by economic and social grievances. Police are more inclined to think that Negroes are basically violent and that they have been misled by

TABLE 12–5. Views of Policemen and Educators about Negroes: Percentage Agreeing with Various Statements

	Police	Educators
Negroes are basically violent.	28%	8%
Riots are caused by police brutality.	9	33
Riots are caused by nationalists and militants.	77	46
Criminal elements are involved in riots.	69	33
Unheard Negro complaints are involved in riots.	31	70

Source: Supplemental Studies for the National Advisory Commission on Civic Disorders (Washington, D.C., July 1968), p. 96.

militants and criminals. Educators are more inclined to think that riots are caused not by the basic violence of Negroes but by the unwillingness of whites to listen to their complaints.

The goal of the police is generally not to reduce the long-term problems of the ghetto but to effect short-term control of riots. They wish to suppress riot activity vigorously, and they are angered by the leniency they perceive in judges and courts.[30] Police in the ghetto also have strong negative attitudes toward Negro civil rights groups and toward federal poverty agencies. They perceive the civil rights groups as contributors to violence and the poverty agencies as misguided social reform institutions that do not understand the legitimacy of force.

[29] Gallup Opinion Index, Report No. 25 (July 1967), p. 19.
[30] Because their occupation is a hazardous one that tends to develop strong in-group ties, the police also view lack of public support as a major problem. However, they need not worry about lack of support among the white community; 54 percent of the whites favor Mayor Daley's order to shoot looters on sight, and an even higher proportion favor a national holiday to honor the police (Gallup Opinion Index, Report No. 37, July 1968, p. 17). Clearly, the police are emerging as heretofore unappreciated heroes in the eyes of whites.

The attitudes of the police are understandable in view of the recruitment and socialization processes through which they pass. Police are recruited from the social classes most likely to have anti-Negro biases—the lower-middle and working classes. Moreover, very few police have had college training. Since we know that education is positively correlated with tolerance, we would expect that the police, being disproportionately representative of the uneducated classes, would be as typically intolerant as the average lower-class white. In addition to the initial anti-Negro bias, occupational socialization probably strengthens the attitudes of policemen. The element of danger in policemen's jobs makes them naturally suspicious. Also, since policemen are engaged in enforcing rules, they become overly concerned with authority, and are politically and emotionally conservative. Jerome Skolnick observes: "It was clear that a Goldwater type of conservatism was the dominant political and emotional persuasion of police. I encountered only three policemen (out of 50) who claimed to be politically "liberal," at the same time asserting that they were decidedly exceptional."[31]

Add to these police attitudes the fact that the crime rate in ghettos is unusually high, and we have the makings of another vicious circle. One officer describes the operation of this circle:

The police have to associate with lower-class people, slobs, drunks, criminals, riff-raff of the worst sort. Most of these . . . are Negroes. The police officers see these people through middle-class or lower-middle-class eyeballs. But even if he saw them through highly sophisticated eyeballs he can't go into the street and take this night after night. When some Negro criminal says to you a few times, "You white motherfucker. . . ," well it's bound to affect you after a while. Pretty soon you decide they're all just niggers and they'll never be anything but niggers. It would take not just an average man to resist this feeling, it would take an extraordinary man to resist it, and there are very few ways by which the police department can attract extraordinary men to join it.[32]

Ghetto Schools. Another agent of white society in the ghetto is the schools. Federal courts have not ruled that communities have any duty to correct *de facto* racial imbalance, and *de facto* school segregation in Northern ghettos—that is, segregated housing patterns coupled with neighborhood schools—has continued unabated, even as token integration has been achieved in the South. Approximately three quarters of all Negro pupils in Northern cities attend *de facto* segregated schools—that is, schools in which 90 percent or more of their classmates are black. In Table 12–6, we observe that whereas in the South there has been some progress toward integration, in the North the process of segregation is actually increasing.[33] This increase in *de facto* segregation in the North has occurred because the

[31] J. H. Skolnick, *Justice without Trial* (New York: John Wiley, 1967), p. 61.
[32] James Q. Wilson, *Varieties of Police Behavior* (Cambridge, Mass.: Harvard University Press, 1968), p. 43.
[33] "Racial Isolation in the Public Schools," *A Report of the United States Commission on Civil Rights*, 1967, pp. 3–7.

Negro population in the central cities has grown and because school officials have taken little action to achieve racial balance.

TABLE 12–6.
Percentage of Negroes Attending Schools in Which a Majority of Pupils Are Negro, in Selected Cities

	1950	1966	Percent Change
Charlotte	100%	96%	−4
Cleveland	84	94	+10
Philadelphia	85	90	+5
	1960		
Dallas	100	90	−10
Detroit	91	92	+1
Oakland	61	83	+22
Richmond	100	98	−2
	1961		
Newark	85	90	+5

Source: "Racial Isolation in the Public Schools," *A Report of the United States Commission on Civil Rights* (Appendix), 1967, compiled from pp. 12–19.

Although the majority of both races prefer integration, at least at the level of verbal commitment, white parents oppose many of the measures that would make integrated education possible. White parents have successfully fought busing of students in most Northern cities. What whites have in mind, when they say that it is permissible for blacks and whites to attend the same schools, is a balance in which most of the children are white. For example, although a majority of whites approve the idea of integration, two thirds of them would not want to send their child to a school where more than half are black. One third of the whites object to sending their children to schools in which approximately half the pupils are black.[34]

In spite of the psychological advantages accruing to Negro children from genuinely integrated schools, and in spite of the increases in educational achievement that occur, there is also strong resistance among educational elites to racial balancing in classrooms. An example of such resistance is the behavior of superintendents. Crain found that superintendents of large school districts generally professed to be "color blind." In general, they oppose the classification of schools as "segregated" or "integrated." However, by refusing to consider racial balance a problem for schools, they impede the process of integration. The official ideology of some members of the educational establishment—"keeping politics out of the schools"—means avoiding social and political issues and minimizing public criticism. It also means, as Crain observes, that ". . . the interaction between civil rights leaders and school superintendents has the preconditions for conflict. They literally do not speak the same language."[35]

[34] See Paul B. Sheatsley, "White Attitudes toward the Negro," in Parsons and Clark, *The Negro American*, pp. 303–324.
[35] Robert L. Crain, *The Politics of School Desegregation* (Chicago: Aldine Publishing Co., 1968), p. 123.

A polarization of attitudes between the black and white masses, resulting in differing perceptions of the same events, is developing. Consider the different perceptions of Negro violence. Since whites believe that Negroes are treated equally with whites, they feel that the riots are caused by agitators, Communists, and hoodlums. In Detroit, for example, 70 percent of the whites believed the riots were completely irresponsible, unjustifiable, and the work of criminals. In contrast, 71 percent of the blacks believed that the riots were the result of widespread mistreatment and social injustice.[36] Clearly, Negroes do not see riots as random or individual behavior, but instead as a spontaneous protest against unfair economic deprivation. Remove these conditions, they argue, and you will remove the cause of the riots. The essential difference between the attitudes of blacks and whites, therefore, is that to whites the riots have little social meaning but to blacks they are of great social significance.

Strangely, although whites do not attach any social significance to the riots, they view them as planned rather than spontaneous. The conspiracy theory of riots dominates the attitudes of whites. Whites also believe that only a tiny minority of the Negro population riots or is in sympathy with violence, though they simultaneously exhibit some tendency to believe that Negroes are more violent by nature than whites. But among Negro explanations for the riots, phrases like "want to be treated like a human being" occur time and time again. These phrases are rarely heard as whites explain riots. When asked, for example, "What do you think is the most important thing the city government can do to keep a disturbance from occurring?" about half the whites, but only one tenth of the Negroes say "more police control."[37]

The polarity of Negro and white attitudes is well illustrated in the reaction of both groups to the explosive symbol "Black Power." Whites, responding negatively, see "Black Power" as synonymous with "black rule," but the majority of blacks see the symbol as meaning "black pride" and a fair share of the economic rewards of American society.

At the beginning of this chapter it was pointed out that the survival of the American political system depends upon how well the ruling elites are able to cope with the internal tensions of American society. In light of this fact, it is significant that elite perceptions of black urban violence have been quite similar to those of the masses. The results of a poll conducted by the *Congressional Quarterly,* shown in Table 12–7, indicate that 62 percent of the Southern Democrats and 59 percent of the Republicans in Congress think that outside agitators were of great importance in the urban violence, whereas only 17 percent

---

[36]Alberback and Walker, "The Meanings of Black Power," p. 17.

[37]"The Uses of Violence," in *Supplementary Studies for the National Advisory Commission on Civil Disorders,* p. 48.

of the Northern Democrats share this view. Only 31 percent of the Southern Democrats and 28 percent of the Republicans, compared to 69 percent of the Northern Democrats, believe that a neglect of the social and economic problems of Negroes was a factor of considerable importance. A majority of all three groups believe that joblessness and idleness among the young are major factors, but the Southern Democrats and Republicans are inclined to attribute this joblessness and idleness to the individual Negro rather than to the economic system. Fifty-seven percent of the Southern Democrats and 42 percent of the Republicans, but only 5 percent of the Northern Democrats, believe that Supreme Court decisions were of major importance in causing violence.

Given the views of the Republicans and Southern Democrats, it is not surprising that the devices they propose to prevent recurring violence tend to be repressive. Seventy-seven percent of the Southern Democrats and 65 percent of the Republicans, in contrast with 44 percent of the Northern Democrats, want to inflict greater penalties upon rioters to prevent them from repeating their behavior. Sixty-six percent of the Northern Democrats want to institute massive federal aid to the cities, but only 14 percent of the Southern Democrats and 4 percent of the Republicans wish to do so. Sixty-four percent of the Southern Democrats and 52 percent of the Republicans, compared to 49 percent of the Northern Democrats, think that larger and better paid police forces would be effective in controlling riots. Forty-six percent of the Southern Democrats and 47 percent of the Republicans, in contrast to only 7 percent of the Northern Democrats, wish to pass legislation voiding the Supreme Court decisions that increased the rights of defendants in criminal cases. However, the Southerners and the Republicans oppose gun-control legislation (see Table 12–7).

Mayors were also included in the *Congressional Quarterly's* survey. The survey indicated that mayors of large cities, where most of the rioting has occurred, are substantially more realistic in their appraisal of the causes and cures of riots than mayors of small towns. For instance, 74 percent of the mayors of cities under 50,000 believe that outside agitators were a major factor, compared to 68 percent of those who were mayors of cities of 50,000 to 250,000 population and only 36 percent of the mayors of cities in excess of 250,000. Whereas 46 percent of the small-town mayors think that irresponsible attitudes among Negroes were responsible, only 14 percent of the mayors of large cities share this attitude. A majority of mayors in big cities want greater penalties, but this majority was only 57 percent, compared to the overwhelming 90 percent of the mayors of small towns. The majority of big-city mayors also want increased federal economic aid, but only a small minority of the small-town mayors want this aid (see Table 12–8).

Riot, Revolution, or Repression? We have classified urban violence as a phase in a social movement. Why did it occur in the 1960s, and what is the next phase? Table 12–9

TABLE 12–7.
Congressional
Perceptions of the
Causes and Cures
of Black Urban
Rioting

	Northern Democrat	Southern Democrat	Republican
Causes			
Poor police-community relations	44%	25%	15%
Outside agitators	17	62	59
Communists	8	38	20
Neglected social and economic problems	69	31	28
Joblessness and idleness among the young	87	54	62
White indifference to Negro needs	57	21	12
Lacking responsibility among Negroes	33	55	55
Supreme Court decisions	5	57	42
Irresponsible news media	33	55	36
Resentment against congressional inaction	7	6	4
Insufficient federal aid	58	12	8
Cures			
Greater penalties	44	77	65
Federal Marshall Plan	60	14	4
Greater state and local effort	86	66	68
Private sector involvement	69	44	52
Larger, better paid police force	49	64	52
Greater expenditure for police anti-riot training	43	38	43
Legislation to void Supreme Court decisions	7	46	47
Gun control legislation	49	18	6
Emphasis on church and family values	54	85	80

Source: *Congressional Quarterly Weekly Reports*, 36 (September 8, 1967), p. 1738.

indicates that racial violence increased steadily up to 1968, when it experienced a moderate decline.[38] What is the meaning of this very recent decline in rioting? Is this a short-term or long-term trend?

The reason for the increase in racial violence seems to be that Negroes now have hopes of bettering their condition. Totally subservient people seldom revolt. When things are looking up, but not far enough up, violence is likely to erupt. It is not those who have accepted poverty as a way of life but those who are rising in the social order who become the most intense advocates of change.

James C. Davies has pointed to the disparity between expectations and actual rewards, rather than the absolute level of reward deprivation, as the key factor in revolutionary movements.[39] It is Davies'

[38] Bryan T. Downes and Stephen W. Burks, "The Black Protest Movement and Urban Violence," a paper prepared for delivery at the annual meeting of the American Political Science Association, Washington, D.C., September 2–7, 1968. See also James C. Davies, "Toward a Theory of Revolution," *American Sociological Review*, 27, 1 (February 1962), 6.

[39] James C. Davies, "Toward a Theory of Revolution," p. 6.

TABLE 12–8.
Mayoral Perceptions
of the Causes
and Cures of
Black Urban Rioting

	Size of Town		
	Under 50,000	50,000 to 250,000	250,000 or more
Causes			
Poor police-community relations	16%	34%	36%
Outside agitators	74	68	36
Community	33	36	25
Neglect of social and economic problems	35	40	47
Joblessness and idleness among the young	72	73	92
White indifference to Negro needs	29	38	50
Lack of personability among Negroes	68	52	23
Supreme Court decisions	41	50	46
Irresponsible news media	55	54	43
Resentment against congressional inaction	6	8	8
Insufficient federal aid	22	37	46
Cures			
Greater penalties	90	77	57
Federal Marshall Plan	23	48	57
Greater state and local effort	55	60	57
Private sector involvement	48	48	75
Larger, better paid police force	49	64	52
Greater expenditure for police anti-riot training	43	38	43
Legislation to void Supreme Court decisions	57	66	36
Gun control legislation	27	34	15
Emphasis on church and family values	83	73	71

Source: *Congressional Quarterly Weekly Report 36* (September 8, 1967), p. 1,740.

theory that masses do not revolt until they *perceive* the possibility
of actually bettering their lot in life, while at the same time *perceiving*
that their attempts to do so are being thwarted. Persons with a long-
standing history of deprivation, or those who are severely repressed,

TABLE 12–9.
Yearly Breakdown
of Information on
Hostile Outbursts

Data on Hostile Outbursts	1964	1965	1966	1967	1968	Total
Number of cities having outbursts	16	20	44	71	64	215*
Number of outbursts	16	23	53	82	65	239†
Total number of days of hostility	42	31	92	236	122	523
Total number arrested	2,000	10,245	2,216	16,471	18,675	49,607
Total number wounded	580	1,206	467	3,348	2,341	7,942
Total number killed	9	43	9	85	46	191

*Many of the same cities have incidents each year. That is why this figure is so high.
†Smaller (less violent) incidents are under-reported.
Source: Bryan T. Downs and Stephan W. Burks, "The Black Protest Movement and Urban Violence," a paper prepared for delivery at the annual meeting of the American Political Science Association, Washington, D.C., September 2–7, 1968, p. 15.

are not likely to perceive any real hope of alleviating their distressed condition. Only when forces not of their own making cause them to hope—justifiably or not—that conditions can become better will they perceive that change is possible and seek further gains. Thus, expectations tend to rise as perceptions of material or social well-being rise.

Davies postulates that so long as the gulf between their expectations and their perception of actual conditions does not grow too immense, the deprived and repressed minorities will not engage in revolutionary activity. However, if their perception of want satisfaction does not keep pace with their rising expectations, the underprivileged will eventually revolt, for there is a critical point at which the gulf becomes intolerable.

Negro violence in America lends itself to analysis through the use of Davies' model. Two factors have contributed to the rise in Negro expectations: (1) The Southern Negro emigration to the Northern cities, with the concomitant anticipation of economic betterment; and (2) the symbolic rewards flowing from federal desegregation policies. Although these factors conspired to raise the expectations of Negroes, they failed to make good their promises. Moreover, the white backlash tended to dull symbolic gratification as well as impede the progress of further reform.

That Negro expectations were on the ascendant as long ago as 1954 is attested to by the fact that, in that year, 64 percent of them, compared to only 53 percent of the whites, thought that life would be getting better for them.[40] The riots and violence of recent years testify that Negro expectations have not been sufficiently realized.

The extent to which the urban revolt becomes a revolution—that is to say, the extent to which diffuse and vaguely defined violence becomes organized and carefully channeled violence—depends in the long run upon white elite reaction. Separatism and support for violence among Negroes is not confined to a few radicals. Most Negroes—even most rioters—favor racial harmony, but nationalism attracts a substantial minority. More Negroes have participated in riots than many whites realize; it is likely that between 10 percent and 30 percent have actually participated in various hostile outbursts. Further, fully 60 percent of those who have participated would be willing to do it again; and 54 percent of all Negroes who did not and would not riot are sympathetic with the rioters. Clearly, the rioters are not outcasts in the eyes of other Negroes. They are not outside agitators but authentic leaders within the black community.[41]

Urban violence, then, is a black counter-elite movement directed against both white and black established elites. As is the case when established elites lose control of any social movement, the mode of action is violent and unstable. Nobody is really in charge.

[40]Thomas F. Pettigrew, "Social Evaluation Theory: Consequences and Applications," Nebraska Symposium on Motivation, 1967, p. 295.
[41]Supplementary Studies for the National Advisory Commission on Civil Disorders, p. 55.

Summary   In many ways, the recent political activism among blacks conforms to elite theory concerning mass movements. It is unstable, unpredictable, and can produce violence; it expresses resentment toward the established order; it is made up of people who seldom participate in democratic politics; and it has produced a variety of counter-elites. But the racial issue differs from other national and international issues in that the white masses have definite opinions about it. Therefore, white elites are not free to do as they please with the problem.

An especially destructive aspect of the racial problem is that, although the American nation is supposedly committed to equality for all men, to recognition of minority rights, and to individual dignity, the treatment of Negroes over the course of American history has directly contradicted these ideals. After centuries of slavery and segregation, black masses are poorly educated, unskilled, poverty-stricken, frequently unemployed, still segregated, and, consequently, subject to a variety of social pathologies. Although blacks feel that whites are to blame for the present condition of Negroes, most whites refuse to accept this responsibility, or even to admit that inequities still exist.

White liberal elites are willing to grant legal equality to Negroes, and are willing to accept individual blacks as equals if these blacks accept the prevailing elite consensus. But even white liberals are not willing to accept black masses, or to take concerted action to bring black masses up to the economic level of the average white.

Historically, white elites have been willing to sacrifice Negro interests in order to preserve national unity—in the years before the Civil War, in the Compromise of 1877, throughout the long period of legal segregation, and in the moderate, go-slow period of recent civil rights legislation. The Supreme Court, as the governmental institution furthest removed from the white masses, was the first to stand up for Negro rights. Elected white elites did not respond to black requests until faced with a prolonged campaign of nonviolent civil disobedience and public demonstrations; even then, elected elites made only minimal, largely symbolic concessions.

Negro middle-class groups such as the NAACP, in achieving the elimination of legal discrimination, activated the black masses, who then turned to a goal that was unacceptable to the middle-class black— absolute equality instead of equality of opportunity. New black counter-elites emerged to lead the black ghetto masses. At the same time, white liberals, although willing to give lip service to the black cause, were too deeply involved in other areas with higher priority—the war in Vietnam, the Cold War, and the maintenance of a large defense establishment—to actually effect any changes in the condition of the blacks.

When the civil rights movement became violent, black elites lost control and the "rules of the game" were violated, which moved white elites, assisted occasionally by their black counterparts, to repress "illegitimate" behavior. Still, mass-oriented black counter-elites continued to gain influence.

As a result of the disparity between heightened black expectations and the failure of white elites to come through with concrete progress toward economic equality, mass urban violence erupted. White masses reacted to black violence with hostility, fear, and the desire to repress the blacks; white elites took steps to effect the repression with stricter anti-riot laws and stronger police forces.

Through the civil rights movement, the black masses have been roused from their apathy to political activism, and have made progress in eliminating legal discrimination. At the same time, the aspirations of blacks have risen considerably, but frustration and bitterness resulted when they were not fulfilled. Moreover, as a result of the white backlash, tensions between blacks and whites are higher than ever. If American elites can help the blacks achieve economic equality, prevent further urban violence, and pacify the white masses, they will indeed have proved the viability of American democracy.

Selected Additional Readings

Clark, Kenneth B. *Dark Ghetto: Dilemmas of Social Power.* New York: Harper & Row (Harper Torchbook edition), 1967. *Dark Ghetto* is a particularly incisive analysis of the life of American blacks in urban ghetto areas and of the pathologies this life produces.

Matthews, Donald R., and James W. Prothro. *Negroes and the New Southern Politics.* New York: Harcourt, Brace, & World (paperback), 1966. This is one of the pioneering works on the changing political role of the Southern Negro. It considerably updates some of Myrdal's earlier comments on Southern politics.

Myrdal, Gunner. *An American Dilemma.* Vol. I: *The Negro in a White Nation.* Vol. II: *The Negro Social Structure.* New York: McGraw-Hill (paperback), 1964. Originally published in 1944, this remains one of the most comprehensive studies available dealing with the situation of the Negro in America. It draws broadly from many disciplines.

Report of the National Advisory Commission on Civil Disorders. New York: Bantam Books, 1968. Popularly called "The Kerner Report," this volume is the most comprehensive study of major urban riots in the United States available today. It presents a detailed discussion of the factors underlying past riots and offers recommendations for avoiding such confrontations in the future.

Parsons, Talcott, and Kenneth B. Clark (eds.). *The Negro American.* Boston: Beacon Press (paperback), 1967. This volume is a collection of excellent articles dealing with the social, psychological, economic, and political position of the Negro in American society.

Pomper, Gerald. *Elections in America: Control and Influence in Democratic Politics.* New York: Dodd, Mead, & Co. (paperback), 1968. Chapter 9 contains a discussion of the development of the civil rights movement in America. The emphasis is on the changing status of Negroes in American society and on the impact such change has had on American voting patterns.

13

**The Few and
the Many: Elitism
and American
Politics**

Elitism asserts that society is divided into the few who have power and the many who do not. According to elite theory, elites—not masses—allocate values for society. Elites are not typical of the masses in backgrounds or attitudes. Elites share a consensus on behalf of the basic values of the system, and public policy reflects prevailing values of elites rather than demands of masses. Elitism also asserts that changes in public policy are incremental rather than revolutionary, and that the movement of non-elites into elite positions is slow and limited only to non-elites who have accepted elite values. Finally, elitism asserts that elites influence masses more than masses influence elites.

Masses are generally apathetic, but defeat or humiliation in war, economic dislocation, or threats to personal safety may occasionally activate mass movements. Mass movements threaten democratic values—individual liberty, majority rule, due process of law, limited government, and private property. Counter-elites express mass sentiments—populism, extremism, racism, anti-intellectualism, and equalitarianism. The responsibility for the survival of democratic values rests with elites, but elite reactions to mass movements may also result in the loss of democratic values.

Admittedly, these propositions run contrary to the *symbols* of American politics. But do they describe the *realities* of American politics? Let us set forth a series of propositions that are related to elite theory and that can be supported with historical and social science evidence derived from the American political experience.

The Constitution and Structure of American Government

Elite theory provides us with an interpretation of the Constitution of the United States and the basic structure of American government. The following propositions can be derived from our analysis of Constitutional politics:

1. The Constitution of the United States was not "ordained and established" by "the people." Instead, it was written by a small, educated, talented, wealthy elite in America, representative of powerful economic interests—bondholders, investors, merchants, real estate owners, and planters.

2. The Constitution and the national government that it established had its origins in elite dissatisfaction with the inability of the central government to pay off its bondholders, the interference of state governments with the development of a national economy, the threat to investors and creditors with state issuance of cheap paper money and laws relieving debtors of contractual obligations, the threat to propertied classes arising from post-Revolutionary War radicalism, the inability of the central government to provide an army capable of protecting Western development or a navy capable of protecting American commercial interests on the high seas, and the inability of America's elite to exercise power in world affairs.

3. Ratification of the Constitution was achieved through the political skills of the elite. The masses of people in America did not participate in the writing of the Constitution nor in its adoption by the states, and they probably would have opposed the Constitution had they the information and resources to do so.

4. The Founding Fathers shared a consensus that the fundamental role of government was the protection of liberty and property. They believed in a republican government by men of principle and property. They opposed an aristocracy or a governing nobility, but they also opposed mass democracy with direct participation by the people in decision making. They were fearful of mass movements that would seek to reduce inequalities of wealth, intelligence, talent, or virtue. "Dangerous leveling" was a serious violation of men's rights to property.

5. The structure of American government was designed to suppress "factious" issues, that is, threats to dominant economic elites. Republicanism, the division of power between state and national governments, and the complex system of checks and balances and divided power were all designed as protections against mass movements threatening liberty and property.

6. The text of the Constitution itself contains many direct and immediate benefits to America's governing elite. Although all Americans, both elite and mass, may have benefited by the adoption of the Constitution, the advantages and benefits in that document for America's elite provided the impelling motive for their activities on behalf of the new Constitution.

Evolution of American Elites

According to elite theory, the movement of non-elites into elite positions must be slow and continuous to maintain stability and avoid revolution. Furthermore, potential elite members must demonstrate their commitment to the basic elite consensus before being admitted to elite positions. Elite theory recognizes competition among elites, but contends that elites share a broad consensus about preserving the system essentially as it is. It views public policy changes as a response to elite redefinition of its own self-interest, rather than as a product of direct mass influence. Finally, elite theory views changes in public policy as incremental rather than revolutionary. All of these propositions can be supported with reference to America's political history:

1. America's elite membership evolved slowly with no serious break in the ideas or values of the American political and economic system. When the leadership of Hamilton and Adams — Federalists — was replaced by that of Jefferson, Monroe, and Madison — Republicans — the policies of American government changed very little, owing to the fundamental consensus among elite members.

2. As new sources of wealth were opened in an expanding economy, America's elite membership was opened to new groups and individuals who acquired wealth and property and who accepted the national consensus about private enterprise, limited government, and individualism. The West produced new elites, which were assimilated into America's governing circle. Public policies were modified, but not replaced. The Jacksonians wanted a more open elite system where men of new wealth could acquire influence, but they were no more in favor of "dangerous leveling" than the Founding Fathers.

3. The Civil War reduced the influence of the Southern planters in America's elite structure and paved the way for the rise of the new industrial capitalists. The Industrial Revolution produced a narrowly self-interested elite of industrial capitalists. Mass movements resulted — Populism and free silver — but they met with failure.

4. Although industrial elites were never ousted from power, they were prevailed upon to assume a more public-regarding attitude toward the welfare of the masses. Economic collapse undermined the faith of elites and non-elites and the rugged individualism of the nineteenth-century industrial elite. But even economic collapse did not bring revolution; it did not result in the emergence of new elites. Instead, the Great Depression, the victories of fascism in Germany and communism in the Soviet Union, and growing restlessness of the American masses combined to convince America's elites that a more public-regarding philosophy was essential to the maintenance of the American political system and their prominent place in it.

5. The new liberal establishment sought to preserve the existing social and economic order, not to overthrow it. Eventually, Franklin D. Roosevelt's philosophy of noblesse oblige — elite responsibility for the welfare of the masses — won widespread acceptance within America's established leadership. The change from isolationism to world-wide involvement of America's foreign policy was a product of this new redefinition of American elite responsibility.

6. Political conflict in America has centered on a narrow range of issues. Consensus rather than conflict has characterized America's elite history. Political rhetoric and campaign slogans should not obscure the fundamental consensus of America's elites. Whatever the popular political label has been — "Federalist," "Democratic,"

"Whig," "Republican," "Progressive," "Conservative," or "Liberal"—America's leadership has been essentially conservative.

7. America's elites have been deeply divided on the nature of American society only once. This elite cleavage produced the Civil War—the nation's bloodiest conflict. The Civil War was a conflict between Southern elites—dependent on a plantation economy, slave labor, and free trade—and Northern industrial commercial elites—who prospered under free labor and protective tariffs. But before, during, and after the Civil War, Northern and Southern elites continued to strive for compromise in recognition of shared consensus on behalf of liberty and property.

8. Policy changes, even those seemingly as revolutionary as the New Deal, did not cause any serious break in the ideals and values of the American system. Nor did they result from demands by "the people." Instead policy changes, including the New Deal, occurred when events threatened the system; governing elites—acting on the basis of enlightened self-interest—instituted reforms to preserve the system. Even the reforms and welfare policies of the New Deal were designed to strengthen the existing social and economic fabric of society with a minimum of dislocation for elites.

The Character of American Elites

Elite theory does not limit its definition of elites to those who participate in *governmental* decision making. On the contrary, an elite member is anyone who participates in decisions that allocate values for society. Power in America is organized into large institutions, private as well as public—corporations, banks and financial institutions, universities, law firms, churches, professional associations, and military and governmental bureaucracies. Several propositions were developed in our analysis of power and the institutional structure of America:

1. Great potential for power is lodged in the giant institutions and bureaucracies of American society. High positions—in industry, finance, government, education, and the military—and great wealth do not necessarily guarantee great power. Those who occupy high positions in the institutions of society may have potential power, yet be restrained in the actual exercise of it.

2. Power is being exercised when the institutional structure of society limits the scope of public decision making to issues that are relatively harmless to the elite. Institutions facilitate the achievement of some values and they obstruct the achievement of other values. For example, the structure of American corporations tends to maximize the values of profit and investment security in decision making.

3. Elites are recruited disproportionately from the upper socioeconomic classes. This is true of governmental, corporate, financial, and military elites.

4. There is considerable overlap in high elite positions. Top governmental elites generally have occupied key posts in private industry

and finance or have held influential positions in education, arts and science, and social, civil charitable associations.

5. Economic power is increasingly concentrated in the hands of a few men who occupy key posts in giant corporations. The concentration of economic power in America is a product of the growing concentration of corporate enterprise, a system of interlocking directorates, and a corporate ownership system in which control blocs of stock are owned by financial institutions rather than by individuals. In addition, both wealth and income are unequally distributed in America.

6. The economic system is inextricably intertwined with the political system. Often, no clear line of division exists between government, business, and military enterprise. References to the military-industrial complex suggest the interdependence of military affairs, political decision making, and corporate profits.

Elite-Mass Differences and Interactions

Elite theory suggests that elites are distinguished from the masses not only by their socioeconomic background but also by their attitudes and values. Elites give greater support to the principles and beliefs underlying the political system. Our analysis of elite and mass attitudes suggests the following propositions:

1. Elites give greater support to democratic values than masses. Elites are also more consistent than masses in applying general principles of democracy to specific individuals, groups, and events.

2. Extremist and intolerant movements in modern society are more likely to be based in lower classes than in middle and upper classes. The poor may be more liberal on economic issues, but when liberalism is defined in noneconomic terms — as support for civil liberties, for example — then the upper classes are more liberal and the lower classes more conservative. Masses demonstrate anti-democratic attitudes more often than elites. Mass movements exploit the alienation and hostility of lower classes by concentrating upon "scapegoats."

3. The masses are less committed to democratic "rules of the game" than elites and more likely to go outside these rules to engage in violence. Mass activism tends to be undemocratic, unstable, and frequently violent.

4. The survival of democracy depends upon the commitment of elites to democratic ideals rather than upon broad support for democracy by the masses.

5. Political apathy and nonparticipation among the masses contribute to the survival of democracy. Fortunately for democracy, the anti-democratic masses are generally more apathetic than elites. Only an unusual demagogue or counter-elite can arouse the masses from their apathy and create a threat to the established system.

6. Occasionally mass apathy is replaced by mass activism, which is generally extremist, intolerant, anti-democratic, and violence-

prone. Conditions which encourage mass activism include defeat or humiliation in war, economic dislocation, or perceived threats to personal safety.

7. Counter-elites appeal to mass sentiments and express hostility toward the established order and its values. Both "left" and "right" counter-elites are anti-democratic, extremist, impatient with due process, contemptuous of law and authority, and violence-prone. Counter-elites express racial prejudices, populism, equalitarianism, anti-intellectualism, and simplistic solutions to social problems.

8. Although "left" counter-elites are just as anti-democratic as "right" counter-elites, their appeal is limited to small numbers of alienated blacks, college students, and intellectuals. In contrast, "right" counter-elites have mobilized mass support among large numbers of farmers, workers, and middle-class Americans. George C. Wallace is a typical mass counter-elite, not only in his appeal to racial sentiments but in his appeal to other mass values.

9. Although elites are relatively more committed to democratic values than masses, elites may abandon these values in crisis periods. When war or revolution threatens the existing order, elites themselves may deviate from democratic values to maintain the system. Dissent is no longer tolerated—the mass media are censored, free speech curtailed, counter-elites jailed, police and security forces strengthened.

10. Elite-mass communication is very difficult. Most of the communication received by decision makers is from other elite members rather than the masses. The decision maker's perceptions of mass attitudes are likely to be affected by his own values; consequently he interprets public opinion to support his own position.

11. Although elites are relatively free of mass influence, this freedom varies with the issue. The masses are ignorant about most political issues and consequently cannot convey any message to decision makers about them. But on issues of race and civil rights mass attitudes are well-formed. Decision makers have a reasonably accurate perception of mass attitudes on civil rights and are more likely to vote their perception of mass attitudes than their own feelings on civil rights questions.

12. The masses believe that elected decision makers should behave as instructed delegates, but very few decision makers consider themselves delegates. Instead decision makers believe they are free agents who should follow the dictates of their own conscience.

Elections and Elite Accountability

Elite theory contends that the masses do not participate in policy making, and that the elites who do are subject to little direct influence from apathetic masses. But many scholars who acknowledge that even "democratic" societies are governed by elites seek to reaffirm democratic values by contending that voters can influence elite behavior by choosing between competing elites in elections. In other words, elitism is sometimes challenged by modern pluralists on the grounds that elections give the masses a voice in policy making by holding governing elites accountable to the people.

Our analysis suggests that elections are imperfect instruments of accountability. But even if the people can hold *governmental* elites accountable through elections, how can corporation elites, financial elites, union leaders, and other private leadership be held accountable? The accountability argument usually dodges the problem of *private* decision making and focuses exclusive attention on *public* decision making by elected elites. But certainly men's lives are vitally affected by the decisions of private institutions and organizations. So the first problem with the accountability thesis is that, at best, it applies only to elected governmental elites. However, our analysis of elections also suggests that it is difficult for the voters to hold even *governmental* elites accountable.

1. Elections are primarily a symbolic exercise that helps tie the masses to the established order. Elections offer the masses an opportunity to participate in the political system, but electoral participation does not enable them to determine public policy.

2. Competing candidates in elections do not usually offer clear policy alternatives; hence it is seldom possible for the voter to affect policy by selecting a particular candidate for public office.

3. Voters are not well-informed about the policy stands of candidates, and relatively few voters are concerned with policy questions. The masses cast their votes in elections on the basis of traditional party ties, personality of the candidates, group affiliations, and a host of other factors having little relation to public policy.

4. Mass opinion on public policy is inconsistent and unstable. Relatively few voters (generally well-educated upper-class voters from whom elites are drawn) hold reasonably consistent political ideologies. Mass opinion is unguided by principle, unstable, and subject to change.

5. Available evidence suggests that elites influence the opinions of masses more than masses influence the opinion of elites. Mass publics respond to political symbols manipulated by elites, not to facts or political principles.

6. The only reasonably stable aspect of mass politics is party identification. But party identification in the mass electorate is unaccompanied by any wide policy gaps between Democrats and Republicans. Democratic and Republican voters hold fairly similar opinions on most issues.

7. It is difficult to use election results to ascertain majority preferences on policy questions because (a) campaigns generally stress the presentation of political ideologies rather than the *content* of the ideologies; (b) victory for a party or a candidate does not

necessarily mean that the voters support any particular policy position of the candidate; (c) voters frequently misinterpret the policy preferences of a candidate; (d) often a candidate's voters include not only advocates of his position, but some who oppose his position and some who vote for him for other reasons; (e) a candidate may take positions on many different issues, so he cannot know which of the policy positions he has taken resulted in his election; (f) for voters to influence policy through elections, winning candidates would be bound to follow their campaign pledges.

8. Elections are means for selecting personnel, not policy. Voters choose on the basis of a candidate's personal style, filtered through partisan commitment. A candidate's election does not imply a policy choice by the electorate.

9. At best, elections provide the masses with an opportunity to express themselves favorably or unfavorably about the conduct of past administrations, but not to direct the course of future events. A vote against the party or candidate in power, however, does not identify the particular policy being censured. And there is no guarantee that an ousted official's replacement will pursue any specific policy alternatives.

10. Few individuals participate in any political activity other than voting. One third of the adult population fails to vote even in presidential elections.

Party Competition Elitism asserts that elites share a consensus about the fundamental values of the political system. This elite consensus does not mean that elite members never disagree or never compete with each other for preeminence. But elitism implies that competition centers on a narrow range of issues and that elites agree on more matters than they disagree. The single elite model suggests that parties agree about the direction of public policy and disagree only on minor details. Our analysis of the American party system suggests the following propositions:

1. American parties share consensus both on basic democratic values and on major directions of American policy. They believe in the sanctity of private property, the free enterprise economy, individual liberty, and limited government. Moreover both parties have supported the same general domestic and foreign policy—including social security, a graduated income tax, counter-cyclical fiscal and monetary policies, anti-communism, the Cold War, and the Korean and Vietnamese wars.

2. The American parties do not present clear ideological alternatives to the American voter. Both American parties are overwhelmingly middle class in organization, values, and goals. Deviation from the shared consensus by either party ("a choice not an echo") is more likely to lose than attract voters.

3. Both parties draw support from all social groups in America, but the Democrats draw disproportionately from labor, workers,

Jews, Catholics, and Negroes, and the Republicans draw disproportionate support from rural, small town, and suburban Protestants, businessmen, and professionals.

4. Democratic and Republican party leaders differ over public policy more than Democratic or Republican mass followers. The consensus about welfare economics extends to Democratic leaders, Democratic followers, and Republican followers; only the Republican leadership is outside this consensus, with a more laissez-faire position. However, all party differences observed fall well within the range of elite consensus on the values of individualism, capitalism, and limited government.

5. American parties are dominated by small groups of activists who formulate party objectives and select candidates for public office. The masses play a passive role in party affairs. They are not really "members" of the party; they are "consumers."

6. Among party activists, power is generally diffused, not centralized. Power within parties is not in the hands of a single elite, but rather a "stratarchy" of elites. The exceptions to this rule are the few large city machines, particularly in the Democratic party.

7. Party activists differ from the masses, because they have the time and financial resources to be able to "afford" politics, the information and knowledge to understand it, and the organization and public relations skills to be successful in it.

8. The choice of party nominees is a choice of party activists, not a choice of the masses of party members.

9. With neither party proposing a serious modification of the status quo, there is a low sense of electoral crisis. Thus, the stakes in electoral outcomes in any American election are not very great. This contributes to the relative ease with which public offices are transferred between the "in" party and the "out" party.

10. The American party system strengthens the national consensus. Serious political issues strain the American party system; the system appears unable to handle any real issues. Both the black movement of the 1960s and the lower-class (Wallacite) white reaction took place outside the framework of the Democratic and Republican party system. In 1968 a majority of Americans did not vote for either the Republican or Democratic candidates for president.

The Interest Group System

Pluralism asserts that organized interest groups provide an effective means of participation in the political system for the individual. It contends that the individual can make his voice heard through membership in the organized groups that reflect his views on public affairs. Pluralists further contend that competition among organized interests provides a balance of power to protect the interests of the individual. Interest groups divide power among themselves and hence protect the individual from rule by a single oppressive elite.

Earlier we pointed out that pluralism diverges from classical democratic theory. Even if the plural elite model accurately portrays the reality of American politics, it does not guarantee the implementation of democratic values. Our analysis of interest groups produced the following propositions:

1. Interest group membership is drawn disproportionately from middle and upper class segments of the population. The pressure group system is not representative of the entire community.
2. Leadership of interest groups is recruited from the middle and upper class population.
3. Business organizations predominate among organized interest groups.
4. Organizations tend to become conservative as they acquire a stake in the existing social order. Therefore, pressures for substantial social change must generally come from forces outside the structure of organized interest groups.
5. Generally mass membership groups achieve only symbolic success and smaller more cohesive groups are able to achieve more tangible results.
6. There is a great deal of inequality among organized interest groups. Business and producer groups with narrow membership but cohesive organization are able to achieve their tangible goals at the expense of broad, unorganized groups seeking less tangible goals.
7. Organized interest groups are governed by small elites whose values do not necessarily reflect the values of most members.
8. Business groups and associations are the most highly organized and active lobbyists in Washington and in the state capitals.

Governmental Decision Making

Elite theory does not focus exclusively on governmental decision making. Decisions made by non-governmental elites may affect the lives of Americans more profoundly than any decision made by government officials. Often government officials merely ratify and give legitimacy to decisions made by non-governmental elites. But the governmental elites are distinguished from non-governmental elites because they may *legitimately* enforce their decisions with physical compulsion. And, because their decisions extend to the whole of society, they can resolve conflicts between segments of society.

The Founding Fathers were concerned with the *potential* for power in the hands of governmental elites. They were particularly concerned that a mass movement, or "majority faction," might gain access to the legitimate use of force and threaten established elites. To reduce this risk, they designed a complex system of separation of powers and checks and balances. If the checks and balances system seems to handcuff government, make it easy for established groups to oppose change, and make it difficult for elites to exercise authority over private interests, then the system is working as intended. Our analysis of the authoritative elites in America—president, executives, Congress, and courts—produced many propositions consistent with elite theory:

1. Governmental decision making involves combined bargaining and compromise among the dominant interests in American society. Governmental elites in America do not command; they seek accommodation with non-governmental elites.

2. Accommodation and compromise is the prevailing style of interaction in American politics. This style is made possible by the underlying consensus among elites. If elite differences were fundamental, it would be impossible to find accommodations or compromises.

3. A system of responsible, competitive, and ideological parties might enable the masses to play a more important role in policy making than the existing system of elite interaction. But majority rule might threaten to overrun important interests in America—economic, social, sectional, and religious interests. Majority rule might also create cleavages that would destroy the nation. Brokerage politics is the price of unity. The Founding Fathers preferred decision making by elite accommodation to the formation of popular majorities.

4. While elites occasionally conflict with each other, the more common form of elite interaction is mutual accommodation—"you scratch my back and I'll scratch yours."

5. Elites seldom conflict over the basic directions of American public policy. Instead conflict, when it occurs, centers upon marginal changes in public policy. In "incrementalism," governmental elites limit their consideration of policy alternatives to those that differ only slightly from the pattern of existing policy. Incrementalism accurately portrays the style of governmental decision making.

6. The president is the first among equals of America's elites. His real power depends not on his formal authority but on his abilities of persuasion.

7. The masses have an attachment to the president that is unlike their attachment to any other official or symbol of government. More than any other official, the president is able to sway mass opinion. Yet the president must still function within the established elite system. The choices available to him are limited to alternatives for which he can mobilize elite support. Despite the president's access to mass opinion, he can be effectively checked by other public and private elites.

8. Important presidential decisions are usually made in consultation with key elite members inside and outside of government. These decisions reflect elite consensus, and, moreover, are incremental—they involve marginal shifts in public policy rather than radical changes in national purposes or objectives.

9. Congress tends to represent locally organized elites, who inject a strong parochial influence in national decision making. Congressmen are responsible to national interests that have a strong base of support in their home constituencies.

10. A congressman's relevant political constituency is not the general population of his district, but its local elite. Less than half the general population of a congressman's district knows his name; fewer still have any idea of how he voted on any major issue. Only a tiny fraction ever express their views on a public issue to their congressman.

11. With the possible exception of civil rights questions, most congressmen are free from the influence of popular preferences in their legislative voting. However, a congressman's voting record generally reflects the socioeconomic makeup of his home district. Congressmen are products of the social system in their constituency; they share its dominant goals and values.

12. Congress seldom initiates changes in public policy. Instead it responds to policy proposals initiated by the president, executive and military elites, and interested non-governmental elites. The congressional role in national decision making is usually a deliberative one, in which Congress responds to policies initiated by others.

13. Congressional committees are important to communication between governmental and non-governmental elites. "Policy clusters," consisting of alliances of leaders from executive agencies, congressional committees, and private business and industry, tend to develop in Washington. Committee chairmen are key members of these policy clusters, because of their control over legislation in Congress.

14. The elaborate rules and procedures of Congress delay and obstruct proposed changes in the status quo. The rules and procedures of Congress strengthen its conservative role in policy making. It is a difficult process for a bill to become a law; congressional procedures offer many opportunities to defeat the legislation and many obstacles to the passage of legislation.

15. An elite system within Congress places effective control over legislation in the hands of a relatively few members. Most of these congressional "establishment" members are conservative congressmen from both parties who have acquired great seniority and therefore control key committee chairmanships.

16. Most bills that are not killed before the floor vote are passed unanimously. The greatest portion of the national budget is passed without debate. What conflict exists in Congress tends to follow party lines more often than any other factional division. Conflict centers on the implementation of domestic and foreign policy; seldom is there any conflict over the major directions of policy.

17. Some of the nation's most important policy decisions have been made by federal courts rather than by the president or Congress. Courts are an integral component of America's elite system. Sooner or later most important policy questions end up in courts.

18. Federal court review of national and state laws is an additional safeguard against majority attacks on liberty and property. Judges are deliberately insulated against the will of popular majorities.
19. The Supreme Court is best understood as an elitist institution rather than as a "conservative" or "liberal" institution in American government. When the dominant elite philosophy was rugged individualism, the court reflected this fact, just as today it reflects the dominant liberal public-regarding philosophy.
20. The social backgrounds of judges are not unlike other governmental elites in reflecting close ties with the upper social strata of society.

The Nature of Sub-elites

The existence of political sub-elites within the larger American political system permits some decentralization of decision making. Decentralization, or decision making by sub-elites, reduces potential strain on the consensus of national elites. Each sub-elite is allowed to set its own policies in its own state and community, without battling over a single national policy to be applied uniformly throughout the land. Let us summarize the propositions that emerge from our consideration of American federalism and our comparative analysis of elites in states and communities.

1. Debate over state versus national power reflects the power of various interests at the state and national level. Currently, the liberal public-regarding elites dominant at the national level generally assert the supremacy of the national government. In contrast parochial, conservative, rural interests dominant in some states and communities but with less power at the national level, provide the backbone of support for "states rights."
2. Although national elites now exercise considerable power in states and communities, particularly through federal "grant-in-aid" programs, this growth of national power has not necessarily reduced the power of state and local governments. State and local government activities are not declining, but growing and expanding.
3. Differences in the economic development levels in the states are reflected in differing levels of mass political participation and party competition. Voter participation and party competition are higher in states with a relatively wealthy, well-educated urban population. Low voter participation and one-partyism characterize rural, low income states with poorly educated populations and a history of discrimination and segregation against blacks.
4. Economic elites in states and communities are generally ranked as the "most powerful groups" by legislators.
5. States with the most cohesive elite system are likely to be one-party states, not competitive two-party states; states in which political parties show little cohesion and unity; and states that

are poor, rural, and agricultural. Wealthy urban, industrial states have more elite groups, but it is difficult for a single elite to dominate the political scene.

6. Scholars have described American communities in terms reflecting both single elite and plural elite models. Yet even the plural elite studies conclude that "the key political, economic, and social decisions" are made by "tiny minorities." They also find that these "tiny minorities" are recruited from the upper and middle class community. Few citizens participate in community decisions that affect their lives.

7. There is conflicting evidence about the extent of competition among community elites, the extent of elite concentration, the fluidity of elites, the ease of access to elite membership, the persistence of elite structures over time, the relative power of economic elites, and the degree of mass influence. Some scholars have reported a polycentric structure of power with different elite groups active in different issue areas and a great deal of competition, bargaining, and sharing of power among elites.

8. Businessmen are not equally powerful in all cities. But business support generally bestows great prestige on a policy proposal, lends a conservative image to proposals for change, and tends to insure financial support.

9. Elite structures in communities are related to the community's size, economic function, and social composition. Small communities with a homogeneous population, a single dominant industry, a weak party structure, and few competing organizations, are more likely to be governed by a single cohesive elite. Larger communities with social and economic diversity, a competitive party system, and well-organized competing interest groups are more likely to have plural elite systems.

10. Monolithic power structures are associated with a lack of political confidence among residents and with a widespread belief that political activity is useless. A plural elite system is associated with a sense of political effectiveness among citizens and with adherence to the rules of the game by leaders.

Mass Activism— The Civil Rights Movement

How do American elites cope with mass activism? Generally, established elites can depend upon mass apathy. But occasionally mass activism replaces apathy, and this activism is extremist, unstable, and unpredictable. America has experienced a long history of mass movements led by a wide variety of counter-elites from Shays' Rebellion of the eighteenth century to recent black militancy. But the place of the Negro in American society has been the central domestic issue of American politics. We chose to examine the movement for black equality within the context of elite theory to observe political activism among subservient people and the reaction of dominant elites to this activism. In many ways, the recent political activism among blacks is typical of mass movements—it is unstable and unpredictable, it expresses resentment toward the established order, it is made up of people who seldom participate in democratic politics and do not always understand the "rules of the game," it is highly flammable and can produce violence, it has produced a variety of counter-elites, and it has threatened the established order. However, we must be cautious in developing generalizations about mass movements based upon black experience in America. For blacks must contend not only with white *elites,* but also with white *masses.* Contrary to the general assumption of elite theory, the white masses *do* have opinions about civil rights and race relations, and elite behavior is more circumscribed by mass opinion than is normally the case. Hence, the relationship between white elites and black masses is complicated by the role of the white masses. Yet elitism offers many insights into the nature of the black struggle in America and the way in which this nation has responded to black demands.

1. Prevailing myths and symbols of the American nation are drawn from democratic theory; these include a recognition of the rights of minorities, a commitment to the value of individual dignity, and a commitment to the value of equal opportunity for all men. Although committed to these abstract ideals, white elites have consistently failed over the course of American history to implement these ideals in public policy.

2. Centuries of slavery and segregation have left black masses poorly educated, unskilled, poorly housed, poverty-stricken, frequently unemployed, segregated, and subject to a variety of social pathologies. White elites generally expect individual blacks to solve these problems individually. Black counter-elites charge that white elites created these problems and are obliged to resolve these problems with black masses as a group.

3. White elites are willing to accept individual blacks on a near-equal basis only if these blacks accept the prevailing consensus and exhibit white middle-class values. White elites are less willing to accept black masses who have not assimilated prevailing middle-class values.

4. Public-regarding liberal elites are prepared to eliminate legal barriers to provide equality of opportunity under the law for individual blacks, but they are not prepared to take massive action to eliminate absolute inequalities ("leveling"), which would bring black masses up to average white standards of living.

5. Historically white elites have been willing to sacrifice the interests of Negroes to avoid cleavage among themselves that would impair national consensus and unity. The propensity to sacrifice black interests for white unity was evidenced in the years before the Civil War, in the Compromise of 1877, throughout the long period of segregation, and in the moderate, go-slow approach of recent civil rights legislation.

6. The first governmental institution to act and achieve equality of opportunity for Negroes in America in the twentieth century was the Supreme Court. This institution was structurally the farthest removed from the influence of white masses, and was the first to apply liberal public-regarding policies to the blacks. Elected elites who are more accessible to white masses were slower to act on Negro rights than appointed elites.

7. Elected white elites did not respond to black requests until faced with a prolonged campaign of nonviolent civil disobedience, public demonstrations, and creative disorder and crises. Generally elites have responded by making the most minimal changes in the system consistent with maintaining stability. Often these changes are only symbolic. No revolutionary changes have been contemplated by elites even when they are faced with massive civil disorder.

8. The elimination of legal discrimination and the guarantee of equality of opportunity has been achieved largely through the efforts of Negro middle-class groups who share a dominant elite consensus and who appeal to the conscience of white elites to extend that consensus to include blacks.

9. The successes of black elites in achieving symbolic goals has helped to activate black masses. Once activated, these masses have turned to goals that went beyond accepted elite consensus — for example, demands for *absolute* equality have replaced demands for equality of opportunity. New mass-oriented black counter-elites have emerged to contend with established middle-class black elites. Middle-class black elites have relatively little influence with masses in the ghettos. Mass counter-elites have less respect for the "rules of the game" than either white elites or established middle-class black leaders.

10. Liberal public-regarding white elites have wanted to extend equality of opportunity to individual blacks, but other goals had higher priority — notably the war in Vietnam, the Cold War in Europe, and the maintenance of a large defense establishment. Consequently, many of the appeals from established middle-class black leaders are set aside, and the demands of black masses ignored.

11. Mass urban violence in the ghettos has confounded both white elites and the established Negro leadership. Black leaders reprimanded black masses, and the cleavage between black leaders and black masses became apparent. Mass-oriented black counter-elites have developed new slogans and tactics to exploit mass activism and violence.

12. Urban violence is a form of political activity on the part of black masses in the ghetto. The rioters (counter-elites) are representative of the black masses in socioeconomic composition but they express greater racial hostility and a higher level of political information and awareness than the masses.

13. White masses have reacted with hostility toward mass violence by blacks even though white masses were not the objects of this violence. Black violence is directed against symbols of white authority, but white masses accept that same authority as legitimate.

14. Established liberal elites who had supported the elimination of legal discrimination and efforts to achieve equality of opportunity reacted negatively when black masses violated the accepted "rules of the game" and demanded absolute equality. White elites, both "liberal" and "conservative," have taken steps to insure "law and order." They have condemned rioters as "criminals" and "riff-raff," passed a law making it a federal crime to cross state lines to stir the masses to riot, and increased police security forces and improved their tactics and training in quelling mass disturbances.

15. The traditional apathy of the black masses has been replaced with an activism that is unstable and promises violence. This change from apathy to activism has occurred as a result of rising expectations of black masses, brought about by symbolic gains in the civil rights movement. The civil rights movement, although well within the established elite consensus in goals and techniques, has activated black masses. It has increased their aspiration levels and inspired impatience and hostility toward the "white establishment." The civil rights movement had to awaken Negroes to their plight in American society to make progress in eliminating discrimination; but the price of this awakening has been a major increase in the aspiration levels of the masses and a subsequent frustration and bitterness when these new aspirations went unfulfilled.

The Uncertain Future of American Democracy The future of American democracy depends on the wisdom, responsibility, and resourcefulness of the nation's elite. Although it is customary in a book on American government to conclude that the nation's future depends on an enlightened citizenry, this reflects the *symbols,* rather than the *realities* of American politics. It is the irony of democracy that the responsibility for the survival of liberal democratic values depends upon elites, not masses.

Threats to the liberal democratic order may originate from either elites or masses. Today the threat of mass counter-elites is clearly in evidence—the Wallace movement, the right-wing extremists, the black militants, the student radicals. Democratic systems are particularly vulnerable to anti-democratic mass movements, since democracies invite mass participation. But it is also possible that democracy will collapse as a result of elite overreaction to the threats of these counter-elites.

Democracy cannot be taken for granted. America has seen many individuals and groups engage in political activity outside the rules and procedures of the democratic process. Moreover, individuals and groups have pursued values at variance with the liberal values of the Founding Fathers. Finally, we have observed that both the procedures of the democratic process and the values of liberal society are not widely shared by the masses of Americans and are occasionally abandoned by America's elites. We have little cause for complacency about the survival of democracy.

Postscript, Part 1
What to Do about the Establishment:
Prescription for Elites

Thomas R. Dye

Mass governance is neither feasible nor desirable. Widespread popular participation in national political decisions is not only impossible to achieve in a modern industrial society, it is incompatible with the liberal values of individual dignity, personal liberty, and social justice. Efforts to encourage mass participation in American politics are completely misdirected. To believe that making American government more accessible to mass influence will make it any more humane is to go directly against the historical and social science evidence. It is the irony of democracy that masses, not elites, pose the greatest threat to the survival of democratic values. More then anything else, America needs an enlightened elite capable of acting decisively to preserve individual freedom, human dignity, and the values of life, liberty, and property. Our efforts must be directed toward insuring that the established order is humane, decent, tolerant, and benign.

Elitism is a necessary characteristic of *all* societies. The elitism we have ascribed to American society is not a unique corruption of democratic ideas attributable to capitalism, war, the "military-industrial complex," or any other events or people in this nation. There is no "solution" to elitism, for it is not *the* problem in a democracy. There have been many mass movements, both "left" and "right" in their political ideology, which have *promised* to bring power to the people. Indeed, the world has witnessed many "successful" mass movements which have overthrown social and political systems, often at great cost to human life, promising to empower the masses. But invariably they have created *new* elite systems which are at least as "evil," and certainly no more democratic, than the older systems which they replaced. Revolutions come and go—but the masses remain powerless. The question, then, is not how to combat elitism or empower the masses or achieve revolution, but rather how to *build* an orderly, humane, and just society.

Let us summarize some of the reasons why mass democracy is neither feasible nor desirable. First of all, in a large society the influence of a single individual on societal decisions, even assuming political equality, is so tiny as to render participation in mass democracy fruitless. As the society grows larger, the individual shrinks—in influence, power, liberty, and the capacity for shaping the decisions which affect his life. As Rousseau observed: "Thus, the subject remaining always one, the relation of the sovereign increases in proportion to the number of citizens. From which it follows that the more the state grows, the more liberty diminishes." The chance that a particular individual in a society of 200 million people can affect the outcome of an election, a referendum, or other societal decision is infinitesimal. An individual who has only one two-hundred-millionth of a say in the outcome of issues cannot be personally effective. This would be true even under conditions of perfect equality.

Inequalities among men are inevitable, and these inequalities produce differences in political power. Men are not born with the same abilities, nor can they acquire them by education. Modern democrats who recognize that inequality in *wealth* is a serious obstacle to political equality propose to eliminate such inequality by taking from the rich and giving to the poor, to achieve a "leveling" which they believe is essential to democracy. But despite their mass appeal, these schemes consistently run astray—in part because of the ingenuity of the men who have acquired wealth in defeating them. But *even if* inequalities of *wealth* were eliminated, differences among men in intelligence, organizational skills, leadership abilities, knowledge and information, drive and ambition, and interest and activity would remain. Such inequalities are sufficient to assure oligarchy, even if wealth were uniform. Moreover, de Tocqueville's warning about equality deserves consideration:

I believe that it is easier to establish an absolute and despotic government among a people in which the conditions of society are equal than among any other; and I think that if such a government were once established among such a people, it not only would oppress men, but would eventually strip each of them of several of the highest qualities of humanity.[1]

Moreover, it is impossible for a mass to govern. The mass must delegate governing responsibilities to representatives, and by so doing they create a governing minority who will be distinguished from the masses in behavior, role, and status. This is true no matter what system of accountability is established. Delegation of authority creates a governing elite. Yet delegation is essential, if for no other reason than that people are unwilling to spend all of their time in decision-making activity—attending meetings, acquiring information, debating, and so on. Organization inevitably means oligarchy. Mosca demonstrated that even European socialist parties espousing democracy were in fact oligarchies:

When his work is finished, the proletarian can think only of rest, and of getting to bed in good time. His place is taken at meetings by the bourgeois, by those

---

[1] Alexis de Tocqueville, *Democracy in America*, Vol. 2 (New York: Vintage Books, 1955), p. 336.

who come to sell newspapers and picture postcards, by clerks, by young intellectuals who have not yet got a position in their own circle, people who are glad to hear themselves spoken of as authentic proletarians and to be glorified as the class of the future.[2]

The authoritarianism of "revolutionary" parties today confirms Mosca's earlier observations. Participatory democracy is a romantic fiction.

The masses are incompetent in the tasks of government. They have neither the time, intelligence, information, skills, nor knowledge to direct the course of a nation. Robert Dahl writes:

It is precisely because human lives *are* important and because there *are* differences in competence that we want competent authorities to be in charge of the plane, the ship, the operating room. When your own life is at stake, you want the authority of the best pilot, the best physician, the best judge. If your plane or ship is hit by a hurricane you will not, I imagine, insist that the captain consult with you and the other passengers on every decision he makes.[3]

Governing a nation is a task which is too important, too vital, too complex, and too difficult to be left to the masses. While of course there is no guarantee that the elites will not make mistakes, there is even less reason to believe that the masses could avoid disaster.

The masses are anti-democratic and therefore cannot be relied upon to govern democratically. Despite a superficial commitment to the symbols of democracy, the people are not attached to the ideals of individual liberty, toleration of diversity, freedoms of expression and of dissent, or equality of opportunity. On the contrary, these are more likely to be the values of elites. Masses are authoritarian, intolerant, anti-intellectual, nativistic, alienated, hateful, and violent. Mass politics is extremist, unstable, and unpredictable. The masses are not committed to democratic "rules of the game"; when they are politically activated, they frequently go outside these rules to engage in violence. Moreover, mass politics frequently reflects the alienation and hostility of the masses by concentrating upon "scapegoats." The scapegoats can be any minority who are somehow differentiated from the majority of the mass—Jews, Negroes, Catholics, immigrants, students, intellectuals, etc.

The masses are fatally vulnerable to tyranny. Extremist movements—reflecting authoritarianism, alienation, hostility, and prejudice—are more likely to be based in masses than elites. Hannah Arendt writes: "A whole literature on mass behavior and mass psychology demonstrated and popularized the wisdom, so familiar to the ancients, of the affinity between democracy and dictatorship, between mob rule and tyranny."[4] The masses, feeling in themselves the power of the

---

[2] Gaetano Mosca, *The Ruling Class* (New York: McGraw-Hill, 1939), p. 332.

[3] Robert Dahl, *After the Revolution* (New Haven: Yale University Press, 1970), p. 121.

[4] Hannah Arendt, *The Origins of Totalitarianism* (New York: Harcourt Brace Jovanovich, 1951), pp. 309–310.

majority, cannot be trusted to restrain themselves in dealing with dissenting minorities. Tolerance of diversity is a quality acquired only through years of socialization. The authoritarianism of the masses is unavoidable, given their authoritarian childhood experiences and family relationships, their limited education and restricted cultural opportunities, their monotonous job experiences, and their orientation toward immediate gratification. Efforts to re-educate or resocialize the masses are futile. Two hundred years ago Jefferson proposed universal free public education as a prescription for mass ignorance, incompetence, and alienation. Today the masses in America average 12 years of free public education, but, if anything, they appear less capable of governing in a wise and humane fashion than the masses of Jefferson's time.

The dilemma of American politics today is not really much different from that faced by the Founding Fathers in 1787 — how to protect in-individuals in a democratic system where majorities rule from the ex-cesses and injustices of *majorities*. James Madison warned that protec-tion against *majority* oppression "is the real object to which our in-quiries are directed." So it must be today. The question is not how to control the elites, but how to restrain the masses. The threat to demo-cratic values is not from ruling minorities, but from unrestrained majorities.

Clearly mass threats to democratic values cannot be restrained by an exclusive reliance on repression. Restrictions on mass political activity — the forcible break-up of revolutionary parties, restrictions on the public appearances of demagogues, the suppression of literature expressing hatred or advocating revolution or violence, the equipping and training of additional security forces, the jailing of violence-prone radicals and their co-conspirators, and so on — will not in itself ensure mass quiescence. More important, repression in a free society is a contradiction. We cannot logically curtail liberty in order to preserve a free society — even the liberty of a demagogue. James Madison con-sidered and rejected repression as a means of controlling mass move-ments, and pointed out the inconsistency of repression in a free society:

Liberty is to faction [mass movements] what air is to fire, an aliment without which it instantly expires. But it could not be less folly to abolish liberty, which is essential to political life, because it nourishes faction, than it would be to wish the annihilation of air, which is essential to animal life, because it imparts to fire its destructive agency.[5]

In short, repression is not really a serious instrument for an elite com-mitted to the values of individual dignity, personal freedom, and toler-ance of diversity.

[5] James Madison, Alexander Hamilton, John Jay, *The Federalist*, No. 10.

To strengthen the American elite system and develop its capacity to act decisively to preserve freedom, human dignity, and the values of life, liberty, and property, America's leadership *should:*

1. *Preserve fundamental constitutional principles designed to modify mass influence in government.* The Founding Fathers devised a series of constitutional arrangements to restrain majorities and protect democratic values. These include Republicanism — decision-making by representatives chosen by the people rather than decision-making by the people themselves; federalism — the division of powers between the national and state governments; separation of powers — the fragmentation of government authority among different national bodies chosen by separate constituencies for different terms; checks and balances — an elaborate system of overlapping powers and responsibilities among national governmental bodies; and judicial review — an appointed court with lifelong members as the final defender of democratic values against the encroachments of popularly elected officials. These arrangements, which make it difficult for majority preferences to become public policy, must be strengthened — not modified, "reformed," or weakened — if we are to avoid the evils of "an unjust and interested majority" which will "outnumber and oppress the rest."

2. *Avoid crises which directly threaten mass security and well-being.* A steady level of either poverty or affluence favors the stability of the social and political system; but marked changes in economic conditions make the masses insecure and vulnerable to the appeals of counter-elites. The actual level of mass well-being is less important than the level of mass anxiety and insecurity. Marked discontinuities in economic conditions, or even the threat of these, must be avoided. Another source of anxiety and insecurity among the masses is the perceived level of personal safety. Elites must provide for mass safety from acts of violence through effective police, court, and penal systems. Otherwise, counter-elites promising "law and order" will move the masses to override traditional democratic values in their search for personal safety. Finally, it is essential that elites avoid humiliation and defeat in war. War itself may strengthen the established elite system and mobilize the masses on behalf of national goals; nothing inspires patriotism in the masses more than decisive military victory. But prolonged and fruitless military efforts, and defeat and national humiliation, undermine the legitimacy of the government. The revelation of impotency or incompetency in government, the loss of men, territory, and resources, all undermine the confidence of the masses in the established order.

3. *Maintain elite legitimacy and authority.* Elites can maintain their legitimacy with the masses by (a) producing reasonably satisfying governmental outputs, and (b) inspiring mass attachments to the system and its values. As indicated earlier, reasonably satisfying governmental outputs must include economic security, personal safety, and either peace or victory in war. Mass attachments to the system and

its values, developed in a long process of political socialization which begins in childhood and extends through the entire adult life, must become a fully recognized responsibility of all elites. Competition among established elites must be responsible — that is, it must take place within established procedures and values. Established elites must avoid appeals to mass sentiments (demagoguery), including attacks on the integrity of the system and its leadership, appeals based on anti-intellectualism and social prejudice, attempts to inspire mass fears or hatreds, and so on. Public education must be made an effective means to political socialization: It must be recognized that the schools inculcate the values of the political system and this inculcation must be deliberate, considered, and effective. More importantly, it must be recognized that the mass media, particularly television, are major influences on mass attitudes and behavior. Children spend more hours in front of television sets than in the classroom, and adults who never read the front pages of newspapers regularly watch network newscasts. Television reaches the masses as has no other instrument of communication in history. Hence elites must insure that the mass media function responsibly on behalf of democratic values, and resist the temptation to program to the values of mass audiences. Finally it is essential that elites be willing to use force effectively against extremist opposition. It is true that moderate democratic regimes frequently find it difficult to do so. But it is essential that the government renounce bargains, compromises, or accommodations with revolutionary elements acting outside of the established rules of the game. Debate and dissent must be tolerated; but disruption and violence must be swiftly and effectively halted.

4. *Encourage the development of community and group identifications among the masses and refocus mass attention on individual, group, and community problems.* The masses are most vulnerable to extremist political movements when family, group, and community affiliations are weakened or severed and when their lives seem to them to be without purpose or responsibility. Lacking a sense of purpose or responsibility and a sense of group or community identification, the individual in the mass becomes isolated, atomized, and alienated. In contrast, when individuals are involved in their family, their profession, their hobbies, their friends and enemies, their church, trade union, or other social groups, their ward or township or county, they can develop a sense of purpose, responsibility, and personal effectiveness. Moreover, if the masses are involved in family, job, church, social group, hobby, and so on, they are unavailable for mass political activity.

Elites can act directly to strengthen community life by returning authority and responsibility to local governments. The masses look upon their local governments as more manageable, more accessible, and more responsive to individual desires than the national government, and consequently feel less alienated and ineffective in relation to them.

And it is true that the sub-elites who govern the nation's communities do tend to reflect local environmental conditions in their decision-making. Returning power to local governments would enable a larger number of sub-elites to exercise some authority and responsibility. Mass political activity could be re focused from the national level to the local level. Americans feel much more capable of understanding and affecting local issues than they do national issues. Of course, the risk is that some sub-elites will not reflect in their local decision-making all of the democratic values of the national elite. One can envision, for example, some Southern communities resuming discrimination against blacks in public education if all national controls were removed from public education. But it is not impossible to devise safeguards against policies by sub-elites which are detrimental to national values. And even if national values were not applied uniformly throughout the land, this would not be too high a price to pay to divert mass attention from national to local affairs.

5. *Insure the openness of the elite system for upwardly mobile segments of the masses.* It is essential that individuals in the masses *feel* that they have the opportunity to rise to positions in the elite. The masses can accept a great deal of inequality in society if they believe they have the opportunity themselves to rise to the top. Even individuals who have come to realize that their upward mobility is at an end can accept inequality if they believe they once had the opportunity to rise within the system and they can rationalize the reasons why they did not do so. On the other hand, a caste system which withholds any opportunity for, or erects artificial (for example, racial) barriers to, individual advancement among the masses cannot inspire mass support. Moreover, openness in the elite system siphons off potentially revolutionary leadership from the lower classes, and the elite system itself is strengthened when talented and ambitious individuals from the masses are permitted to enter governing circles. Of course, only those individuals from the masses who have demonstrated their commitment to the elite system and its political and economic values can be admitted into the ruling class. But it is essential that there be regular "circulation of elites."

6. *Avoid raising the expectation levels of the masses, and engender bitterness and frustration when expectations go unfulfilled.* The disparity between mass expectations and actual rewards, not the absolute level of mass deprivation, is the key factor in revolutionary movements; the masses do not revolt until they *perceive* the possibility of actually bettering their lot in life. When elites hold out the hope that conditions can become significantly better, or that radical change is possible, or that social evils can be eradicated quickly, they raise the expectation levels of masses, inviting extremist political activity when expectations are not met. Elites must insure that the gulf between mass expectations and mass perceptions of actual conditions does not grow too great. This means that elites must act and speak responsibly

about what the masses can reasonably expect within the framework of the existing system. Aaron Wildavsky brilliantly summarizes what elites should *not* do:

A recipe for violence: Promise a lot; deliver a little. Lead people to believe they will be much better off, but let there be no dramatic improvement. Try a variety of small programs, each interesting but marginal in impact and severely under-financed. Avoid any attempted solution remotely comparable in size to the dimensions of the problem you are trying to solve. Have middle-class civil servants hire upper-class student radicals to use lower-class Negroes as a battering ram against the existing local political systems; then complain that people are going around disrupting things and chastise local politicians for not cooperating with those out to do them in. Get some poor people involved in local decision-making, only to discover that there is not enough at stake to be worth bothering about. Feel guilty about what has happened to black people; tell them you are surprised they have not revolted before; express shock and dismay when they follow your advice. Go in for a little force, just enough to anger, not enough to discourage. Feel guilty again; say you are surprised that worse has not happened. Alternate with a little suppression. Mix well, apply a match, and run. . . .[6]

Liberal elites must come to realize that only incremental change in the condition of the masses is possible, and that it is irresponsible to lead the masses to believe anything else.

7. *Refrain from exaggerating societal problems.* Elites must *not* encourage masses to believe that "society" is responsible for their problems, that individual efforts to cope with problems are useless, and that only massive governmental programs can improve the quality of life. The prevailing impulse of today's liberal public-regarding elite is to *do something* and *do good.* In the absence of any serious social or economic problems such an elite is tempted to create them out of rhetoric, in order to provide itself with the opportunity for "doing good." Elites in government and the mass media are particularly prone to exaggerating social problems in order to advance themselves and their "solutions." But it is short-sighted indeed for an elite to undermine mass support for the system in order to indulge its taste for "service," "reform," and "good deeds." Moreover, the exaggeration of societal problems frequently leads to massive governmental "solutions" which only make things worse.

8. *Rekindle a sense of unity and purpose by setting forth common national goals.* Common goals and a sense of national purpose can serve to unify the masses, stabilize the social order, and lend legitimacy to governing authorities. An absence of striving, goal-oriented behavior invariably generates boredom, particularly in an affluent society. Boredom, in turn, generates a demand for radical change — any kind of change, even violence, cruelty, nihilism, or "revolution for the hell of it." If the masses feel that society is directionless, that their lives have no particular meaning or purpose, then they are vul-

[6] Aaron Wildavsky, "The Empty-Head Blues: Black Rebellion and White Reaction," *The Public Interest* (Spring 1968), p. 3.

nerable to counter-elites who offer to fill the void in their lives. If there are no national goals toward which the masses believe elites are striving, then the masses are less likely to accept elite activity as legitimate. Of course, it is essential that the goals set forth by elites affect all individuals and groups in much the *same* fashion. If the goals set forth by elites affect blacks differently from whites, or poor differently from rich, or young differently from old, etc., then the goals will divide rather than unite the nation. For example, goals such as finding a cure for cancer, cleaning the air and water, and exploring outer space, are generally less divisive than eliminating poverty, ending *de facto* segregation, or reforming the welfare system. Mass sentiments must be directed toward a recognized *common* good or against a recognized *common* enemy.

Postscript, Part 2
  What to Do about the Establishment:
Democracy without Irony

L. Harmon Zeigler

About the "irony of democracy" delineated in this book many students ask a fundamental and frightening question: What is to be done? Some illustrative comments reveal the general pessimism among students: "How can I, merely an 18-year-old freshman from Central Oregon, ever attempt to wage battle against the all-powerful elite?" *"The Irony of Democracy* certainly does not make me eager to take advantage of the opportunity to register to vote. I almost feel it is futile." Obviously, there is frustration, a sense of helplessness, and anger over our claim (p. 359) that "the future of American democracy depends upon the wisdom, responsibility, and resourcefulness of the nation's elite."

If the book has created anger and frustration along with (we hope) a clearer perception of reality, then the situation may not be as bleak as we have suggested. The first necessity for any constructive change is an understanding of how influence really is distributed.

I believe that the anti-democratic tendencies of the masses can be changed, thus reducing the dangers in mass political participation. However, by suggesting how to reduce the dangers I do *not* wish to be interpreted as suggesting that the fundamental premise of this book will be changed. Elites, not masses, will always govern America: "Revolutionary" movements are led by elites, and even the much-heralded "counter-culture" is dominated by a few intellectuals. The only way to avoid elite rule is to decentralize decision-making to the point of absurdity. (Even the New England town meeting drew sparse attendance.) A particularly relevant example of the inevitability of elite rule is community control over schools and other governmental functions, now so much in demand. The phrase itself is illusory, because there is really no *community* as such, but rather an articulate group of community leaders who wish to contest for power with an established elite (in most cases the central administration of schools). Paul Goodman's definition of decentralization, while not incorrect in its assumptions, misses the point: "Decentralizing is increasing the number of decision-making units and the number of the initiators of public policy; increasing the awareness of individuals of the whole function in which they are involved; and establishing as much face to face association with decision-makers as possible. *People are directly engaged in the function*."[1] Goodman's point is correct, up to a point, for (obviously) increasing the number of decision-making centers increases opportunities to influence decisions. But do not assume that the word "people" means "masses," for it does not. Further, do not assume that the content of decisions would be altered appreciably by a shift in the locus. A social system which has institutionalized the consensus values we have described in this book is not likely to be appreciably changed by tinkering with political institutions.

At this point in the development of our society, institutional reforms (e.g., making political parties "more democratic," abolishing the seniority system in Congress, etc.) are futile. I am in complete agreement with Richard Flacks that

fundamental social change in an advanced industrial society is not initiated immediately through the political system, nor is it likely to result from mass insurrections and rebellions. Instead, fundamental social change occurs only after a prolonged period of ferment and conflict within the principal cultural, social and economic institutions of the society.[2]

Leaving aside for the moment Flacks' comments upon insurrections, let me emphasize the point that political institutions cannot be viewed as agencies of change but rather must be viewed as reflections of the dominant values of society. Changing the shape of an institution without changing its underlying value structure is futile. The next logical question is: What kind of change do I want, and how do I propose to achieve it? My basic concern is not the content of policy but the probability of expanding the alternatives considered by policy makers, by increasing the number of articulate publics to which policy makers respond. In other words, the pluralist description of the American political system which we reject above as not being accurately descriptive, is one which I hope can be realized.

One short-term method is protest. Since my colleague has chosen to address himself to the governing elite, to advise on methods of assuring domestic tranquillity, let me address myself to those who by their protest have indicated dissatisfaction with the American political system. Protests are *prima facie* evidence of little political power. (The protests of the 1960s and early 1970s, beginning with the civil rights demonstrations and culminating in student uprisings, have in every case been undertaken because of the realization that "normal" channels of political influence were not accessible.) Consequently, as stated clearly in the text, one cannot expect that long-term social change can develop out of protest activity.

[1] Paul Goodman, "Notes on Decentralization," in Irving Howe (ed.), *The Radical Papers* (Garden City, N.Y.: Doubleday, 1966), p. 190 (emphasis added).

[2] Richard Flacks, "On the New Working Class and Strategies for Social Change," unpublished paper, p. 8.

But the implications for the social and political action required for substantial change must also be spelled out. The realities of the situation are not encouraging. Protest, even peaceful protest, is not viewed with favor by either elites or masses. In spite of overwhelming evidence on this point, student protesters persist in the belief that their actions will "awaken the public." Indeed, these actions will awaken the public, and its elite representatives will respond, but the response will be grim and repressive. That the backlash to protest, especially student protest, is inevitable must be understood if my argument against the possibility of radical change through protest is to be understood. As Wilson and Lipsky have argued, the protesters' basic problem is that they have no resources to exchange for political benefits, and their protests reduce even further the opportunities for coalitions with groups who have actual or potential resources.[3] It is consequently of little political significance that blacks and students form an alliance, for both groups suffer from the same problem: no exchangeable resources. Take, for example, protests about the Vietnam war. According to the Survey Research Center, adult "doves" were quite antagonistic toward Vietnam war protesters: A clear majority were negative, and almost one-fourth declared themselves extremely hostile. Thus the natural target for a coalition — that part of the adult population opposed to the war — was alienated.[4]

Whether or not student protesters consciously sought coalition with those who shared their values, their tactics achieved the opposite effect. That any alternative tactic of protest could succeed in building coalitions is doubtful. But clearly the fierce hostility of the mass suggests that it is in no mood to tolerate dissent, even when peaceful. It may be helpful to potential protesters to know that, in spite of media coverage sympathetic to the youthful protesters, adults (even doves) approve of what has been labeled a police riot at the 1968 Democratic Convention in Chicago. The adult population also thought that the four slain Kent State students got what they deserved. That part of the electorate which was *not* alienated by students (and which agreed with their goals) came to less than 3 percent.[5]

It is my personal experience that student protest leaders practice selective perception with consummate skill. If there were to be "power to the people," then the student protesters would find themselves in a far worse situation than those who were so brutally attacked at the Chicago convention. A genuine "people's revolution" in America would begin with a reign of terror in which first radical students and then blacks would be threatened with brutal extermination. Still, the rhetoric remains unchanged. Especially frustrating to

[3]James Q. Wilson, "The Strategy of Protest: Problems of Negro Civic Action," *Journal of Conflict Resolution*, 3 (September 1961), pp. 291–303; Michael Lipsky, "Protest as a Political Resource," *American Political Science Review*, 68 (December 1968), 1144–1158.

[4]Philip E. Converse, *et al.*, "Continuity and Change in American Politics: Parties and Issues in the 1968 Election," *American Political Science Review*, 69 (December 1969), 1087.

[5]*Ibid.*, p. 1088.

one who seeks social change is talk of the "worker-student alliance." Consider, for example, the following:

The S.F. State student strike has gained more and more support from *the people in the community,* exactly because the students are fighting for the needs of not only blacks, browns and yellow people, *but the majority of white working people as well.*[6]

Such statements ignore not only the available evidence, but also the fundamental separation of radical students from mainstream America. Whatever the intentions, student protesters are popularly identified as the bearers of "counter-culture" values, which are and *always* will be at odds with the Protestant ethic of most Americans.

The major error of student protesters was to allow the "movement" to become encumbered with vast amounts of ideological baggage and with life styles which Americans simply cannot accept. Most Americans believe in the ethic of hard work, accept inequality, do *not* believe that "society" causes the obvious inequalities in the distribution of income, and reject with fierce antagonism the noncompetitive values of the counter-culture. Lane and Lerner have cogently stated the seriousness of the clash between the old and the new cultures:

The counter-culture proposes substantially different values for Americans. It challenges the orienting and self-justifying beliefs of middle America in such a way that to embrace some of its truths would require that these men develop a political ideology that is cognitively abstract, emotionally differentiated, and morally complex. In brief, middle Americans would have to become intellectuals.[7]

Of course, this is precisely the point of *The Irony of Democracy,* and why radical political movements accomplish only repressive political responses. As Slater puts it: "If the matter is left to a collision of generational change it seems to me inevitable that a radical right revolution will occur as a last ditch effort to stave off change."[8]

My argument is neither for nor against the values of either the old or the new cultures, but is simply that social change is not accomplished by confrontation politics. Indeed, these tactics have so far accomplished just the reverse of the intended goals. For instance, popular support of the Cambodian invasion was intensified by widespread antagonism against student protest. This brings me to an interesting point of Slater's; he argues that radical pressure and liberal reform are complementary—that radical pressure from students makes it possible

[6] Robert Avakian, "Worker–Student Alliance?", in Maurice Zeitlin (ed.), *American Society, Inc.* (Chicago: Markham Publishing Co., 1970), p. 505.

[7] Robert E. Lane and Michael Lerner, "Why Hard-Hats Hate Long Hairs," *Psychology Today* (November 1970), p. 105.

[8] Philip E. Slater, *The Pursuit of Loneliness* (Boston: Beacon Press, 1970), p. 126.

for liberal leaders to gain maneuverability. Whether true or not (and I argue that it is not), the point is not germane to a discussion of strategies for fundamental change, for the radical-liberal thrust creates a counter-thrust toward repression: The structure and locus of decision making do not change. Further, since 1968, events have shown that if any elite group has gained maneuverability it is *not* establishment liberals. The winding-down of the war in Vietnam (which may well leave a permanent occupation force in Southeast Asia) is not a result of a radical-liberal thrust, but simply a realization on the part of the predominant elites that the war cannot be won, and that the majority of Americans are sick of the war and will respond favorably at the polls if it is concluded, one way or another. Against this "gain," consider the substantial losses in individual freedom and privacy from the elite response to radical pressure. Scores of state legislatures have "cracked down" by passing laws stringently regulating student behavior. Perhaps the most extreme — and most chilling as a portent of a possible future — is the West Virginia law absolving police officers, in advance, of any responsibility for deaths occurring during a riot, and providing that all participants in any riot are equally guilty for the death of any police officer. The various "anti-riot" and crime control bills which are now the law of the land make possible the prosecution of individuals for their *thoughts*. Wire-tapping and other forms of electronic surveillance make individual privacy nearly an obsolete concept. If the survival of democracy depends upon the wisdom of elites, as it now does, then we are at the most crucial period in the history of the nation. As the authors of the most recent study of the American electorate point out: ". . . It is obvious to any 'rational' politician . . . that there are several times more votes to be gained by leaning toward Wallace than leaning toward McCarthy."[9]

A further point to be made about the "youth revolt" is that it is not anything of the sort. The vanguard of the new generation is exactly that — an elite, or "an elite-to-be." The evidence is clear that, at least politically, there is no youth culture. For instance, outside the South, Wallace captured a disproportionately high vote among those under 30. While expressing in extreme form the values of traditional America, Wallace attracted large numbers of younger voters. So let the college radical avoid deceiving himself:

Although privileged young college students, angry at Vietnam, saw themselves as sallying forth to do battle against a corrupted and cynical older generation, a more head-on confrontation at the polls, if a less apparent one, was with their own agemates who had gone from high school to the factory instead of college, and who were appalled by the collapse of patriotism and respect for the law that they saw around them.[10]

9 Converse, *et al., op. cit.,* p. 1105.
10 *Ibid.,* p. 1104.

Such a finding should not be surprising, for we are simply seeing the elite-to-be trying and failing, primarily because of their unwillingness to recognize the irony of democracy.

So the first order of business for the new elite is to get over its naiveté concerning popular support and to engage in behavior which can result in significant social change. Here again let the reader be aware that I am maintaining that social change (even if it involves radical restructuring of power) is elite-initiated. The task of the new elite is formidable. If it is to bring "power to the people" (read "different" people), it must initiate action which will decompose the consensual elite into smaller, weaker factions. This can only be done, as Rudi Dutschke so cogently said, by "a long march through all the institutions of society." Where does the march begin? While I have spent some time pointing out the futility of protest, I would be guilty of the same naiveté if I did not acknowledge some effect of campus turmoil; but the effect (at least any *benevolent* effect) has been upon the students themselves. I cannot argue a cause-and-effect relationship between campus activity and the attitudes of students, but certainly one can presume that the greatest effect of a shattering of consensus occurs among those who are either participants in protest or whose values are ready to be shaken. Evidence indicates that the college population is ready for change. For instance, 28 percent of the freshmen in American universities describe themselves as politically left, or far left. The percentage increases for each successively higher learning level, until 59 percent of the graduate students assign themselves this rating.[11] While such self-ratings are difficult to assess exactly, at least one cautious conclusion can be safely drawn. A *few* medical students, law students, and business students are looking less toward personal financial achievement and more toward aiding society's underclass. At the same time, students, including many who are ideologically leftists, are as negative about extreme left groups (for instance, Students for a Democratic Society) as is the general population.

This rejection of far-left organizations, general sympathy with *some* far-left ideas, and occasional personal commitment to the ideas of the counter-culture are encouraging, but clearly not cause for rejoicing. Here I take clear exception to the argument of Charles Reich.[12] He asserts that there is an emerging culture that is noncompetitive, more "humane," and less materialistic and confining (he calls it Consciousness III), which will spread through the entire population by the force of its own appeal and without the need for broad-gauged, concerted proselytizing. Like me, he finds the new-left activism of the 1960s a failure but offers no other alternative than: "when self is recovered the power of the corporate state will be ended as miraculously as a kiss breaks a witch's evil enchantment."[13] I urge students not to take such

[11] *The Gallup Political Index,* 1971, p. 36.

[12] Charles A. Reich, *The Greening of America* (New York: Random House, 1970).

[13] *Ibid.,* p. 295. For an alternate, more realistic appraisal, see Joe Olexa, *Search for Utopia* (doctoral dissertation, University of Oregon, 1971).

statements seriously. If those who reject the old culture simply conduct their personal lives in a manner somewhat different from the traditional style (even to the point of living in communes), then, unless one seriously expects most adults to reverse their values, social change will be left to participants in the "old culture." Further, Consciousness III is hardly as idyllic as it is portrayed to be by Reich. Although it includes some genuinely humane values, it also includes hard narcotics, violence (presumably Charles Manson is a liberated person), and substantial evidence of merely superficial changes in life style. For example, Reich attaches considerable importance to clothes and rock music. I cannot find much evidence that such symbols of change are very meaningful. That someone wears his hair long, likes rock music, and smokes grass are not usually good indicators of his political values. (In fact, most people do at least one of these remarkably revolutionary things at one time or another.) So Consciousness III is not coherent but inarticulate. Its spread, beyond the campuses of our colleges and universities, is superficial, and it contains no viable political expression.

To develop a viable political expression, today's youthful elite must recognize their minority status and thus give up dreams of rapid change through either the "normal" political process or confrontation politics and violence. Not only will change not come about through confrontation politics, it will not come about by playing within the rules. As in the past, American democracy today does not answer to the demands of unpopular minorities. The occasional election of radicals (for instance, three to the Berkeley city council in 1971) should not be taken as an indicator of any change in the American electorate. Even the forthcoming 18-year-old vote will not seriously alter the political balance of power. As I have argued, while the Vietnam war and the attendant protest may have radicalized the university population to the left, "a sizeable segment of southern and northern working class youth were being radicalized to the right."[14] Approximately 11.5 million persons between 18 and 20 years old will be eligible to vote, but only 4 million will be college students. Of these 4 million a rough estimate of the "far left" contingent would be a million and a half.[15]

A plan of action, then, will necessarily be long-term. Some premises of the new left, I believe, can form the basis of a coherent program of fundamental change. First, it is entirely reasonable to argue that the hostility of the masses to democracy is not due to innate or latent anti-democratic attitudes, but to their exclusion from the decision-making system, whether by an oppressive establishment or by their own choice because they see participation as futile for them. Participation in decision making could therefore make the masses less of a threat to democracy. Also from the new left and worth taking seriously is the idea that "participatory democracy" is a means as well as an end. For whereas new left advocates of participatory democracy do

[14] Seymour Lipset and Earl Raab, "The Wallace Whitelash," *Transaction,* 7 (December 1969), p. 28.
[15] See Richard M. Scammon and Ben J. Wattenberg, *The Real Majority* (New York: Coward-McCann, 1970), for an elaboration of this point.

not recognize the disaster which would occur if their dream were *suddenly* realized, they are correct in their assumption that fundamental change must ultimately be supported by broad segments of the population. However, they are incorrect in their assumption that fundamental change must come about *from* the grass roots.

I believe that an individual gains in responsibility and awareness by active participation in decisions; that the *act* of participation is a socializing experience. Bachrach, who proposes industrial democracy as a means of increasing participation, argues that "political education is most effective on a level which challenges the individual to engage cooperatively in the solution of concrete problems affecting himself and his immediate community."[16] He therefore advocates using the factory community as a microcosm of society. But this is too little and too late. By the time a person is employed in a factory his attitudes towards participation are usually fixed. Dahl cogently gives the causes: ". . . affluent American workers . . . tend to be consumption oriented, acquisitive, privatistic, and family centered. This orientation has little place for passionate aspiration toward effective citizenship in the enterprise (or even in the state!)."[17] Clearly, then, the work place is not industrial society's New England town meeting.

Why should it be otherwise? In our supposedly democratic society, the single institution with which virtually every person has early and sustained experience is one of the most authoritarian institutions in the society. From the age of six and until the student leaves school, he is subject to the control of one of the most arbitrary and anti-democratic institutions known to man: the public school. If one goes from a public school to, say, a factory, he will never have had the opportunity to participate in a decision which affects him directly. Since our readers must know what public education is like, much detail is not necessary here. Still, some essential points need to be made. Public schools approach "total institutions"; they resemble prisons or mental hospitals. The students have no choice but to attend them, have little or no choice over what and when they will learn, and are seriously constrained in their personal behavior by rules which they cannot change. They are inmates; the teachers are the guards. While teachers have somewhat more freedom than students, their performance is judged largely on the basis of whether or not they maintain order. The principal is the warden. His role is to keep the operation running smoothly. Consequently, not only is the freedom to be an individual denied, but also the militancy, by both students and teachers, that is a reaction to this denial, is discouraged. To allow a disruption of order is to make the principal suspect in the eyes of his superior, the superintendent. There is a place for everyone on the hierarchical ladder. As long as everyone knows and keeps his place the school is considered to be functioning efficiently.

---

[16] Peter Bachrach, *The Theory of Democratic Elitism* (Boston: Little, Brown and Co., 1967), p. 103.
[17] Robert A. Dahl, *After the Revolution?* (New Haven: Yale University Press, 1970), pp. 134–135.

In such a system, survival rather than education is the goal. To say that the major function of the schools is not to educate may sound extreme, but it is accurate. Silberman calls this phenomenon "education for docility,"[18] which, performed admirably by public schools, is *not* a perversion of societal expectations. Schools are expected by adults to maintain discipline and respect for authority, even at the expense of students' self-inquiry. Students who suffer the most from such an authoritarian system do not in most cases find the situation intolerable. The majority think that discipline is "about right."[19]

In conjunction with the authoritarian social structure of the school, the curriculum (and classroom environment) is generally free of the controversy and give and take of political debate. Teachers of social studies, for instance, believe that "good citizenship," "obedience and respect for authority," and similar virtues are far more important than the development of critical thinking. As Ehman puts it, "Teachers are more interested in perpetuating the *status quo* and transmitting values than rationally analyzing controversy and values of the society."[20] To illustrate, a survey of a "progressive" midwestern high school indicates that nearly two thirds of the seniors wanted to discuss the war in Vietnam, but only thirty percent reported that their teachers actually were willing to.[21]

Thus, both the social structure and formal curriculum of the school operate to make political cripples of youth. Not only are they deprived of the right to participate, they are taught absolute nonsense about the political process. In their own personal lives and in their formal instruction they are led to believe that politics has little or nothing to do with conflict resolution. In their conflicts with those in authority the result in most cases is termination of the conflict by the authority. Further, students are unable to state alternative choices for resolving a particular conflict.[22]

How can participatory democracy in any form be expected to succeed if the school is a de-politicizing agent? Clearly, this process must be reversed. How? We must recognize, first, that change will not come from those who currently have power in public education, and, second, that students do not now have the skills necessary to expand their power. I am not suggesting that they do not *want* to expand their power, but the evidence on this point is conflicting. Both the Harris and Gallup polls have uncovered substantial student discontent about authority. However, both polls suggest that students are as ambivalent in their attitudes as are most adults. Thus, clear majorities of students want more of a voice in decisions about curriculum, teachers, school

[18] Charles E. Silberman, *Crisis in the Classroom* (New York: Random House, 1970), pp. 113–157.

[19] "Second Annual Survey of the Public Schools," *Idea Reporter,* 1970, p. 3.

[20] Lee H. Ehman, "Normative Discourse and Attitude Change in the Social Studies Classroom," *The High School Journal* (November 1970), 78.

[21] Richard C. Remy, "Teachers, Students, and the War in Vietnam: A Research Note on Controversial Issues in the Classroom," *Ibid.*, p. 139. For contrary evidence see Richard M. Merelman, *Political Socialization and Educational Climates* (New York: Holt, Rinehart and Winston, 1971), p. 160.

[22] John P. DeCacco, "Curriculum for the Seventies: Social Science or Civic Education?", unpublished paper, p. 6.

rules, and student dress. Yet they accept discipline as fair, generally do not object to dress codes, believe that their teachers are good, are satisfied with their curriculum, and, in general, do not question the benevolence of the administration of the school.[23] What emerges, then, is a desire for participation without any clear understanding of the meaning of participation. It is hardly surprising that when students at the university level succeed in realizing their demands for participation, very few take the opportunity to participate.

Students, then, must be informed not only about methods of increasing their participatory responsibilities, but also about alternative ways of engaging in the educational experience. Up to this point, the educational reform movement has been a failure. Most "innovations" (generated, incidentally, by university-related intellectuals working primarily through the U.S. Office of Education) have been "blunted on the classroom door."[24]

We must get beyond the classroom door. We must educate children at a very early age about the necessity of participation in decisions. But to do this we must have a clearly defined strategy. The most feasible way of inducing a change in public schools is to destroy their virtual monopoly on the schooling of children. A free market for educational services would not only provide an alternative to the public-school monopoly, but would also force the existing schools to compete. A recent study found business administrators to be much more innovative and audacious than school administrators.[25] School administrators might become more innovative if they were placed in a market situation at least as competitive as that of business executives.

To implement the proposal to destroy the public-school monopoly on education, an unusual coalition of liberal and conservative thinkers has proposed the "voucher plan." Briefly, a voucher plan combines public funds with parental (and, one would hope, student) choice in a new relationship. Under the plan, an educational-voucher agency would receive all federal, state, and local educational funds for which children in a particular area are eligible. The agency would then issue a voucher to every family with school-age children. The value of the voucher would approximate the current annual per pupil expenditure for education. Parents would then use the vouchers to shop around for schools of their choice.

The immediate advantages of such a system are apparent. First, it would give parents the unique opportunity to make a personal choice about the expenditure of public funds. Probably their sense of frustration (as reflected in the nationwide taxpayer's revolt) would diminish. Whatever one thinks of the ability of the average parent to make decisions about education, they could hardly do worse than what the pub-

[23] Silberman, *op. cit.*, p. 157.

[24] John I. Goodlad and M. Frances Klein, *Behind the Classroom Door* (Washington, Ohio: Charles A. Jones Publishing Co., 1970), p. 97.

[25] Julius S. Brown, "Risk Propensity in Decision-Making: A Comparison of Business and Public School Administration," *Administrative Science Quarterly*, 15 (December 1970), 473–481.

lic schools now offer. In any case, one of the notions suggested by Bachrach's discussion of the factory could be more easily attained through the voucher plan. People would be *required* to make decisions. I think that such a radical decentralization of decision making beyond the local community to the family would have immediate benefits by involving vast numbers of people in crucial decisions, an educational process which can broaden the alternatives of the participants.

A further advantage, and perhaps the most important one, is to acknowledge the wisdom of Adam Smith and John Stuart Mill, both of whom believed that a public monopoly on education would crush spontaneity and variety. Given an open competition for public funds,

> even if no new schools were established under the voucher system, the re-
> sponsiveness of existing schools would probably increase. But new schools
> will be established. Some parents will get together to create schools reflecting
> the special perspectives of their children's special needs. Educators with
> new ideas — or old ideas that are out of fashion in the public schools — will also
> be able to set up their own schools. Entrepreneurs who think they can teach
> children better and cheaper than the public schools will also have an oppor-
> tunity to do so.[26]

Under such a plan the truly "experimental" schools would increase considerably. Schools with genuine student power do exist, and can serve as a model. For instance, Adams High School in Portland, Oregon, now regarded as an educational rarity, would become a common (although not pervasive) phenomenon. Adams High School is based upon the belief that ordinary teen-agers are able to accept responsibility for their education by planning their own studies and managing their own time. The school is also operated from the assumption that the social climate of the school may have a greater effect on student learning than does the curriculum. Thus, except for the requirement that they come to school, there are virtually no rules. For students accustomed to the rigid structure of most schools, the shock of Adams was no doubt intense. But the evidence indicates that most have come around to making their own choices. As one student put it, "At least you feel like a person here." One might suspect that — as is usually the case — the children of the privileged would be better equipped to cope with the open environment of Adams High School. But the student body of 1600 is drawn from all social strata, including working-class whites and blacks.[27]

Schools like Adams will certainly not immediately become the norm. As we have stated, most parents like things the way they are, and would probably not send their children to such a school. However, as

---

[26] *Educational Voucher* (Cambridge, Mass.: Center For the Study of Public Policy, December 1970), p. 2.

[27] Neil Postman and Charles Wingartner, *The Soft Revolution* New York: Dell Publishing Co., 1971), p. 78. I do not wish to suggest that Adams High School will be an immediate success. For students used to an authoritarian system, such an abrupt change can hardly be immediately beneficial. The process of individual responsibility must be begun much earlier. Further, open schools have a difficult time operating in a traditional political structure. Pressure from parents has forced Adams to become more conservative in its social structure.

open schools increased in number and demonstrated their effectiveness, student pressures on traditional schools would increase. Their awareness of their oppression would be strengthened, and they would be strengthened, and they would have alternatives.

The task of establishing a voucher system is, unfortunately, a problem in political influence. The educational establishment (National Educational Association, American Association of School Administrators, and even the "militant" American Federation of Teachers) is solidly opposed to it. Significantly, the first serious efforts at planning and implementing the voucher system were financed by the Office of Economic Opportunity, and not the U.S. Office of Education. The plans for Adams High School and the voucher system were both developed at Harvard. So we are back in the game of interest group (elite) politics. However, voucher systems will be operating in a very few school districts under the auspices of the Office of Economic Opportunity. OEO hopes to fund many more programs, and, at this writing, has plans for a six million dollar budget to expand the voucher system. So the strategy of change has begun.

What I am proposing goes beyond the currently fashionable notion of "community control" and does so because the evidence suggests that decentralization of authority would result in increased pressures toward intolerance of diversity. The fact that the voucher plan is federally financed is not unique. As Coleman has suggested, local authorities have more of an interest in maintaining stability than do national governments.[28] Although Coleman was speaking primarily of education, his point can be applied generally. Even if we define community as "neighborhood" (e.g., a geographical sub-unit within a larger legal community), I still adhere to my basic premise. As the community-power-structure literature suggests, small communities tend to be governed by a single, cohesive elite. Further, as Altshuler notes, experimental evidence indicates that pressure towards conformity and consensus is greater in smaller than in larger groups.[29]

This pressure towards consensus is exactly what we must avoid. Such pressure has lead to the "unrealistic conflict" of the 1960s. What we have witnessed is intensive and violent social conflict between small minorities and adamant majorities. What we must achieve is widespread and non-violent social conflict within all strata of society.

Is educational reform sufficient to achieve such widespread conflict? Put another way, can open schools have any impact upon a relatively closed society? Or, for that matter, can open schools survive at all? Even if they can, can those who emerge from them have much of a chance to participate effectively in the political decision-making process?

Such questions are vexing, because they involve an irritating dilemma. On the one hand, there can be no genuine alternatives to exist-

[28] James S. Coleman, "The Struggle for Control of Education," in C. A. Bowers, *et al., Education and Social Policy* (New York: Random House, 1970), p. 78.

[29] Alan A. Altshuler, *Community Control* (New York: Pegasus, 1970), p. 35.

ing schools without widespread changes in other social institutions. On the other hand, genuine educational change should be the catalyst for other fundamental social change. As Everet Reimer argues:

True education is a basic social force. Present social structures could not survive an educated population even if only a substantial minority were educated. Something more than schooling is obviously in question here, more than a college degree, even a Ph.D., indeed, almost the opposite of schooling is meant. People are schooled to accept a society. They are educated to create or re-create one.[30]

In order for such an educated minority to survive, and for a true alternative educational system to create this minority, the present linkage between formal education and economic success (even survival) must be weakened. The role of education in self-actualization is radically constrained by the necessity of making a living. Indeed, the most widely cited reason (sanction?) for not dropping out of school is that you will end up on welfare. As long as education is the key to survival in a competitive world, meaningful innovation is unlikely. The simplest and least bureaucratically complex method of weakening the links between education, jobs, and income is through the institution of the guaranteed annual income. Such a proposal differs considerably from the traditional welfare schemes currently employed because it makes no assumption about willingness to work. Space prohibits a detailed description of how a guaranteed annual income might work. However, the general idea is that each citizen is guaranteed, preferably by a constitutional amendment, the right to an income sufficient for him to live with dignity. While the economic implications of such a scheme are of considerable importance, let us concentrate upon the educational and political consequences. Freed of the necessity of preparing their "products" for a niche in the economic structure, schools would have enough "slack" to respond to the innovations I have suggested. The reduction of such pressure would also allow individuals to take a less vocational and more humane view of their educational opportunities.

Combined with the destruction of the public monopoly of education, the recognition of a public obligation for an adequate standard of living would lead to some predictable and desirable political consequences.

A population socialized from an early age to participate in decisions, and free to develop as individuals, would probably insist upon continued participation in decisions about work. (Although the Protestant Ethic denies it, most people would continue to work.) In such a situation, the notion of industrial democracy seems quite feasible. Given the viable option of exiting from an unpleasant work situation, an in-

[30] Everet Reimer, *An Essay on Alternatives in Education* (Cuernavaca, Mexico: CIDOC, 1970), p. 3/13.

[31] See Robert Theobald, ed., *The Guaranteed Income* (Garden City, N.Y.: Doubleday, 1967), for a more exhaustive discussion.

dividual would be free to demand more voice in the conduct of the organization's affairs.[32] I am not suggesting that workers would necessarily wish to participate personally in the management of a firm, but it is quite likely that some form of worker representation in management decisions could be achieved. Whether such participation results in sharing power or controlling the enterprise is not as important a question as it may appear. In West Germany, for example, workers' representatives share managerial functions; in Yugoslavia, workers' councils have authoritative decision-making power. In both cases, however, professional management is as powerful in running the affairs of the firm as it is in the United States.[33] The important common ingredient of any industrial democracy plan is the provision of an *opportunity* to influence decisions affecting the on-the-job environment. A cautionary note: it is significant that proposals for industrial democracy come from the intellectual left and not from the ranks of organized labor. Until there is a genuine demand for participation, opportunities will be ignored.

Another obvious opportunity for participation—assuming again an increased *desire* for participation—is the neighborhood. When one speaks of returning power to local governments, in many cases (e.g., in very large cities), the governments are not local at all. For any appreciable increase in participation, sub-units of cities must be created. Here, in contrast to industrial democracy, some demands (most spectacularly Ocean Hill–Brownsville, in New York City) have filtered up from the bottom. However, there is still no widespread public clamor. My assumption is that demands for neighborhood government will increase slowly in the wake of educational reforms. People seeking opportunities to influence policy—ordinarily a minority—will try to reduce the impediments of an over-bureaucratized and overcentralized governmental apparatus.[34]

At the risk of redundancy, I wish to emphasize that movements toward decentralization must be accompanied by educational and economic innovations, or the result will simply be one more vindication of Michel's "iron law of oligarchy" (see p. 200). The failures of the poor to participate in the community election program illustrate quite well the futility of providing opportunities for participation to people who lack the skills and resources for effective participation. One should also keep in mind that decentralized decision making depends for success upon the individual's belief that there is a benefit to be gained at least equal to the cost of participation. This latter point can be illustrated by reference to one of today's most crucial problems: pollution of the environment. It is puzzling to hear (admittedly not

[32] See Albert O. Hirschman, *Exit, Voice, and Loyalty: Response to Decline in Firms, Organizations, and States* (Cambridge, Mass.: Harvard University Press, 1970).

[33] Eric Rhennon, *Industrial Democracy and Industrial Management: A Critical Essay on the Possible Meanings and Implications of Industrial Democracy* (London: Tavistock Publications, Ltd., 1968).

[34] There is a burgeoning literature on the details of neighborhood government. For a survey, see Altshuler, *op. cit.;* Milton Kotler, *Neighborhood Government* (Indianapolis: Bobbs-Merrill, 1969).

simultaneously) advocates of community control demand effective regulation of the environment. Obviously a small community could not deal effectively with a corporate giant. The point is that a neighborhood government should have decision-making authority consistent with the principle that those who make the decisions will have to live with the consequences of the decisions.

The goal of these efforts is to increase the number of people with skill and resources sufficient to enable them to compete effectively in the political process. Dahl has correctly identified the most serious flaw in any plan for institutional reform: severe inequality in the distribution of political resources.[35] It is not entirely clear what a political resource is. However, at a minimum, people must have time, interest, and ability. Currently, as we know, these attributes are disproportionately concentrated in the higher social classes. By suggesting ways of reforming education, the distribution of income, the environment of the job, and the opportunities for local participation, I am offering the possibility of reducing such inequalities. Accordingly, one would expect that the process whereby political leaders are recruited would be altered. The wider distribution of resources and skills would reduce the extent to which a single social class has monopolized the political recruitment process. Elite consensus could be substantially reduced by the destruction of this monopoly. A reasonable outcome of this diffusion of skills and resources would be the inclusion in "normal" political debate of ideas which are currently excluded from the agenda of the elites. As the range of issues expanded, existing political institutions charged with the responsibility of representation would fragment. The two-party system, which we have described as representative of the values of the middle class, would be replaced by a larger number of more ideologically committed parties.

The upshot of such fragmentation would be an increase in political conflict, both locally and nationally. While we are accustomed to try to minimize conflict in our political process, a high level of conflict — an intense ferment in our social, political, and economic institutions — is a necessary precondition for a truly pluralistic society.

[35] Robert Dahl, *op. cit.*, p. 115.

Index

McCarthyism, 21
McClelland, David C., 312
McClosky, Herbert, 132–133, 137–138, 140–141, 172, 197–199
McCloy, John J., 99
McCulloch v. *Maryland*, 61
McElroy, Neil H., 97
McKinley, William, 82
McNamara, Robert S., 98, 105, 116, 126
Madison, James, 31, 34, 43, 44–45, 47, 49, 62, 64, 65, 92, 241, 295, 366 (*see also The Federalist*)
Majority rule, 8
    elite opposition to, 244
Managerial elite, 108–112 (*see also* Corporate managerial elites)
Marbury v. *Madison*, 51, 63, 280
Marshall, Chief Justice John, 51, 61, 280, 281
Marshall Plan, 122
Marshall, Justice Thurgood, 283
Martin, Luther, 28, 36
Mass media, 159–163 (*see also* Television)
    and the presidency, 249
    print vs. television, 160
    Vietnam coverage, 162–163
Masses:
    attitude toward democratic values, 19–21, 131–133
    attitude toward state and local government, 288–290
    contradictions in political beliefs, 174–178
    and elites, communication between, 155–164
        differences in values, 19–21, 347–348
    mass activism, 20–21, 150–154, 356–359
    political apathy, 148–150, 356
    populist values, 21
    and the presidency, 249–250
    television influence on, 159–163
Massialas, Byron G., 143–144
Matthews, Donald R., 141, 274–275, 318
Mellon, Richard King, 103, 104
Meredith, James, 322
Merelman, Richard M., 147
Messinger, Sheldon L., 234
Michels, Roberto, 200, 217, 386
Milbrath, Lester, 187, 191
Military elite:
    military-industrial complex, 114–120
    "military mind," 120
    social background of, 119–120
Mill, John Stuart, 8, 171
Miller, Warren, 159, 184, 262, 263
Mills, C. Wright, 91, 112
Missouri Compromise of 1820, 70
Mitchell, John M., 101
"The mobilization of bias," 156–157
Monopolies, 75–80
Monroe, James, 64
Montesquieu, Baron, 50, 241
Moore, Barrington, Jr., 204
Moos, Malcolm, 114
Morgan, J. Pierpont, 76–77, 81, 83

Morris, Gouverneur, 43
Morris, Robert, 32, 37
Mosca, Gaetano, 4–5, 364–365
Moynihan, Daniel P., 101–321
Munn v. *Illinois*, 75
Myrdal, Gunnar, 309–310, 314

Nagel, Stuart, 95
National Advisory Commission on Civil Disorders, 310–311
National Association for the Advancement of Colored People (NAACP), 313
National Labor Relations Act of 1935, 87
National Urban League, 313
Natural aristocracy, 10
Negroes (*see also* Civil rights movement):
    American ambivalence toward, 309–311
    and Civil War, 68–73
    ghetto life, 324–333
    identity problems, 328–329
    and local elections, 187
    masses vs. middle class, 328
    matri-focal family patterns, 312, 328
    perceptions of citizenship, 147–148
    rioting, 140, 190–191, 338
    slavery and effects of, 311–313
    social class structure, 328
    voting rights, 171–172
Neustadt, Richard, 247
New Deal, 85–87, 346
New Freedom program, 83
New Jersey Plan, 41
Nie, Norman, 160
Nixon, Richard, 118, 169, 256–258
Nixon administration, elites in, 100–101
North Atlantic Treaty Organization (NATO), 122

Office-holding qualifications, 42–44
Oligarchy, 304
Olson, Mancur, 221
Organizations (*see also* Interest groups; Lobbyists):
    collective and selective benefits, 221
    conflict of interest in, 214, 233–234
    conservative influence of, 234–236
    dominance by minorities, 227
    integration of individuals in, 232–234
    motivation for joining, 217–223
    voluntary membership, 216–217

Packard, David, 100
Paine, Thomas, 32, 296–297
Parties, political (*see* Political parties)
Parenti, Michael, 232
Patrons of Husbandry, 74–75
Patterson, Herbert P., 114–115
Patterson, William, 41
Pennock, Roland, 10
Pentagon papers, 126
Pinckney, Charles C., 43, 64
Plessy v. *Ferguson*, 313, 314
Plural elites, 11–12, 14–15 (*see also* Elites)
    community, 300–302, 356

States:
    bipolar elite structure, 297–298
    dominant elite among lesser elites, 296–297
    elite structures in, 294–298
    federal grants-in-aid to, 292–294
    federal power in, 292–294
    governmental elites, 96, 287–290, 355
    interest group elites, 294–298
    plural elite structure, 298
    public attitude toward government, 288–290
    single unified elite system, 295–296
    states' rights, 291–292
    voter turnout, 290
States' rights, 291–292
Stockholders, 106, 108–110
Stevenson, Adlai, 121
Steiner, Gary, 160
Stokes, Donald, 159, 262, 263
Stouffer, Samuel A., 131–132, 136
"Stratarchy," 200–201
Student Nonviolent Coordinating Committee (SNCC), 318
Sub-elites (*see* State governmental elites, Local governmental elites)
Supreme Court, 280–284, 355 (*see also* specific cases)
    civil rights law, 283
    constitutional powers of, 51–52
    and desegregation, 314–315
    and the New Deal, 281, 282
    and railroads, 75
    as reflection of elite philosophy, 281, 284
    and segregation in the South, 313
    social background of judges, 283–284
    and social Darwinism, 282
Swanson, Bert, 303–305

Taft, William Howard, 247–248
Taney, Chief Justice Roger, 67, 70, 281–282
Tauber, Alma F., 324–325
Tauber, Karl E., 324–325
Television, 159–163 (*see also* Mass media)
    liberal bias of, 161
    Vietnam coverage, 162–163
Textbooks, in public schools, 143–145
Three-fifths Compromise, 42
Thurmond, Strom, 315
Trow, Martin, 136–137

Truman, David, 6, 155, 274, 278
Truman Doctrine, 122
Truman, Harry S, 122, 247
Turner, Frederick Jackson, 66

Unions as lobbyists, 219, 224, 227–228

Vanderbilt, Commodore William H., 74, 82
Verba, Sidney, 191, 232–233
Vietnam War, 123–128, 168, 169, 184, 255–258
    and Korean War, compared, 184
    television coverage of, 162–163
Villard, Henry, 74
Violence (*see also* Civil rights movement):
    as alternative to voting, 140–141
    television coverage of, 161–162
"Virginia Dynasty," 64–65
Virginia Plan, 40–41
Voting qualifications, 42–44

Wahlke, John C., 159
Wallace, George C., 21, 23–24, 148–150, 151–154, 207, 208, 283
Warner, W. Lloyd, 299
Warren, Chief Justice Earl, 283
Wars, and the liberal establishment, 121–128
Washington, Booker T., 313
Washington, George, 32–35, *passim*, 37, 47, 61
Wealth, inequality of, 107–108
Weber, Max, 198
Webster, Daniel, 67
Weeks, Sinclair, 100
Welch, Robert, 23
Western elites, 66–68
Western territory, slavery question in, 70, 72
Wheeler, Burton K., 297
Whig party, 71
White, William S., 275
Wildavsky, Aaron, 17, 301, 370
Willkie, Wendell, 203
Wilson, Charles E., 98, 105
Wilson, James Q., 375
Wilson, Woodrow, 83, 266

Yancey, William L., 322

Zeigler, Harmon, 234